THE MODERNS

Inflatable Sculpture

The Jewish Museum: New York City July 2nd to August 24th

Kip Coburn Charles Frazier David Jacobs

Otto Piene Vera Simons Susan Lewis Williams

Arnold Saks

Poster, *Inflatable Sculpture*, Jewish Museum, New York, 1969. The graphic concept of "inflatable" is visualized with clarity. Design: Arnold Saks

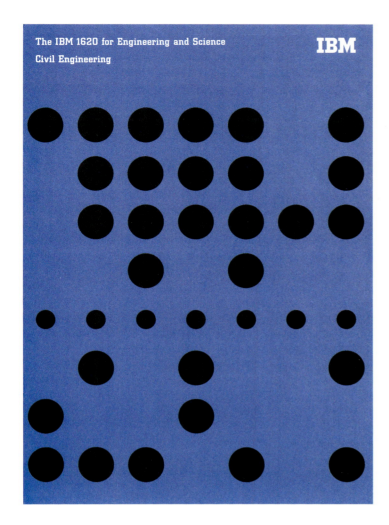

Brochure cover, *The IBM 1620 for Engineering and Science: Civil Engineering*, IBM Data Processing Division, 1960. One in a series of seven brochures illustrating the importance IBM attaches to its corporate design program, created by Eliot Noyes and Paul Rand in the 1950s. Design: Mary L. Beresford

Magazine cover, *Interiors*, Whitney Publications, New York, vol. 113, no. 3 (October 1953). Bauhaus artist Xanti Schawinsky's abstract design of implied ripples and shadows on sunlit water communicates soothing movements and constant flow. Design: Schawinsky

AGE OF THE AUTO

1958

The automobile industry has given more people more jobs than the last two wars put together.

P.L. Smith, M.D., Yeadon, Pa.

Booklet front and back covers, *Age of the Auto*, the Composing Room, no. 3 in a series of 4, 1960. This 16-page insert from the series *About U.S. Experimental Typography* by American Designers was originally printed in *Der Druckspiegel*, the graphic arts magazine published in Stuttgart, Germany, to show European graphic designers the work of American designers while giving them something characteristically American to read.
Text: Percy Seitlin; Design: Lester Beall

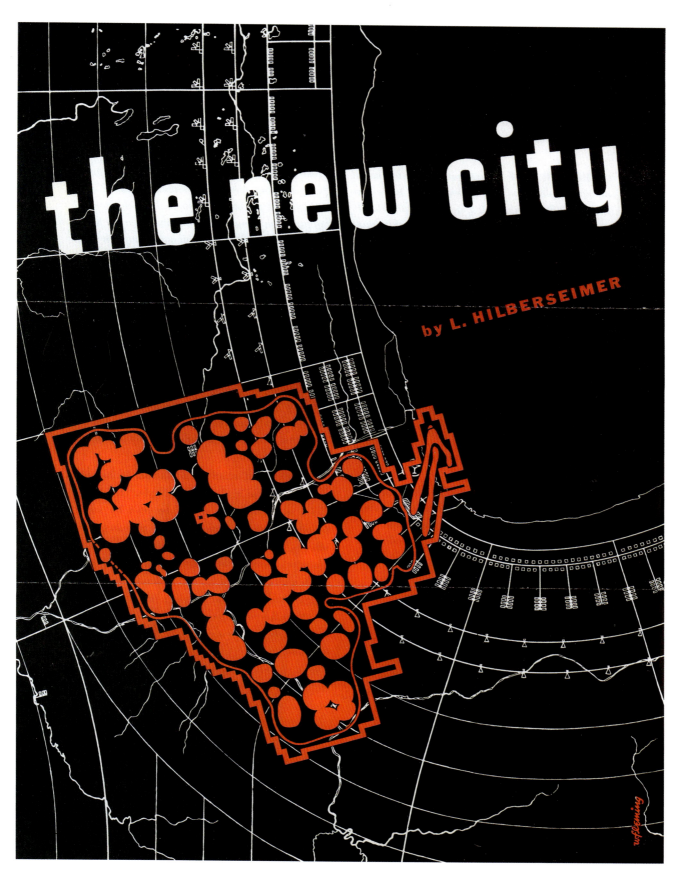

the new city

by L. HILBERSEIMER

Book prospectus, *The New City: Elements of Planning*, by Ludwig Karl Hilberseimer, Paul Theobald and Company, 1944. This book is based on the ideas Hilberseimer, who was a professor of city planning at Illinois Institute of Technology, began to develop as founder of the department of city planning at the Bauhaus Dessau in the 1920s. William Fleming's design represents a proposed replanning of Chicago; superimposed in red is a reconstructed plan of the stone-age settlement at Glastonbury, England. Design: William Fleming

Booklet cover, Go Tourist Class, Hamburg–
American Line, North German Lloyd, 1936.
Design: Paul Smith with art direction by H.
A. Donderi

THE MODERNS
MIDCENTURY AMERICAN GRAPHIC DESIGN

STEVEN HELLER
GREG D'ONOFRIO

ABRAMS, NEW YORK

Editor: Eric Himmel
Design: Kind Company
Production Manager: Anet Sirna-Bruder

Library of Congress Control Number: 2016961384

ISBN: 978-1-4197-2401-5

Printed and bound in China
10 9 8 7 6 5 4 3 2 1

Abrams books are available at special discounts when
purchased in quantity for premiums and promotions as
well as fundraising or educational use. Special editions
can also be created to specification. For details, contact
specialsales@abramsbooks.com or the address below.

ABRAMS The Art of Books
115 West 18th Street, New York, NY 10011
abramsbooks.com

ON LOVE

ORTEGA y GASSET

aspects of a single theme

elaine lustig

meridian Books M84 $1.35/Canada$1.45

Book cover, *On Love: Aspects of a Single Theme*, by José Ortega y Gasset, Meridian Books, 1957. Design: Elaine Lustig Cohen

To our loyal friend and mentor, the late Elaine Lustig Cohen. More than a pioneer woman graphic designer, she was a faithful advocate of all things modern. We dedicate this book to her career as a designer, artist, and archivist, but mostly for her unfailing generosity, counsel, and influence toward all designers, artists, and scholars. This book is a testament to her devotion to creating the discipline of graphic design history—and being part of that history.

Sounds from the Alps

Album cover, *Sounds from the Alps*, Westminster
Recording Company, c. 1960. These repeated,
rhythmic, painterly brushstrokes conceptually
express the mountains and valleys and musical
sounds of the region—especially yodeling.
Design: Rudolph de Harak

Print **America'sGraphicDesignMagazine May/June1961**

RUDOLPH DE HARAK

Magazine cover, *Print*, May/June 1961. Rudolph de Harak, the magazine's guest art director, experiments with Kodalith photographic distortion emphasizing the waviness of the American flag. Design: De Harak

01 INTRODUCTION

Midcentury Confluences

Modernism was composed of disparate movements of the early to mid-twentieth century that shared the same philosophical and aesthetic currency. It was a confluence of avant-garde art and design spread throughout the industrial world by visionary artists and designers, theorists, and dogmatists with emblematic styles based on disruptions in European culture, politics, and society. It was the end of the ancien régime and the start of the new order. It was left, right, and center—communist, socialist, democrat, syndicalist, and fascist—held together by common disaffection, even disgust, with antiquated ideas about art and design. Lots of isms arose under the banner of Modernism: Constructivism, Cubism, Dadaism, Expressionism, Futurism, Productivism, Purism, Suprematism, Vorticism, Zenitism, and (an ism by any other name) De Stijl. The progenitors of Modernism were form givers with grand, often idealistic, ideas that inspired later generations of form makers, many of whom contributed to broader shifts in commercial graphic design, advertising, and typography. Some were individualists; others hewed to rigorous formulas.

Modernism in graphic design derived from outgrowths of these larger movements. Modernist typography emerged from inventions such as Parole in Libertà (Words-in-Freedom) by Italian Futurists and *Die neue Typographie* (the New Typography), a coinage of the German typographer Jan Tschichold in the late twenties that essentially summed up the typographic impulses of Dutch De Stijl, Russian Constructivism, German Bauhaus, and other like-minded European schools. The Bauhaus, in particular, was a wellspring of bold Gothic, or sans serif, typefaces often set in lowercase in asymmetrical compositions. *Die neue Typographie,* which evolved into the so-called International Typographic Style, informed the typographic practices of all the designers in this book. Toward the end of the fifties, an "orthodox," or more formulaic, version of International Typographic Style coalesced in Switzerland. The "Swiss Style" became a flash point around which adherence to and apostasy from the rigors of Modernism revolved. In Swiss Style, type is further purified and placed invisibly on an underlying grid, emphasizing readability and clarity of communication. As disseminated by the journal *Neue Grafik* from 1958 to 1965, Swiss Style functional design ideas, which were especially useful in corporate environments, also infiltrated American practice. Yet even among the orthodox, there were differences in method and manner between the organized and systematic Zurich school and the organic and artistic Basel school. In spite of rules and movements, typography evolved within functional parameters and individual preferences.

The Moderns focuses on sixty-three graphic designers, including the principals and disciples who brought Modernist graphic design to the United States as well as acolytes who continued the legacy in the design capitals of New York, Chicago, and Los Angeles from around 1937 with the founding of the New Bauhaus to 1970, the height of the International Typographic Style. Our aim is to highlight a curated group that, like Modernism itself, had varying viewpoints and methods yet was bound by governing principles of function, clarity, and simplicity held together through geometry, abstraction, and minimalism, as well as photography, typography, and collage. This is not an encyclopedia of all those who joined the "movement," but a selection of those who we believe were most instrumental in bringing Modernism into American graphic design for the purpose of selling products and ideas in the commercial and cultural arenas. Modernism prevailed in so many stylistic variations and nuances that it is difficult to represent all the participants who played catalytic roles.

A handful of important figures are not included here: Charles Coiner, art director at the N. W. Ayer & Son advertising agency, Dr. Mehemed Fehmy Agha, art director at Condé Nast, and Egbert Jacobson, director of the design department at Container Corporation of America, all of whom gave direct and indirect opportunities to many of the designers in this book; the Austrian immigrant Joseph Binder, who was a leader in airbrush-pictorial modern styling; and Walter Landor, whose business identity design work enhanced various commercial brands. Their respective absences are not intended to slight their accomplishments, which are significant but not entirely within our focus. A more difficult omission is László Moholy-Nagy, whose work and influence as an educator, painter, sculptor, photographer, and designer are so widely studied that it would be impossible to do him justice in the space allowed here.

European émigré artists and designers (including five Bauhaus students and faculty) were so influential in bringing European expressions of Modernism to America that we cover their contribution in an opening section of the book. Working alongside them, and often learning directly from them, was a first generation of native American moderns who established themselves in the very late thirties and early forties, most of whom were active during the fifties and sixties. Over time, a number of slightly younger Modernists emerged in the postwar world, and they are also part of our story.

American Modernists came in many flavors. Of these, we recognize a few: The rational moderns (including, in this book, Jacqueline Casey, Ivan Chermayeff and Thomas Geismar, John and Mary Condon, Donald and Ann Crews, Rudolph de Harak, Burton Kramer, John Massey, Tomoko Miho, Reid Miles, Arnold Saks, and Barbara Stauffacher Solomon) practiced objectified, systematic design in the tradition of the Swiss Style. The exuberant moderns (including Saul Bass, Lillian Bassman, Lou Dorfsman, Gene Federico, William Golden, George Lois, Alvin Lustig, Georg Olden, Paul Rand, Louis Silverstein, Alex Steinweiss, and Bradbury Thompson) were known for making "big ideas" come alive through type. The eclectic moderns (including Lester Beall, Peter Bradford, Robert Brownjohn, Richard Danne, Louis Danziger, Ray Eames, Neil Fujita, Morton Goldsholl, Charles Goslin, Irving Harper, E. McKnight Kauffer, Ray Komai, Roy Kuhlman, Matthew Leibowitz, Herb Lubalin, Elaine Lustig Cohen, Charles E. Murphy, Tony Palladino, Alexander Ross, Arnold Shaw, Deborah Sussman, and Lance Wyman) routinely broke the rules and veered away from the dominant Swiss Style, bringing more personal and expressive elements to their work.

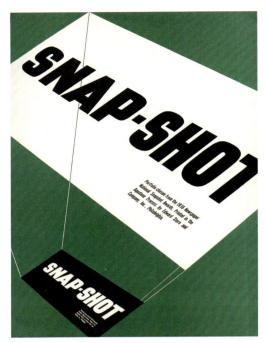

Brochure cover, Newspaper National Snapshot Awards, reproduced from *The Printing Art Quarterly* 66, no. 4, 1936. Design by Charles Coiner, acclaimed art director for N. W. Ayer & Son.

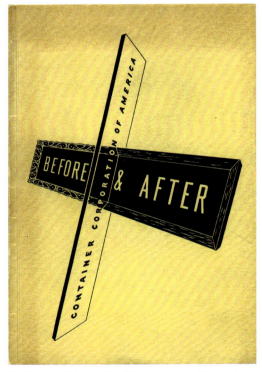

Booklet cover, *Before & After, A Monograph,* no. 2 in a series, Container Corporation of America, Chicago, 1940. This small promotional booklet discussed the ethos of the Container Corporation of America art department and the benefits of "good" packaging design, using examples and text on the evolution of design, type styles, pictorial design, simplification, and more. Art direction: Egbert Jacobson

There was also a class of "idiosyncratics," rebels who were ideologically opposed to or aesthetically ambivalent toward Modernism and drawn to historical revivalism. You will not find in this volume, for example, Push Pin Studios, the devoutly eclectic and profoundly influential purveyor of popular culture and commercial art, which revived the denigrated styles of Victorian, Art Nouveau, and Art Deco, and by having done so reintroduced narrative illustration to the design equation. Nor are there Peter Max and Tom Daly (Daly & Max), who did likewise through their use of stylized illustration and rare wood types. Quite a few art directors and designers also fit into this eclectic category, among them Bob Cato and John Berg, whose CBS record album cover designs were archetypes of the genre; Robert Scudellari, who did book jackets that were not stylistically constrained; Otto Storch, whose format for *McCall's* magazine was alternately the paradigm of the new ornamentation and a paean to functionalism; Art Paul, whose approach to *Playboy* magazine was to invest in concept-driven and metaphoric illustration; Arnold Varga, whose advertisements for the Joseph Horne Company updated the passé art of decoupage; and Ed Benguiat, who injected a nineteenth-century spirit into twentieth-century typography. All were contemporary, but not modern.

To confuse matters even more, some of the modern pioneers with eclectic tendencies could be downright post-Modernist (if such a rubric has any meaning) when it suited them. Despite Herbert Bayer's excoriation of Victorian ornamental typefaces in advertising as "bad taste under the disguise of functionalism par excellence," he designed posters for Aspen, Colorado, using ornamental typography combined with modernistic collage. Bradbury Thompson routinely used nineteenth-century engravings from Diderot as a foil for his modern typography. Alexander Ross, Matthew Leibowitz, and Lester Beall also employed a diverse mix of Dada and Surrealist techniques in their compositions. And Herb Lubalin, the master of talking type, did his share of Victorian layouts—when, of course, the subject called for it.

Making Modern

Many of the graphic designers who began working before World War II were Depression-era children from immigrant or poor families who were introduced to commercial art in high school as an alternative profession to other labors. For this generation, modern design would symbolize a break from their parents' old-world ties, and design education rose to the challenge of meeting their desire for change. Leon Friend, who wrote, with Joseph Hefter, one of the first textbooks that used Modernism as a paradigm for commercial art (*Graphic Design: A Library of Old and New Masters in the Graphic Arts*, 1936), was one of the most influential teachers. As head of the art department at Brooklyn's public Abraham Lincoln High School, he exposed his students (including Alex Steinweiss, Gene Federico, and Seymour Chwast) to such important European and American graphic designers as Jean Carlu, A. M. Cassandre, and E. McKnight Kauffer, teaching them to emulate these models. Teachers such as Howard Trafton at the Art Students League and Herschel Levit and Tom Benrimo at Pratt Institute in New York further opened doors to the expressive realms of graphic design. When Alexey Brodovitch launched his Design Laboratory at the Philadelphia Museum School of Industrial Art in 1933, it was with the unspoken intent of introducing European advertising design to American students. In 1937 in Chicago, László Moholy-Nagy founded the New Bauhaus (later the School of Design and the Institute of Design), where he invited György Kepes to join the faculty; Moholy-Nagy, Kepes, and the Russian-born architect Serge Chermayeff were heroic figures to many of the designers who came out of the school. Their pedagogies and European ethos had impact far beyond the scope of their respective tenures. In 1942, Chermayeff established the Bauhaus-inspired design department at Brooklyn College, where Kepes and Robert Jay Wolff taught. In the early forties, Herbert Bayer and Paul Rand taught advanced advertising design classes at the American Advertising Guild, in New York. Before and after World War II, new design schools attracted European émigré faculty members. At Black Mountain College in North Carolina, Josef Albers held court among such European teachers as Alexander "Xanti" Schawinsky, Leo Lionni, and Will Burtin (the native-born but European-influenced Alvin Lustig was there too). In 1941, Brodovitch brought his Design Laboratory to New York's New School for Social Research, immeasurably broadening his reach. There were further developments well after the war ended. The first graduate program in graphic design in the United States, founded at Yale University in New Haven in 1951, was initially headed by Alvin Eisenman and soon included Albers, Herbert Matter, and Lustig on the faculty. The Center for Advanced Visual Studies, which Kepes founded fifteen years later at the Massachusetts Institute of Technology (MIT) in Cambridge, offered a neo-Bauhaus approach. The Chouinard Art Institute in Los Angeles and the School of Visual Arts, Parsons School of Design, and the Cooper Union for the Advancement of Science and Art in New York all trained leading Modernist designers.

Museums and galleries also gave their stamps of accreditation. As he originally conceived the Museum of Modern Art in 1929, founding director Alfred H. Barr Jr. envisioned a program that would "expand beyond the narrow limits of painting and sculpture in order to include … typography [and] the arts of commerce and industry." Architect Philip Johnson launched the Department of Architecture in 1932, and soon it came to embrace design in the spirit of the Bauhaus, where works in different media were held up to equal aesthetic standards. In 1938, Herbert Bayer (with assistance from Walter and Ise Gropius) designed the exhibition and catalog for the museum's "Bauhaus 1919–1928" exhibition, which offered the general public a first look at this influential movement. Later, curator Mildred Constantine, who shaped the museum's design exhibitions and collections from 1943 through 1970, helped to popularize difficult-to-categorize collections, or what she called "fugitive material." With design exhibitions including "Olivetti: Design in Industry" (1952), "Signs in the Street" (1954), and "Lettering by Hand" (1962), she fostered a new discipline of curatorial studies in the applied and decorative arts. She also gave career-defining solo exhibitions for individual graphic and product designers such as Alvin Lustig and Massimo Vignelli, as well as thematic poster exhibitions—too many to name—that featured both veteran and up-and-coming Modernists.

In 1936, the Composing Room opened the first gallery in New York—first named PM, later A-D, and finally 303—dedicated to graphic design, with a small exhibition of Herbert Matter's posters. The Composing Room was a type shop that also advanced the art and craft of type design and made a remarkable contribution to design history and practice. It produced educational programs, including lecture series, single and group exhibitions in the gallery, catalogs, and one of America's most influential graphic arts periodicals, PM (for "production manager"), later called A-D (for "art director"), which was published bimonthly between 1934 and 1942. The program, conceived and sustained for almost forty years by the Composing Room's cofounder, Robert Leslie (1885–1986), was rooted in graphic arts traditions, yet it was motivated by new approaches, even if these rejected tradition. Despite his own preference for classical typography, "Doc" Leslie (he was a medical doctor), or "Uncle Bob," as he was affectionately called, gave Modernism's designers a platform from which to publicize their experiments.

New York was not the only gallery mecca in the United States. In Chicago, the Katharine Kuh Gallery's "Advance Guard of Advertising Artists" (October 1941) offered a significant perspective on modern graphic design and its relationship with commerce. The exhibition included nine American and European pioneers of avant-garde design,

including Frank Barr, Herbert Bayer, Lester Beall, E. McKnight Kauffer, Herbert Matter, Paul Rand, and Ladislav Sutnar, as well as Moholy-Nagy and Kepes, who helped to put it together. "Now that the world is at war and it is increasingly difficult for us in America to maintain an intelligent and critical contact with the European art scene," wrote Kuh, "we must concentrate our attention at home on nurturing the most important values and particularly those values which most logically develop from our own activities."

In Chicago, the design patron Walter P. Paepcke, founder and president of Container Corporation of America, made a space both real and figurative for the moderns, hiring Egbert Jacobson as director of its design department. Beginning in 1936, the department pioneered a modern design program for the company, consisting of a trademark, stationery, packaging, printed forms, products, publications, vehicle identification, and exterior and interior signage for buildings—as well as very visible advertising campaigns. Container Corporation of America's advertising agency, N. W. Ayer, headed by Charles Coiner and later by Leo Lionni, commissioned émigré designers and artists, among them Xanti Schawinsky, Fernand Léger, A. M. Cassandre, Kepes, and Bayer, to illustrate advertisements for the company's "Great Ideas of Western Man" campaign.

The moderns were also made visible through numerous consumer and trade magazines. Both the design journals from Europe (*Arts et Métiers Graphiques*, *Campo Grafico*, *Commercial Art/Art and Industry*, *Neue Grafik*, *Journal of the Ulm School for Design*, *Gebrauchsgraphik*, *Graphis*, *Typographica*, *Typographische Monatsblätter*, also called *TM*), Japan (*Idea*, *Graphic Design*) and their American counterparts (*Art Direction*, *Advertising Arts*, *Westvaco Inspirations*, *PM* and *A-D* journals, *Print*, *Dot Zero*, *CA: The Journal of Commercial Art*, *Western Advertising*) promoted the best of the old and new. *Fortune*, *Harper's Bazaar*, *Portfolio* and *Vogue*, among others, gave an outlet to American and European pictorial Modernists by the score. Curated and juried graphic compilations (*International Poster Annual*, *Modern Publicity*) further put forth the variety of Modernism in play.

The Great Depression and World War II were stimuli for perpetuating modern design and familiarizing the public with its look. In 1933, Coiner directed a unified design system for the National Recovery Administration (NRA), established by the Roosevelt administration to bring industry, labor, and government together to create codes of "fair practices." The NRA logo was ubiquitous and led in 1939 to Coiner's branding campaign for the U.S. Office of Civilian Defense. Each of these initiatives led directly to further investment by the government in graphic design. Almost every government agency and all service branches employed civilian and military graphic designers to produce cautionary and informative graphics. The best known was the U.S. Office of War Information, whose graphics chief, Francis Brennan, former art director of *Fortune* magazine, believed that posters should be "war art," combining the sophisticated style of contemporary art with the promotion of war aims. He hired scores of designers and illustrators, to promote strength at home and abroad.

Eclectic and Modern

Graphic design advanced through a dialectic between the proponents of the modern and advocates of eclectic form. European Modernism, which formed the foundation of postwar American design, attracted those who were ambitious to do more than just rote commercial art. As a teenager in the thirties, Paul Rand was introduced to the Bauhaus, and he speaks for many of his contemporaries about its influence: "I was intrigued with that kind of work which focused on ideas and not banalities; which stressed painting, architecture, typography and showed how they interrelated." Rand and his fellows snatched design out of the printing shop or agency bullpens and forged a real profession.

Belief in "the rightness of form" was a key to the modern design gestalt, but formalism at the expense of serendipity, wit, and humor produced dry, cold results. The moderns practiced economy; promoted the virtues of white space, asymmetry, and hierarchy; used color functionally when possible; and imbued their work with measured expression. They inhaled geometry and exhaled remarkably complex mathematical compositions. Some outright rejected expressionist approaches, favoring the systematic Swiss Style of visual organization that was successfully applied to global corporate communications, product, and exhibition design where order was imperative. But for genres like posters, record album covers, and book jackets, a wide range of design and typographic methods was preferable.

Typefaces and typography are never created in a vacuum. Practical and commercial motivations prevail, but theoretical and artistic rationales are never entirely in the shadows either, and choices are routinely informed by conscious concerns and unconscious impulses, which inevitably change with time. The moderns, who more or less followed the lead of the Bauhaus and the New Typography associated with it, preferred sans serif faces, especially Akzidenz-Grotesk, which was originally released by the H. Berthold typefoundry in Berlin in 1896 as "Accidenz-Grotesque" by "royal type-cutter Ferdinand Theinhardt," to express messages with clarity, simplicity, and ideological (typographic, that is) purity. Futura, the geometric "typeface of the future," designed by German Paul Renner in 1927, was frequently used by Ladislav Sutnar, Paul Rand, and countless other purveyors of modern aesthetics. Certain elegant serif and industrial slab serif faces, including Girder, Memphis, and Cairo, as well as Didot, a favorite of Alexey Brodovitch that was adapted by CBS for its identity, were also imbued with Modernism's flair.

Reduction of visual noise in everything from advertisements to book design was the stated goal of the more rigorous postwar graphic design moderns, who practiced the International Typographic Style emanating from Switzerland. Swiss Style did not reach its critical mass until the introduction of one particular typeface named after the famously neutral nation. Arguably, the most indelible typeface of the period was Helvetica (a.k.a. Swiss), designed in 1957 by Swiss type designer Max Miedinger with help from Haas Type Foundry president Eduard Hoffmann. If there are other typefaces that have triggered the same intense feelings among designers as Helvetica, bring them on. Some adore the face while others hate it, often for the same reason: neutrality.

Helvetica prompts paroxysms of joy and fits of rage because the face represents a clear Platonic ideal—or a turgid generic sterility. Helvetica was the answer to the unsatisfactory optical imperfections found in earlier grotesques (sans serifs). "Conceived in the Swiss typographic idiom, the new Helvetica offers an excitingly different tool to the American graphic designer and typographer," reads promotional text in a D. Stempel typefoundry specimen sheet from the late fifties. "Here is not simply another sans serif type but a carefully and judiciously considered refinement of the grotesk letter form." Helvetica was perfectly consistent with the needs of corporate identity.

The prime influencers justifying the value of design—graphic and industrial—to the interdependent business environment viewed global communication as key to economic stability. The corporate identity design experts included Lester Beall (Connecticut General Life Insurance), Will Burtin (Upjohn), William Golden (CBS), Egbert Jacobson (Container Corporation of America), Herbert Matter (Knoll), Ladislav Sutnar (Sweet's Catalog Service), and many others in this book who created distinctive marks and uniform standards. It can be argued that the pacesetter for Midcentury Modern corporate identity was IBM. Its chief during the fifties, Thomas Watson, famously announced, "Good design is good business." IBM was not the only design-savvy corporation, but when it hired Eliot Noyes as its design consultant and he, in turn, recruited Paul Rand to revamp its graphics, American corporate identity was truly born.

IBM's first logo (with contoured Gothic lettering in the shape of a globe) was designed in 1924, when "high-tech" business machines came with mahogany cabinetry and Queen Anne legs. So it is not so ironic that a typeface derived from nineteenth-century slab serifs came to symbolize the computer age. After all, the future was kind of scary. In fact, in the thirties, when the IBM logo was redesigned using Beton, a slab serif typeface whose name is German for "concrete," visions of the future were actually amalgams of the old and the slightly newer. IBM did not fully embrace Modernism until the early fifties, when Eliot Noyes replaced Queen Anne with progressive product and industrial design. In 1956, Paul Rand redesigned the IBM logo using a Constructivist-inspired slab serif called City, designed in 1930 by Georg Trump, because he felt it was important to retain something of IBM's earlier Beton identity. In 1962, when Rand added emblematic stripes to the IBM logo, City was transformed into a typeface that truly symbolized a company with its eye on the future, slab serifs and all. These stripes did more than act as a mnemonic; they implied that a logo was more than a mash-up of stylized letters or word and image—it was a symbolic entity that embodied corporate legacy and reputation. And the fifties and sixties were the era of these new communicative entities.

For every action there is a reaction. Modernism (ultimately derided as Corporate Modernism) came under fire from a growing number of eclectic designers for what had evolved into cool sterility (although the work in this book is rarely dry or formulaic). In the mainstream, this reaction (or rebellion) against the sterile extreme was represented notably by Push Pin Studios, founded in 1954 by Milton Glaser, Seymour Chwast, and Edward Sorel, with Reynold Ruffins joining shortly after. Its inventive methods awoke a somnambulant postwar field and altered advertising and book design. Although Push Pin was not fanatically avant-garde, through its reinvention of discarded mannerisms it did spark a profound shift in commercial art away from the cold rationalism of Corporate Modernism on the one hand, and the staid conventions of common commercial practice on the other, into new realms of pictorial expression.

Like the moderns, Push Pin believed design could make a significant difference to the well-being of society, not only by making messages more accessible through clear systems, but by brightening daily life through expressive form. Its means of achieving this goal, however, was through visibility in the marketplace. Just as Push Pin ushered in the reprises of Victorian and Art Nouveau as the basis for contemporary visual language, a distinctly past-future, anti-Modernist new offshoot known as Psychedelia (because it was influenced by hallucinogenic drugs) became the sweet code of youth during the late sixties. It, too, brought back Art Nouveau as an influence on typography. This was anathema to true moderns. Art Nouveau's youth-culture underpinnings were a clear slap in the face of, at the very least, orthodox moderns such as Josef Albers. In fact, Victor Moscoso, who—along with Stanley Mouse and Alton Kelley, Rick Griffin, and others—was a pioneer of psychedelic posters, studied with Albers and enjoyed doing everything he was told

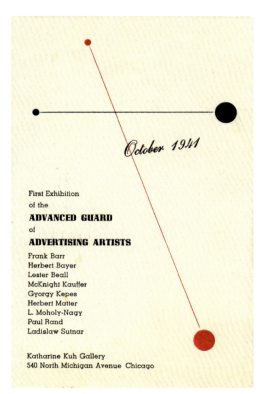

Exhibition announcement mailer, "First Exhibition of the Advanced Guard of Advertising Artists," Katharine Kuh Gallery, Chicago, October 1941. An editor's note in *A-D Journal* (Oct.–Nov., 1941) stated the exhibition was "one of the most successful ever held at the gallery according to Miss Kuh. Business men jammed the place, especially during lunch hours." Design by Frank Barr, typography teacher and supervisor of the printing workshop at Chicago's Institute of Design during the early 1950s

Booklet cover, *A Portfolio of Student Work from the School of Design at Yale University*, c. 1954. From the Alvin Lustig introduction: "The whole design program at Yale represents an interesting effort to synthesize the two apparently conflicting concepts in American education at this moment, that of the specialized expert, the product of the technical training school, versus the intellectually trained 'rounded gentlemen' of the traditional university. The School of Design accepts women students."

not to do, including intentionally vibrating colors. These nouveau Art Nouveaus enjoyed the formal intricacies of letterforms as much as any formal Modernist would, and they became obsessed with drawing the ornate negative spaces between letters. The youth-culture design form went mainstream when Photo-Lettering, America's largest phototypesetting house, introduced "Psychedelitypes," a collection of zany faux Art Nouveau faces. Psychedelic design was integrated into the mainstream at breakneck speed. But there was a more significant typographic shift that began in the late fifties and sixties—phototype technology—and its maestro was Herb Lubalin.

Back in the early sixties BC (before computer), Lubalin became known for expressive and illustrative typography that was made possible through photo manipulations. His primary work, like that of so many other designers before him (Beall, Burtin, Leibowitz, Steinweiss, and Ross) and some of his contemporaries (Troller, Giusti, Kramer, Wolff), was pharmaceutical advertising. The complex and often-indecipherable content of drug advertisements for Ciba-Geigy, Pfizer, Upjohn, Hoffmann-La Roche, and others, for drugs with unpronounceable names, demanded clever and decoratively symbolic solutions. Lublin was among the designers tasked with creating accessible allegories for drugs that would otherwise languish in obscurity. But his eclectic Modernism was best evidenced through his design of the typeface Avant Garde, which more than any other sixties or seventies typeface was emblematic of its time. He predicted (along with his typographic business associate Aaron Burns) as early as 1960 that since type was rapidly moving off the page and onto the television screen, typographers would need to rethink the aesthetics of type. He argued that typographers should abandon delicate Didots, the subtleties of which were lost on the cathode-ray tube, and rely instead on bold, more readable sans serifs. He further argued that large print advertisements on the sides of moving vehicles explained why passersby had become conditioned to reading fleeting messages. With the public's eyes pulled in different directions on message-laden streets, it was incumbent on graphic designers to devise new kinetic reading methods that were at once legible, eye-catching, and stylish. Passive typography—the kind that quietly, and sometimes elegantly, sat on a page—was not viable in a telekinetic world. Like the screaming headlines in tabloid newspapers, television demanded increasingly dramatic type displays. Technology had been influencing typographic aesthetics since the days of Johannes Gutenberg, but the act of moving typefaces around in telekinetic space demanded that typographers reappraise the essential cultural role of type: Was it still a neutral vessel for words and ideas, or a component of—indeed, a player in—a larger communications drama? One thing was certain: Type in motion could never be entirely neutral.

Motion typography arguably redefined Modernism in the fifties. It was so costly and time-consuming that only designers with patience and ambition even attempted to make type perform on the screen. But in the late fifties and sixties, film-title-sequence designers, including Saul Bass and Pablo Ferro, experimented with teaching type to perform on screen. Ferro, who began inking comic book pages for Stan Lee, also introduced dancing type for eccentric TV commercials that combined cartoon lettering with Victorian circus type into improvisational compositions. By utilizing quick-cut editing, stop-motion animation, and simultaneously projected images, he helped condition viewers to receive multiple graphics and produced typographic tours de force. Modernism had become star of stage and screen, but at the same time it was voraciously absorbing popular culture and morphing into something new.

Advertisement, "Tonnage," Young & Rubicam, 1960.
The figurative typographic expression underscores the
association with form and content. Design: Don Egensteiner

Advertisement, "Authority," Plant Engineering, 1959. Noel Martin
produced many catalogs beginning in 1947 at the Cincinnati Art
Museum and later at the Cincinnati Contemporary Arts Center.
He was a member of Ladislav Sutnar's small circle of friends and
in 1953 included in "Four American Designers," a graphic design
exhibition at the Museum of Modern Art in New York, along with
Herbert Bayer, Leo Lionni, and Ben Shahn. Design: Martin

Landscapes of Modern Design

The fifties and sixties were decades of ecological shifts in the broad landscape of graphic design and typography. The players and their roles are numerous and intersecting. It could be considered a formative period or a transitional one, the bridge from the pre-computer to the computer era. The Modernism celebrated in this book is not one size fits all. Although the designers included were nourished by the previous generations or their contemporaries, they also tried to avoid formulaic solutions. The overarching "look" or "feeling" of the era does, in retrospect, reveal a movement toward something, but there are numerous options and plenty of tangents. In design school, it might be de rigueur to copy the plaster cast or the professor's method, but once basic principles are learned, adaptation and reinvention kick in. The moderns we have selected to examine run along a broad spectrum of conceptual and visual thinking, supported by the idea that design is a method of aesthetically and intellectually bringing order out of chaos—of making concrete and appealing a grand mishmash of information, ideas, and communications—and of serving humankind.

This book would not be possible if graphic design were ignored as cultural effluvia. Yet codifying graphic design history has gone through a few developmental stages since the first edition of Philip B. Meggs's *A History of Graphic Design* in 1988. By outlining a lengthy legacy dating back to cave paintings, Meggs legitimized graphic design's ephemeral legacy and provided context as an applied art. However, he inadvertently formed a canon that ignored various designers who had made inroads. Subsequent editions, and a handful of alternative historical texts (see the bibliography), have been more inclusive, and that is also a goal of this book. We have sought to add names to the canon. These include Peter Bradford, John and Mary Condon, Donald and Ann Crews, Charles Goslin, Ray Komai, Roy Kuhlman, Charles E. Murphy, Tony Palladino, Peter Piening, Alexander Ross, Arnold Shaw, Barbara Stauffacher Solomon, and Rudi Wolff. And while Walter Allner, Neil Fujita, Burton Kramer, Reid Miles, Arnold Saks, and Dietmar Winkler are known in certain quarters, they have been ignored by current generations. Recognizing the contributions of these relatively unknown figures is essential to understanding how Modernism evolved and where it fits today. In addition, the better-known practitioners are not just here for context, but to introduce aspects of their output that have been ignored.

That said, a note about how graphic design history evolves: Before Philip Meggs's work, the history was mostly anecdotal, delivered in lectures and through professional-promotional profiles in trade magazines, which provide the majority of original sources today. Louis Danziger and his former student Keith Godard deserve credit for pioneering formal design history seminars, which brought the stories to light and led to Meggs's books. Subsequently, a slew of writers and researchers created databases of designers' portfolios, archives, and oral histories. The history has been built brick by brick. One designer speaks well of another, and that person becomes part of the folklore. Originality has been celebrated, but even that has needed a push. The designers who are best known are often the most vociferously promoted, either by their own efforts or those of others—through shows, competitions, and magazine articles. But obscurity still threatens the rest. There is no dearth of publishers anxious to produce books like this. The obstacles are the legions of rights and license holders, who make it difficult to access works for reproduction. While intellectual property should be respected, access should not be stopped by gatekeepers. This is why some designers who should be in books like this, and this book in particular, are absent from the history of Modernism in graphic design, which still has a way to go before it is complete. •

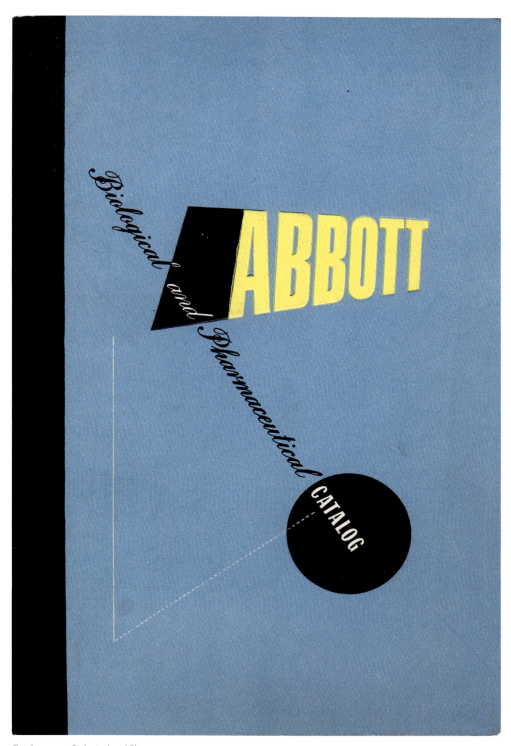

Catalog cover, *Biological and Pharmaceutical Catalog*, Abbott Laboratories, North Chicago, Illinois, 1938. Design attributed to M. Martin Johnson

Front of a double-sided paper insert, "Kromekote: Salesmaker for the World of Music," Champion Papers, c. 1962. George Giusti's brightly colored design is both abstract and reductive. It captures the essence of the premium smooth paper's surface while communicating the message directly to record makers. Design: Giusti

ÉMIGRÉS

02

Josef Albers
1888–1976

Albers teaching about angularity and proportions at Black Mountain College, 1946. Photo: Genevieve Naylor

When the Nazis shut down the Bauhaus in 1933, Josef Albers, born in Bottrop, Germany, and one of the country's foremost art and design "Jungmeisters" (young masters) since 1920, became the first of the school's instructors to safely immigrate to the United States (four years before Walter Gropius and László Moholy-Nagy), where his reputation as an artist and educator prospered. He had a profound influence on art and design theory and practice, notably through his book *Interaction of Color* (1963), as well as his classes at Black Mountain College, where he taught with his wife, Anni (1899–1994), starting in 1933, and Yale University, where he was chairman of the Department of Design from 1950 to 1958. One of the few graphic design jobs he did in America was what Nitzan Hermon, founder and former creative director of VVVVVV, a communication and technology design studio at the New Museum in New York, called "a visual and audible exploration of early lounge music" for Command Records. It was, in the argot of the moment, a mash-up of Bauhausian Precisionist art and cool sixties sounds.

Between 1959 and 1961, Albers, then in his early seventies, designed seven minimalist, abstract geometric album covers for Command Records that were at once rhythmic, harmonious, and, in short, perfectly musical. The three-year collaboration with the record company's cofounders, Enoch Light (1905–1978), a musician and innovative sound-recording engineer, and George Schwager, produced a nexus of design and audio that resonates today. Other than a cover for the catalog of the Museum of Modern Art's "Machine Art" exhibition in 1934, this is arguably the only commercial work that Albers produced, although his color theories and pedagogy had an incalculable impact on commercial designers.

Command Records (originally Command Performance Records) was founded in 1959 so that Light and Schwager could release conservative orchestral and easy listening music. Toward the end of the fifties, however, Light started experimenting with stereo and other technologies, including optical sound recording onto 35 mm magnetic film, in order to create new ways of experiencing recordings in home environments. Around this time, Command's art director, Charles E. Murphy, introduced Albers, who had just left teaching at Yale, to Light, and together they worked on Command's "new vision."

Using Albers gave Light an opportunity to bypass the clichés built into music industry packaging conventions. "The idea behind Light's approach to this series of records, with their emphasis on precision, subtlety, and nuance, allowed for a far more abstract approach to the album covers," wrote Alexander Tochilovsky, director of the Herb Lubalin Study Center of Design and Typography at Cooper Union in New York. "The use of squares and of grids of dots are consistent with his Modernist pursuit of the simplest and most effective means of communicating the intended subject, and with his interest in interactions." Albers's first cover, for *Provocative Percussion*, offers a visual interpretation of the music: "The dots break off the grid and bounce up in an elegant way that alludes to the music's dynamic range and of the stereophonic 'bouncing'

occurring in the recordings." Incidentally, this was also the first use of the gatefold album jacket, credited to Light, who used the extra space to document the music.

Albers's covers for Command were not the first to pair graphic Modernism with experimental music. Yet the albums are rare icons in the modern canon that spoke to the integration of sight and sound. "Enoch, Murphy and Albers have brought something new to life, through the context of Albers's packaging and Enoch's hifi experimentation," Hermon said. "And although the shift to Modernism was a gradual one—it is interesting to see the obvious effect that this collaboration had, especially in the confines of exotica and early lounge music."

Although Albers's graphic design work in the United States was limited, Nicholas Fox Weber, executive director of the Josef and Anni Albers Foundation, wrote, "No medium better conveys Josef Albers's comprehensive commitment to the Modernist sensibility than his work in graphic design. Though not extensive, his typographic efforts over more than half a century retain an immediacy that bespeaks his evolving yet always consistent aesthetic."

Moreover, his contributions as a teacher and author were major. Black Mountain College became a proving ground for American Bauhausian pursuit. "Asked what he hoped to accomplish at the school, Albers replied in his scant English, 'To open eyes.' As with Moholy-Nagy, 'vision' was the modernist password," wrote Achim Borchardt-Hume. Albers was quoted as saying, "Learning is better than teaching because it is more intense: the more is being taught, the less can be learned."

Albers ran the Department of Design at Yale University during its defining years, when its undergraduate and graduate degree programs began. Setting a modern course, he invited leading practitioners to teach at various levels. He also taught color-theory courses at Pratt Institute, New York. Today, Albers is best known as an artist. He began his investigative Homage to the Square series of hundreds of artworks in 1950 and continued for twenty-five years. The key to these explorations, Albers explained, was an illusion: A central square, lying between inner and outer ones, subtly takes on the hue of its neighboring squares. From this series came his 1963 book, *Interaction of Color*, considered the definitive treatise on color, which taught students the indelible and incredible impact of color and its interactions through perceptual studies that transformed the language of the visual world. These transformations constituted a legacy of art and design and are still used in color-theory course work today. •

001

001
Album cover, *Provocative Percussion, Vol. III* by
Enoch Light and the Light Brigade, Command
Records, Grand Award Record Company,
New York, 1961. The series of album cover
designs for Enoch Light's Command Records
reveals Josef Albers's commitment toward a
Modernist graphic vocabulary. His suggestive
and visual musical metaphors are playful
experiments in rhythm, color, line, shape,
space, and Gestalt principles.

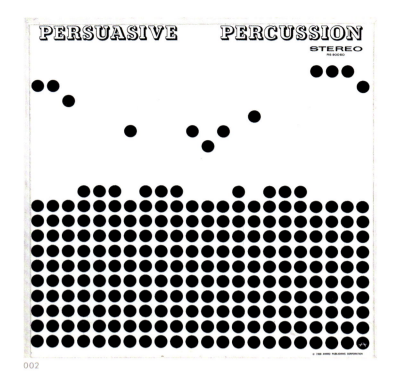

002

003

002
Album cover, *Persuasive Percussion* by Enoch Light and the Light Brigade, Command Records, Award Publishing Corporation, Harrison, New Jersey, 1959. Enoch Light describes this record as "the most unusual record you have ever put on your turntable. It is a unique mixture of entertainment, excitement, beauty, and practicality."

003
Album cover, *Persuasive Percussion Volume 3* by Enoch Light and the Light Brigade, Command Records, Grand Award Record Company, New York, 1960

004

005

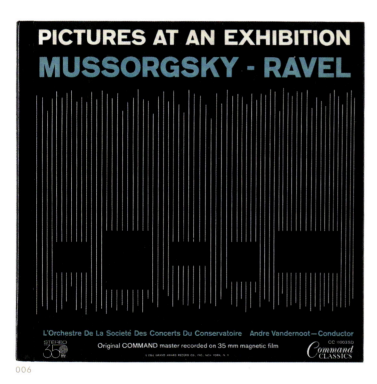

006

007

004
Album cover, *Magnificent Two-Piano Performances* by Leonid Hambro and Jascha Zayde, Command Classics, Grand Award Record Company, New York, 1961

005
Album cover, *Provocative Percussion* by Enoch Light and the Light Brigade, Command Records, Award Publishing Corporation, New York, 1959

006
Album cover, *Pictures at an Exhibition* by Modest Mussorgsky and Maurice Ravel, Command Classics, Grand Award Record Company, New York, 1961

007
Album cover, *Provocative Percussion Volume 2*, Command Records, Grand Award Record Company, New York, 1960

Walter Allner
1909–2006

Allner in his New York studio, c. 1950.
Photo: Dan Weiner

Walter Heinz Allner, a Bauhaus-trained graphic designer and art director of *Fortune* magazine from 1962 to 1974, introduced Modernist typographic sensibility to American magazine design. In addition to overseeing the magazine's design, he created seventy-nine covers, which ranged from poster-like, minimalist graphic abstraction to complex photographic collage. The consequence was that much of his cover art projected a Pop Art sensibility that expressed the personality of America's leading financial monthly.

Born in Dessau, Germany, Allner enrolled at the Bauhaus in 1927 when he was eighteen, two years after it moved from Weimar to his hometown, and six years before the Nazis shut it down. "Behind the vast, glass and metal facade, which I, in speechless wonder, had watched going up, my life began," he wrote in 1983. At the Bauhaus, he studied typography, poster design, and painting under key masters of the modern movement, including Josef Albers, Wassily Kandinsky, and Paul Klee. While on a short leave from the Bauhaus, he worked at the Gesellschafts- und Wirtschaftsmuseum in Vienna with the progressive philosopher, sociologist, and economist Otto Neurath, the innovator of universal sign-symbols known as isotypes, which form the basis for contemporary pictorial iconography.

Allner was always peripatetic; he worked in the Netherlands under Piet Zwart, the influential Dutch modern typographer, in 1930, and in Paris with the Art Deco poster artists Jean Carlu and A. M. Cassandre. Yet it was Josef Albers's Precisionist abstract geometric graphics that had the most influence on the streamlined art and design that Allner later brought to *Fortune*.

With his signature approach, Allner ran his own design partnership, Omnium Graphique, in Paris in 1934–36. At that time, he devoted himself to abstract painting and exhibited at the Salon des Surindépendants and the Salon des Réalités Nouvelles in Paris; there he became a progenitor of an art form he called "new realities." He was also art director of the publishing house Formes, Editions d'Art Graphique et Photographique, where he worked with Man Ray. He eventually returned to magazine design as editor under Walter Herdeg of the Swiss design journal *Graphis*, from 1945 to 1948. In 1948, he founded the *International Poster Annual* for the Swiss publisher Zollikofer, in St. Gall, with art direction by Cassandre, and he edited it until 1952. He also edited the book *A. M. Cassandre: Peintre d'affiches*, adding to his reputation as one of the world's leading experts on poster history.

Upon immigrating to the United States in 1949, he was a freelance design consultant for RCA, Johnson & Johnson, the American Cancer Society, ITT, and IBM. The Outdoor Advertising Association of America commissioned him to design all of its twenty-four-sheet billboards for a national traffic-safety campaign. He designed an advertising poster, "Enjoy LIFE Every Week," for *Life* magazine in 1951; in the same year, he joined *Fortune* magazine, where he remained until 1974, working initially as an assistant to Leo Lionni on a major redesign and then as art director. He said in an unpublished talk in 1987 at the University of Bridgeport, in Connecticut, that when the magazine first appeared on European newsstands, in the early 1930s, it was considered the "epitome of modernism—precisely because—its conservative layout not withstanding—it visually glorified American industry."

In 1965, after taking a course at MIT, he experimented with the first computer-designed cover on a national magazine for the annual Fortune 500 issue. A company press release at the time proudly noted that the image, consisting of arrows in upward flight behind large illuminated numerals, was generated on a computer's oscilloscope and then photographed. Long before the personal computer revolutionized the methods used to produce graphic design, Allner predicted the integration of aesthetics and advanced technology, and so he worked directly with computer engineers whenever he could.

"Allner's interest in science, coupled with a venturesome spirit, has led him into exciting new design fields," wrote John Lahr in *Print* magazine in 1966. This spirit was evident in *Fortune* covers, notably one in which he arranged for dozens of windows on twenty floors of the Time & Life Building in New York to be illuminated at night to spell out "500." Allner said of his *Fortune* covers that each one "has to be something of a surprise" even in his own eyes. Regardless of the medium, Allner's work was always in sync with principles he learned at the Bauhaus: succinctness, rejection of embellishment, and aesthetic integrity. "He relies on the purity of form pared down to its essentials," wrote Dennis Wepman.

After retiring from *Fortune* in 1974, Allner taught Communication Design at Parsons School of Design and lectured throughout the United States and Europe. His motto for students and professionals was, "Raise the aesthetic standard—the public is more perceptive than you think." He also continued to design posters based on Bauhausian principles: shunning superfluous ornamentation and conveying messages with brevity and simplicity. "I try to be concise. The idea to communicate should be positive and direct," Allner noted. "My initial effort is always directed towards finding a symbol, a form, or a trademark, which will translate the subject as concisely as possible, and will also permit a simple graphic interpretation of the greatest possible impact."

Allner's design for *Fortune*, and also for the trade magazine *Modern Packaging*, underscored Modernism's legacy of conceptual simplicity coming out of an age of clutter. Allner was a modern master, and as designer Steff Geissbuhler eulogized, "He is one of the very last genuine Bauhaus students." •

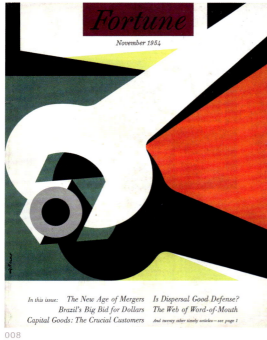

008

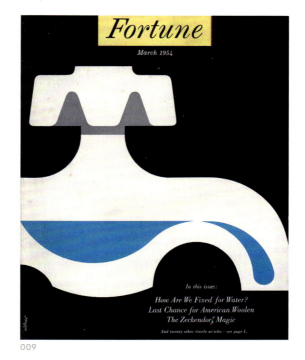

009

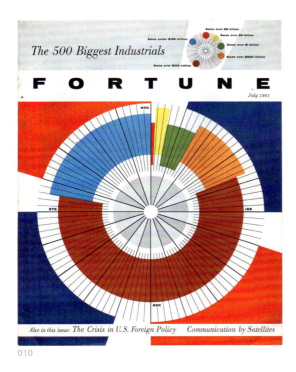

010

011

008

Magazine cover, *Fortune*, November 1954. A stylized wrench illustrates an article on the swiftly changing U.S. capital-goods market and its impact on the economy. Influenced by information authority Otto Neurath, Allner mastered the clarity of communication by developing a direct and concise graphic language.

009

Magazine cover, *Fortune*, March 1954. This faucet represents the article "How Are We Fixed for Water?" about the water resources and problems in the United States.

010

Magazine cover, *Fortune*, July 1961. Allner's information graphic uses color and line to illustrate *Fortune*'s directory of the 500 largest U.S. industrial corporations.

011

Magazine cover, *Fortune*, January 1959. This cover marks the start of a yearlong series of articles focusing on the influences shaping the U.S. market, with the first being "The 1960's: A Forecast of the Technology." The top band is a photograph by Martin *Munkácsi* of New York construction workers.

012

013

012
Album cover, *Johann Christian Bach—Four Compositions* by Paul Sacher conducting the Vienna Symphony Orchestra, Columbia Masterworks, Columbia Records, 1954. The cover artist is incorrectly identified as Robert Allner. The optical-like design is a captivating balance of logical and precise angular forms, paired with flat black-and-white transitions and tensions.

013
Advertisement, "Edmund Burke on the People's Liberty: The People Never Give Up Their Liberties but under Some Delusion," part of "Great Ideas of Western Man" campaign, Container Corporation of America, 1954

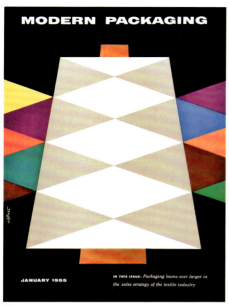

014

015

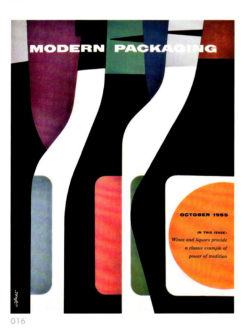

016

017

018

019

014–019
Magazine covers, *Modern Packaging*, January 1955, February 1955, October 1955, March 1957, April 1959, and April 1963. Allner's stylized and energetic graphic forms aptly illustrate each issue's featured article: textiles, canning, wine and liquor, people of packaging, and packaging shows/exhibitions.

Herbert Bayer

1900–1985

Bayer in his Aspen, Colorado, studio, c. 1946 (detail)

In 1969, *Print* magazine's thirtieth-anniversary issue comprised a special collection of essays titled "Great Graphic Designers of the 20th Century." It portrayed a profession on the cusp of great demographic and technological change. Among the elders portrayed, Herbert Bayer's name stood out. "Herbert Bayer: The Bauhaus Tradition"—written by a like-minded devotee of orthodox Modernism, the Swiss master Josef Müller-Brockmann—emphasized Bayer's prominence among graphic design eminences and positioned him as a beacon at a time when the ideals of prewar European Modernism were at odds with design practice in the United States. In 1938, Bayer designed the exhibition, catalog (coedited with Walter and Ise Gropius), and related printed ephemera for the Museum of Modern Art's historic 1938 exhibition "Bauhaus 1919–1928." This was the first time the Bauhaus was the subject of an exhibition in America, and it was the thirty-eight-year-old Bayer's most important contribution upon first arriving in his new land.

Born in Haag, Austria, Bayer left Berlin in 1938 and immigrated to New York, where he practiced for eight years. Recalling his arrival, he said, "I was impressed by America, impressed by the idea of freedom." In turn, more than any other graphic designer, Bayer was responsible for synthesizing modern art and American modern mise-en-page, exhibitions, typography, and photography. The 1939 self-promotional brochure *Things to Come* marked a high point in design, in which Bayer played a fundamental role in bridging the gap between European avant-garde design and the new American aesthetic. Perhaps borrowing its title from the 1936 science fiction film *Things to Come* (with a screenplay by H. G. Wells), the brochure's energetic, imaginative, and dreamlike graphics are unfamiliar yet hint at the emerging new forms. It's this balance between modern art and science that Bayer mastered.

"Bayer grew up in a world of great artistic movements," wrote Müller-Brockmann in *Print*, "which established essential foundations and goals in all areas of visual design." He was referring to the Modernist avant-garde, whose notions of the "rightness" of form and content had a powerful influence on contemporary corporate practice. Bayer was both a student and then an instructor at the Bauhaus, which was a source of inspiration and a raison d'être for his career. There was no typography or advertising workshop at the school in 1921 when Bayer arrived from Austria, where the twenty-one-year-old had apprenticed under an artist in Linz. His main focus was on learning mural painting under Wassily Kandinsky, but he also joined a group of students who were experimenting with László Moholy-Nagy on typography projects that employed asymmetry, easy-to-read sans serif typefaces, red and black lines, and eye-catching grammatical signs.

Bayer was twenty-three when Walter Gropius recognized his gifts and put him in charge of teaching typography and advertising. In three years as a teacher, Müller-Brockmann wrote, Bayer established himself as "one of the pioneers of modern visual communication" in type, photography, and display design; at twenty-five, he "developed the idea of functional typography from the ground up." Müller-Brockmann argued that Bayer's strict discipline and acute intelligence hinged on the absence of "fashionable artiness"—though over time his designs, curiously, became just that in terms of how Modernism was executed for certain clients. "Although Bayer at first worked lines, squares, dots and other geometric elements in with type to achieve greater forcefulness, he later abandoned such aids." In 1925, "to counteract the flood of bad typefaces," Bayer designed the Universal Alphabet, a lowercase, sans serif face constructed out of arcs, angles, and vertical and horizontal lines. "The shapes of the letters are pared down to a minimum without depriving them of their typical character and improving their legibility."

As orthodox as his work might appear, Bayer was quick to understand the limitations of style and was therefore not rigidly opposed to using an "invented free-form shadow type particularly suited to advertising . . . when a suggestive psychological effect is desired." Müller-Brockmann praised Bayer for his ability to analyze a problem and grasp its psychological meaning, which he then translated into visual terms.

In the late twenties in Berlin, Bayer worked as an art director for German *Vogue* and a design director at Dorland Studio, Germany's largest international advertising firm. In the United States, for eight years in New York and then in Aspen, Colorado, from 1946 on, he found consulting art directorships with the John Wanamaker department stores, the J. Walter Thompson advertising agency, and Dorland International. Through his intense relationship with Walter P. Paepcke, president of Container Corporation of America, he helped to create the legendary advertising campaign "Great Ideas of Western Man," which lasted from 1950 to 1975 and drew on the talents of many artists and designers. His *World Geo-Graphic Atlas*, published by Container Corporation of America in 1953, is a masterpiece of information design on a massive scale. Bayer was also thrust into the role of consultant for Paepcke's Aspen development project, for which he spearheaded the restoration of Victorian buildings including the Wheeler Opera House and the Hotel Jerome, selecting color schemes. A strong blue, known as "Bayer Blue," persevered for some fifty years, but it is now disappearing.

Bayer directed Container Corporation of America's design program until his retirement in 1965. He continued as art and design consultant to the Atlantic Richfield Company until his death, overseeing what was for a time the world's largest corporate art collection. He also worked as an architect, an interior designer, a painter, and sculptor. •

020

020

Self-promotional brochure, *Things to Come*, 1939. From the interior text: "American advertising art is in transition. New forms, new—a more graphic approach, a more essential appeal is emerging from the experiments of yesterday. It is Herbert Bayer, more than any other living artist, who is responsible for this shaping process and for its most original and vigorous direction. . . .

Master of mise en page, industrial designer, director of exhibits, type creator, photographer, painter and poster artist, his work represents the finest synthesis of modern art mediums in advertising. An adventurer of esthetics, an engineer of the arts, Herbert Bayer brings to American advertising an original practicality, a sound and imaginative impetus."

021

022

021
Magazine cover, *Harper's Bazaar,*
"College Fashions," Hearst Corporation,
August 1940. A precursor to the pop-art
movement of the mid- to late 1950s,
this striking cover geared toward women
readers repeats and delicately shifts
overexposed photographs combined with
vibrant flat lipstick colors. Art direction:
Alexey Brodovitch

022
Poster, *Mont Tremblant*, 1939. Shortly
after his arrival in the United States,
Bayer worked for Mont-Tremblant, a ski
destination in Quebec, Canada, for which
he designed this heroic photomontage
poster in a modern and surrealistic manner.

023

024

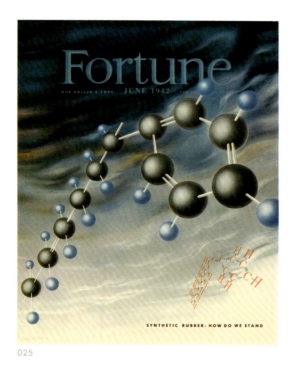

025

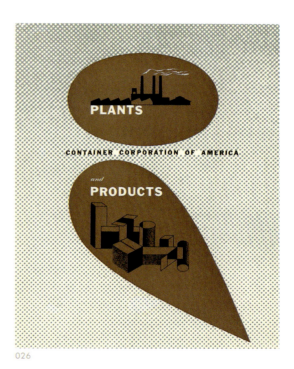

026

Journal covers, *Wine and Liquor Retailer: Devoted to Package Store Merchandising*, Atlas Publishing Company, January 1941 and August 1942. Between 1940 and 1942, Bayer designed about twenty-seven covers for *Wine and Liquor Retailer* in which he experimented with a variety of methods and techniques including photomontage, collage, illustration, hand lettering, and more.

Magazine cover, *Fortune*, June 1942. Bayer's cover introduces the article "Synthetic Rubber: How Do We Stand?" with an interpretative illustration of synthetic rubber's chemical structure.

Catalog cover, *Plants and Products*, Container Corporation of America, 1948. This publication traces the company's growth in terms of materials, products, facilities, and production.

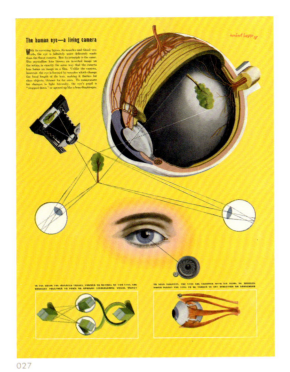

027

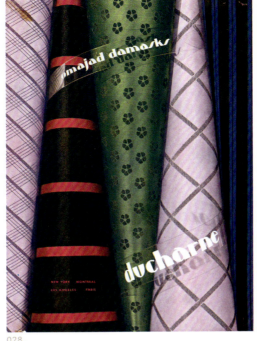

028

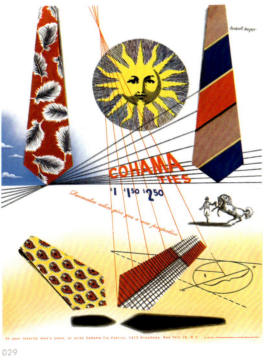

029

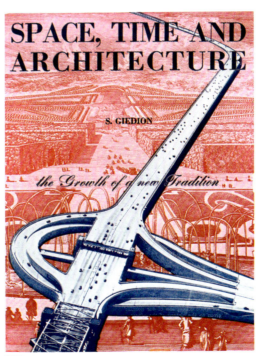

030

027

Advertisement, "The Human Eye—A Living Camera," *Life*, December 18, 1939. Printed to supplement the article "The Eye: Mankind's Efficiency Depends on Its Most Precious Sense"

028

Advertisement, "Omajad Damasks," Ducharne, 1945

029

Advertisement, "Cohama Ties: Sunmaker Colors Give You a New Perspective," Cohama Men's Wear Fabrics, c. 1945

030

Book jacket, *Space, Time and Architecture: The Growth of a New Tradition*, by Siegfried Giedion, Harvard University Press, 1941

031

Magazine cover, *House & Garden*, Condé Nast Publications, August 1945. From the interior: "A plan, elevation and bird's-eye perspective of one of the first prize-winning houses in House & Garden's Blueprints for Tomorrow architectural contest. The design was submitted by Lester C. Tichy. Howard Beyer [an incorrect identification of Bayer] has worked out an abstract composition from the parts, which go to make it up."

House & Garden
A Condé Nast Publication

Prize Houses – 21 Building pages

August 1945
Price 35 Cents 40 Cents in Canada
COPYRIGHT 1945, THE CONDÉ NAST PUBLICATIONS INC.

031

Alexey Brodovitch

1898–1971

Brodovitch in his *Harper's Bazaar* New York office, 1937. Photo: George Karger

With Russian bravado, Alexey Brodovitch commanded generations of students and assistants (including designers and photographers Richard Avedon, Lillian Bassman, Hiro, Marvin Israel, Harvey Lloyd, Irving Penn, and Garry Winogrand, among many others): "Astonish me!" In the mid-twentieth century, these two words were as essential in freeing the design world from cliché as "We hold these truths to be self-evident" is to democracy itself. Many of these visual talents significantly helped to mold the mass media during the fifties and sixties, and they brought forth other Brodovitchians. "Astonish me!"—that charged phrase from the maestro of majestic magazines—triggered changes in editorial pacing and configuration that continue to inspire.

The influential art director of *Harper's Bazaar* from 1934 to 1958, Brodovitch, born in Ogolitchi, Russia, "played a crucial role in introducing into the United States a radically simplified, 'modern' graphic design style forged in Europe in the 1920s from an amalgam of vanguard movements in art and design," wrote Andy Grundberg when the American Institute of Graphic Arts (AIGA) posthumously awarded Brodovitch its 1987 AIGA Medal for lifetime achievement, for his expressively elegant typography, dynamic and dramatic photography, and signature use of white space. In his magazine and advertising art direction and teaching, Brodovitch made photography "the backbone" of modern design, and he "fostered the development of an expressionistic, almost primal style of picture-taking that became the dominant style of photographic practice in the 1950s," added Grundberg.

A White Russian exiled in Paris after the Russian Revolution, Brodovitch cut his teeth as a graphic designer at the storied typefoundry Deberny et Peignot, where he produced distinctive, striking, sometimes poster-like typographic editorial pages for *Arts et Métiers Graphiques*, a bimonthly art and design journal edited by Charles Peignot. During this early sojourn in France, he won first prize in a poster fair for the Bal Banal, a 1924 artists' ball organized by the Russian artists in Paris, which kicked off his career as an original stylist and earned him commissions to design posters for major French companies. Brodovitch was also a prolific advertising art director, producing catalogs and publicity for Madelios, the men's department of the Aux Trois Quartiers department store. He experimented with Art Moderne and Constructivist design styles, consistent with the modern ethos of the twenties.

America beckoned in 1930, when the Philadelphia Museum of Art invited Brodovitch to create an advertising art department, which became known as the Design Laboratory, in the museum's school. In Philadelphia, he was also a designer at N. W. Ayer, the advertising agency that was a haven for émigrés. In 1934, Carmel Snow, the editor of *Harper's Bazaar*, appointed him art director to give Dr. Mehemed Fehmy Agha's *Vogue* a run for its money. The next twenty-four years "became a veritable Periclean age for the publication," noted a biography of Brodovitch published in 1972. "Brodovitch brought an entirely new sense of orchestration, scale, pitch, flow, line, accent and form to the magazine. By then a man of two

cultures, he was able to join the maturity and sophistication of European sensibility with the dynamism of America."

By introducing some of photography's and illustration's greatest modern talents, including Bill Brandt, Henri Cartier-Bresson, A. M. Cassandre, Saul Steinberg, and even Salvador Dalí to American readers, while nurturing a new generation too numerous to name, Brodovitch secured an incredible legacy. He also revolutionized how fashion was rendered and perceived in magazines: "Clothes were presented not as pieces of fabric cut in singular ways, but as signs of a fashionable life," wrote Grundberg. As art director for Saks Fifth Avenue and I. Miller, Brodovitch had a similar influence on fashion advertising.

Brodovitch created the most innovative American graphic design magazine of the era, a veritable homage to *Arts et Métiers Graphiques*, titled *Portfolio*, only three issues of which were published, in 1949–50. Edited by editor turned art director turned editor Frank Zachary, *Portfolio* was filled with profusely illustrated articles on Alexander Calder, Charles Eames, Paul Rand, Saul Steinberg, and other artists and art themes. Zachary often cited Brodovitch as his mentor for helping conceive the magazine's contents and creating its elegantly tactile design, through the use of die-cuts, transparent pages, multipage gatefolds, and other complex graphic devices. *Bazaar* was Brodovitch's flagship; *Portfolio* was his laboratory.

In his quest to be astonished, Brodovitch had no tolerance for mediocrity. "A student's worst offense was to present something Brodovitch found boring," Grundberg noted, even though he "did not formulate a theory of design." To be modern or not made no difference if the result was uninspired. Isms were contemptible; genius was all that mattered. •

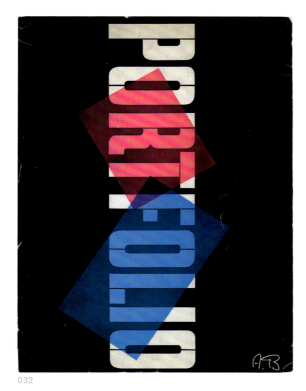

032

033

034

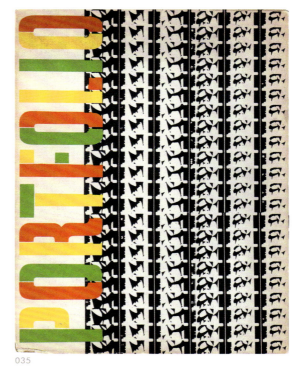

035

032–035

Magazine covers, *Portfolio: A Magazine for the Graphic Arts*, Zebra Press, no. 1 (Winter 1950), with transparent colors printed over type (front and back); no. 2 (Summer 1950), with an embossed logo and tissue-paper kite design by Charles Eames; and no. 3 (1951), with Alexander Calder film stills by Herbert Matter. *Portfolio* editor Frank Zachary said he learned more about magazine design and pacing from Brodovitch, who would lay all the spreads out on the floor to determine how the layouts worked best together.

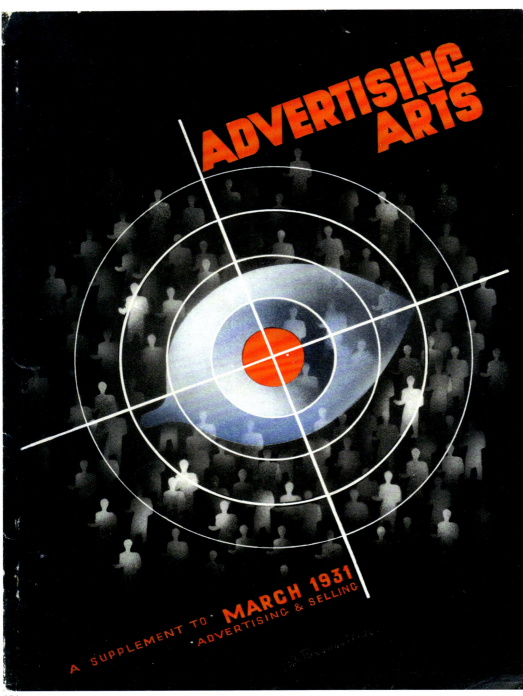

036

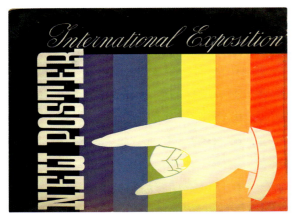

037

036
Magazine cover, *Advertising Arts,*
supplement to Advertising and Selling (F. C.
Kendall, editorial director), March 1931.
Brodovitch made his cover using a piece of
Bristol board freehand, without sketches.
With an airbrush, he covered the surface
of the board with black, and then he used
poster paints. A stencil of the little man
was cut out of ordinary paper, and the
figure was airbrushed in over the black
background, using white paint and the
stencil. The white circles were made with a
compass and ruling pen, while he lettered
on tracing paper. On the back of the
tracing paper, the lettering was drawn first
with white and black lead pencil. Then it
was rendered with a brush.

037
Catalog cover, *New Poster, International*
Exposition of Design in Outdoor Advertising,
The Franklin Institute of the State of
Pennsylvania, 1937

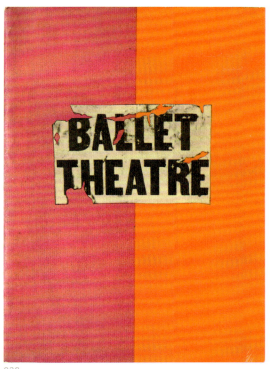

038

039

040

038
Program cover, *Ninth Ballet Theatre Annual*, New York, 1949

039
Advertisement, "Rousseau on the Citizen and the State," part of "Great Ideas of Western Man" campaign, Container Corporation of America, 1962

040
Book cover (front and back), *The Doctors and the Devils*, by Dylan Thomas, Time Reading Program, Time Incorporated, 1964

Will Burtin

1908–1972

Burtin with the model of a basic cell structure developed for Upjohn Company's exhibition "The Cell," c. 1957. Photo: Ezra Stoller

Will Burtin, born in Cologne, Germany, the son of a French chemist, believed that striving to understand molecular biology, endocrinology, and bacteriology was as important to his design practice as studying the typography of Didot and Bodoni. He was a master of making complex data accessible through graphic concepts, which included creating pages of text as elegant as they were informative. The role of the graphic designer, he wrote in *Print* in 1955, was to increase the average man's understanding "between what the reading public knows and what they should know." There was no higher calling.

His professional life was therefore devoted to mastering information design in a modern manner. Indeed, such technical material might have remained forever relegated to colorless textbooks if Burtin had not become the champion of exquisite functionality. This was no better realized than through his designs for the Upjohn Company—one of America's largest producers of pharmaceuticals—from 1949 to 1971. Burtin refused to shy away from the complexity of science; rather, he used visual means to cast it in an accessible light.

Burtin fled Hitler's Germany in 1937 after Minister of Propaganda Joseph Goebbels ordered him to design posters for the Nazis as the ministry's director of design. He adopted Thomas Jefferson's dictum "To learn how to keep learning is the mark of civilized man." Burtin believed that designers had to know about more fields than just design—science was integral to all life, and the exploration and prediction of phenomena constituted the holy grail of civilization. For the sake of clarity, scientists reduce time, space, and thought to abstract symbols, and that was what the designer did too. "The designer stands between these concepts, at the center, because of his unique role as communicator . . . interpreter, and inspirer," Burtin wrote in *Graphis* in 1949.

Burtin's graphic design for Upjohn's identity, packaging, advertisements, catalogs, and, particularly, *Scope*, the company's in-house magazine, was direct and consistently on message. Originally designed by Burtin, then Lester Beall until Burtin returned, *Scope* possessed elegant typography, with graphics sprinkled throughout as signposts that guided the viewer through a hierarchy of information. Burtin took this to an even greater level of virtuosity. Edited for physicians, *Scope* was intended to improve the understanding of modern therapeutics, establish goodwill, and help sell Upjohn's products, yet Burtin gave it entry points that allowed access to the average reader as well. His ability to transform technical language into visual symbols provided readers with a clear grasp of the material.

For the professional reader, arcane medical articles were not cluttered with dreary text boxes and drab flow charts. "The choice of format was . . . of great importance, not only to give the new journal the distinction we wished it to have but to appeal appropriately to the physician," explained Burtin in *Print*. The house organs already in existence ran the gamut in design from the most conservative to the most modern, and from those that used design sparingly to those that were highly and almost flamboyantly ornamental. With conservatism regarded as inappropriate for a journal devoted to a rapidly progressing science, contemporaneous design seemed mandatory, but without looking frivolous, which would seem out of place. Burtin's use of photographs of microscopic imagery gave the work an abstract quality that suggested modern art. Even the covers of *Scope* were designed not only to be attractive but also to suggest the content. In the modern spirit, design was used not for its decorative effect but as an integral tool for clarifying scientific presentations.

"Integration" was a defining practical trait for Burtin. "In designing booklets, posters, ads, exhibits, and displays, I noticed that the integration of job components towards a dramatic end-product asked for a measure of discipline difficult to define," he wrote. But he did define it, as the marriage of order and instinct—learning everything there is about a particular subject and then allowing instinct to drive the design.

Burtin designed "Integration: The New Discipline in Design," an exhibition for the A-D Gallery in 1948, which demonstrated how he, and by extension others, clarify scientific information for general consumption. "Understanding of space and time relations is a main requirement in visual organization. In printed design images are superimposed on paper surfaces. The spaces inside and between letters, between lines of type, their relationship to illustration, are vital factors, which determine the eye's access to the basic information," he explained.

Even earlier, at *Fortune*, where he worked as an art director from 1945 to 1949, Burtin had developed ways of conveying information through the design of charts, maps, graphs, and diagrams that made complex data discernible and understandable. Ladislav Sutnar noted in his 1961 book *Visual Design in Action* that Burtin developed two basic strategies: the purist approach, in which charts and diagrams were compressed into a two-dimensional projection that unambiguously framed the information; and the dramatized approach, the grouping of visual data with poster-like impact, as in a chart that graphically used radical cropping and contrasts to grab reader attention. For this latter, Burtin often used an airbrush to make scientific diagrams so concise and beautiful that they functioned both as art and as information.

"Who said that science cannot achieve beauty," Burtin argued in *Print*. "What nonsense, that art cannot contain scientific truth! It is human limitation, deficiency of understanding, that make one or the other not do what they can do." For Burtin, art was a means of obtaining knowledge and communicating it to all generations. Being a designer was being a scientist. •

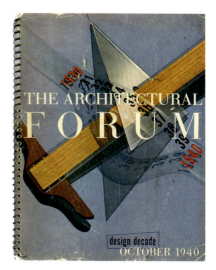

041

041

Magazine cover and original art, *Architectural Forum*, "Design Decade 1930–1940," published by Time, vol. 73, no. 4 (October 1940). The drafting tools of an engineer reveal a precise composition of light, shadow, form, and texture. "The lack of ornament in contemporary design has been noted by any number of critics," wrote the issues editor. "It would be absurd, however, to ignore the extraordinary richness of form in the modern scene, or the amazing variety of textures, colors and patterns at the disposal of the designer. . . . Through the machine, the arts have come off their crumbling pedestals and gone back to workshop. Which is where they belong, and where they always were in great periods."

042

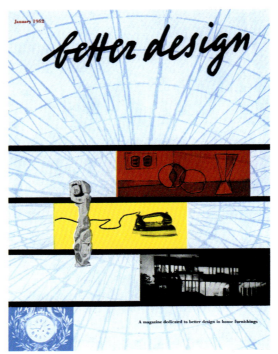

043

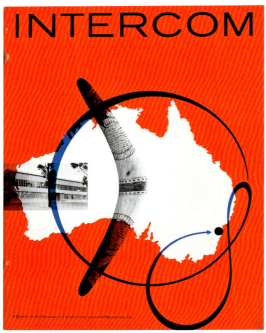

044

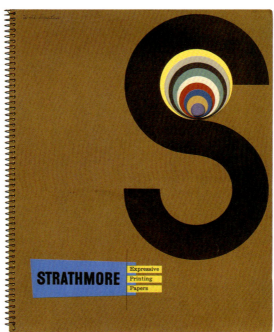

045

Magazine cover, *Design +*, "Florida Issue," no. 1 (1950)

043
Magazine cover, *Better Design*, January 1952. Dedicated to better design in home furnishings. Design editor: Will Burtin

044
House organ cover, *Intercom*, a quarterly publication of Upjohn International Operations, Upjohn Company, Summer 1959

045
Booklet cover, *Expressive Printing Papers*, Strathmore Paper Company, 1952. By puncturing a hole in all the pages, Burtin creates an effective illusion of three-dimensional depth. This experimental approach is a departure from the standard two-dimensional printing methods and allows the reader to experience the product (a variety of paper colors) in one single piece of work.

RESTRICTED

GUNNERY IN THE A-26

AIR FORCE MANUAL NO. 56 • NOVEMBER 1944 • RESTRICTED

046

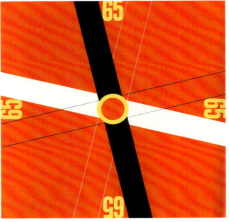

047

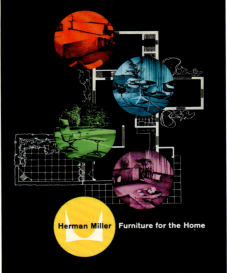

048

046
Manual cover, *Gunnery in the A-26, Air Force*, Army Air Forces Training Aids Division, Office of Strategic Services (OSS), Manual no. 56, November 1944. A transparent crescent shape and cropped images illustrate the complex process of maneuvering speed and the bomber's gunnery skill.

047
Conference program cover and interior page, "Vision 65: World Congress on New Challenges to Human Communication," Southern Illinois University (SIU), Carbondale, October 21–23, 1965. Organized by Burtin and sponsored by the International Center for Typographic Arts (Aaron Burns, director) in cooperation with SIU, "Vision 65" "concerned itself with the broad emergent problems of communications and challenges posed by the technological and social developments in ways which will significantly stimulate the individual and the community."

048
Product brochure, *Furniture for the Home*, Herman Miller, c. 1958

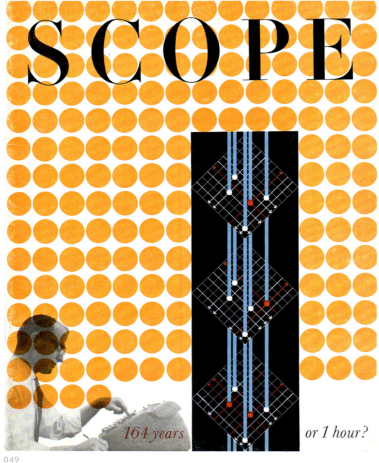

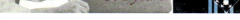

049

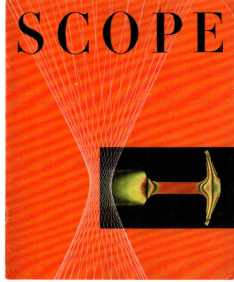

050

051

052

049
House organ cover, *Scope*, Upjohn Company, Kalamazoo, Michigan, vol. 4, no. 11 (1957). Burtin's cover illustrates a feature article on the development of the modern computer, or "electronic brain," and its ability to compute in one hour what the human brain may do in 164 years.

050
House organ cover, *Scope*, Upjohn Company, Kalamazoo, Michigan, vol. 4, no. 9 (Summer 1956)

051
House organ cover, *Scope*, Upjohn Company, Kalamazoo, Michigan, vol. 3, no. 8 (Summer 1952)

052
House organ cover, *Scope*, Upjohn Company, Kalamazoo, Michigan, no. 5 (September 1943)

053

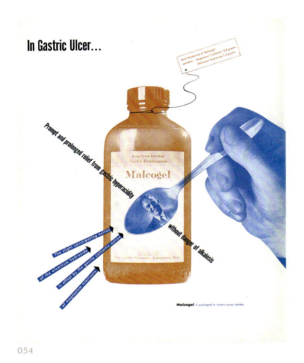

054

055

053
Brochure cover, *Heredity and Beyond*,
issued on the occasion of an education
exhibit, "Heredity and You," held in the Time
& Life Building, New York, 1967

054
Advertisement, "In Gastric Ulcer . . .
Malcogel," *Scope*, no. 5 (September 1943)

055
Advertisement, "Full Capacity for Men and
Machine, A Unicap a Day," *Scope*, no. 5
(September 1943)

George Giusti

1908–1990

Giusti in his Bronx, New York, apartment and studio, c. 1943

George Giusti, whose designs for books, records, and ads dominated the late forties to midfifties mass media, combined the artist's eye with an architect's logic. Giusti trained as a student at the Reale Accademia di Belle Arti di Brera in Milan; Ludwig Mies van der Rohe and Piet Mondrian were his models, and Paul Klee was his inspiration. Becoming a serious painter was one goal; becoming an engineer, reflecting a boyhood ideal, was another. Many of his best advertising and magazine paintings and drawings reveal a bent for physics combined with Precisionist rendering.

Like many others of his generation, Giusti nurtured Bauhausian instincts for unorthodox approaches to systematic design; this was balanced with classical skill and an exuberant Italian flair. After a stint with a Milanese ad agency, he worked in Lugano, Switzerland, as an art director before moving to Zurich, where he opened an advertising and editorial design studio. In 1938, he was invited by Herbert Matter to work on the Swiss Pavilion at the 1939–40 New York World's Fair, and he decided to stay in the United States. His early American work—much of it posters and propaganda materials for government agencies during World War II, postage stamps and posters for the Museum of Modern Art in New York, *Fortune* covers, and more than twenty advertisements for Davison Chemical Corporation and the American Optical Company—involved detailed airbrushed illustrations and photography showing real objects in symbolic fashion. For a long time, his work was primarily representational, leaning toward surreal spatial realms. Then, in the early fifties, a linear, abstract surrealism flowered, and what ensued was illustrative design language involving various media—painting, metal sculpture, and collage.

"Giusti is taken up with the discovery of pictures for things that are not accessible to the normal visual powers of the human eye," wrote Georgine Oeri. "Jobs in which a pictorial interpretation has to be found for the revelations of modern science suit him and attract him." Even after he started simplifying, employing abstract glyphs and geometric figures reminiscent of the art of Paul Klee and Joan Miró, his work conveyed distinct messages and moods, representations and emotions. "He often used the form of the human face as his creative point of departure for graphic projects," explained historian R. Roger Remington. His faces often recalled primitive masks filled with modern joy. "He had a jeweler's concern for precision and craftsmanship," wrote Remington, quoting historian Philip B. Meggs that Giusti's greatest gift was the "ability to reduce forms and images to a simplified, minimal essence."

This is the distinctly European quality that Walter Herdeg, the Swiss impresario of international design and founder of *Graphis* magazine, greatly admired—and why Giusti's illustrations graced so many magazine covers. Frank Zachary, the art director of *Holiday* magazine, used Giusti for covers that expressed both essential and symbolic aspects of nations, cities, and people featured inside the magazine. Giusti's method, which included a lot of dimensional, object-centric, abstracted constructions, was at once exotic and American.

He began a prolific relationship with *Fortune* magazine (and Time publications in general) in 1941, after art director Francis Brennan assigned him work. Of that period, he wrote in a "Questionnaire for Fortune Artists": "For an artist it was a real beginning. Immediately I got a prominent assignment which culminated with a contract as art consultant for J.R. Geigy Pharmaceuticals," where, from 1960 to 1967, his iconography interpreted hard-to-represent concepts of illness and good health. Other clients included *Modern Packaging* and *Interiors* (*Interiors + Industrial Design*) magazines and Container Corporation of America.

There were, however, few better platforms for Giusti's conceptual mind and aesthetic than book covers and jackets and record covers—especially jazz. His typography almost always played second fiddle to his illustrations, which, like imagery by Saul Bass, Paul Rand, and Leo Lionni, were poster-like in their graphic strength and color intensity. His brand of Modernism did not require a total commitment to geometry, although many of his pieces relied on that, but to the freedom to invent. The most recurring aspect of Giusti's later work was the ability to retain a modern spirit while inhabiting different forms. Perhaps it was the improvisational quality or the lightness of hand, but even today his Modernism evokes both its own time and time beyond.

In an autobiographical entry in *Who's Who in America*, Giusti wrote: "The true artist delves deeply into his own fantasies. But he is not an idle dreamer; his feet are on firm ground. The unconscious is a bottomless reservoir from which he draws the raw material for his creativity. With his conscious mind he takes the nebulous and translates it into logical and useful concepts. Thus he turns dreams into reality and relates them to the present. It is impossible to be creative without this interchange between fantasy and the real."

For many years prior to his death, Giusti's work was characterized by his use of metal in architectural, sculptural, and graphic design projects. Metal sculpture portraits of the likes of Pope Paul VI, Richard Nixon, Mao Zedong, Golda Meir, and Mick Jagger are startling in their caricatural likenesses. He also used metal for conceptual graphic design that raised his simple expression onto a higher plane. •

May 1952

GEORGE GIUSTI

056

Magazine cover, *Interiors*, May 1952. This informal, organic composition of "bird" patterns makes a strong visual statement by mixing bright colors and photographic, painterly, and abstract forms.

Put permanence into products with Western Brass...because brass is tough to start with...because time, use and environmental attack only mellow it. You'll make it better with durable brass. You'll make it best with Western Brass; it's "tailor-made" to your individual needs.

You'll get modern styling, ageless appeal, with Western Brass... because solid brass adds a classic note to contemporary design, keeps any design forever young and beautiful. You'll make it better with beauty-rich brass. You'll make it best with "tailor-made" Western Brass.

057

058

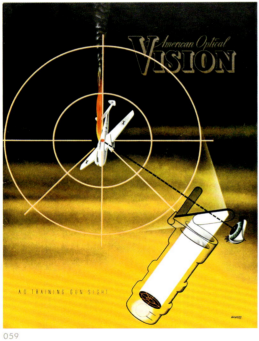

059

060

060

057–058
Advertisements, "Western Brass," Olin Mathieson, 1960

059
House organ cover, *American Optical Vision*, "AO Training Gun Sight," American Optical Company, vol. 28, no. 2 (August 1944)

060
House organ cover, *American Optical Vision*, "AO Variable Density Goggle Produced for Armed Forces," American Optical Company, vol. 28, no. 3 (November 1944)

061

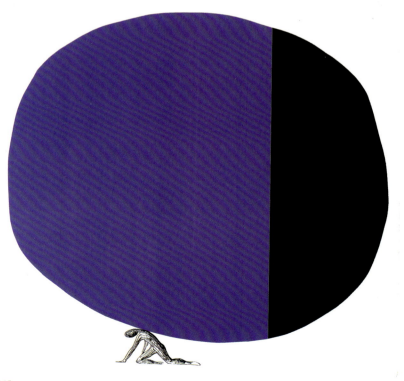

062

061
Brochure cover, *New Pertofrane Rapid Relief for the Depressed Patient*, Geigy, mid-1960s. Giusti effectively illustrates the rapid relief of depression by signaling movement with gradated and contrasting colors and transparency.

062
Advertisement, "Tofranil in Depression," Geigy, December 1963. For this medication, Giusti uses large areas of flat color, empty space, and visual tension to illustrate the patient's struggle with depression.

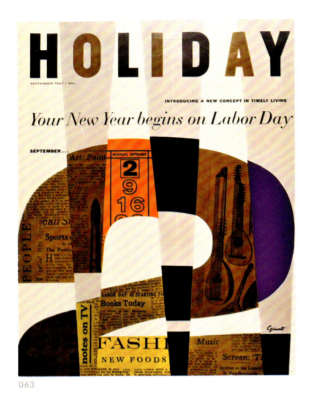

063

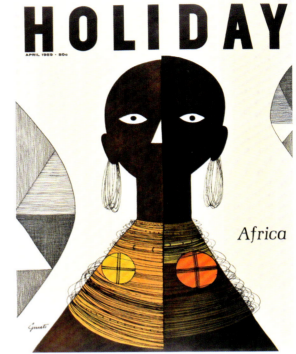

064

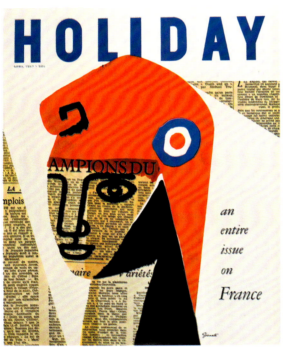

065

063
Magazine cover, *Holiday*, "Your New Year Begins on Labor Day," September 1957

064
Magazine cover, *Holiday*, "Africa," April 1959

065
Magazine cover, *Holiday*, "An Entire Issue on France," April 1957

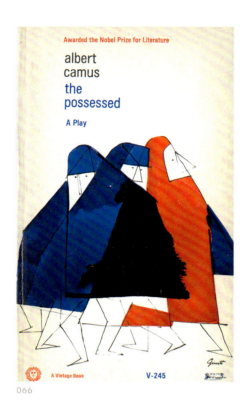

066

067

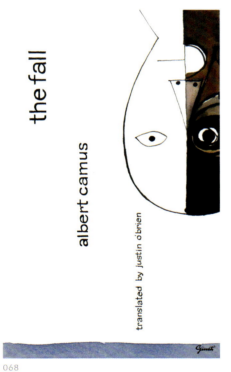

068

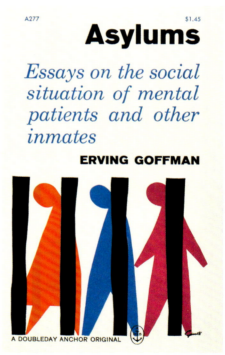

069

066
Book cover, *The Possessed: A Play in Three Parts*, by Albert Camus, Vintage Books, Knopf, 1960

067
Book cover, *Caligula and 3 Other Plays*, by Albert Camus, Vintage Books, Knopf, 1962

068
Book cover mechanical, *The Fall*, by Albert Camus, n.d. (unpublished)

069
Book cover, *Asylums: Essays on the Social Situation of Mental Patients and Other Inmates*, by Erving Goffman, Anchor Books, 1961

György Kepes

1906–2001

Kepes in his Wellfleet, Massachusetts, house designed by Marcel Breuer, 1949

"For those who are unaware of György Kepes," wrote Rudolph de Harak, "let me simply say that he is a visionary and visual experimenter, whose achievements in various media are extraordinary and of great importance to this century." While that can be said of many moderns in this book—especially émigrés who, before fleeing the storms of war and repression, helped transform visual language in art and design—Kepes, like his good friend and fellow Hungarian László Moholy-Nagy, possessed a range of experience that was essential in shaping generations of Modernists after him. Most notably, as founder and director of MIT's Center for Advanced Visual Studies (CAVS) from 1967 to 1974, he showed the world how light, color, kinetics, and photography could play a role in communications and aesthetics.

Born in the town of Selyp, Hungary, Kepes moved to Budapest with his family in 1914. There, from 1924 to 1928, he studied painting at the Royal Academy of Fine Arts, influenced by Lajos Kassák, the socialist Hungarian avant-garde painter. His introduction to Russian Constructivism came, in part, through exposure to the many leftist avant-garde journals, including *Munka* (*Work*), then circulating in Central Europe. Kepes ended his life as a painter, but design entered his life in the twenties, he told de Harak, because "I didn't want to be just a painter. I was emotionally involved in the Hungarian peasant's life." Painting was too static and "too limited in terms of social message communication." In 1930, with the Great Depression looming, he decided to become a filmmaker and wrote to Moholy-Nagy, whom he had never met but assumed would be a soul mate. "He invited me to work with him in Berlin."

In Berlin in the early thirties, he designed book jackets, stage sets, and exhibitions to pay the bills, and thanks to Moholy-Nagy, eleven years his elder, Kepes met Modernism's unique range of iconic personalities: "Gropius was in Berlin, as was [Marcel] Breuer. . . . I met [Soviet filmmakers Aleksandr] Dovzhenko and Dziga Vertov there," he recalled. Berlin at the time was "the last tick before the death of Germany, or at least the Weimar culture." He also met the satiric photomontage artist John Heartfield, who was designing covers for the magazines *Arbeiter-Illustrierte-Zeitung* and *Das neue Russland*. Although, by his own admission, Kepes could not do nearly as well, he felt that "if [Heartfield] could do it, I could also"—and he did, for about a year. Kepes said often: "I was interested in doing something where I felt I may help a little to change the mood of history."

With Nazism on the rise, Kepes left Berlin in 1936 at Moholy-Nagy's urging, first for London, where he met his future wife, the artist, writer, and children's book illustrator Juliet Appleby (1919–1999), and then for the United States in 1937. In London, he was art director for the department store Simpson Piccadilly, doing "everything, from window displays to graphic design." London was one of the "important intermezzos in my existence." In the United States, Moholy-Nagy was appointed director of the New Bauhaus, in Chicago, and asked Kepes to head the Light

Workshop. "We did not know what to teach," said Kepes. "It was an interesting excursion in the wilderness."

Moholy-Nagy was not getting along with the students, and amid a wealth of problems the trustees withdrew all funds. This led Kepes to start what he called "a mini-school," with fifteen or more students. He taught an idea that "as the eye is the agent of conveying all impressions to the mind, the achieving of visual communication requires a fundamental knowledge of the means of visual expression. Development of this knowledge will generate a genuine 'language of the eye,' whose 'sentences' are created images and whose elements are the basic signs, line, plane, halftone gradation, color, etc."

In 1938, Kepes started writing his classic book *Language of Vision*, with the help of Egbert Jacobson, director of design at Container Corporation of America, among others, who were better English speakers. The core idea, based on Gestalt psychology, was the insistence that, "visual communication is universal and international; it knows no limits of tongue, vocabulary, or grammar, and it can be perceived by the illiterate as well as by the literate."

Kepes left Chicago in 1943 for Brooklyn, by way of Texas. Invited by Serge Chermayeff, he taught at Brooklyn College, where his students included Arnold Shaw and Saul Bass, who said, "He changed my life. He turned me around and I became a designer because of him. He opened the door for me that caused me to understand design and art in another way."

In 1946, Kepes was offered a position at MIT by Bill Wooster. "At MIT, I had some difficulty in finding my own kind of inner balance," he told de Harak. But gradually he developed a program that involved the commixture of physics and perception out of which he developed his books *The New Landscape in Art and Science* (1956) and the six volumes of anthologies in a series titled Vision + Value (1965–66).

Over time, his feelings about how design could change life faded a little: "Life was editing my goals." Interdependence was one of those ideals. Image making did not always live up to his desires about the intellect and ethics. "It would be a great benefit for all of us if we could re-pose our interest in these issues I believed in so many years ago," he said, adding that he did not give up his beliefs, he just edited them "in a certain minor key." While keeping the modern flame, Kepes noted that he had "a mixed response and a mixed-up response" to the International Typographic Style of graphic design. "I like it, but I feel it lacks physiognomy. Expressive power," he said. He confessed, "I feel often almost let down that there is not a stretching out. It's all of a coordinated design, but not a courageous exploration."

Nonetheless, Modernism was clearly his life's blood. He told de Harak: "I feel much more sympathy and a warmer response to what you are doing, or what people are doing, who know the whole spectrum of design and choose, in an appropriate moment, the right idioms." •

Cahiers d'Art

12ᵉ ANNÉE

070

070
Unpublished experiment, *Cahiers d'Art, 12 Année*, 1937. This black-and-white montage combines photograms, circles joined by thin lines, spliced lettering, and torn-edged paper collage.

György Kepes

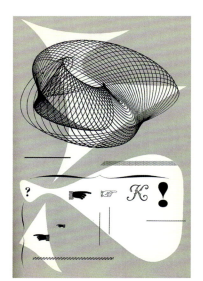

071

Gyorgy Kepes
Typographical
Experiment

072

071

Title page for insert and typographical exercise, reproduced from *PM: An Intimate Journal for Production Managers, Art Directors, and Their Associates* 6, no. 3 (February–March 1940). The issue features a sixteen-page insert written and designed by Kepes, with an introduction by his colleague and friend László Moholy-Nagy.

072

Typographical experiment, reproduced from *Advance Guard of Advertising Artists*, Katherine Kuh Gallery, 1941, the Kepes-designed catalog for an exhibition on modern graphic design and its relationship with commerce. The exhibition brought together for the first time nine American and European pioneers of avant-garde design: Frank Barr, Herbert Bayer, Lester Beall, E. McKnight Kauffer, Kepes, Herbert Matter, László Moholy-Nagy, Paul Rand, and Ladislav Sutnar.

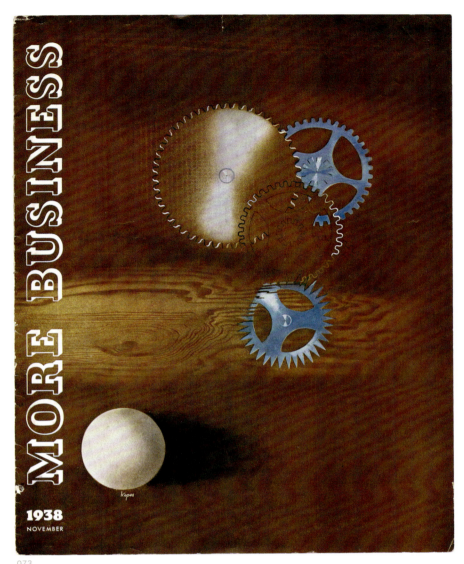

073

074

075

073
Journal cover, *More Business: The Voice of Letterpress Printing and Photo-Engraving*, American Photo-Engravers Association, vol. 3, no. 11 (November 1938). This special issue was devoted to the 1937 opening of the New Bauhaus, subsequently the School of Design, in Chicago. László Moholy-Nagy and Kepes described the school's training with illustrated texts and European avant-garde page designs; Moholy-Nagy wrote "New Approach to Fundamentals of Design" and Kepes wrote "Education of the Eye," with additional texts and illustrations on photography, photomontage, photograms, color photography, volume and space, sciences, and a lettering article by Hin Bredendieck.

074
Prospectus cover, *School of Design in Chicago*, László Moholy-Nagy, director, 1940. A lens refraction, compass, and technical drawing signal new tools and freedoms of expression. From the interior: "Our concern is to develop a new type of designer, able to face every requirement, scientific and technical, social and economic, not because he is a prodigy but because he has the right method of approach," says Moholy-Nagy.

075
Advertisement, "School of Design in Chicago," László Moholy-Nagy, director, 1940. This advertisement ran as a full page on the back of *Direction* magazine 3, no. 8 (November 1940), and reads: "Integration of art, science and technology. Workshop training with basic tools and machines of industry. For information: School of Design in Chicago, 247 East Ontario Street."

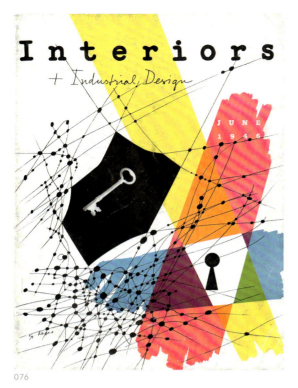

076

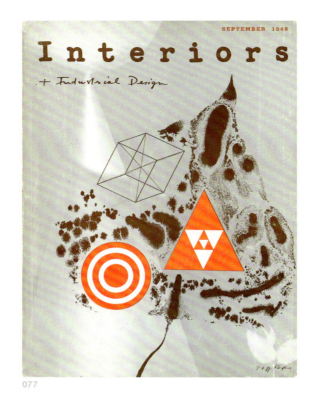

077

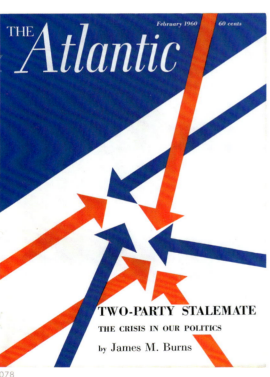

078

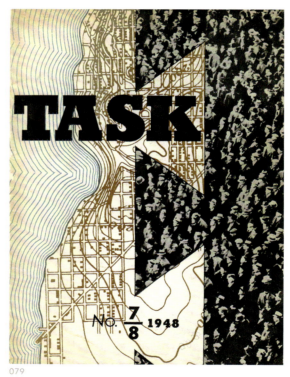

079

076

Magazine cover, *Interiors*, Whitney Publications, vol. 105, no. 11 (June 1946)

077

Magazine cover, *Interiors*, Whitney Publications, vol. 108, no. 2 (September 1948). Design: György and Juliet Kepes

078

Magazine cover, *Atlantic Monthly*, February 1960

079

Magazine cover, *TASK*, Cambridge, Massachusetts, nos. 7–8 (1948). From the interior: "[TASK] was founded before the war to examine the physical, social and economic aspects of city and resource planning, and of housing and architecture." This is the first postwar issue.

080

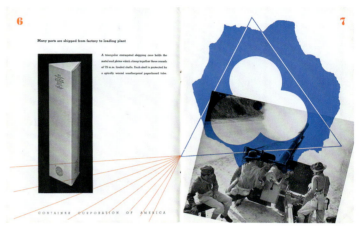

080
Catalog cover and interior spreads, *Paperboard Goes to War*, Container Corporation of America, Chicago, 1942. This pictorial catalog records some of the paperboard products (fiber, corrugated shipping containers, folding cartons) manufactured for war industries. From the interior: "Food, ammunition, tank and airplane parts and the other myriad necessities of this mechanical war are now being packed in paperboard to make production and delivery easy and safe."

Leo Lionni

1910–1999

Lionni in his New York office, c. 1955

Leo Lionni was a Renaissance man in modern guise—teacher, author, critic, editor, painter, sculptor, printmaker, designer, cartoonist, and children's book illustrator who held a doctorate in economics. Born in Amsterdam, he was the son of a diamond cutter from a well-to-do Sephardic Jewish family; his mother was a singer. Her brother, Piet, an architect, allowed his adoring five-year-old nephew to play with his drafting supplies. And two other uncles, both collectors of modern art, fed his artistic inclinations. At that time, Amsterdam was governed by a socialist party that favored a progressive educational system. "There was great emphasis on nature, art, and crafts," recalled Lionni.

Graphic design provided a means to bring Lionni's art and design passions together. He came under the influence of Futurism when that radical movement was at its height. By 1931, Lionni was part of the second Futurist wave. "I was living the life of the avant-garde: We had blue plastic furniture and Breuer chairs," he said. He painted turbulent abstract pictures typical of the era, and his work had such flair that it caught the eye of Filippo Tommaso Marinetti, codifier of the movement, who pronounced Lionni to be "a great Futurist."

With Marinetti's support, Lionni's paintings were exhibited in shows throughout Italy. On the eve of one such exhibition, Marinetti received a telegram announcing that the Nazis had shut the Bauhaus. "We sat up the entire night," recalled Lionni, "and decided to send a telegram back inviting all the Bauhaus artists to Italy, and offered our homes for them to stay in indefinitely." Not only was Lionni indignant and fearful about Nazi repression, but he also considered the Bauhaus to be his true home: "I never really felt comfortable as a Futurist, even though Marinetti proclaimed me to be the heir of aero-dynamic painting. I actually resented it; I had *never* even been in an *airplane* before. I am really Dutch. I felt closer to De Stijl, and I responded to the patterns and symmetry of the tulip fields. In fact, I rarely ever put type or image on angles unless there was a good reason to do it."

Lionni soon devoted himself to advertising design, "simply for the joy of putting good imagery onto pages," he said. He also attended the University of Genoa, in 1935, but when the darkest elements of Fascism began to shroud Italy, he immigrated to Philadelphia, taking a job with the N. W. Ayer advertising agency after a fortuitous meeting with the distinguished art director Charles Coiner, who assigned him to create ads for *Ladies' Home Journal*. Lionni's big break occurred in the early forties when an N. W. Ayer multimillion-dollar client, Ford Motor Company, was unhappy with new ad proposals. Lionni created a series of ads that earned him the job. In one week, he went from a fifty-dollar-a-week assistant to a five-hundred-dollar-a-week art director on one of the largest accounts in the United States, and others came his way. For one account, he hired the neophyte Andy Warhol to do sketches for Regal Shoes.

As the art director for Container Corporation of America's "International Series," Lionni returned to his Modernist roots. For one project,

he asked Fernand Léger, who was then living in New York, to create a painting. The company's president, Walter P. Paepcke, asked if Léger would also do it in black and white as a newspaper ad. Lionni made a line drawing of the painting, which he showed to Léger. Seeing the "rough," the painter said, "That's as good as I would do it," and signed the Lionni sketch, which was later printed.

In 1948, Lionni began to get restless as an advertising designer. He left the agency, moved to New York, opened a small office, and joined *Fortune* magazine as an art director. "I told them I would do it on a freelance basis, three days a week, and that I wanted an assistant who would go to all the meetings." He stayed on for eleven years.

Lionni redesigned *Fortune* twice. In each case, he eschewed cold functionality for a more human approach. He introduced Century Schoolbook, his favorite typeface. "I don't know much about type, but Century Schoolbook is a human face." During Lionni's tenure, painters were encouraged to do illustrations and picture essays, and illustrators were commissioned as graphic journalists—not to render prescribed imagery, but freed to draw on and interpret firsthand experiences. Lionni urged artists "to do things which they were not accustomed to doing."

Lionni consulted with Henry Luce on many projects for Time publications, including a prototype design for *Sports Illustrated*. He also maintained outside clients, including the Museum of Modern Art, for which he designed the catalog for the exhibition "The Family of Man" (1955), and Olivetti, where he did ads, brochures, and showroom design.

His most satisfying accomplishment was a short tenure as coeditor and art director of *Print*. During the midfifties, Lionni elevated the magazine's graphic design commentary, making it a platform for varying disciplines. He opened up the design community to invention, through coverage of international trends and national currents. Still, his professional career, except for a few found moments to study mosaics, had been in the service of others. "Everything I had done was a happy compromise that I've never felt ashamed of in the least." At the age of fifty, at the peak of his endeavors, Lionni left Time and became a picture book author.

For Lionni, the children's book was an organic synthesis of all his talents, beliefs, and obsessions; it wed humor, color, and abstraction with the desire to teach. According to Bruno Bettelheim, Lionni "is an artist who has retained his ability to think primarily in images, and who can create true picture books. . . . It is the true genius of the artist which permits him to create picture images that convey much deeper meaning than what is overtly depicted."

Lionni's endeavors were enlivened by youthful innocence, sage-like logic, and humor. Moreover, in word and deed, he was an unfaltering rationalist, a devout humanist, and a passionate Modernist. •

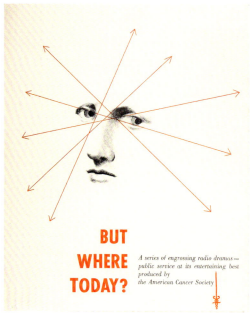

BUT WHERE TODAY?

A series of engrossing radio dramas—public service at its entertaining best produced by the American Cancer Society

081

which way out?

for family counseling call

AFFILIATED WITH FAMILY SERVICE ASSOCIATION OF AMERICA

082

KEEP 'EM ROLLING!

DIVISION OF INFORMATION
OFFICE FOR EMERGENCY MANAGEMENT
WASHINGTON, D.C.

083

081
Booklet cover, *But Where Today? A Series of Engrossing Radio Dramas—Public Service at Its Entertaining Best*, American Cancer Society, 1952

082
Poster, *Which Way Out? For Family Counseling Call*, Family Service Association of America, 1956. Lionni reiterates the question about a serious subject visually with a symbolic illustration.

083
Poster, *Keep 'Em Rolling!*, Division of Information, Office of Emergency Management, U.S. Government Printing Office, 1941

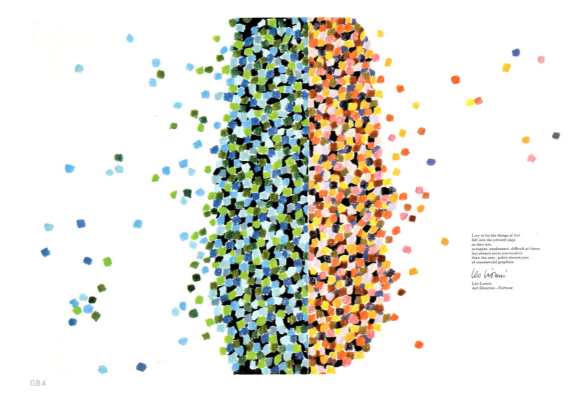

084

085

084

Advertisement, *Fortune*, July 1957. "I try to let the things of Art fall into the printed page as they are, arrogant, unpleasant, difficult at times but always more provocative than the easy, polite stereotypes of commercial graphics."

085

Advertisement, *Fortune*, January 1960. "The simple convolutions at the right demonstrate how powerful a one and a half-page design can be—and how big the space looks. It suggests how the use of certain looping forms and the exploitation of bleed can create a feeling of activity and spaciousness."

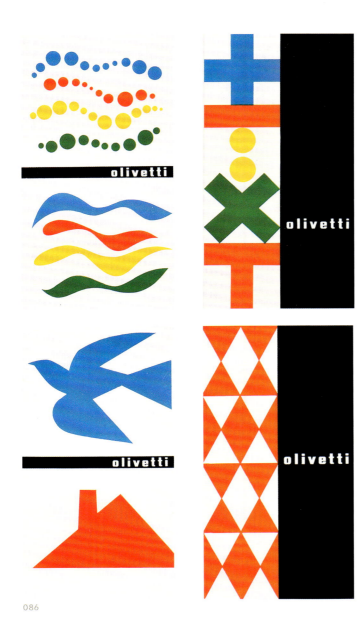

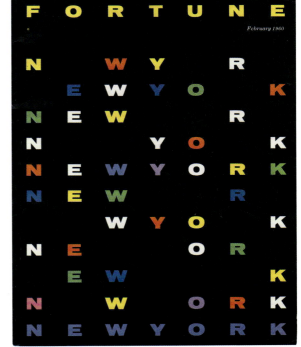

LEO LIONNI

Product brochure covers, Olivetti Corporation of America, New York, c. 1957. Consultant art director: Lionni

Product brochure cover, *Fully Automatic Carriage Printing Calculator*, Olivetti Corporation of America, New York, c. 1955–57. Consultant art director: Lionni

Magazine cover, *Fortune*, February 1960. From the interior: "The cover of this special issue suggests one of New York's great spectacles: thousands of lighted office windows shining through the early darkness of a winter afternoon."

Herbert Matter

1907–1984

Matter self-portrait in his Tudor City, New York, studio, c. 1936

Herbert Matter's most historically emblematic work was done in Europe. His signature posters for the Swiss Tourist Office (1934–36) are among the most familiar of the genre that László Moholy-Nagy called "typofoto." While these posters successfully communicate their immediate message through a skillful application of photomontage, on a more lasting note, they transcend a momentary promotional campaign through dramatic scale and perspective shifts. In America, his most important work included his twenty-five montage and photographic covers and interiors for *Arts & Architecture* magazine (1943–46), while his symbolic *Fortune* covers helped define American futuristic styling, and his design of *Plus*, the experimental, short-lived architectural and interior magazine, extended this forward-looking graphic experience.

Matter's work is well known, the photographer-designer himself not so much. This is not surprising, as Matter was exceedingly modest. "The absence of pomposity was characteristic of this guy," noted Paul Rand, a friend for four decades and fellow Yale graphic design professor. Throughout Matter's creative life, he was devoted to narrowing the gap between so-called fine and applied arts, but the deed was often best accomplished through works rather than through words.

Matter was born in Engelberg, a Swiss mountain village. There he was exposed to the treasures of one of the finest medieval graphic arts collections in Europe. In 1924, he attended the Ecole des Beaux-Arts in Geneva before heading back to Engelberg as a freelance designer. But after two years, the allure of Modernism brought him to Paris, where he attended the Académie Moderne in 1928–29 under the tutelage of Fernand Léger and Amédée Ozenfant, who encouraged Matter to expand his artistic horizons.

In Europe during the late twenties and early thirties, the creative scope of graphic design appeared to be boundless; it entered daily life in meaningful and visible ways. Journalistic, imaginative, and manipulated photography were revolutionary influences, and, since he was smitten with the camera, Matter began to experiment with the Rolleiflex for design and self-expression.

Inspired by the work of El Lissitzky and Man Ray, Matter was intrigued by photograms as well as the perceptual magic of collage and montage. In 1929, he was hired as a designer, typographer, and photographer for Deberny et Peignot. There he learned the nuances of fine typography while he assisted A. M. Cassandre and Le Corbusier. But in 1932, expelled from France for not having the proper papers, he returned to Switzerland to follow his own path.

"Herbert's background is fascinating and enviable," recalled Rand. "He was surrounded by good graphics and learned from the best." It is no wonder that the famed posters Matter designed for the Swiss Tourist Office had the beauty and intensity of Cassandre and the odd vantage points, dramatic contrast, and vertical angles of heroic Russian Constructivist posters by photomontage artists Gustav Klutsis and the Stenberg brothers.

In 1936, Matter was offered round-trip passage to the United States as payment for his work with a Swiss ballet troupe. He traveled with the company across America and then decided to remain in New York. At the urging of a friend, he met Alexey Brodovitch, who had been collecting Matter's travel posters (two of which were hanging on Brodovitch's studio wall). Matter soon began taking photographs for *Harper's Bazaar* and Saks Fifth Avenue. Later, he affiliated himself with a photographic firm, Studio Associates, located near the Condé Nast offices, where he produced covers and inside spreads for *Vogue*.

During World War II, Matter designed advertisements for Container Corporation of America, which at the time was among the more progressive design-centric corporations. In 1946, he became the chief graphic design consultant at the office and furniture design company Knoll, molding its graphic identity for two decades, until 1966. "Herbert had a strong feeling for minute details, and this was exemplified by the distinguished typography he did for the Knoll catalogues," explained Alvin Eisenman, former head of the Graphic Design Department at Yale and a longtime friend.

In 1952, he was asked to join the Yale faculty as professor of photography and graphic design. "He was a marvelous teacher," said Eisenman. "His roster of students included some of the most important names in the field today." In 1954, he was commissioned to create the corporate identity for the New Haven Railroad; his NH logo, with its elongated serifs, was once widely known and admired. It also contained a secret visual pun that continues to vex students (the slab serifs of the H form the wheel bed of a train).

Matter's affinity for modern art was evident in his closest friendships. In 1944, he was asked by the Museum of Modern Art to direct a movie on the sculpture of his intimate friend and neighbor Alexander Calder. It was his first attempt at cinema, and thanks to the sympathetic and deep understanding that only one kindred artist can have for another, the completed film was one of the finest in its genre. From 1958 to 1968, he was the design consultant for the Guggenheim Museum, applying his elegant typographic style to its posters and catalogs, many of which are still in print. He worked in Gertrude Vanderbilt Whitney's former studio in MacDougal Alley with his wife, Mercedes Matter, who founded the Studio School just around the corner. During the late fifties and early sixties, he was an intimate participant in the New York art scene, counting Jackson Pollock, Willem de Kooning, Franz Kline, and Philip Guston as friends. In 1960, he started photographing the sculpture of Alberto Giacometti, another spiritual intimate, for a comprehensive book.

Paul Rand, in a poem for a 1977 Yale exhibition catalog, best describes the clarity and power of Matter's design: *Industry is a tough taskmaster./Art is tougher./Industry plus Art, almost impossible./Some artists have done the impossible./Herbert Matter, for example.* •

Fortune

ONE DOLLAR A COPY OCTOBER 1943 TEN DOLLARS A YEAR

HERBERT MATTER

Magazine cover, *Fortune*, October 1943.
The design illustrates the highly technical,
ultra-precision ball bearing manufacturing
process developed at SKF Industries. By
blending black-and-white photograms

and photographs with primary colors and
geometric forms, Matter communicates the
process abstractly with tonality, texture, and
motion. Art direction: M. Peter Piening

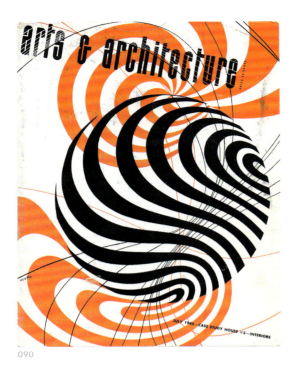

090

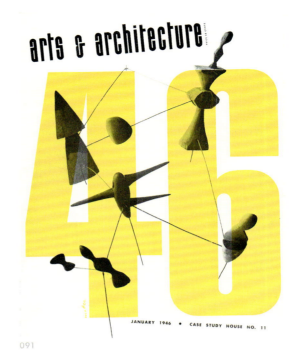

091

092

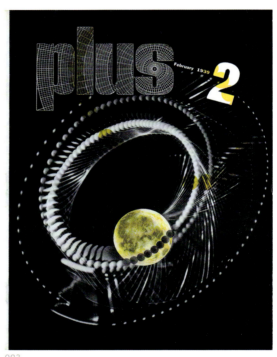

093

090
Magazine cover, *Arts & Architecture*,
July 1945

091
Magazine cover, *Arts & Architecture*,
January 1946. A playful and expressive
abstract design combining large numbers
with a photograph of Alexander Calder's
Constellations, made of small, hand-carved
biomorphic wood forms linked by tightly
pulled wire.

092
Magazine cover, *Plus: Orientation
of Contemporary Architecture*, no. 1
(December 1938). From the editors: "In all
the controversy that has revolved around
the subject of modern architecture, one
small fact has often gone unobserved:
Modern . . . has its extremists, its
moderates, and its conservatives. Far
from being a reflection on the movement,
however, this lack of unanimity bears
testimony to its strength and long standing."

093
Magazine cover, *Plus: Orientation of
Contemporary Architecture*, February
1939. Matter experiments with slow-motion
photography in this photomontage using
Alexander Calder's *Mobile in Motion* image
from 1936.

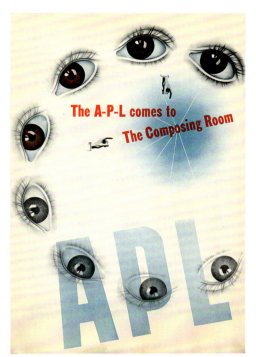

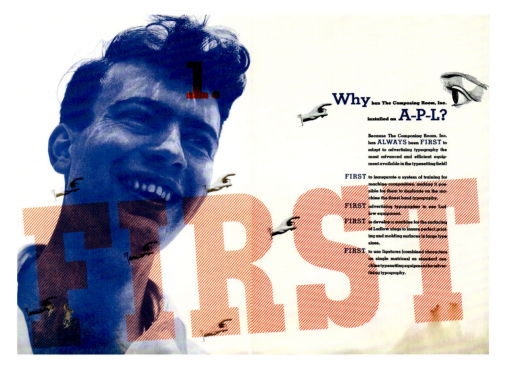

094

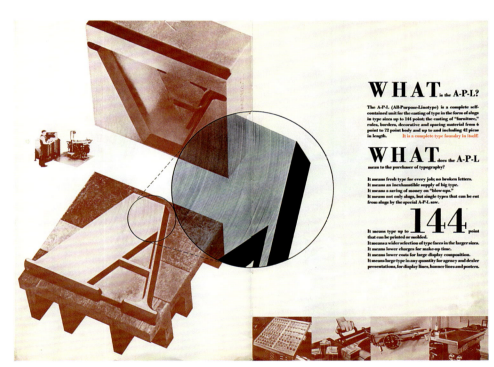

095

094
Product booklet cover and interior spreads, *The A-P-L Comes to the Composing Room*, Composing Room, New York, 1937. "The A-P-L (All-Purpose-Linotype) is a complete self-contained unit for the casting of type in the form of slugs in type sizes up to 144 point; the casting of 'furniture,' rules, borders, decorative and spacing material from 6 point to 72 point body and up to and including 42 picas in length."

095
Logo, *New Haven Railroad*, 1954. After hundreds of sketches, Matter achieved this well-balanced "NH" with elongated, machine-like slab-serifs graphically suggesting railroad tracks. Design assistance: Norman Ives

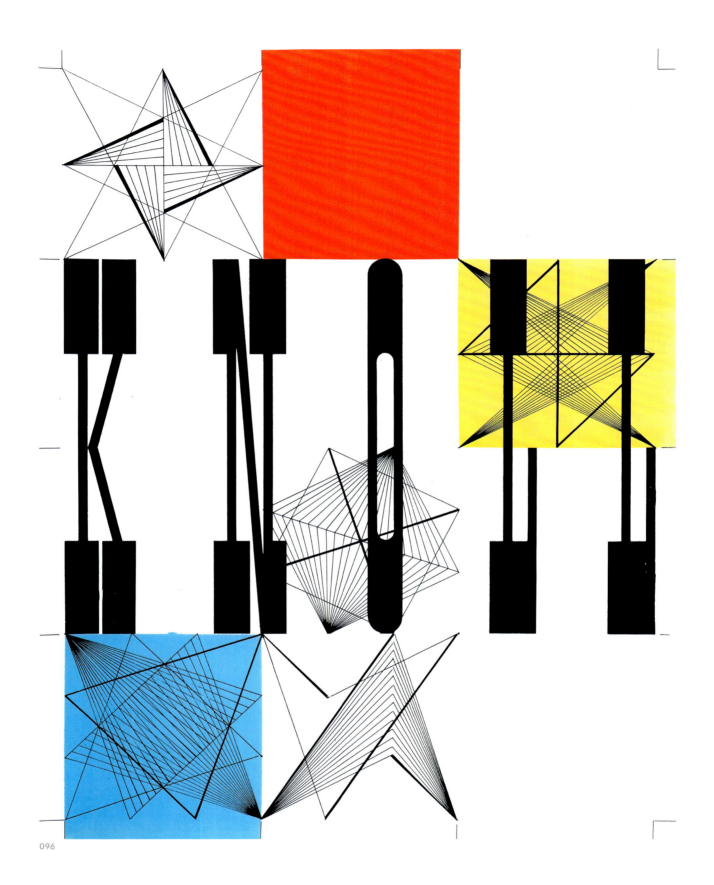

096

096
Poster with original crop and printer marks
visible, *Knoll*, Knoll Associates, New York,
c. 1948

097

098

099

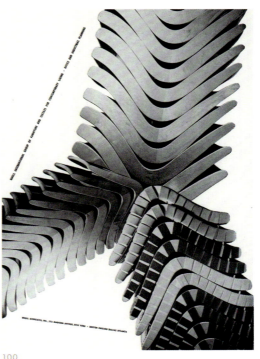

100

097
Advertisement, "Knoll Associates and Its Overseas Branches Extend Their Greetings at the New Year," Knoll Associates, New York, 1955

098
Advertisement, "From the Collection of Molded Plastic Chairs Designed by Eero Saarinen," Knoll Associates, New York, 1951

099
Advertisement, "Knoll Associates Inc. 1947–1948," Knoll Associates, New York, 1947

100
Advertisement, "Knoll International Group of Furniture and Textiles for Contemporary Living, Office and Industrial Planning," Knoll Associates, New York, 1951

Erik Nitsche

1908–1998

Erik Nitsche did not wield Modernist formulas like a cookie cutter. Rather than adhering to Modernist orthodoxy, Nitsche focused on finding a methodology for clean systems and order, impelled by his restlessness at doing mostly illustrative work during the early part of his career. He insisted that he was as good—and certainly as prolific, if not more so—than any other designer of his age, speculating that had it not been for his asocial tendencies ("I preferred to do the work, not talk about it") and a few poor business decisions along the way (he turned down a job at IBM that later went to Paul Rand), he might be as well known today as the other acknowledged pioneers. In fact, he worked for many of the same clients. Judging from the sheer volume of work bearing his signature or type credit, there are few others who can make this claim.

Nitsche was born into a family of commercial photographers in Lausanne, Switzerland. Paul Klee was a family friend and exerted a profound influence on young Nitsche, who wanted to be an artist. Nitsche attended the Kunstgewerbeschule in Munich where he studied with the famous German typographer F. H. Ehmcke and eventually won a prestigious award for a poster competition for an annual Munich ball. Paris beckoned; there he was hired by Maximilien Vox, an enterprising typographer, advertising designer, and writer who headed his own typography agency designing everything from packages to letterheads.

From about 1930 to 1935, Nitsche produced hundreds of illustrations and political cartoons for weekly publications such as the French *Vu* and the German *Simplicissimus* and *Der Querschnitt*, as well as scores of advertisements for magazines and newspapers. Sensing the larger troubles to come, he decided to leave Europe for the United States in 1934. He landed in Hollywood, where he got a job designing sets and curtains for a musical called *All Aboard*. But Hollywood was obsessed with attitude and class, and Nitsche was a devout social recluse. In 1936, he packed his bags.

In New York, he found that it was surprisingly easy to get work. His assignments included witty editorial and fashion illustration, studio photography, and a modicum of layout. Fashion became his bread and butter for quite a while, and he also painted covers for *Fortune*, *Vanity Fair*, *Stage*, *Arts & Decoration*, and *House Beautiful* that were either comical or decorative.

After a chance meeting with the publishers of *Air Tech* and *Air News* magazines, he was hired as art director with total control. What for many designers would have been a hellish assignment—to design charts and graphs about aerodynamics—was pure heaven for Nitsche. He savored designing "meaningful" technical data for such things as hydraulic systems and cross sections of airplanes. The greatest compliment to him came from former Bauhaus master László Moholy-Nagy, who had seen the magazines and asked a mutual acquaintance, "Who is that doing the Bauhaus in America?"

Nitsche was developing two approaches that would eventually blend into a seamless style. The first incorporated abstract drawings. These appeared on Decca Records albums, of which he designed more than two hundred, and in some advertising work. The second was elegant typography that combined a line or two of Gothic type, such as Akzidenz-Grotesk (and later Helvetica), with a classic serif face, like Garamond or Didot. He rejected the strict Swiss Style, referring to it as "a little too cold for our uses," and stayed "pretty much with the classical typefaces."

Nitsche left the hustle of New York City in 1945 for Pound Ridge, New York; then, after becoming art director for Dorland International in 1950, he moved to Ridgefield, Connecticut. He also did work for the Gotham Agency, a small-sized advertising firm that handled the General Dynamics account. The advertisements that he created for this multinational corporation transformed him from a boutique designer into one of the world's most effective—and Modernist—corporate designers.

General Dynamics was incorporated in 1952 as the parent of ten different manufacturing firms that were administering to the defense needs of the United States. General Dynamics' president, John Jay Hopkins, argued that General Dynamics could benefit mankind through scientific research, and presenting a good public face was essential to this goal. Nitsche's ads introduced his abstract drawing style to give a futuristic aura that suggested General Dynamics' progressive aspirations.

The corporate clarion was a series of six posters, designed by Nitsche, promoting Atoms for Peace, featuring symbolic abstract imagery. These posters established a tone for all future General Dynamics graphics, as well as a paradigm for how the marriage of science and engineering would be visualized by kindred companies. Like a battlefield general, Nitsche built a total corporate advertising and identity campaign. He developed an editing, layout, and cropping method for the General Dynamics annual reports that emphasized cinematic pacing, following a principle of dynamic flow based on scale, repetition, and juxtaposition. Nitsche's crowning achievement, however, came when he edited and designed the company's history. *Dynamic America*, which took him about four years to complete, told the story of the nation's military and industrial development as seen through the lens of General Dynamics.

Nitsche was phased out at General Dynamics in 1964, a few years after Hopkins's death, and he turned to book packaging. Toward the end of his life, the eighty-nine-year-old designer was building eight-foot models of sculptural toys that he called "Polichinelles." When asked about them, he snapped in his German accent, "Let's talk about the future." •

101

101
Mini subway car card, *Say It Fast . . .
Often . . . in Color,* New York Subway
Advertising Company, no. 3, 1947

102

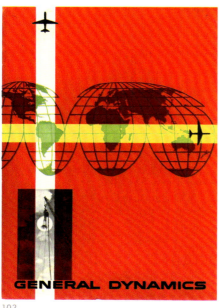

103

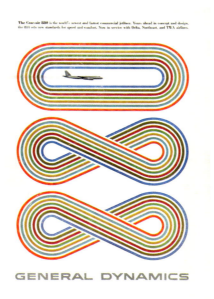

104

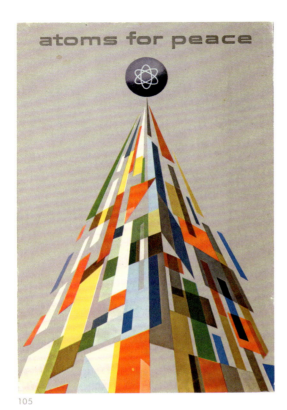

105

106

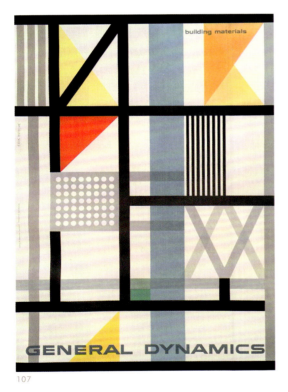

107

108

105
Booklet cover, *Atoms for Peace*, General Dynamics, 1955

106
Poster, *Electronic Intelligence*, General Dynamics, 1958. Copy from an advertisement of the same design: "Guide a plane. Spot a marauder. Interrogate a thunderhead. Electronic sentinels—gathering, analyzing and integrating information — will enhance man's domination over his environment . . . and help preserve him from his follies."

107
Poster, *Building Materials*, General Dynamics, 1954

108
Poster, *Undersea Frontiers*, c. 1960. Copy from an advertisement of the same design: "Nuclear-powered, undersea vessels may soon carry pioneers on voyages of discovery to the unknown continents that lie beneath the ocean's surface . . . teeming with a limitless wealth of minerals, metals, foods and energy."

109

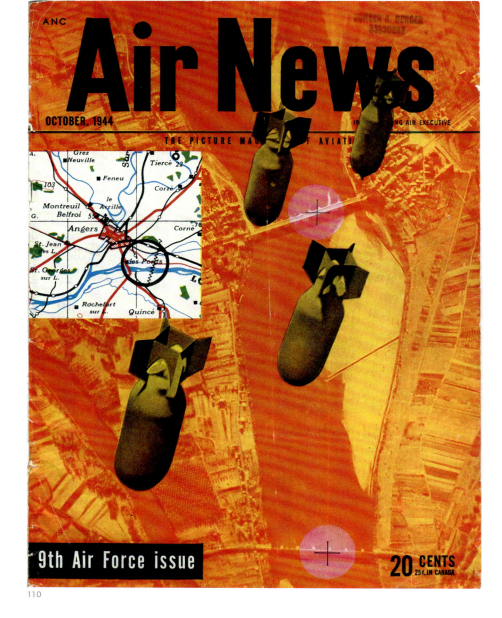

110

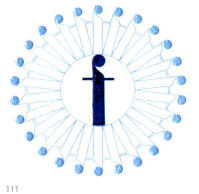

111

109
Poster, *All About Eve*, Twentieth Century Fox Film Corporation, 1950. "It's all about women . . . and their men!"

110
Magazine cover, *Air News: The Picture Magazine of Aviation*, "9th Air Force Issue," vol. 7, no. 4 (October 1944). The cover depicts the U.S. 9th Air Force B-26 bomber group destroying the railway bridges over the Loire River at Les Ponts-de-Cé, Angers, on August 1, 1944.

111
Logo, *Wm. Filene's Sons Company*, Boston, c. 1950. A lowercase f is surrounded by a circle of twenty-six tightly fit and animating f's, reflecting the store's many departments.

112
Album cover, *Béla Bartók: Violin Concerto* by Tibor Varga with the Berlin Philharmonic Orchestra and conductor Ferenc Fricsay, Decca Records, 1951

113
Album cover, *Schubert: Quintet in A Major* by Franz Schubert, Adrian Aeschbacher, Rudolf Koeckert, Oskar Riedl, Josef Merz, and Franz Ortner, Decca Records, 1953

114
Album cover, *Brahms: Variations on a Theme by Haydn / Franck: Symphonic Variations for Piano and Orchestra* by Ferdinand Leitner and Géza Anda, Decca Records, 1951

115
Album cover, *An Andrés Segovia Program* by Andrés Segovia, Decca Records, 1952

116
Album cover, *Walter Piston: Sonata for Violin and Piano / Nicholas Lopatnikoff: Sonata no. 2 for Violin and Piano* by Joseph Fuchs and Artur Balsam, Decca Records, 1951

M. Peter Piening

1908–1977

Piening in his Syracuse University office, 1964

Born in 1908 of Danish parents in Grabow, Germany, M. Peter Piening studied design from 1926 to 1928 at the Bauhaus before receiving his PhD in philosophy at the University of Berlin. After his studies, he worked in Berlin at the esteemed Ullstein Verlag before moving to Paris, where he worked part-time at Condé Nast's *Vogue*, beginning an association that ultimately brought him to New York in 1934. Piening was creatively and intellectually influenced by Bauhaus teachers László Moholy-Nagy, Paul Klee, Ludwig Mies van der Rohe, and Josef Albers, and he practiced an original and inventive method of design expression.

From his early arrival in the United States, Piening held down prominent ad agency positions at N. W. Ayer and J. Walter Thompson in New York. He worked as art editor at *Life* magazine in 1937 and as art director at *Fortune* in 1941–44, before the magazine was taken over by Will Burtin in 1945. At *Fortune*, Piening helped shape the magazine's overall design program, as he introduced "modern" enhancements and redesigns of the interior pages and covers by removing the traditional double-framed ornamental border and, in some instances, the more traditional shaded and beveled logo. His editorial experience landed him projects with *Architectural Record*, *Town & Country*, *Cosmopolitan*, and *Living for Young Homemakers*, along with a staggering number of industry trade publications.

One of his early and most important designs in America was for the cover of the June–July 1938 issue of *PM: An Intimate Journal for Production Managers, Art Directors, and Their Associates* (see p. 320), a leading trade journal exhibiting ambitious work from influential practitioners of the period. In Piening's black-and-blue design, distinctly influenced by Surrealism and Constructivism, a sans serif P and a slab serif M float in illusionistic space amid pictorial planes and frames. This signaling of the old and the new or integration of arts and craft encapsulates Piening's Bauhaus education and best represents the issue's significant thirty-two-page article, "The Bauhaus Tradition and the New Typography," by L. Sandusky; it was the first survey of Bauhaus thinking in an American periodical, and it featured the work of avant-gardes, recent émigrés, and American Modernists selected by Lester Beall and Sandusky. Beall designed the interior pages.

Piening commissioned *Fortune* covers by fellow Modernists John Atherton, Hans Barschel, Herbert Bayer, George Giusti, Peter Vardo, and Herbert Matter, and the eight he designed himself are modern masterpieces. For "Reconversion in Typewriters" (August 1944), he designed an abstract image evoking an industrial process using forms suggestive of a typewriter. His later *Architectural Record* cover "Hospitals" (June 1947) superimposes a red, biomorphic form (presumably representing the dynamic body) over grayscale, semitransparent, rectilinear planes. This pairing of geometric forms with expressive shapes was a reoccurring theme in his work. A 1946–47 catalog from the Art Students League had this to say about him: "Piening's approach to the subject of art is typically expressed by the following Goethe quote: 'People see what

they know. They do not see the thing until they know it to be seen.' He consistently and energetically endeavors to transmit this thought and apply this formula in his approach to the people who work with him. Paying great attention to natural forms in his work, Mr. Piening believes that to be a good artist you must derive your basic training from nature."

The only known published book on Piening is *Trademarks and Symbols*, published by Syracuse University in 1964. It features a collection of more than sixty trademarks and symbols that he designed in the United States. Piening held trademarks in high regard and once said: "Visual communication is the language of all men. . . . It must be individual, unique in its association of form and content, responsible to both patron and public, and intrinsically active in its function. Like any other work of art, it serves, therefore, as a visual catalyst in the general process of communication towards understanding." His trademarks and symbols were generally simple, composed of geometric shapes, beginning with his very first trademark, for the Lincoln Zephyr (1934), produced under the direction of Charles Coiner at N. W. Ayer. The Zephyr was Lincoln's first aerodynamic car, and Piening characterized its meaning, "a soft, gentle breeze," with thin, concentric teardrop shapes. His trademark for the National Housing Center is characteristic: A circle is cut into the simplified icon of a house, making an ideogram that precisely captures the concept "housing center" and, not incidentally, suggests an arrow pointing upward. It served the organization well, as it was applied and used on an international stage.

Piening's client list reads like a who's who of American life and industry, including Ballet Theatre, Ford, Shell Oil, United States Steel, Douglas Aircraft, Eberhard Faber, Ballantine Beer and Ale, Squibb, and Alcan. His lifelong passion for painting, an independent study that paralleled his design practice, was evident in his numerous abstract and distinctly Cubist designs for American Recording Society albums from 1951 on.

Piening spent a considerable period of his career training students. He taught layout, lettering, design, and typography for seven years at New York's Art Students League and was a professor for adult graphic education classes at New York University. "Many people can draw; fewer people can think; the combination of both makes the creative artist," he said in the 1948–49 Art Students League catalog. In 1958, he joined the faculty at Syracuse University's School of Art, where he remained until his retirement in 1973. •

117
Magazine cover, *Fortune*, "Reconversion
in Typewriters." August 1944. The cover
illustration reflects the feature article about
L. C. Smith & Corona Typewriters, whose
Syracuse plant was reconverting from
making wartime Springfield rifles back to
making typewriters again postwar.

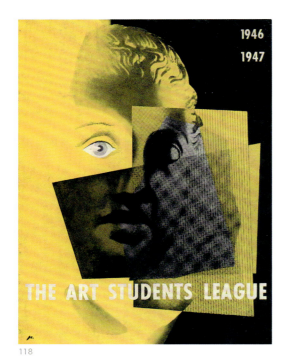

118

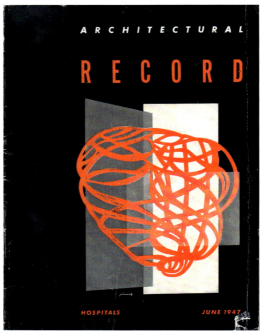

119

122

123

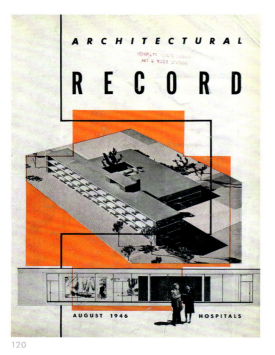

120

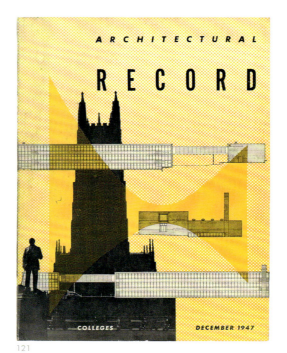

121

118
Catalog cover (attributed to Piening), *The Art Students League 1946–1947*, New York, 1946. This prospectus interior was planned and designed by Michael F. Tomaino under the supervision of Piening.

119
Magazine cover, *Architectural Record*, "Hospitals," F. W. Dodge Corporation, June 1947

120
Magazine cover, *Architectural Record*, "Hospitals," F. W. Dodge Corporation, August 1946

121
Magazine cover, *Architectural Record*, "Colleges," F. W. Dodge Corporation, December 1947

122
Logo, National Housing Center, c. 1964. The simplicity of the mark with an ideal combination of shapes aids in its success. It was used internationally in Denmark, Sweden, Germany, Holland, Belgium, France, Spain, and Italy.

123
Logo, Barden Corporation, precision bearings, c. 1960

124

125

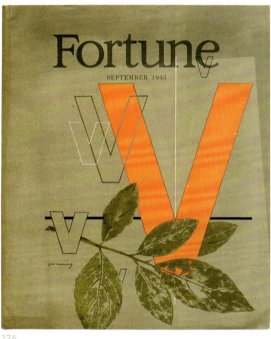

126

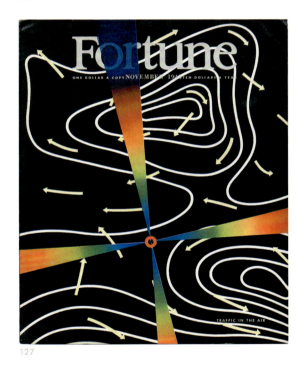

127

124

Magazine cover, *Fortune*, "Middle East Oil," June 1944. This issue's feature article investigates the U.S. government's intention to lay a pipeline between the rich Saudi Arabian oil fields and the distant shore of the Mediterranean.

125

Magazine cover, *Fortune*, "Colonial Policy," October 1944. The flags on the cover refer to colonial powers' responsibilities to the international community during—and after—the uncertain time of World War II.

126

Magazine cover, *Fortune*, September 1945. The cover design celebrates the victory ("V") of World War II and the hopeful aspiration of peace (olive branch). Describing the cover, the magazine states: "The present cover, by Peter Piening, FORTUNE'S art director 1941–44 and now of our experimental staff, was executed in exactly four hours and thirty minutes—by Mr. Piening's own account— four hours in argument as to what symbols to use, thirty minutes in actual application of brush to paper."

127

Magazine cover, *Fortune*, "Traffic in the Air," November 1943. Describing the cover, the magazine states: "The design on the cover . . . represents the directional beams of an airway radio-range station, superimposed on a stylized weather map. Some readers may wonder why we endowed invisible radio beams with the colors of the spectrum. We did so simply because we think it looks handsome." Art direction: M. Peter Piening; Cover: Peter Vardo

Cipe Pineles

1908–1991

Pineles in her *Charm* magazine New York office, c. 1955. Photo: Ed Feingersh

The announcement for "An Evening with One of the Best," a lecture series in the late eighties sponsored by the Art Directors Club of New York, promised to be an illuminating conversation with six veteran advertising art directors and graphic designers. The event was more than a little tainted: The participants were all men. Once upon a time, few would have raised an eyebrow at this, but by the late eighties, women had already become the majority gender, if not in advertising, then in graphic design. One woman who should have definitely been invited to participate was Cipe Pineles. As art director of *Glamour*, *Overseas Woman*, *Seventeen*, and *Charm*, the Viennese-born Pineles had as much, if not more, influence on publication design and illustration in America as any member of the Art Directors Club. She was the first female member of the organization (founded in 1921). Pineles had been proposed for membership in the late thirties but was repeatedly turned down until, the story goes, her first husband, William Golden (she was later married to Will Burtin), refused to join in 1948, saying that he wanted no part of a men's club. Pineles was admitted the next day. She was the second woman inducted into the Art Directors Club Hall of Fame, in 1975.

Pineles immigrated to the United States with her family in 1923. As a Pratt Institute graduate, she started looking for work in the early thirties, eventually landing a job with Contempora, a consortium of internationally renowned designers, artists, and architects, where she designed modish fabric designs and displays. In 1933, she was hired as an assistant to Dr. Mehemed Fehmy Agha, art director of *Vanity Fair* and *Vogue*, where she received an invaluable education. "We used to make many versions of the same feature. If we did, let's say, twenty pages on beauty with twenty different photographers we made scores of different layouts in order to extract every bit of drama or humor we could out of that material. Agha drove us to that because he was never happy with just one solution. And he was right too. We learned that magazine design should never play second fiddle to advertising," Pineles explained. Five years later, she was appointed art director at *Glamour*, a poor relation to *Vogue*, targeted at women who could not afford the high cost of high fashion. While money had been no object at *Vogue*, at *Glamour* Pineles would have to do whatever she could on a meager budget. She made the proverbial silk purse, but was so indignant over Condé Nast's treatment of the magazine that she left *Glamour* in 1944 to become art director of *Overseas Woman*, a U.S. Army magazine for American servicewomen stationed abroad. From there she moved to *Seventeen*, a magazine that defined the teenage market for girls.

"That was the best job I had because the editor was attuned to the audience, and no matter what anybody else did, she and I knew that for seventeen-year-olds the subjects had to be done in a special way," Pineles recalled. She personalized her art direction in the sense that if she showed a cape, she chose the model, the accessories, and the atmosphere in which the garment was presented. Often, she also conceived the issue's theme.

Pineles transformed American illustration from a saccharine service to an expressive art. "I avoided illustration that was weighed down by cliché or convention, and encouraged that which was unique to the editorial context," Pineles said. She launched the illustration careers of the likes of Seymour Chwast and Robert Andrew Parker and commissioned illustration from painters Ben Shahn, Jacob Lawrence, Yasuo Kuniyoshi, Raphael Soyer, and Robert Gwathmey. She was convinced that the audience of teenage girls was intelligent enough to appreciate sophisticated art. Rather than force her artists to mimic a text, Pineles allowed them to paint what they felt. "If it was good enough for their gallery then it was good enough for me," she explained. The artists also made her design differently. "My sense of magazine pacing was altered because I had to separate one artist from another by distinctly different stories. And I was forced to use different typography than I had been used to so as not to compete with the illustration."

Her photographic sense was equally unconventional. Pineles found fashion to be a fascinating subject and was interested in the effect it had on the way people felt about themselves. She despised the haughtiness of *Vogue*'s fashion photography and urged *Seventeen*'s photographers to focus on real-life situations. "Make the models look normal," she charged.

Pineles was not inclined to change her magazine formats, especially typographic styles, simply to announce change for its own sake. She resisted design fashion: "Changing the typeface for the headlines or the body type were outside manifestations. Although they would make the reader think that the magazine had changed . . . actually, in order to make substantial alterations the contents [of the magazine] had to be tackled [before anything else]," she explained. Nothing was formulaic. Type was selected according to the same expressive mandates as illustration.

Pineles described herself as personally responsible for interpreting in visual terms the contents of a publication, from appointing photographers and artists to certain features, to deciding to use many typefaces or just one. "But most important is the talent to harness it and create momentum so that the reader will keep turning the pages." •

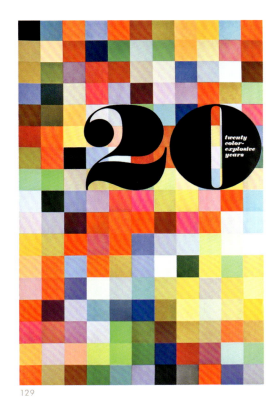

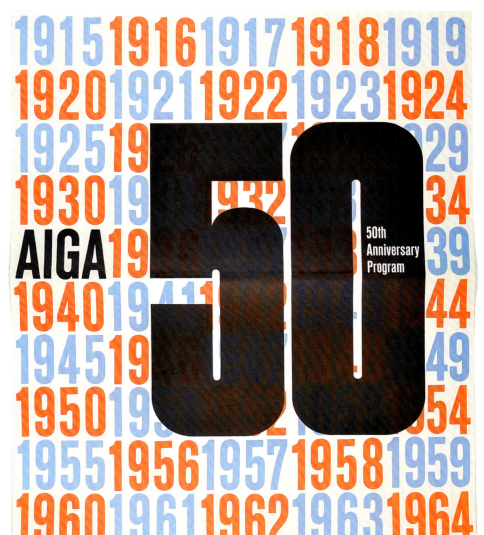

128

Cover and logo, *Lincoln Center Journal*,
"Festival '68," June 1968. Design: Pineles
and Will Burtin

129

Promotional cover, *House & Garden*,
"Twenty Color-Explosive Years," Condé Nast
Publications, 1965

130

Cover, *AIGA 50th-Anniversary Program*,
1965. Design: Pineles and Will Burtin

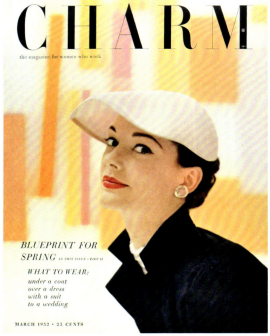

131

132

133

134

131
Magazine cover, *Charm: The Magazine for Women Who Work*, March 1952. Art direction: Pineles

132
Magazine cover, *Charm: The Magazine for Women Who Work*, January 1954. Art direction: Pineles; Photo: William Helburn

133
Magazine cover, *Seventeen*, Hearst Communications, July 1949. Two individual photographs designed as one composition. Art direction: Pineles; Photo: Francesco Scavullo

134
Magazine cover, *Seventeen*, Hearst Communications, May 1948. Art direction: Pineles; Photo: Francesco Scavullo

135
Magazine cover, *Vogue*, "Christmas Gifts," Condé Nast Publications, December 1, 1939. "Spelling VOGUE and Christmas delight in the world's most fabulous lettering." Photo: Anton Bruehl

VOGUE

INCORPORATING VANITY FAIR

CHRISTMAS GIFTS

NORTH AND SOUTH FASHIONS

DECEMBER 1, 1939
PRICE 35 CENTS

© THE CONDÉ NAST PUBLICATIONS, INC.

CIPE PINELES

Ladislav Sutnar

1897–1976

Sutnar at the University of Michigan, Ann Arbor, 1953. Photo: David H. Reider

The Czech designer Ladislav Sutnar, who immigrated to the United States in 1939 and worked in New York, made a decidedly modern impact. His most noteworthy innovation, introduced during the early sixties, was the parentheses around American telephone area code numbers. The concept, integral to the design of the Bell System's new communication network, instantly became part of the vernacular of everyday life. The Bell System was engaged in the technological upgrade of its huge network, and Sutnar eased public access to both emergency and regular services, while providing Bell with a distinctive identity. Sutnar designed information architecture for a wide range of American businesses. His was the quintessential Modernist mission of creating logical, hierarchical graphic systems that transformed routine business data into digestible forms.

Long before the advent of the "information age," there was information, masses of it begging to be organized into retrievable packages. In the thirties, the Great Depression required industry to focus on retooling factories and improving products, which spawned a new breed of graphic designer whose mission, to modernize antiquated aspects of life, led directly to efficient communications expressed through typographic purity. Sutnar was in the vanguard, driven by the fervent belief that good design applied to the most quotidian products had a beneficial, even curative effect on society.

From 1941 to 1960, as the art director of Sweet's Catalog Service, America's leading producer of trade and manufacturing catalogs that brought together into one source plumbing, electrical, and building supplies, Sutnar developed graphic tools that allowed users to traverse seas of data. Along with his team of researchers, writers, and designers (including Knud Lönberg-Holm, director of research), Sutnar transformed the complex language of product information into concise visual communication. Immediately, he replaced the old-fashioned word brand, Sweet's Catalog Service, with a sans serif S (for Sweets) in a circle. This economical letter mark was the cornerstone of an overall corporate design program that he continued to innovate throughout his tenure, employing a language of signs, symbols, and iconography. The S was identifiable and memorable, as were Sutnar's other brand icons, which are analogous to the friendly computer symbols used today and were inspired, in part, by El Lissitzky's iconographic tabulation system in Vladimir Mayakovsky's 1923 book of poems, *For the Voice.* Sutnar also made common punctuation—commas, colons, and exclamation points—into linguistic traffic signs by enlarging, fattening, and repeating them, which was reminiscent of the Constructivist functional typography of the twenties.

He sought a universal graphic language, yet he possessed a graphic personality that was so distinctive from others practicing the International Typographic Style that his work did not even require a credit line. It was based on functional needs, not overly complicated visual conceits, and so never obscured his clients' messages: "The lack of discipline in our present day urban industrial environment has produced a visual condition, characterized by clutter, confusion, and chaos," wrote curator Allon Schoener in the now-famous book that resulted from his 1961 traveling exhibition, "Ladislav Sutnar: Visual Design in Action." "As a result the average man of today must struggle to accomplish such basic objectives as being able to read signs, to identify products, to digest advertisements, or to locate information in newspapers, books, and catalogues. . . . There is an urgent need for communication based upon precision and clarity. This is the area in which Ladislav Sutnar excels."

Sutnar introduced the theoretical constructs that for him defined "good design" in the forties, when such definitions were rare in American commercial art. Design then was based partly on instinct but mostly on market convention. This went against the Sutnar grain. He sought to alter visual standards by introducing "the sound basis for modern graphic design and typography," which, as he asserted in *Visual Design in Action,* is "a direct heritage of the avant-garde pioneering of the twenties and thirties in Europe. It represents a basic change that is revolutionary." More than an exhibition catalog, *Visual Design in Action* was a testament to the historical relevance of Modernism and the philosophical resonance of Sutnar's focus on the functional beauty of total clarity. It is as spot-on about the power of design and "design thinking" today as it ever was. Sutnar was not a seer; he simply understood what made graphic design a useful tool.

His lasting contribution is to have synthesized European avant-gardisms into a lexicon that rejected "formalistic rules or art for art's sake." While he modified aspects of the New Typography, "He made Constructivism playful and used geometry to create the dynamics of organization," observed designer Noel Martin, who in the fifties was among Sutnar's small circle of friends. Sutnar used tight frameworks to allow a variety of options. His structurally strict yet creatively flexible systems for clarifying otherwise dense industrial data placed him in the pantheon. His American work, including interior and exterior graphics for Carr's Department Store (1956–57), advertisements for Vera Scarves, identity for Addo-X, and other stunningly contemporary works, is important for his dedication to total design schemes.

Sutnar harnessed avant-garde principles, injecting visual excitement into even the most routine material. While his basic structure was decidedly rational, his juxtapositions, scale, and color were rooted in abstraction. Underlying Sutnar's mission was the urge to introduce aesthetics, via design, into daily routine so that, yes, even a plumbing catalog should be a joy. "There is just one lesson from the past that should be learned for the benefit of the present," he wrote in 1959, that "painstaking, refined craftsmanship" should always underscore modern design. •

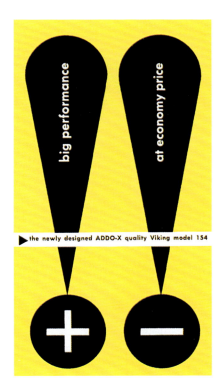

big performance

at economy price

▶ the newly designed ADDO-X quality Viking model 154

+ −

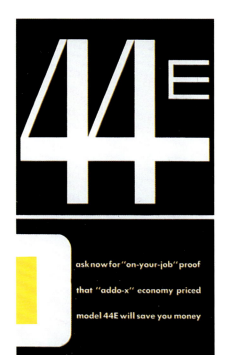

44E

ask now for "on-your-job" proof

that "addo-x" economy priced

model 44E will save you money

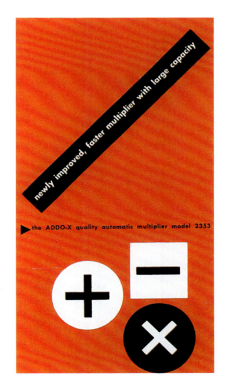

newly improved, faster multiplier with large capacity

▶ the ADDO-X quality automatic multiplier model 2353

+ − ×

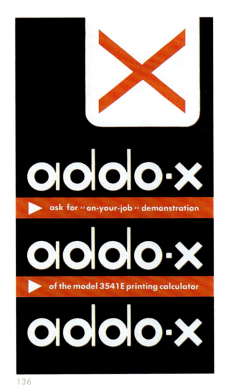

oıolo·x

▶ ask for "on-your-job" demonstration

oıolo·x

▶ of the model 3541E printing calculator

oıolo·x

136

oıolo·x 2341E

oıolo·x 2341E

oıolo·x 2341E

completely automatic multiplication

at conventional adding machine cost

ask for "on-your-job" demonstration

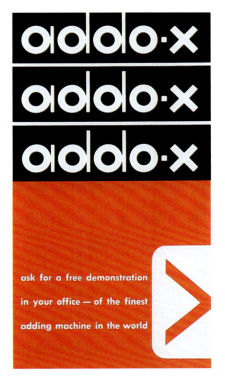

oıolo·x

oıolo·x

oıolo·x

ask for a free demonstration

in your office — of the finest

adding machine in the world

136
Direct mailers, *Addo-x*, c. 1956–59. A
business machine company, it had a unique
geometric logo with only four simple shapes.
When applied to the printed covers and
combined with product symbols, the results
are quickly identifiable and memorable,
reflecting the craftsmanship of the Swedish
company's products. Repetition and color
add to the visual unity and strength.

137
Book cover, *TGM*, Masaryk Institute, New York, 1960. Published on the 110th anniversary of the birth of Thomas G. Masaryk, founder and first president of Czechoslovakia

138
Poster, *II–Olympiad in America*, Workers Gymnastic Federation of USA and Eastern Divisions of SGU Sokol, 1947

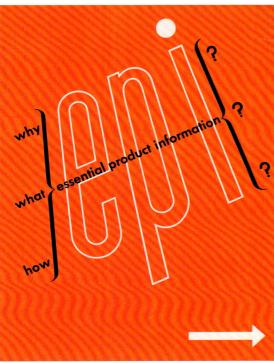

139

140

141

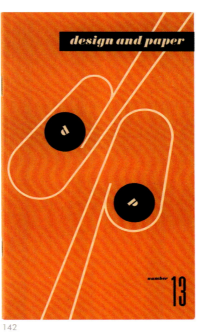

142

139
Brochure cover, *EPI: Why, What, How, Essential Product Information?* Sweet's Catalog Service, 1942. From the interior: "The increasing need for speed in war production is reflected in increasing demand for product information. In order to be useful such product information should be comprehensive, concise, and coordinated."

140
Advertisement, "Utility, Simplicity, Beauty – Effective Design," Sweet's Catalog Service, 1955. "Product information should be designed, subject to the usual standards— utility, simplicity, beauty."

141
Promotional booklet, *Shape, Line and Color*, Design and Paper no. 19, Marquardt, New York, 1945. It discusses shape for coordination, shape for identification, line for indication, color for articulation, and color for stimulation. "In the hands of a skillful designer . . . these design elements have functions of unsuspected variety," said Sutnar.

142
Promotional booklet, *Controlled Visual Flow*, Design and Paper no. 13, Marquardt, New York, 1943. Sutnar believed that "Visual Flow may be accomplished by simplification and coordination of design factors for the most efficient and continuous transmission of information."

143

144

145

143
Logo, Sweet's Catalog Service, 1941.
The versatile and functional S in the visual
identity program for Sweet's Catalog
Service, the premier publisher and
distributor of American industrial trade
products and service catalogs

144
Catalog front and back covers, *Harco
Masts—Towers*, Harco Steel Construction
Company, Elizabeth, New Jersey, 1944

145
Catalog interior spread, *Cuno Continuously
Cleanable Filters*, Cuno Engineering
Corporation, Meriden, Connecticut, 1944

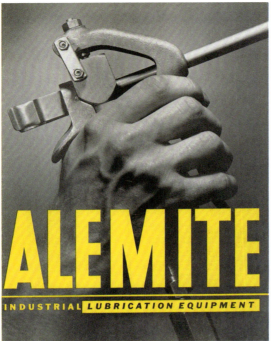

146

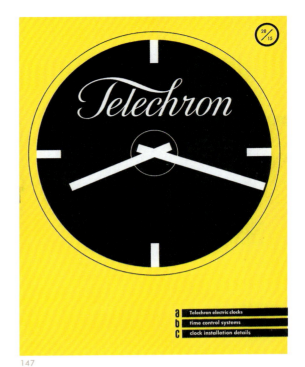

147

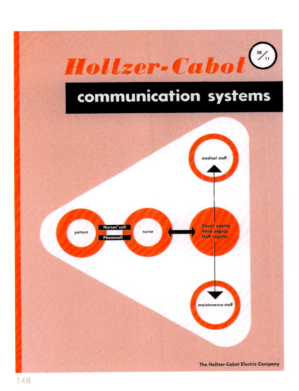

148

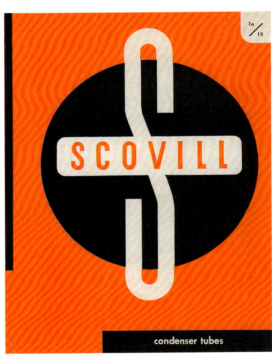

149

146
Catalog cover, *Alemite Industrial Lubrication Equipment*, Stewart-Warner Corporation, Chicago, 1941

147
Catalog cover, *Telechron*, Warren Telechron Company, Ashland, Massachusetts, 1944

148
Catalog cover, *Holtzer-Cabot Communication Systems*, Holtzer-Cabot Electric Company, Boston, 1944

149
Catalog cover, *Scovill Condenser Tubes*, Scovill Manufacturing Company, Waterbury, Connecticut, 1943

Fred Troller

1930–2002

Troller in his Port Chester, New York, studio, c. 1967

The Zurich-born, Rye, New York, transplant Fred Troller was one of the most enthusiastic progenitors of Swiss Style and the International Typographic Style in the United States. Influenced by the ideals of the Bauhaus and "receptive to the visual charms of a newly emerging (American-influenced) popular culture," wrote Karin Gimmi in her history of the Geigy Chemical Corporation's graphic design program, Troller offered a functional and experimental alternative to the wildly retro, ornamental graphic design mannerisms that were fashionable in the sixties.

Troller graduated from the Kunstgewerbeschule Zürich in 1951. He first visited America in 1953, when he and his wife, Beatrice, were cast for a part in *Cinerama Holiday*. Shortly after, he spent a brief period in Mexico as an artist before returning to Switzerland, where he worked as a painter and independent designer between Basel and Zurich, with no allegiance to either school.

Troller made his mark in the United States when Gottfried Honegger hired him to join the Geigy Chemical Corporation in Ardsley, New York, as art director from 1960 to 1966—what may have been "the six most fruitful years at the design studio," said Gimmi. Hiring Troller at Geigy "proved to be ideal in that he represented a cosmopolitan, creative, and, in an artistic sense, very undogmatic and contemporary position." During his reign, Troller championed the clear and direct, functional "Geigy style" to compete with more complicated American advertising design. Yet, unlike the company's Basel office, Troller's Geigy practiced a more expressive, experimental approach, a design freedom tailored to the American market and refreshingly distinct. This corporate image did not attach itself to the aesthetic of one individual or a guideline of standardized rules, but instead followed a general design spirit represented by white space, grids, geometric principles, stylized and abstract graphics, Akzidenz-Grotesk (and occasionally Univers and Helvetica), visual metaphors, experimental photography, new printing techniques, and vivid saturated contrasts. "I feel that the character and philosophy of the company should be visible in everything," said Troller, "no matter whether it is an advertisement, a piece of direct mail or the Corporation's letterhead. Within this philosophy, and within our own graphic style, the designer has the freedom to work out his own solution."

"In 1960 the [Geigy] art department had to provide propaganda material for the 40 group leaders, 275 physicians' sales reps, and 36 hospital reps," said Gimmi. Troller's posters, journals, packaging, advertisements, and brochures introduced a pop-culture sensibility to the company's otherwise economically formal design. For the drug Sterazolidin, a pain reliever for patients with rheumatoid arthritis, he created colorful, stylized X-rays. The result was both an abstract and a symbolic representation.

By the time Troller left Geigy in 1966, not long before it merged with CIBA, the company had made a name for itself in American graphic design, notably with its 1965 landmark exhibition, "Geigy Pharmaceutical," at Gallery 303 at the Composing Room in New York, and later

"Geigy Graphics" at the Princeton University School of Architecture in 1967. "No matter how good the product might be, it will sell better if the company name enjoys a good reputation in the mind of the consumer or the public in general," Troller said.

Troller opened his own design studio, Fred Troller Associates, in Rye, New York, where he specialized in trademarks, advertisements, and annual reports for clients such as IBM, Exxon, Xerox, Polaroid, Cross Siclare, General Electric, and Westinghouse, as well as, most visibly, book jackets for publishers Doubleday Anchor, Random House, and Simon & Schuster. For his paperback covers, Troller deployed Swiss Modernism; as Mark Owens wrote, they emerge from a cultural moment, "dramatizing a world view of arrangements—between bodies and technologies, minds and machine, individuals and ideas." In 1969–70, he created a series of eye-catching destination posters for American Airlines that were more like stop signs than scenic tableaux, where he used the illusion of moving letters to suggest speed.

Troller proudly claimed that his business experience enabled the highest responsiveness to client needs. While this can often be read as boilerplate commercial hype, Troller meant every word. He was a master at squeezing a lot of meaning out of a few images and colors. "His designs successfully combined Swiss rigorousness with American vitality," designer Massimo Vignelli said.

And this served him well as a teacher too. Vignelli said the true test of Troller's pedagogy was his success at "providing a constant supply of talented graphic designers to New York design firms." His career shined not in the glow of awards but through his standards of excellence as both a practitioner and a teacher. He taught and lectured at the Rhode Island School of Design, Cooper Union, the School of Visual Arts, and Philadelphia College of Art. He eventually chaired the Division of Graphic Design at Alfred University in Alfred, New York, retiring in 2000.

As a tribute to the respect Troller earned among his Modernist peers, he was commissioned by Paul Rand to design his tombstone: two stone cubes, with the top one slightly rotated and carved with Rand's name and dates in sans serif letters, evocative of the designer's quintessentially Modernist sensibility. The bottom was in Hebrew.

Of his time spent in the United States, particularly New York, Troller said, "The change of environment to the United States has affected my work in a very positive way. The dynamic climate of New York and the international flavor of its people produce an ambience which stimulates and inspires the creative process." •

New Persantin® brand of dipyridamole   oxygen to the heart   Geigy

150

151

152

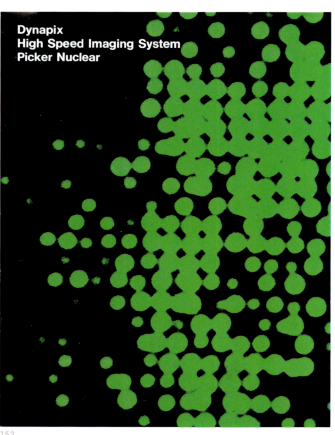

153

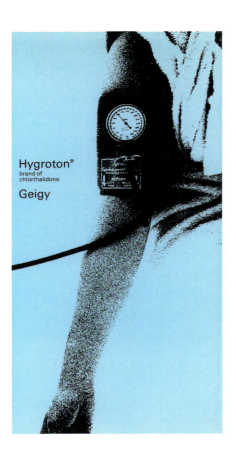

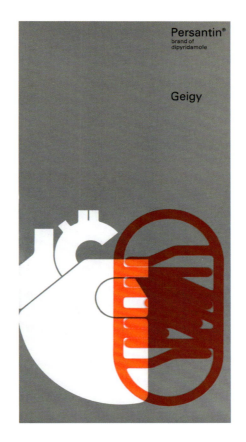

154

154
Advertising inserts, "Hygroton," "Persantin,"
"Dulcolax," and "Preludin," Geigy, New York,
c. 1962. Art direction: Fred Troller

155

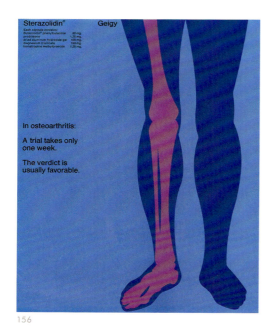

156

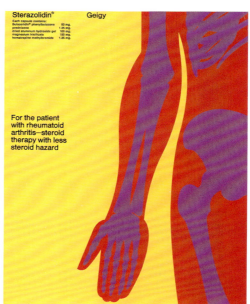

157

155
Advertisement, "Preludin: Inside the Obese Diabetic a Slim One Signals to be Let Out," Geigy, New York, c. 1964

156
Geigy sales sheet, Sterazolidin, "In osteoarthritis: A trial takes only one week. The verdict is usually favorable," Geigy, New York, c. 1964. Troller's stylized and vibrant color x-rays gave Geigy a new, expressive visual vocabulary.

157
Geigy sales sheet, Sterazolidin, "For the patient with rheumatoid arthritis—steroid therapy with less steroid hazard," Geigy, New York, c. 1964

158

159

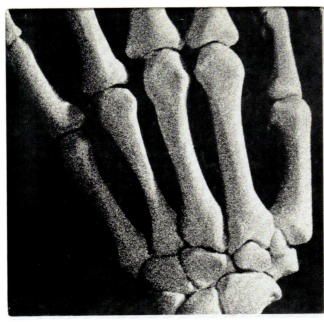

160

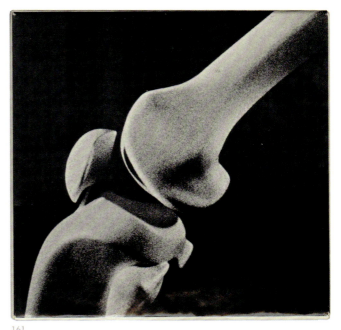

161

158
Physicians' sample packaging (box top), "Tandearil: Helps arthritic hands to move again," Geigy, New York, c. 1964. Art direction: Fred Troller; Design: Markus Low; Photo: Michael Gilligan

159
Physicians' sample packaging (box top), "Tandearil: Helps gouty arthritics to move again," Geigy, New York, c. 1964. Art direction: Fred Troller; Design: Markus Low; Photo: Michael Gilligan

160
Physicians' sample packaging (box top), "Butazolidin Alka in Rheumatoid Arthritis," Geigy, New York, 1966

161
Physicians' sample packaging (box top), "Butazolidin Alka in Osteoarthritis," Geigy, New York, 1966

George Tscherny

b. 1924

Tscherny in his New York studio at 216 East Fifty-Third Street, 1960

Born in Budapest to a Hungarian mother and a Russian father, George Tscherny was raised in Germany from the age of two. A neighborhood movie palace captured his imagination: "I remember the display for *All Quiet on the Western Front*. It had real foxholes, gas masks and helmets," he recalled. "But more impressive was the huge hand-painted poster of a movie star on the side of the building. This was my first awareness of graphic design—and even then I realized it was what I wanted to do."

Then came the Nazis. On November 10, 1938, the fourteen-year-old's life was turned topsy-turvy by Kristallnacht, the Night of Broken Glass, a vivid omen of terror to come. The following month, George and his younger brother escaped across the German border into the Netherlands. Their parents later made it to Newark, New Jersey, and Tscherny and his brother arrived in New York, on what Tscherny called a "floating concentration camp," on June 21, 1941. In 1942, he joined a government-sponsored training unit and then enlisted in the U.S. Army and was sent overseas. One of Tscherny's sergeants was a commercial artist who, in civilian life, worked for one of the big American advertising agencies. After learning about Tscherny's desire to become an advertising artist, he took the young man under his wing.

After the war, Tscherny was accepted into Pratt Institute in Brooklyn. He also met and later married a young dancer, Sonia Katz, who came from a German-speaking Jewish family forced to leave Europe. At Pratt, he took a class in advertising design taught by Herschel Levit and devoured the work of Lester Beall, Bill Golden, and Bradbury Thompson, among others. He also developed his own approach, and he soon became Levit's "prize pupil." Levit recommended Tscherny for his first job with Donald Deskey, whose days as the glamorous industrial designer of the interior of Radio City Music Hall were over. Tscherny left Pratt without graduating and cut his teeth at the Deskey office rendering comps for Procter & Gamble toothpaste and shampoo packages. "By the time I left, two-and-a-half years later, I was still sketching virtually the same packages," he noted.

In 1953, George Nelson hired him as an assistant to design director Irving Harper, who was responsible for designing trade advertising for the Herman Miller Furniture Company. Eventually, he became the head of the graphics department. "Working with Nelson was probably the most important thing that happened to me professionally," Tscherny recalled. "I was literally thrown in with the elite of design. But more important, Nelson was one of the few articulate spokesmen for design then—and his ideas rubbed off on me. In fact, the most enduring lesson was not to bring preconceived ideas to any project. When Nelson designed a chair, for example, he didn't start with the assumption that it had four legs." Nelson had no interest in graphics. "He was interested in building three-dimensional monuments," continued Tscherny. "He had no pressing need to involve himself in my area. That meant I could do almost anything within reason."

Tscherny believed that "design communicates best when reduced to the essential elements," but he resisted Modernism's ideological traps. One of his most significant accomplishments while working for Nelson was to break the cliché of how furniture was advertised, with pretty models posing with the case goods. Tscherny felt that the professional audience wanted to see the product alone, but he intuited that signifying a human presence was important. As a consequence, he developed a method called "the human element implied."

A 1955 advertisement announcing the opening of a new Herman Miller showroom in Dallas was the first time he used this approach. An extraordinarily simple design, it featured two spare lines of sans serif type and a photo of a chair with a cowboy hat resting on the seat. "By including the hat, I suggest Dallas," explained Tscherny, "while at the same time, I show the furniture in use, suggesting the human presence." Evoking a human presence, rather than manipulating pure geometric form, has been the key feature of Tscherny's design.

Tscherny started his own business when he was thirty. However, he was "afraid that it wasn't enough to simply *do* the work. Without a front-man or a partner who spoke well, I would have to *verbalize* what I was doing." The best way to hone persuasive skills, he thought, was by teaching. Teaching design at the School of Visual Arts gave him the ability he needed. "I attempted to teach the kids—as Nelson taught me—not to have preconceptions, but rather to be receptive to new ideas. Indeed, I am happiest when I do what I call 'Talmudic design'; when I look at the problem from top to bottom, ask myself questions, provide answers, and most important, try not to fall in love with any one answer until a mental bell rings."

Silas Rhodes, founder of the School of Visual Arts, said of Tscherny: "One sees popular art raised to the highest level." Indeed, he frequently relies on found objects—not necessarily cultural artifacts, but secret graphic clues that he finds within a problem. One such discovery came when he had to show graphically that Ernst & Ernst, a large accounting firm, was changing its name to Ernst & Whinney, and he found that by using the right typeface, if he turned the E ninety degrees, it would become a W.

Philip B. Meggs wrote that Tscherny's process is one of "selection," a choice of appropriate tools to convey a client's message. Tscherny's approach defies strict categorization, but his recipe for success can be characterized by three principal ingredients: a subtle, yet subversively impish, sense of humor; a refined, yet playful, typography ("In typography I strive for legibility and readability—except when I don't"); and last, but most critical, a genius for transforming decidedly complex problems into disarmingly simple solutions. •

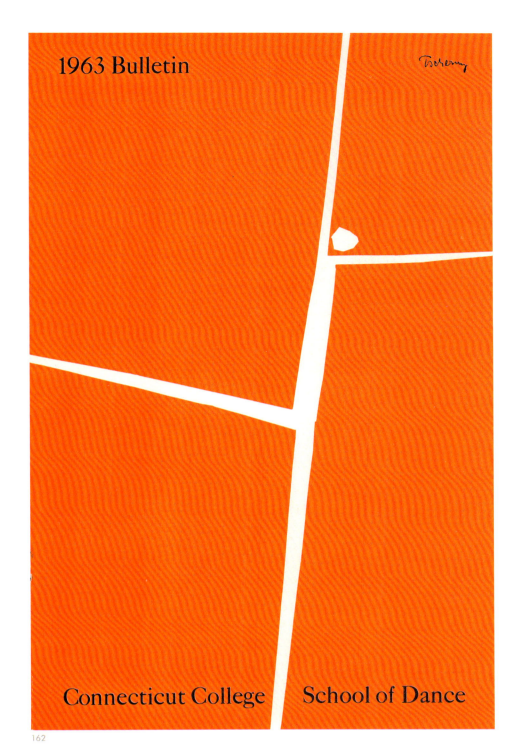

162

163

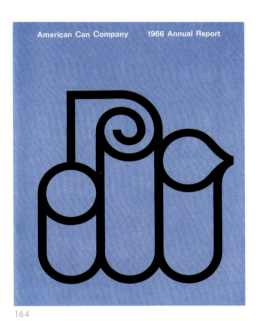

164

162
Bulletin, Connecticut College, School of Dance, 1963. Tscherny's gift is knowing exactly when to stop designing. His methods are instinctive. Design communicates best when reduced to an inescapable and essential form.

163
Annual report, American Can Company, 1965. Text from the inside cover: The new Action A logo represented a "consistent, distinctive and memorable picture" of the company while suggesting "the folding, forming, and printing" of its many products.

164
Annual report, American Can Company, 1966. Text from the inside cover: "The trio of bold, graphic symbols . . . are representative of a strong, modern, dynamic company, as well as the areas of business in which it is engaged: 1) Container and Packaging 2) Products, Consumer and Service Products 3) Chemical Products."

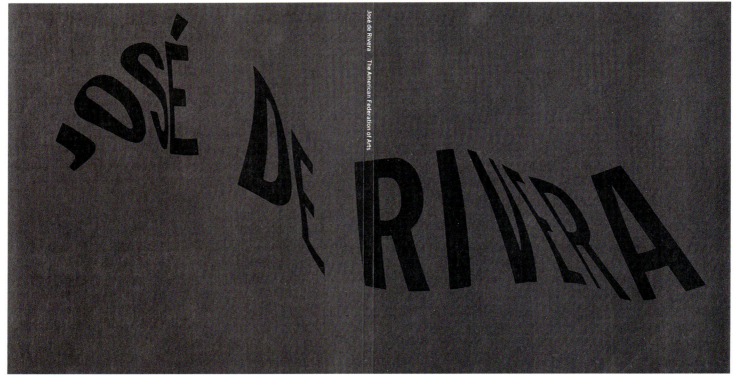

165

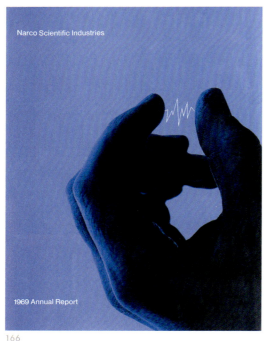

166

167

165
Exhibition catalog front and back covers, *José de Rivera*, American Federation of Arts, 1961. This photographic experiment carefully bends and twists the letterforms to express the artist's curvilinear metal sculptures.

166
Annual report, Narco Scientific Industries, 1969

167
Catalog cover, School of Visual Arts, 1964–65

168

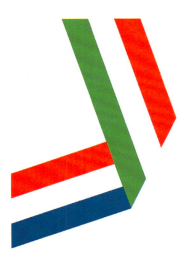

U.S.A. at the TRIENNALE

May 14–July 15, 1968   Milan, Italy

169

Benny Goodman and his orchestra

170

168
Newspaper supplement, *The Mood Is Right*, *New York Times*, 1958

169
Poster, *U.S.A. at the Triennale*, Milan, May 14–July 15, 1968

170
Catalog cover, Benny Goodman and His Orchestra, 1958

171
Advertisement, Aluminum Extrusions, 1954

OVERSEAS NATI**ONA**L AIRWAYS

Quarterly Report

June 30, 1969

172

Leland Hayward Presents

Jerome Robbins' " Ballets: U.S.A."

173

172
Quarterly report, Overseas National
Airways (ONA), June 30, 1969

173
Catalog cover, Jerome Robbins' "Ballets:
U.S.A.," 1958

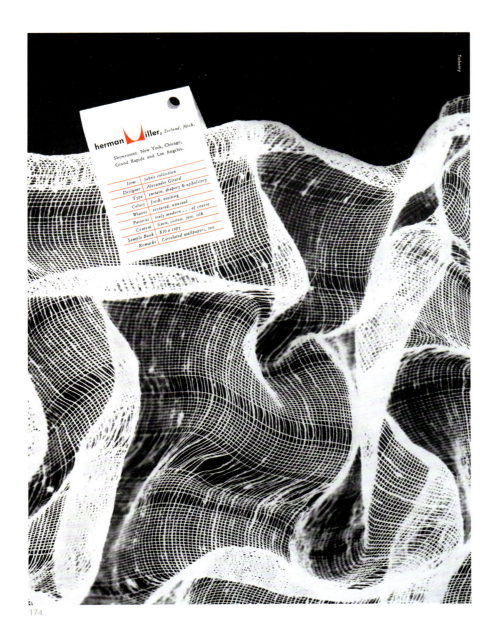

174

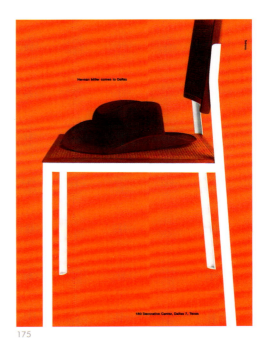

175

176

174
Advertisement, Herman Miller Furniture
Company, 1954

175
Advertisement, "Herman Miller Comes
to Dallas," Herman Miller Furniture
Company, 1955

176
Magazine cover, *Scope*, a student project
at Pratt Institute, 1948

Massimo Vignelli

1931–2014

Vignelli, Unimark International, New York, c. 1965

Massimo Vignelli was a design missionary, dedicated, in his own words, to improving "the world around us, to make it a better place to live, to fight and oppose trivia, kitsch and all forms of subculture which are visually polluting our world." Neither entirely Swiss Style nor American, what can be described as "Vignelli-Modern" was a nuanced interpretation of Italian humanist and purist precepts, derived from the work and thoughts of form givers from antiquity through the early twentieth century.

This high priest of modern graphic design left Italy in late 1965 and, with six others including Bob Noorda, a Dutch-born graphic designer and former art director at Pirelli in Milan, founded Unimark International, a new breed of corporate identity office and the first corporate design firm in the United States to introduce strict design systems. Unimark worked on both corporate and editorial projects. One of the most notable among the latter was *Dot Zero*, intended as a quarterly reference for professionals in the fields of visual communication and design, with art direction by Vignelli. *Dot Zero*, which published five issues between 1966 and 1968, was legendary for influencing how designer-targeted magazines were conceived and ultimately served their constituencies by introducing a critical voice to a rather insulated profession.

Dot Zero was initially designed to help promote Finch Paper, which at that time was a client of Unimark. "We did their CI [corporate identity]," Vignelli explained, "and we suggested to do a design magazine aimed to graphic designers, as a promotional organ for Unimark. . . . Not a how-to magazine! Not a house organ! Not an esoteric issues magazine! Not another Company magazine!" The founders and their writers sought to address several key issues that were not being covered by other design magazines at that time, including the seemingly rarefied areas of design history, semiotics (Marshall McLuhan), architecture (Arthur Drexler), perception (Jay Doblin), art, and anthropology (Lionel Tiger), as well as material culture. Ultimately, Unimark's banner was "showing the kind of graphics we stood for, One typeface, One size, Bold and Regular. Designed on a grid."

Vignelli's training as an architect in his native Italy during the midfifties and his friendship with the Swiss graphic designer Max Huber instilled his love for the grid, color, and vitality. In those early years, Vignelli also began a long-lasting friendship with Umberto Eco, one of the top semioticians in the world. Semiotics is the study of symbology, the notion that every sign (word, letter, image, number, etc.) is arbitrary and has meaning only when it represents an idea or thing. Vignelli understood the semiotic grid as the relationship between semantics (the meaning of the information), syntactics (its visual representation), and pragmatics (the effect of the sign on the receiver). It's a closed-loop system to make sure a design clearly and consistently represents the proper message, and that the audience receives that message as intended.

For Vignelli, the semiotic grid was the sine qua non of communication design and therefore a perfect tool to untangle the jumble of the New York subway system—with its 714 miles of track with some 465

stations—which was physically and visually a mess by the sixties. He devised a modular system of signs, each designed as individual units. Mathematical precision and rationality informed every part of his design program, from these prefabricated signs to typography that was modulated, with the smallest type on the informational panels one-half the size of the type on the directional panels, and that one-half the size of the typography on the station identification signs.

There are many other examples of Vignelli's rational design, but few as vivid as the *Herald*, a new weekly New York newspaper. In the sixties, most newspapers adhered to the same basic, narrow six- and eight-column formats, maintained by heavy-handed makeup editors with little interest in the fine points of design. "It takes people with vision, courage and strong intellectual drive to generate a new newspaper with new style of content and new visual aspect to convey it appropriately," Vignelli wrote in *Vignelli: From A to Z* (2007). The *Herald* was a modern gem: clean and crisp with a very limited yet still hierarchical type palette and generous use of white space. It was also modular, which made for a tighter editorial and advertising layout. The *Herald* prefigured Vignelli's signature designs for other specialty newspapers and magazines, including *European Journal*, *Skyline*, and *IDCNY*.

Vignelli resigned from Unimark International in 1971, and established Vignelli Associates with his wife, Lella, a product and furniture designer. He became the proselytizer-in-chief for design as a curative force, as well as the most fervent crusader for a graphic design history and criticism movement in the United States. He insisted that practice and legacy—making and learning—went hand in glove. Graphic design, he maintained, could never truly be a transcendent profession without rigorous critical analysis and theoretical exploration.

Critics called him a rigid ascetic, but his passion for design was exuberant. Vignelli was not interested in being fashionable, believing that "strength and dignity" would stimulate people's senses. He possessed a sly wit that, if not always overt in his work, came through in his personality. A sixties photograph of Vignelli and his colleagues at Unimark shows them all posing in white lab coats. Vignelli exuded a joy and style through design.

He was committed to creating design that responded to "people's needs not to people's wants." Vignelli made his presence known as spokesperson for design in the twenty-first century. "Design without discipline is anarchy, an exercise of irresponsibility," he wrote. "One of the greatest things about the modern movement was the sense of responsibility," he said in an interview published in *Design Dialogues*: "We have a responsibility to our client not to design something that will become obsolete quickly. . . . We have a responsibility to society to look for meaning in design, structure, in such a way that will last a long time." •

Bertoia, Florence Knoll, Saarinen, Mies van der Rohe, Noguchi have designed for Knoll, Aulenti, Albinson, Cafiero, Christen, Colombo, Mangiarotti, Pearson, Pettit Platner, Pollock, Schultz, and Stephens still do.

Knoll International, in 28 countries, has all these furniture and textile designs.

320 Park Avenue, New York

Knoll International

178

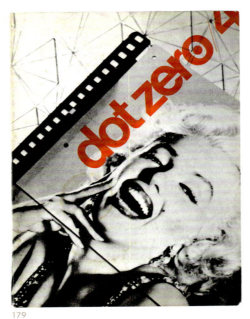

179

177
Poster, Knoll International, New York, 1967. The Helvetica logotype is unique for its' playfully overprinted colors, influenced by Vignelli's friend Max Huber. The backside is illustrated with black line drawings of Knoll's entire furniture collection.

178
Magazine cover, *Dot Zero 3*, Dot Zero, New York, Spring 1967. The cropped and rearranged image of the *World Journal Tribune* newspaper hints at the article inside, "Will Newspapers Ever Enter the Twentieth Century?" by Clay Felker.

179
Magazine cover, *Dot Zero 4*, Dot Zero, New York, Summer 1967. Cover photo of the U.S. Pavilion at Expo 67, Montreal, by George Cserna

180

181

183

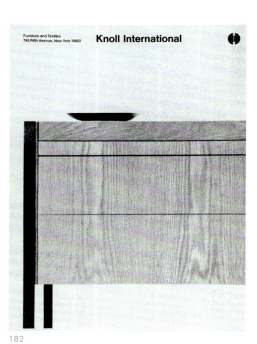

182

180
Catalog cover, *Knoll World*, no. 3, Knoll International, April, 1967. Text from *Knoll World*, no. 1 (January 1967): "In an effort to create a unified corporate look in all its printed matter, Knoll has hired Unimark International as graphic designer. . . . The purpose Unimark sees for itself is to "synthesize fine design and sophisticated marketing procedures for the benefit of the international business community. . . . Once the Knoll graphics program is established, the headquarters for design, printing, and distribution will be the Unimark office in Milan, headed by Bob Noorda. By having our operation in Europe, we'll be able to take advantage of quality printing at a lower cost than here [New York], and better serve the needs of our international licensees."

181
Catalog cover, *Tarif Tissus*, Knoll International, France, 1969

182
Catalog covers, *Furniture and Textiles*, Knoll International, New York, c. 1969

183
Ticket envelope, American Airlines, c. 1969

184

186

185

184
Product sheet, "Max 1," Heller Designs,
Mamaroneck, New York, c. 1970

185
Individual page, *Type face*, Graphic
Standards Manual, New York City Transit
Authority, 1970. "It is vital that all signs
be read easily and understood quickly.
This demands the consistent use of a
distinctive type face throughout the entire
system. Research has shown that the most
'appropriate' type face for this purpose is
a regular sans serif. Of the varius weights
of sans serif available, Standard Medium
has been found to offer the easiest legibility
from any angle, whether the passenger
is standing, walking or riding." Design:
Unimark International / New York

186
Newspaper, *the Herald*, New York, April 18,
1971. Vignelli designed *the Herald* with a
grid of six columns, sixteen modules high,
and one typeface: one size for text, two
sizes for titles, and italics for captions.

Bertoia

Harry Bertoia, sculptor, designs furniture for

Knoll Associates Incorporated
320 Park Avenue,
New York, New York 10022

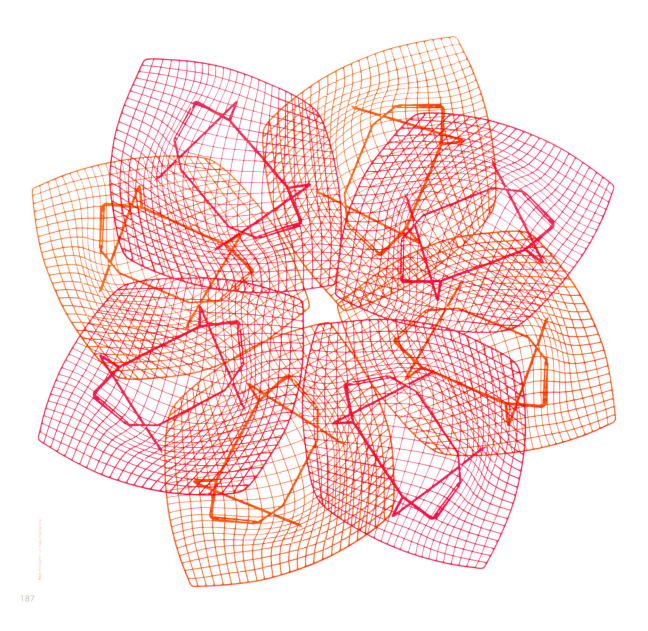

187

187
Poster, *Bertoia*, Knoll Associates, New York, c. 1968. Design: Massimo Vignelli / Unimark International

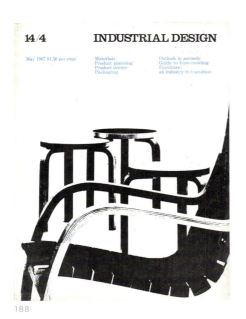

188

189

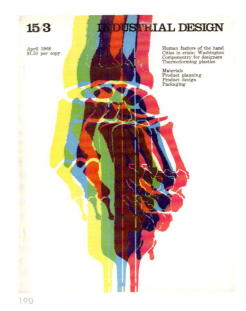

190

191

192

193

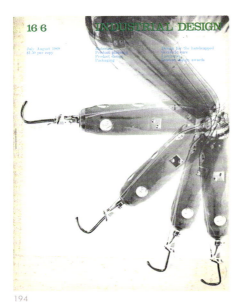

194

188–194

Vignelli became design director for *Industrial Design* magazine in May 1967, shortly after his arrival in the United States. "Because design was based on a grid format, we could accommodate all situations and, importantly, could design the magazine in a single day, achieving the desired tension and speeding the production process," Vignelli stated in *Design is One* (2006).

Magazine covers, *Industrial Design*, Whitney Publications, vol. 14, no. 4 (May 1967) with Gerhard Doerrié; vol. 14, no. 10 (December 1967); vol. 15, no. 3 (April 1968); vol. 15, no. 6 (July–August 1968); vol. 16, no. 2 (March 1969); vol. 16, no. 3 (April 1969); vol. 16, no. 6 (July–August 1969)

Dietmar R. Winkler

b. 1938

Winkler in his MIT studio-office, c. 1965. Photo: Fred Brink

When Dietmar R. Winkler first arrived in the United States in 1959, he brought a postwar European design pedigree: a modern ethos, Constructivist principles, and precision hand skills. American design was ripe for his ideas. From 1965 to 1970, Winkler worked as a designer at the Office of Publications (later renamed the Office of Design Services) at MIT in Cambridge, where European Modernism was shaping practice in the fifties. He was in the right place at the right time to help advance one of America's best-known Modernist academic graphic programs.

Born in the village of Plagwitz, Germany, Winkler studied design at the Kunstschule Alsterdamm, Hamburg, and in 1957, shortly after graduating, secured a position with the emerging pharmaceutical company Chemie Grünenthal, where he learned letterpress printing, prepared precise comps, and handled metal type, as well as dealt with the complexities of modular typography and proportions through the use of a grid system. For Winkler, this on-the-job training formed a foundation for "seeing and responding to the visual world through proportion, not through frozen geometry or the grid."

In America, he spent a year at the Rhode Island School of Design, studying the use of conceptual and language-based metaphors in American advertising. He also explored classical typography, including the early sixteenth-century Italian humanist printer and publisher Aldus Manutius, who became a great inspiration. "It is his perseverance in spite of all the technical problems of his times, which encourage us to commit ourselves to larger and more important issues," he recalled.

Deciding not to return to Germany, Winkler landed a job as an assistant art director at Reach, McClinton & Humphrey in Boston, designing print collateral and magazine advertisements. For the next five years, as a partner and designer in the three-person design firm Leverett A. Peters and Associates, he further established a notable reputation working for such clients as Badger Industries, Cornell University Press, Simmons College, Harvard University, Oxford Paper Company, and WGBH Boston. In 1960, he was awarded the prestigious Gold Medal of the Art Directors Club of Boston.

In 1963, Winkler went back to Germany to tour the D. Stempel and Bauer typefoundries and the Klingspor-Museum in Offenbach, with its extensive modern type collection. He met Hermann Zapf, who he said "spent a whole day showing me the steps between the conception of a type face and the arduous implementation processes leading to the final letterform for print production." This extracurricular education would prove beneficial two years later when Winkler arrived at MIT, where the largely self-taught Muriel R. Cooper, Jacqueline S. Casey, and Ralph Coburn had no formal education in typography.

At MIT, Winkler designed hundreds of brochures, posters, and publications. "I never saw the status of a pamphlet or booklet as less than that of a poster, in the same ways I don't see any difference between art and design," Winkler said. He frequently consulted with his colleague Carl Zahn, a graphic designer, typographer, and director of publications at the Museum of Fine Arts, Boston, who generously shared his expertise regarding the availability of typefaces, paper selections, pricing, and four-color reproduction. Winkler taught his office to think about press and paper size, and binding and folding options. He was the only staffer with the technical skills to prepare his own camera-ready art. He introduced the technique of split fountain printing, and saved on printing costs by using odd paper lots, which had been wrongly trimmed or had small defects.

By the time Winkler joined the office, the graphic vocabulary had been partially established by Cooper, Casey, and Coburn, but it was also shaped by the influences of English, German, and Swiss "visiting designers" invited by editor John Mattill through the years. Winkler built upon the office's early Modernist visions and also influenced its output, including the individual work of Casey and Coburn. Meanwhile, Winkler said, "we all learned from each other" yet "surprisingly there was never organized or spontaneous criticism." He added, "We were always excited about working at MIT, because we were surrounded by contemporary architecture," and it was "quite liberating" to step outside and experience the work of Alvar Aalto, Araldo Cossutta, Le Corbusier, I. M. Pei, Paul Rudolph, and Eero Saarinen, among others; for Winkler, "they represented a new spirit."

Winkler's designs were harmonious and free from embellishment. He never favored strict grids but instead employed dynamic modular systems, in which "the content provides the form and rhythm." He experimented with modular abstraction, repetition, pattern, and, when budget allowed, photography. "I became more and more interested in animation and experimented with ways to express motion or progressions," he said. His 1969 poster design for a course on COBOL programming used manipulated letterforms in a kinetic composition evolving rhythmically down the page. The transparent forms cleverly facilitate the content of the message. "Excellence will always break the back of mediocrity," Winkler insisted.

Winkler left MIT in 1970 and operated as a freelance type and design director, specializing in the development and implementation of publication programs and corporate identification systems for nonprofit organizations and institutions. He also became an active and dedicated educator and lecturer.

Winkler's fifty years of design contributions to American Modernism resonate today. He was instrumental in advancing Swiss and German principles and aesthetics and the emerging International Typographic Style in an American academic environment that sometimes rebelled against the Modernist ethos. •

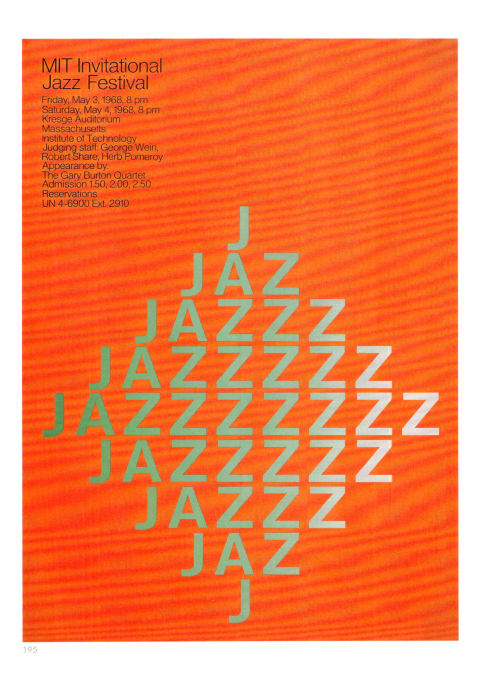

195

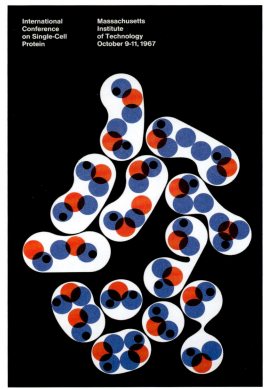

196

197

195
Poster, *MIT Invitational Jazz Festival*, Massachusetts Institute of Technology, 1968. The design explores split fountain printing to achieve color variations, and to take advantage of larger press sizes to allow printing of several publications in different color combinations without spending the extra money; a pragmatic solution given the modest budgets.

196
Folder, *International Conference on Single-Cell Protein*, Massachusetts Institute of Technology, 1967. Winkler experimented with simple graphic motions to visualize the growth and splitting of a cell and to help enliven the two-dimensional page.

197
Poster, *Graduate Education in Ocean Engineering*, Massachusetts Institute of Technology, 1967. This typographic animation represents the movement of waves.

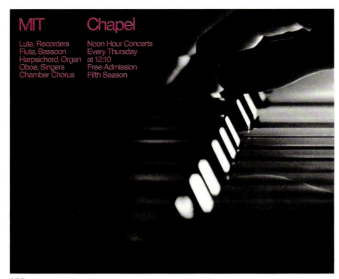

198

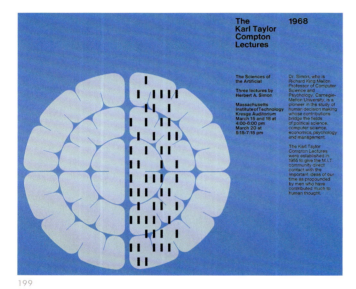

199

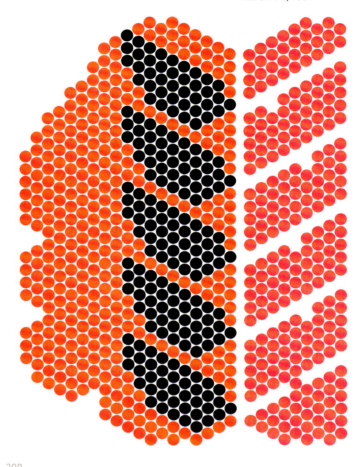

International
Conference
on Malnutrition
Learning
and Behavior

Massachusetts
Institute
of Technology
March 1-3, 1967

200

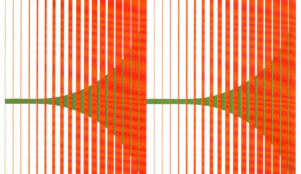

Noonhour
Concert Series
MIT Chapel
Thursday
October 23, 1969
12:10 pm
Concert for
Two Trumpets
and Organ

Robert Hazen,
Trumpet
Peter Conant,
Trumpet
John Cook,
Organ

201

198

Poster, *MIT Chapel Concerts*, Massachusetts
Institute of Technology, 1968. Photo: Fred Brink

199

Poster, *The Karl Taylor Compton Lectures*,
Massachusetts Institute of Technology, 1968.
This promotes the lecture series "Sciences of
the Artificial," which pits the brain against the
machine, symbolized by Hollerith's punch-card
format used in semiautomatic data processing.

200

Brochure, *International Conference on
Malnutrition Learning and Behavior*,
Massachusetts Institute of Technology, 1967.
The cover is a geometric design prepared with
multicolored Dennison round labels.

201

Poster, *Concert for Two Trumpets and Organ*,
Massachusetts Institute of Technology, 1969.
Increasingly interested in experimenting with ways
to express motion, Winkler composed a minimal
and abstract design using only color, shape, and
form to animate the sound of music.

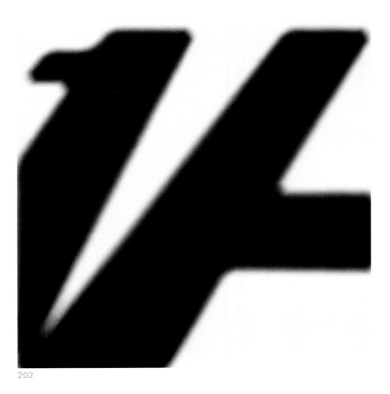

What **will you do now that** **you're 1A?**

A Vietnam Commencement	Moderator	Diane Clemens
MIT Kresge Auditorium Monday May 20, 1968 8 pm	Graduation into what?	Harvey Cox Harvard Divinity School
	What can you do about the draft?	Ira Arluck Norm Daniels
Sponsored by the ad hoc committee for inquiry into social responsibilities	A tribute to the resisters	Louis Kampf
	Poetry readings	Barry Spacks Sidney Goldfarb

202

Lowell Institute School under the auspices of the Massachusetts Institute of Technology

Special Summer Computer Course Introduction to COBOL Programming

203

202
Poster, *What Will You Do Now That You're 1A?*, Massachusetts Institute of Technology, 1968. This "Vietnam Commencement" poster with its soft and out-of-focus image supported administrative efforts to advise students about their legal rights with regard to the military draft.

203
Poster, *Special Summer Computer Course: Introduction to COBOL Programming*, Massachusetts Institute of Technology, 1969. Geometric shapes gradually build to form the acronym COBOL while symbolizing the back-and-forth motion of the different reels of an IBM Mainframe Computer.

Rudi Wolff

b. 1931

Wolff in his William Douglas McAdams office,
New York City, c. late 1950s

Rudi Wolff believes, "The design consultant is of necessity a non-specialist. His range of activity reaches into many fields and disciplines." His projects for significant pharmaceutical clients as art director at William Douglas McAdams and his later ones at his own design consultancy firm, the eponymous Rudi Wolff, Designer, allowed him the creative freedom to develop a personal, well-crafted vision and body of work. His interest in science and study of Cubism, Dada, and the Bauhaus formed the background to much of his work.

In 1938, the seven-year-old Wolff immigrated with his family to New York from Hamburg, Germany. Raised in Manhattan in an upper-middle-class, cultured European home, Wolff attended public school but spent much of his time painting murals in the back of the classroom. This eventually led him to the High School of Music and Art and a short stay at the vocational School of Industrial Art, where an English teacher, aware of his unhappiness at school, suggested that he switch to evening school and apprentice during the day for her husband, the eminent New York wood engraver Bernard Brussel-Smith. In this atmosphere of skill and craft, Wolff learned the art of end-grain wood engraving and became a skilled printer.

At Brussel-Smith's urging, Wolff attended Cooper Union School of Art at night while continuing to work during the day, graduating with a fine arts degree in 1949. His discovery of the power and use of simple two-dimensional design was shaped by courses taught by Carol Harrison and Henrietta Schutz. Wolff credited Harrison for introducing a program in color, painting, and fabric design to Cooper Union that was similar to what Josef Albers was offering at Yale. This period was significant in shaping Wolff's distinctive embrace of Modernism.

While attending Cooper Union, Wolff was employed at a small agency for about a year designing one-column ads for the *New Yorker*, which he called a valuable experience in "constraint." He landed a better opportunity at William Douglas McAdams, a large Madison Avenue medical advertising agency, where he worked on high-profile accounts for such pharmaceutical giants as Upjohn, CIBA, Pfizer, and Hoffmann-La Roche. During this period, Wolff became interested in medicine; he even considered attending medical school, but without having the prerequisite courses, it would have taken much too long.

Wolff started as a comp artist working under art director Victor Trasoff. Shortly after, when Wolff was twenty-two, an account executive persuaded Trasoff to make Wolff a full art director, first for the CIBA account and later for Roche, where he worked with talented photographers and illustrator-artists including David Attie, R. O. Blechman, Jacob Landau, Herbert Matter, Jim McMullan, Robert Osborn, Ben Rose, Ben Shahn, Edward Sorel, Simms Taback and Reynold Ruffins, Rolf Tietgens, and Andy Warhol.

Through the agency, Wolff became friendly with one of the Upjohn heirs who at the time was CEO of the company's important veterinary division. This relationship resulted in creative solutions for the cover and editorial matter of an Upjohn in-house magazine, *Veterinary Scope*. Wolff occasionally visited the office of Will Burtin, who was design director at Upjohn. Although Wolff never worked directly with Burtin, he was influenced by the older man's work, particularly medical and scientific exhibitions, such as "The Cell" (1958) and "The Brain" (1960). Wolff also admired and learned from such modern design luminaries as Lester Beall, Erik Nitsche, and Paul Rand.

The work Wolff produced was aimed at physicians, describing a medicine's healing effects. When asked about this challenge, he said, "The product, usually prominent in general advertising, is considered relatively unimportant in pharmaceutical design. Here the effect of the product (the drug), and not its shape or form, is the pivotal point. Being released from the burden of not having to show or glamorize a particular product, but having to concentrate on a variety of medical states or effects, forces the designer to think in abstract terms." His graphics therefore struck a balance between the conceptual and functional, using sans serif typography, pure flat color, abstract form, figurative photography, light patterns, and other contemporary means. The idea was to capture visual attention while expressing the idea of disease and the possible cure that a particular drug might provide.

In 1968, he opened Rudi Wolff Design at East Seventy-Fourth Street, a consulting firm responsible for advertising, annual reports, corporate communications, exhibition design, editorial content, and film. He conceived and designed "Therefore I Am: The Miraculous Harvest of the New Biology," a 1969 exhibition on biology and genetics for the Xerox Exhibit Center in Rochester, New York. "As a designer," he said, "I felt I could communicate ideas to help a lay audience to better understand the sciences." He worked for many important clients, including the Metropolitan Opera, Xerox, Yale University, Deloitte, Siemens, Whitney Museum of American Art, National Gallery of Art in Washington, D.C., New York Botanical Garden, and Jewish Museum.

Wolff followed a philosophy of "design simplicity" developed from classic European Modernism. He believed that "the most exciting solutions usually derive from the very subject to be dealt with. Without the proper background a correct analysis of the problem is impossible."

From wood engraving to corporate design to science and on to the fine arts, there has always been a direct link between Wolff's interests and his design. Taken together, they played an important role in enriching his body of work and visual virtuosity. •

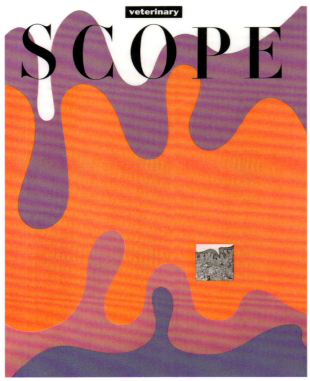

204

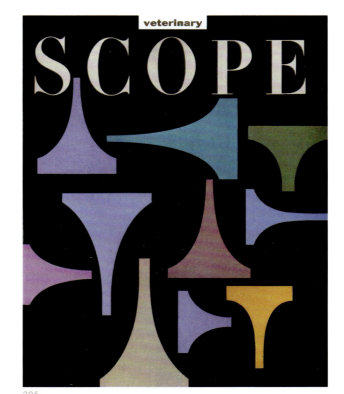

205

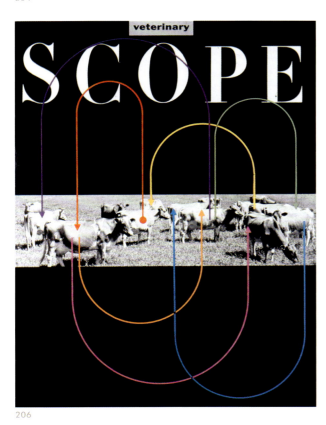

206

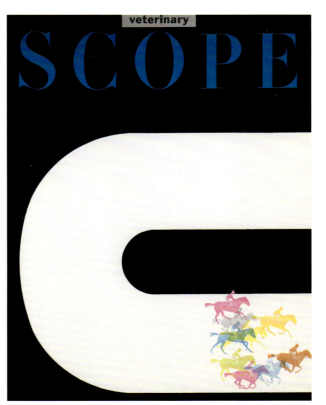

207

204–207
Magazine covers, *Veterinary Scope*, Upjohn
Company, 1958

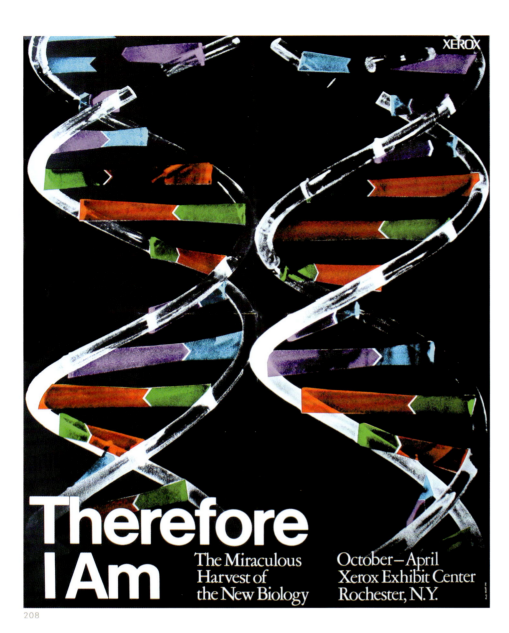

208

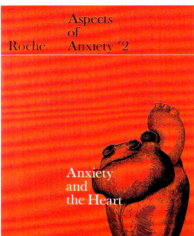

210

209

208

Exhibition poster, *Therefore I Am: The Miraculous Harvest of the New Biology*, Xerox Exhibit Center, Rochester, New York, 1969. The poster illustrates a detail of the eight-foot high DNA exhibition model, an internally lit and revolving plexiglass structure.

209

Logo, Xerox Exhibit Center, Rochester, New York, c. 1969

210

Booklet covers, *Aspects of Anxiety*, "Fight or Flight: The Nature and Meaning of Anxiety," no. 1, and "Anxiety and the Heart," no. 2, Roche Laboratories, 1963

211–218

To convey complex medical ideas, Wolff employed a variety of experimental techniques utilizing typography, photography and darkroom effects, abstract forms, symbolic illustrations, and painterly styles in his pharmaceutical trade advertising for Roche Laboratories and the Upjohn Company, c. 1962–69.

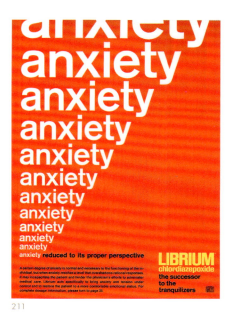

211

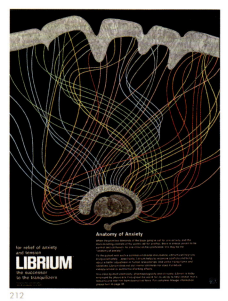

212

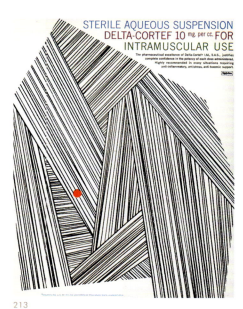

213

214

215

216

217

218

b eall,

lester

320

East

42nd

Street

New York

N.Y.

Mu 4-6784   Mo 4-8360

Self-promotional advertisement, c. 1938. Beall left
Chicago in 1935 for New York City, where he established
his first studio/office in Tudor City. This ad appeared in
the 18th Art Directors Annual of Advertising Art; it shows
Beall's European avant-garde influences, distinctive self-
expression, use of photomontage, and acute ability to mix
and match multiple type styles. Design: Lester Beall

HOMEGROWN

03

Saul Bass
1920–1996

Bass in his Hollywood, California, office, c. 1960

Hollywood, the city of fantasy and glitz, was also a wasteland of formula and convention. The Bronx-born Saul Bass arrived there in 1945, intent on producing unconventional advertising for the movie industry. But the odds were against him. Tried-and-true conceits dictated the look and feel of posters, foyer cards, and ads. The common poster showed something for everybody: bits of romance, action, drama, and, of course, unblemished portraits of the stars.

Bass was not going to become a hack. After reading György Kepes's *Language of Vision* (1944), he became a card-carrying modern reductionist. While working in the New York office of Warner Bros., he toyed with the picture and text components of movie ads, mostly playing with scale, which was the only latitude he was allowed. Of course, it was a creative dead end. "I could only carry it so far, because the other ingredients had to be there," he recalled in *Graphic Design in America*. So he packed up for Hollywood and went to work for Buchanan & Co., the agency that handled Paramount Pictures. Finally, in 1949, he designed his first breakthrough ad, for *The Champion*. It was totally black with a tiny halftone and a little lettered scrawl below it, but it was the auspicious beginning that thrust Bass's mature neo-Expressionist approach to Hollywood publicity into view, launching his career as an innovative advertising and film-title-sequence designer in the fifties and sixties for the likes of Otto Preminger and Alfred Hitchcock.

The tyrannical Preminger, known for his huge ego, nonetheless gave Bass the opportunity to make title-sequence history by making a conceptual shift from mundane title-card lettering superimposed over backgrounds to short prologues in the films. In 1955, he made a bold leap with the print advertising for *The Man with the Golden Arm*, which eschewed a picture of its star, Frank Sinatra, in favor of a pattern of black bars that framed a primitive woodcut-like rendering of a crooked arm, symbolizing the drug-addicted protagonist. Theater owners objected to the absence of the star, but the following tells the story of Bass's subsequent success: Preminger "was sitting with his back to me—he didn't know I was there—talking on the phone, obviously to an exhibitor somewhere in Texas," Bass recalled. "The exhibitor was complaining about the ads and saying that he wanted to have a picture of Sinatra . . . and I heard Otto say to him, 'Those ads are to be used precisely as they are. If you change them one iota, I will pull the picture from your theater.' And hung up on him." Rather than hype the film, the graphic reduced the plot, the story of a tormented drug addict, to an essence—a logo, really—that evoked the film's tension.

The real revolution occurred when Bass animated this simple graphic icon for the title sequence of moving white bars on a black screen, which was transformed into an abstract ballet of erratic shapes. After a few moments, the bars metamorphosed into the arm. "There was a tendency, when I did the title for *The Man with the Golden Arm*, to think it worked because it was 'graphic,'" Bass explained in *Print* magazine in 1960. "If it worked, it was because the mood and feeling it conveyed made it work, not because it was a graphic device." Nevertheless, by creating a graphic symbol that was effective for use in both the print campaign and the opening title sequence, Bass invented a genre that other directors realized was an appealing way to introduce a film by compressing narrative to a graphic device.

But Bass said he was simply returning to the essence of motion pictures as a purely visual medium. "We've come full circle," Bass once explained. "[We] went to a theatrical stage approach with inordinate reliance on dialogue, and now we're back again to a greater reliance on the visual, but in a way that is more real and more current with our lives today."

The Man with the Golden Arm was Bass's first movie within a movie, and it had less to do with specific aesthetics of design than a sense of the story being synthesized into an abstract narrative. All aspects of a movie should fit together like pieces of a puzzle: "In every title I've done, I've been very conscious of the fact that the title has a responsibility to the film, that it is there to enhance the film, to set it up, to give it a beginning—and not to overpower and preempt it," he asserted in *Print*.

Bass continued making title sequences for four decades, many as memorable as the films themselves. Although he was best known for motion design, his graphics derived from his print origins. He was a Modernist with expressionistic instincts that were visible in his packaging, products, corporate identification, logos, and illustration. "His work surrounds us," wrote David R. Brown when Bass received the AIGA Medal for lifetime achievement in 1981. "Pick up the telephone and you're hard-pressed not to recall Bass's ubiquitous Bell System symbol and look. . . . In the supermarket or in the kitchen—Wesson, Quaker, Alcoa, Lawry's, Dixie: Saul Bass. Relax with a magazine, read a book, watch TV, take some pictures—*Saturday Evening Post*, Warner, Minolta: Saul Bass. Give to charity—The United Way, Girl Scouts: Saul Bass. Strike an Ohio Blue Tip match."

One of the keys to unlock Bass's preeminence was his fluency with symbols of all kinds and ability to control their potency through scale and juxtaposition. In Bass can be found the measure of a Renaissance graphic designer as word and image communicator who knew no media, conceptual, or expressive bounds in his mission to help the commercial and cultural worlds show their personalities through his voice. •

219

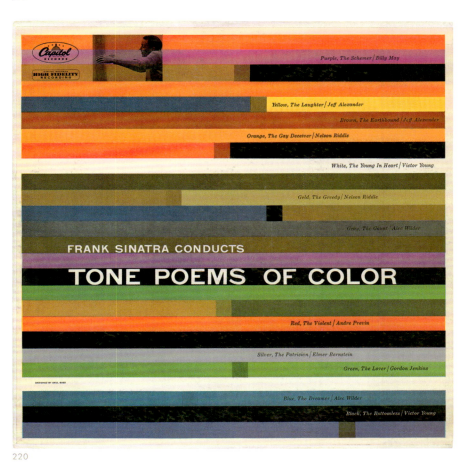

220

219
Album cover, *Blues & Brass* by Elmer
Bernstein, Decca Records, 1956. Bass
pioneered more than modern film-title
sequences; he was the quintessential
multidisciplinary graphic designer who
jumped effortlessly between corporate
identification, printed collateral,
and motion.

220
Album cover, *Tone Poems of Color* by
Frank Sinatra, Capitol Records, 1956

221

222

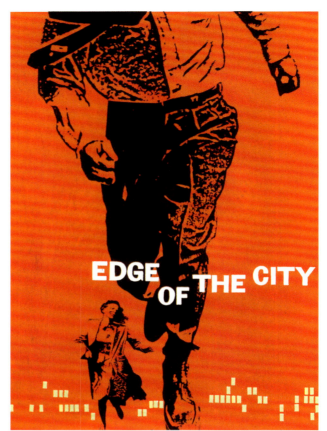

223

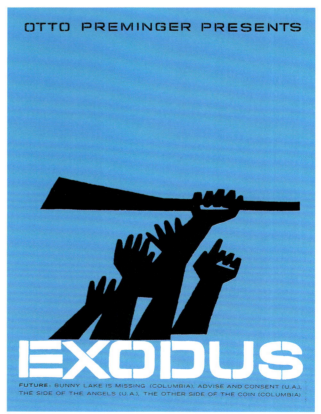

224

221
Poster, *The Man with the Golden Arm*, 1955

222
Poster, *Anatomy of a Murder*, 1959

223
Advertisement, *Edge of the City*, 1957

224
Trade advertisement, *Exodus*, 1960

THE MAGNIFICENT SEVEN · DIRECTED BY JOHN STURGES

225

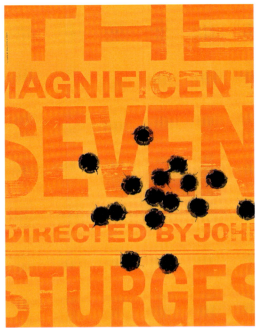

226

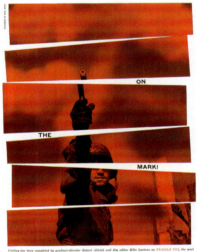

227

225
Unused advertisement, *The Magnificent Seven*, 1960

226
Unused advertisement, *The Magnificent Seven*, 1960

227
Trade advertisement, *"On the Mark!," Fragile Fox* (later renamed *Attack!*), directed by Robert Aldrich, 1956

228

Magazine cover, *Arts & Architecture*,
November 1948

229

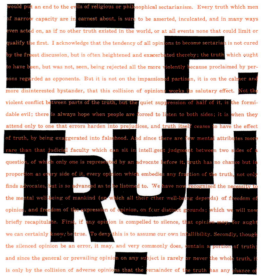

231

232

229
Poster, *Seventh San Francisco International Film Festival*, 1963

230
Poster, *Human Rights Week*, U.S. National Commission for UNESCO, 1963

231
Advertisement, "John Stuart Mill on the Pursuit of Truth," part of "Great Ideas of Western Man" campaign, Container Corporation of America, 1957

232
Logo, Bell System, 1969

Lillian Bassman

1917–2012

Bassman working at home, 246 Lexington Avenue, New York, early 1940s.
Photo: Paul Himmel

Virtually ignored by the fashion industry, girls from thirteen to twenty-one were not a quantifiable-enough market for fashion magazines to bother with until the end of World War II. To help rectify the situation, in 1945 the legendary *Harper's Bazaar* editor Carmel Snow asked a young magazine designer, Lillian Bassman, to create a format for a forthcoming sister periodical. *Bazaar* had been covering college girls in annual fall sections of the magazine, but the new stand-alone *Junior Bazaar* (with emphasis on *Junior*) was intended to compete with *Seventeen*, which had launched a year before, and capture this postwar consumer tidal wave. *Junior Bazaar* was not only in the vanguard of fashion marketing; it gave Bassman's design talents the opportunity to flourish.

Bassman was raised in the Bronx by free-thinking intellectual, Russian immigrant parents; she was brought up "with a mindset that allowed her to live as an independent and unconventional woman," noted William Grimes in his *New York Times* obituary. By way of example, at fifteen she moved in with Paul Himmel, a documentary photographer, whom she would later marry. Before working at *Harper's Bazaar*, Bassman studied at Textile High School in Manhattan. "Meanwhile, she had begun to model for artists, which was a pleasant enough and slightly outré way to make some spending money, and far preferable to babysitting (her entrée into the art world was probably Boris Gorelick, a close family friend who helped found the Artists' Union in 1934)," wrote her son, Eric Himmel. "She was bemused when posing for George Bridgman's famous anatomy class at the Art Students League that he used chalk to outline the musculature on her body, but if she thought he was slightly creepy, she also got the idea: The human form is a more exciting curriculum than anything on offer in high school." In August 1935, she was accepted into the Federal Art Project of the New Deal–era Works Progress Administration, first as a model and then as a muralist's assistant. When *Harper's Bazaar* art director Alexey Brodovitch reviewed her fashion illustration portfolio, he accepted her, tuition free, into his prestigious Design Laboratory at the New School for Social Research, where she switched from fashion to graphic design. Brodovitch hired her as an unpaid apprentice at *Harper's Bazaar* in 1941. Eventually, she became his first paid assistant.

Junior Bazaar demanded a radically different look from "Big *Bazaar*," and Bassman was happy to oblige. With *Harper's Bazaar*, Bassman told the editors of the *Hall of Femmes* book about her, her role was to assist Brodovitch in "producing anything he wanted. Nothing of my own." But with *Junior Bazaar*, which initially credited both Brodovitch and Bassman for art direction, "I began to function on my own," she said.

Brodovitch had not been told that his assistant would command the spin-off's design. He was furious. However, "once he had his name on the masthead," Bassman noted, "he was perfectly happy. . . . He designed a couple of covers, that was all." So the entire magazine became Bassman's personal design laboratory. The new magazine did not have to

appeal slavishly to its advertisers; since the end of the war, only a few manufacturers were geared up for a market of teenage girls. It was an opportunity to take liberties because, she said, "we had nothing to lose."

"Bassman and Brodovitch's prime innovation was to emphasize graphic design," wrote critic and curator Vince Aletti in *Hall of Femmes*. To distinguish the new magazine from the old, the layouts involved playful placement of shapes, overlapping transparent colors, lots of unadorned spaces, and layered photographs. Inside, "fashion pages popped with an irrepressible inventiveness" that included photomontage, vignettes, and lots of simulated movement. "At *Junior Bazaar*," wrote Aletti, "Bassman built an upbeat, unpredictable magazine," with layouts that reveal a contemporary energy and modern spirit.

"It was like playing in kindergarten," Bassman said in *Hall of Femmes* about the ability to discover "new ways of saying things and doing things that were totally different." She said she considered *Junior Bazaar* to be avant-garde in a distinctly European way. Rather than literally selling clothing, Bassman's design promoted attitude. Take the January 1947 cover (with photography by Ernst Beadle) showing the somewhat faint photo, on a yellow background, of the back of a young woman wearing a quiver, readying a bow and arrow to shoot at a graphic representation of a target overprinting part of the woman. Indeed, many of Bassman's cover designs relied on flat over- or underprinted colors and shapes, always with the condensed sans serif word "*Junior*" dwarfing the smaller Gothic face "*Bazaar*."

Bassman recalled that "Kodachrome was not exactly fantastic at the time," so she used color elements on black-and-white surfaces as a way to activate the page. To achieve engaging effects, she routinely manipulated and cut up images. When she was asked in *Hall of Femmes* how the photographers appreciated her process, she said, "We were working with young people who were willing to work along with us. . . . They kind of enjoyed it." Bassman also provided visibility to future photographic stars such as Richard Avedon, who inspired her to become a photographer, Robert Frank, and Louis Faurer. Bassman allowed the photographers to develop their own ideas, and she especially sought out Avedon for new design concepts. This was an impetus for her to learn to shoot and develop her own photographs. Fittingly, in *Junior Bazaar*'s last issue (May 1948), she published a seven-page portfolio of her own photographs, a wedding story titled "Happily Ever After." After that, photography became her métier.

Magazine modernism occurred at different times and with various results in the United States and Europe from the twenties to the fifties. The use of photography and photomontage in image-centric, cinematically paced page spreads was a good indication that a publication had a Modernist aesthetic. •

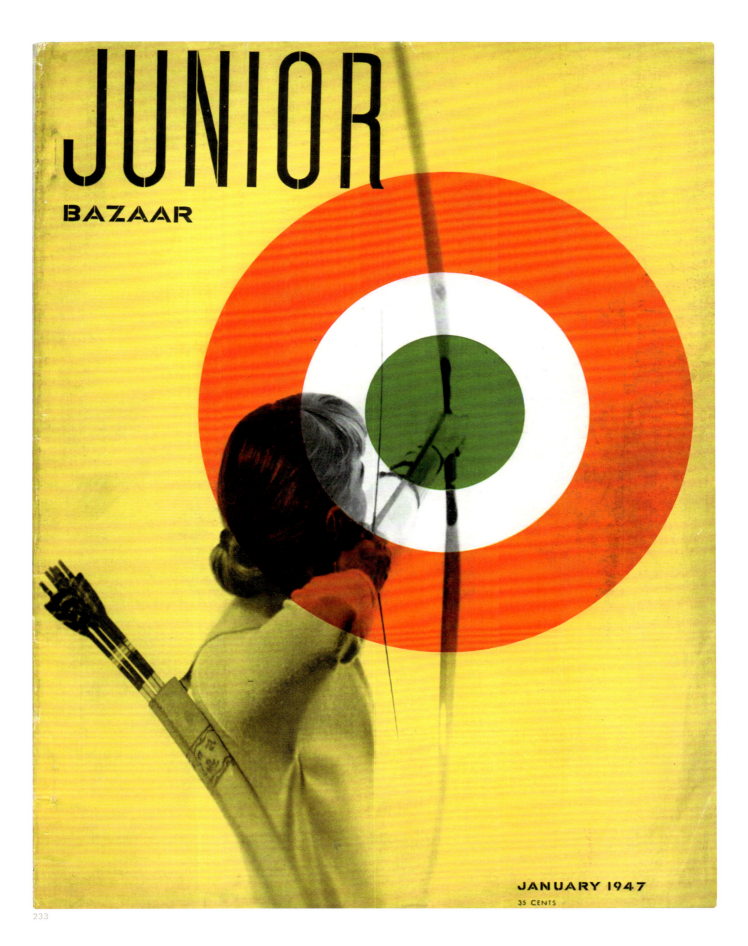

LILLIAN BASSMAN

Magazine cover, *Junior Bazaar*, Hearst
Magazines, New York, January 1947. Art
direction: Alexey Brodovitch and Bassman;
Photo: Ernst Beadle

234

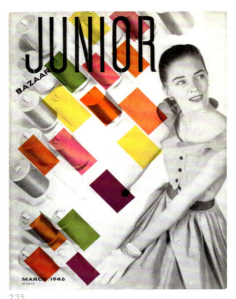

235

236

237

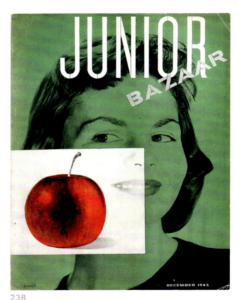

238

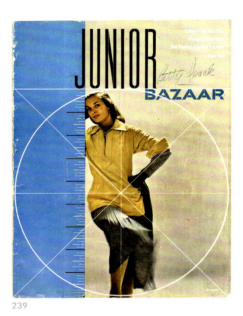

239

234
Magazine cover, *Junior Bazaar*, Hearst
Magazines, New York, November 1945.
Photo: Richard Avedon

235
Magazine cover, *Junior Bazaar*, Hearst
Magazines, New York, March 1946. Art
direction: Alexey Brodovitch and Bassman;
Photo: Richard Avedon and Leslie Gill

236
Magazine cover, *Junior Bazaar*, Hearst
Magazines, New York, April 1946. Art
direction: Alexey Brodovitch and Bassman.
Photo: Leslie Gill

237
Magazine cover, *Junior Bazaar*, Hearst
Magazines, New York, June 1946. Art
direction: Alexey Brodovitch and Bassman;
Photo: Hermann Landshoff

238
Magazine cover, *Junior Bazaar*, Hearst
Magazines, New York, December 1945.
Art direction: Alexey Brodovitch and
Bassman; Photo: Leslie Gill

239
Magazine cover, *Junior Bazaar*, Hearst
Magazines, New York, August 1947. Art
direction: Alexey Brodovitch and Bassman;
Photo: Richard Avedon

240

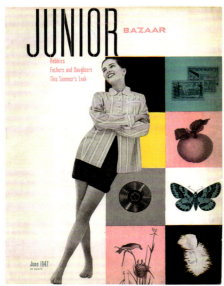

241

240

Magazine interior spread, *Junior Bazaar*, Hearst Magazines, New York, February 1947. Photo: Richard Avedon

241

Magazine cover and interior spread, *Junior Bazaar*, Hearst Magazines, New York, June 1947. Art direction: Alexey Brodovitch and Bassman; Photo: Ronny Jacques

242

Magazine interior spread, *Junior Bazaar*, Hearst Magazines, New York, May 1948. Photo: Leslie Gill

242

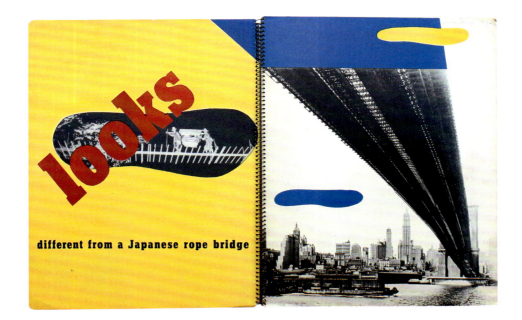

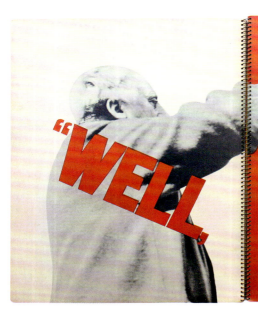

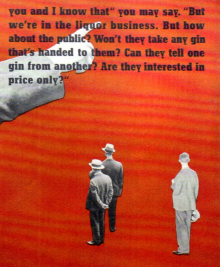

247

247

Large format, spiral-bound promotional book interiors, *Brooklyn Bridge*, Hiram Walker & Sons, 1936. The mundane convention of selling gin comes to life with Beall's distinct graphic language visualized by scale, dynamic double page spreads, carefully cropped photographs, angular type, and large areas of flat color.

248

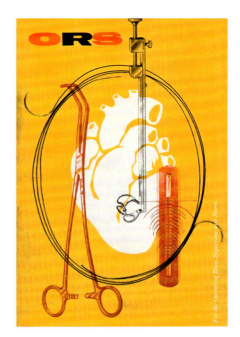

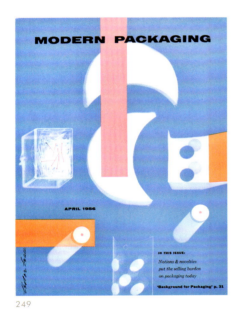

249

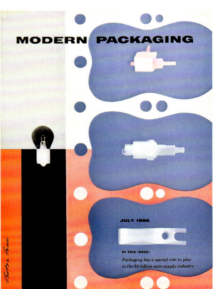

250

248
House organ cover, *ORS: For the Operating Room Supervisor and Nurse,* Davis & Geck, c. 1950s

249
Magazine cover, *Modern Packaging,* April 1956

250
Magazine cover, *Modern Packaging,* July 1956

251

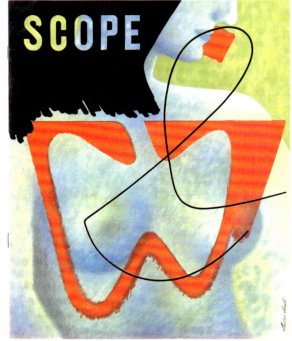

252

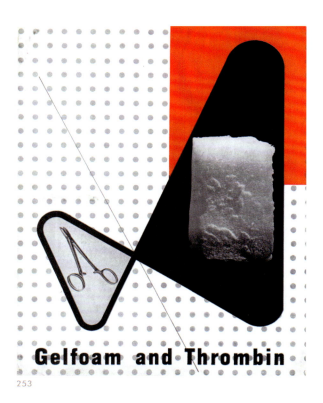

253

254

251
Magazine cover, *Scope*, Upjohn Company,
vol. 2, no. 5 (July 1947)

252
Magazine cover, *Scope*, Upjohn Company,
vol. 2, no. 2 (June 1946)

253
Catalog cover, *Gelfoam and Thrombin*,
Upjohn Company, 1945

254
House organ cover, *What's New*, Abbott
Laboratories, 1939

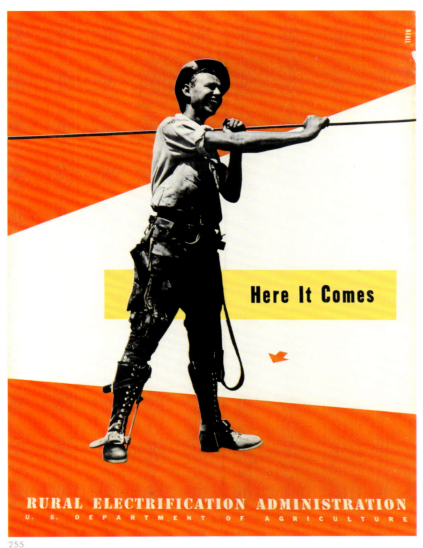

255

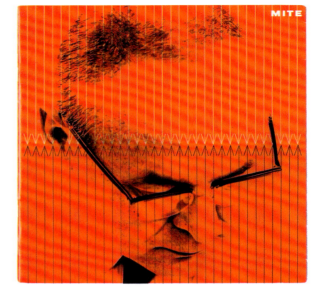

256

257

LESTER BEALL

258

255
Poster, *Here It Comes*, Series 2, Rural Electrification Administration, U.S. Department of Agriculture, 1939

256
Corporate booklet cover, MITE Corporation, New Haven, Connecticut, 1964

257
Cover, *Connecticut General Style Book [and Some Notes on Typographic Design]*, Connecticut General Life Insurance, 1958. The logo uses a stylized and elongated CG, with the G fitting snugly inside the C. The rounded thick corners and distinctive solid shapes represent the company and its many uses of paper and forms.

258
Logo, International Paper Company, 1959

Peter Bradford

b. 1935

Bradford at home in South Salem, New York, 1970.
Photo: Mary Anne McLean

In baseball terminology, Peter Bradford would be called a utility player. Expert at his craft and artful in his execution, he had skills that were utilized across a wide range of genres and platforms, from editorial to architecture and so much in between. He was not a member of the first American modern wave, yet in his way he reinterpreted the ideals of simplicity and dynamic flow that coursed through Modernism's veins.

The Boston-raised Bradford studied at the Rhode Island School of Design. He worked as a designer for I. M. Pei, Time, Whitney Publications, and CBS, and he designed books for Aperture, Xerox, and Encyclopaedia Britannica. Yet arguably, the work that established his Modernist credentials started with the covers for *Industrial Design* that he created in the early sixties, which received accolades from his peers—but disapproval from his superior, Charles Whitney.

In 1960, Bradford left an unsatisfying job at what he called "the strawberry fields" of Time and *Architectural Forum* for an admittedly precarious one as art director of *Industrial Design*. "I was the fifth art director on a magazine that was only six years old. Does that tell you anything?" he wrote in an unpublished acerbic memoir. Publisher Charles Whitney was so pleased with his readers' growing interest in the industrial design articles in his *Interiors* magazine that, at the suggestion of industrial design maestro George Nelson in 1954, he launched a separate magazine that integrated industrial with other applied arts. The first issue of *Industrial Design* (or *ID*) was edited by Jane Mitarachi (later Thompson) and Deborah Allen, with Alvin Lustig as cover designer and art editor. "When I got there," Bradford recalled, "the editor was Ralph Caplan, whiz-bang writer and prime mind of the book."

Caplan appreciated Bradford's rebellious personality, but there was still some tension. Bradford's covers, for instance, went counter to the more poetic Lustig tradition. "I felt safer hand-drawing most of the early cover images," Bradford said about his own dramatic conceptual, expressionistic forms that appeared to be done with the mathematical precision of Op Art. He described his own covers as, respectively, "an ink-lined collage of energetic New York, a thick-nib rendering of a steel furnace, and odd shapings made by extruded foam." For Whitney, his method and the outcome were "too arty." For Bradford, the covers, which richly yet abstractly captured an essence of industrial design, "were a mixed reward," he wrote, "sometimes rich, often not." (Massimo Vignelli took on the art direction in 1968–70, which seemed to satisfy Whitney's tastes.)

Bradford found, however, that the geometric patterned illustrations he created for inside pages were more satisfying—what design critic William Owen described as "a kind of humanistic rationalism." These drawings were more improvisational than his covers. "Haste was my thrust, nearby objects my tools," he wrote. But Whitney was still not pleased with any of it. "He was sure I was plotting against him and his book by contaminating its looks," Bradford ruefully explained. "He didn't imply this he said this."

A few weeks after finally opening his own firm in August 1965, Bradford received a call from architect and critic Peter Blake, who had been named editor in chief of *Architectural Forum* under the new auspices of Urban America. Bradford was not eager to return to the magazine, but Blake implored him to help design an issue about Le Corbusier. This opportunity launched a new phase for Bradford. For the issue's cover, he believed his job was to make the magazine, which was in a deathly rut, as atypical and lively as possible. "I made the largest sign I could manage using Corbu's stencil letters," he wrote. About his feat, he said, "I felt giddy . . . and loved the buck-naked bluntness of the thing."

On the strength of the "LeC" issue, as it became known, Blake had Bradford take on eight more issues of the revived *Architectural Forum*. Subsequent covers were not as audacious but no less unconventional for magazines in general and architectural journals in particular. Bradford's playfully optical tricks were abstract yet still functionally representational. He also earned the design leadership of Urban America's publications, which included other ventures related to declining urban centers and better city planning, as well as its logo. "I found pleasure in rationalizing the goals of Urban America and abstracting them in a mark," he noted, but he added that "as I designed many more marks, I tried to avoid abstractions altogether as ineffective decorous vanities. But everyone seemed to expect and want one, and the designer in me obliged."

In 1966, Bradford was given *City* magazine, a chronicle of urban happenings. Bradford said he was asked to make "an aggressive journal." Here he reached the heights of conceptual design. In one issue, the title, *City*, was formed dimensionally out of real high-caliber bullets, suggesting the racial strife in the cities in 1968. The 3-D illustrator Nicholas Fasciano was commissioned to take "the problem to magical lengths. . . . He built whole physical narratives of our cities." Bradford had Fasciano make a *City* logo out real twisted pipes to illustrate the nightmare of getting federal funds.

Bradford's ethos was to make the reader feel emotion. So his work had to have message and "lots of attitude," he emphasized. He described *City* (with this metaphor for his own work) as "weaponized" text and design. •

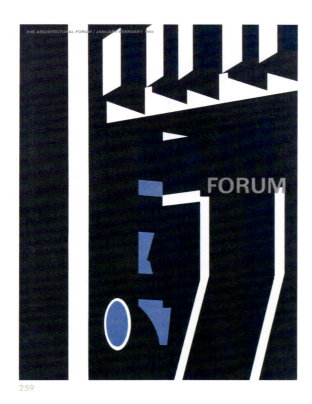

259

260

261

262

259
Magazine cover, *Architectural Forum*, January–February 1966. Abstracted from a Louis Checkman photograph of the Robert Hutchings Goddard Library at Clark University in Worcester, Massachusetts, by architect John Johansen

260
Magazine cover, *Architectural Forum*, November 1965. Shadow patterns on the concrete castings of the McNulty house in Lincoln, Massachusetts, by architects Mary Otis Stevens and Thomas McNulty

261
Magazine cover, *Architectural Forum*, October 1965. A tribute issue devoted to the architect Le Corbusier shortly after his death (August 1965) using his familiar stencil lettering style (Charette) as the single dominant image

262
Magazine cover, *Architectural Forum*, June 1966. Abstract lines of auto traffic curve and overlap beneath the tracks of San Francisco's Bay Area Rapid Transit System

FORUM

263

263
Magazine cover, *Architectural Forum*,
April 1966. A schematic plan for the
proposed campus at Tougaloo College,
Mississippi, planned by Gunnar Birkerts.
Bradford created an expressionistic form of
Modernism, playing with shape and color
and transforming ideas into moods.

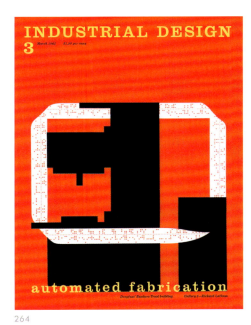

264

265

266

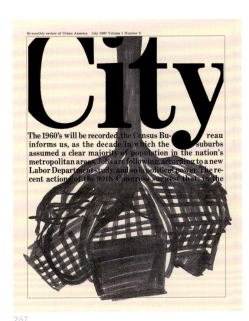

267

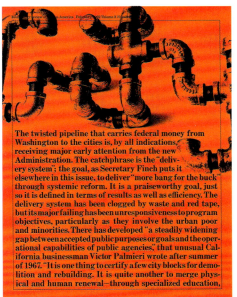

268

PETER BRADFORD

264

Magazine cover, *Industrial Design*, March 1963. A deliberately rigid image emphasizing the trends in manufacturing to computerize and automate processes, leading to closed, often circular, thought paths and resistance to innovation

265

Magazine cover, *Industrial Design*, July 1961. Recent developments in computerized manufacturing techniques enabling the extrusion of multiple arbitrary, asymmetrical shapes in metal and plastic simultaneously

266

Magazine cover, *Industrial Design*, October 1960. A special issue devoted to New York City designers using a line drawing and news clipping collage to suggest the speed, chaos, and commercial complexities of big city business life

267

Magazine cover, *City: Bi-monthly Review of Urban America*, July 1967. The first issue of the flagship magazine for Urban America in Washington, suggesting the emerging power of American suburbs to overpower and suffocate all aspects of metropolitan life

268

Magazine cover, *City: Bi-monthly Review of Urban America*, February 1969. The "pipeline" or delivery system of federal funding to cities is clogged by waste and red tape, and it is failing in its major objectives to deliver succor in the urban poor and minorities. Illustrator: Nicholas Fasciano

Robert Brownjohn

1925–1970

Brownjohn in his New York studio, 1958

Predicting what the Newark-born graphic designer Robert Brownjohn would have accomplished if had lived beyond his mere forty-five years is fruitless yet fascinating to contemplate. When creative people die before their time, one can only speculate over the what-ifs of a life lost. His talent clearly exceeded his life span. How would his reputation have grown?

BJ, as he was known, had already built an impressive design legacy. Among the most conceptually inspiring was a series of witty covers for *Pepsi-Cola World*, the monthly internal magazine for the internationally known soft-drink giant. Each of the covers cleverly combined Pepsi's identity with a seasonal theme, such as November's showing Pepsi bottle caps used to indicate players on a football diagram or February's with the Pepsi logo embroidered on a lace valentine. BJ's book covers and record albums were also exemplary concepts, mostly done in a modern idiom. What could be more iconic than the thumbs-down image illustrating the cover of Bertrand Russell's *Unpopular Essays*. The wit of his cover for *The Art of Dramatic Writing*, with exclamation points replacing the I's, is ingenious. BJ was making major inroads into movies too, with title sequences for the James Bond classics *From Russia With Love* and *Goldfinger*. Filmmaking might have captured his energies, for in 1964 he joined the film production company Cammell Hudson (which later became Cammell Hudson & Brownjohn).

Brownjohn was eighteen when he began at the Institute of Design in Chicago in 1944. Building upon the teachings and aspirations of his mentor and founder of the institute, László Moholy-Nagy, he made architectural tenets the bedrock of his graphic and motion design. "Architecture is the greatest catalyst in design," he reportedly said. "It provides a structural sense and discipline to your composition." BJ was talking about his fascination for the temporal and spatial structure of film, but he also applied this discipline to his graphic work. He subscribed to Moholy-Nagy's idea: "The true artist is the grindstone of the senses; he sharpens his eye, mind and feeling; he interprets ideas and concepts through his own media."

BJ worked with Moholy-Nagy on advertising and exhibitions. He was also awarded special student status in architecture by Serge Chermayeff. Upon graduation, he worked as a planner with the Chicago Plan Commission. Then, in 1949, Chermayeff invited BJ to teach as an instructor at his alma mater, despite his not having an architecture degree. A year later, BJ left for New York, where he joined George Nelson's design office as a designer and worked at various firms on a freelance basis. Among his jobs were abstract cover designs for *Furniture Forum*, which included Walter Gropius and Richard Neutra on the editorial board. He also worked for brief periods with the Herman Miller Furniture Company and with Ed Bartolucci at Bob Cato Associates, where he designed covers for Columbia Records, including his use of Vibrations, a vibrating typeface employed years later for the sixties East Village rock-and-roll venue the Electric Circus. In 1956, he helped define the look of jazz in the city with the cover of *Jazz New York*, a magazine about the first New York

Jazz Festival, and the *American Jazz Annual* for that year, using stencil types, spot colors, and geometric kineticism to evoke the improvisational music discussed therein.

In 1957, Brownjohn joined forces with Serge Chermayeff's son, Ivan, and Tom Geismar. "His goal was not to make things pretty but to arrive at a design that would solve a problem both conceptually and formally," states the Art Directors Club précis for his 1995 induction into its Hall of Fame, describing him as maintaining a fast-paced lifestyle, "which was integral to his art, his theory of graphic design, and his method of working."

BJ was one of the young New York moderns who turned to the city's environment for inspiration, or what his friend Tony Palladino called "graphic turn-ons that later we could apply to jobs. . . . The fresher the essence, the better the job was." Brownjohn also believed that if an idea could not be described over the telephone, it was not simple, clear, and direct enough to work.

Brownjohn, Chermayeff & Geismar was a hit in the commercial design world, yet after three years, in 1960, Brownjohn was on his way out the door. The peripatetic BJ moved his wife and daughter to England, where he worked for J. Walter Thompson as creative director. "His style was a new experience for the JWT staff. He was interested in found objects and typographic 'junk' collected in the street, kept odd hours, was often absent, and spoke his mind," states the ADC.

BJ's daughter, Eliza, was his sounding board. "He would take me to lunch and draw his ideas for a project on the tablecloth and then ask me for my feedback," she said. "I also spent a lot of time with him in his production studio when he was doing his titles, cinema commercials, and other things."

The citation for Brownjohn's 2002 AIGA Medal for lifetime achievement states: "His projects exemplify every aspect of his relationship to design, including his emphasis on content over form and his preferences with ordinary and personal images. . . . His spirit of invention and designs for living in the machine age were balanced with references to the aesthetic models that Moholy-Nagy admired"—the idea that design is integrated with life and vice versa. •

269

269
Album cover, *Si-Si, No-No* by Machito &
His Orchestra, Tico Records, A Division of
Roulette Records, 1957. A uniquely colorful
and vibrating typographic solution acts as a
visual metaphor for the exciting rhythmic pace
and sound of the mambo and cha cha cha
tempo. Design: Robert Brownjohn / Brownjohn,
Chermayeff & Geismar

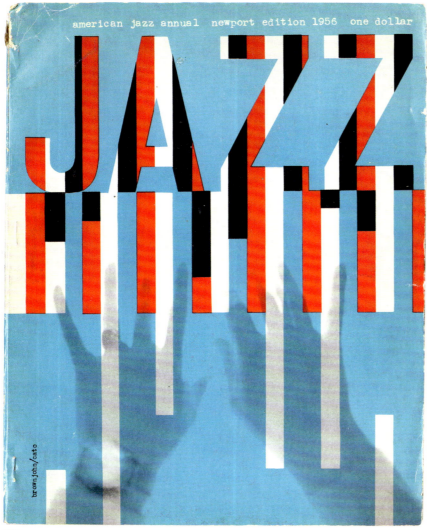

270

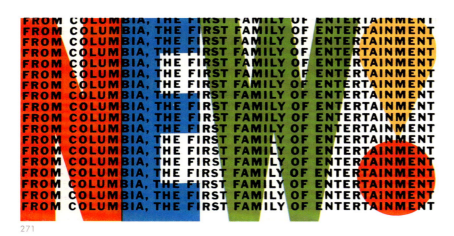

271

272

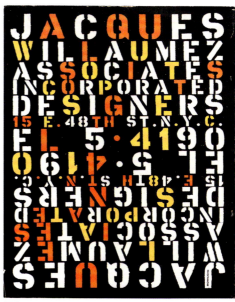

273

270
Cover, *Jazz New York*, First Annual New York Jazz Festival, 1956

271
Booklet cover, *New! From Columbia, The First Family of Entertainment*, Columbia Records, 1958

272
Cover, *American Jazz Annual, Newport Edition*, International Jazz Associates, 1956. Photo: Bob Cato

273
Advertisement, "Jacques Willaumez Associates Incorporated Designers," 1956

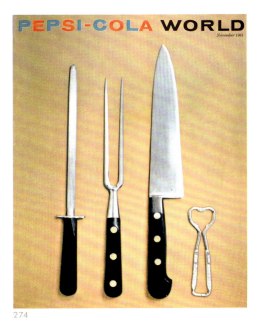

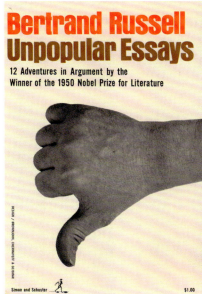

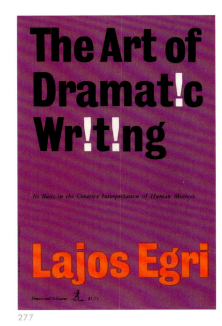

274

276

277

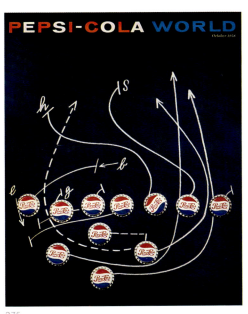

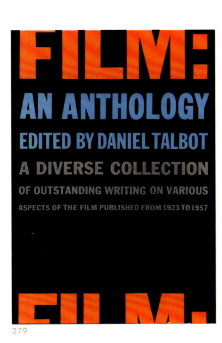

275

278

279

274
Magazine cover, *Pepsi-Cola World*, Pepsi-Cola Company, November 1961. Design: Brownjohn, Chermayeff & Geismar

275
Magazine cover, *Pepsi-Cola World*, Pepsi-Cola Company, October 1958. Design: Brownjohn, Chermayeff & Geismar

276
Book cover, *Unpopular Essays*, by Bertrand Russell, Simon & Schuster, 1964. Design: Brownjohn, Chermayeff & Geismar

277
Book cover, *The Art of Dramatic Writing*, by Lajos Egri, Simon & Schuster, 1960. Design: Brownjohn, Chermayeff & Geismar

278
Book jacket, *The Optimist*, by Herbert Gold, Little, Brown, 1959. Design: Brownjohn, Chermayeff & Geismar

279
Book jacket, *Film: An Anthology*, edited by Daniel Talbot, Simon & Schuster, 1959. The movement of film is expressed in this typographic treatment. Design: Brownjohn, Chermayeff & Geismar

Jacqueline S. Casey

1927–1992

Casey as a judge at "Creativity on Paper" exhibition, sponsored by *Art Direction* magazine, 1966

Jacqueline S. Casey practiced an inspired and functional Modernism. From 1955 to 1989, she was a designer in the Office of Publications (later renamed the Office of Design Services) at MIT, and in 1972 she was appointed its director. Casey said of her design, "My work combines two cultures: The American interest in visual metaphor on the one hand, and the Swiss fascination with planning, fastidiousness, and control over technical execution on the other."

Born in Quincy, Massachusetts, Casey attended the Massachusetts College of Art (MassArt), where she received a bachelor's degree in fine arts with a focus on fashion design and illustration. After graduating in 1949, she worked briefly in fashion, advertising, and interiors but never secured a job worthy of her interests; frustrated, she said, "I broke the negative cycle by traveling through Europe for three months" and returned "with the decision to focus my life on something related to the arts . . . to develop my visual sensitivity."

Casey landed a job at MIT's Office of Publications in 1955 designing summer session materials, recommended by her friend and fellow MassArt alumna Muriel R. Cooper (1925–1994), a pioneer feminist, designer, educator, and researcher with her own legacy as the first design director for the MIT Press. In the early fifties, the office had established "a graphic-design program enabling all members of the university community to benefit from free, professional design assistance," wrote Philip B. Meggs. The department's founder and director, John Mattill, was a science writer-editor whose Modernist vision was the guiding spirit for the early development of academic graphics. Cooper, who started as a freelance designer in 1952, was the department's first office employee responsible for handling its graphics.

"In my early days at MIT, a designer working on summer materials would interview faculty and have a mini-course in a subject such as radioisotopes from the professor in charge. There was an opportunity to learn something new every day," Casey recalled. In 1957, when Cooper left MIT on a Fulbright Scholarship, Casey became active in promoting a creative environment, responsible for designing posters, catalogs, and other printed collateral to help promote MIT events, programs, academic lectures, and art exhibitions, ranging from science to music to technology. Of her designs, Casey told Liz McQuiston in the 1988 book *Women in Design*, "My job is to stop anyone I can with an arresting or puzzling image, and entice the viewer to read the message in small type and above all to attend the exhibition."

Eventually, the office grew to include two additional full-time designers: Ralph Coburn (b. 1923) from 1957 to 1988 and Dietmar Winkler from 1965 to 1970. Coburn, a proficient Modern painter, was "instrumental in fostering minimalist typography and design," and he "became very comfortable in experimenting with different typographic systems." Coburn "did not just adopt Swiss Design," said Winkler, "he explored and expanded upon it . . . into a very personal approach."

Over the years, Mattill invited European designers to work on summer session materials, including former Bauhaus student George Adams-Teltscher, Denis Postle and John Lees of England, Walter Plata of Germany, and Paul Talman and Thérèse Moll of Switzerland. American designers also made important contributions, among them Nancy Cahners, Bob Cipriani, David Colley, and Harold Pattek. Casey "had great trust in her colleagues' abilities," Winkler said, and furthermore, "we shared between us the same values."

Of all the visiting designers, the one who left a lasting impact on Casey was Moll, who worked at MIT for a brief period in the summer of 1958. Moll had been a friend and assistant to Karl Gerstner in Basel. "She introduced the office to European typography [and was] well trained in the design of modular systems. This use of proportions in designing publications series became a useful tool," Casey said. "It is important to have a process in which logic determines where things are placed. I use the grid because I won't build a page without first laying the foundation."

The MIT Office of Design Services played a critical role in helping popularize the Swiss gospel and the International Typographic Style throughout the United States during the sixties and beyond. Casey was heavily influenced by Gerstner, Armin Hofmann, Josef Müller-Brockmann, Emil Ruder, and Anton Stankowski and was well informed about contemporary photographers, artists, musicians, and writers. "The most constant part of my approach to design has always been the search for information. . . . It starts out with gathering material: an interview with the client, taking notes and establishing the client's objectives, a library visit . . . determining the purpose of the communication, the audience, looking for any hint of special significance to make a more accurate and vital statement." Her designs were unified but rarely standardized. She explored modular abstraction, empty space and scale, and visual metaphors and language. Intrigued by the aluminized, silver paper that Tomoko Miho used in her *Great Architecture in Chicago* poster, she went on to experiment with metallic materials and inks. "Casey's posters weave their magic through beautiful compositions and handsome typographic treatments," noted Joseph P. Arnell. "But they are far more than pretty faces. Through a marriage of ideas and images, words and pictures, her posters make us stop, look and think. Then, they challenge us to understand."

For Casey, who retired in 1989, "MIT was much more than a workplace. It was her identity and life, her home," Winkler said. For more than thirty years, she was an accelerator of change, not only for MIT but for designers worldwide. "While MIT has its roots in tradition, the university represents all that is experimental, exciting, and future orientated. For me designing is highly personal and private," Casey summed up. "My objective is to design a product with an accurate visual and verbal message that can be understood by the audience." •

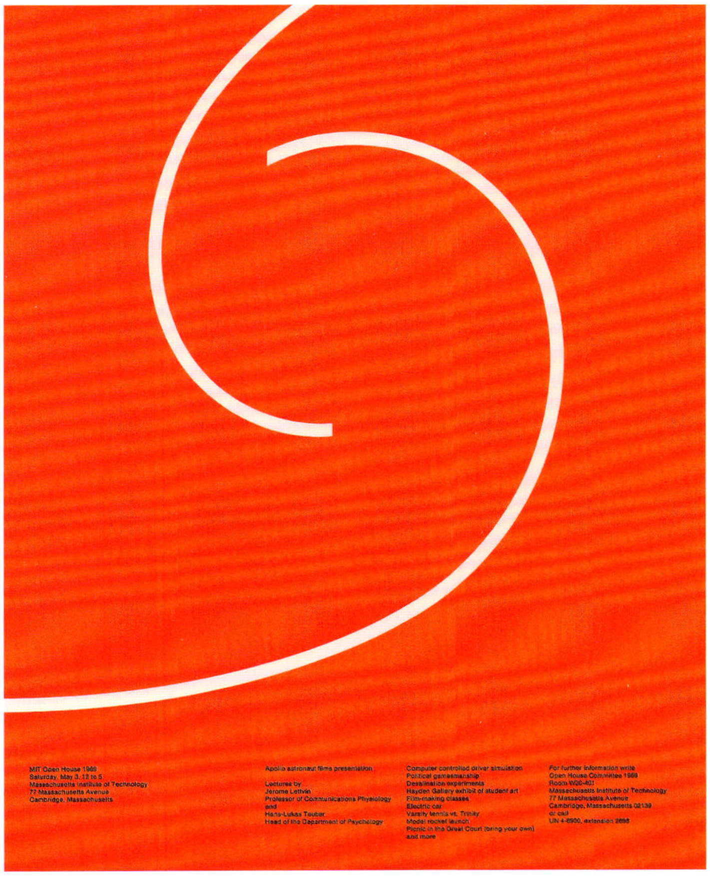

Faculty-Student Exchange Program

A faculty-student exchange program has been formed in order to promote cooperation among its member institutions in various scientific and technical fields. Students have the member colleges and universities will spend a semester at M.I.T. taking courses or doing research. Each student will be provided with the incremental costs, including transportation, for the semester at M.I.T.

Students in the fields of biology, chemistry, engineering, and physics are encouraged to apply. Preference will be given to juniors.

Application deadlines are April 1, 1972, for the fall semester of 1972, and November 1, 1972, for the spring semester of 1973.

For further information and application forms, please write:
Faculty-Student Exchange Program
Massachusetts Institute of Technology
Room 8-214
Cambridge, Massachusetts 02139

Member institutions include:
Alabama A. and M. University
Bennett College
Fisk University
Hampton Institute
Massachusetts Institute of Technology
Norfolk State College
North Carolina A. and T. University
Virginia State College

MIT Open House 1969
Saturday, May 3, 12 to 5
Massachusetts Institute of Technology
77 Massachusetts Avenue
Cambridge, Massachusetts.

Apollo astronaut films presentation

Lectures by
Jerome Lettvin,
Professor of Communications Physiology
and
Hans-Lukas Teuber,
Head of the Department of Psychology

Computer controlled driver simulation
Political gamesmanship
Desalinization experiments
Hayden Gallery exhibit of student art
Film-viewing classes
Electric car
Varsity tennis vs. Trinity
Model rocket launch
Picnic in the Great Court (bring your own)
and more

For further information write
Open House Committee 1969
Room 9W2-401
Massachusetts Institute of Technology
77 Massachusetts Avenue
Cambridge, Massachusetts 02139
or call
UN 4-6900, extension 2866

280

281

Symposium
on the occasion of the dedication of the
Center for Space Research
Massachusetts Institute of Technology
Kresge Auditorium
April 25, 1966, 9:00 am
The public is invited

Report:
Selected Research Activities
of the Center for Space Research

Opening Remarks
Jerome B. Wiesner
Provost, MIT

Introduction
John V. Harrington
Director of the
Center for Space Research, MIT

Speakers
Herbert S. Bridge
Professor of Physics, MIT

William L. Kraushaar
Professor of Physics
University of Wisconsin

Wickler R. Markey
Professor of
Aeronautics
and Astronautics, MIT

Bruno B. Rossi
Institute Professor, MIT

Nevin S. Scrimshaw
Head of the Department of
Nutrition and Food Science, MIT

Eugene B. Skolnikoff
Professor of Political Science, MIT

Informal reception and open house
Center for Space Research
2:00 pm.

Center for Space Research

282

280
Poster, *MIT Open House*, Massachusetts Institute of Technology, 1969

281
Poster, *Faculty–Student Exchange Program*, Massachusetts Institute of Technology, 1972. Exchange between faculty and students is symbolized by an oversize, carefully cropped white X and by the three colored triangles occupying the letter's negative space.

282
Poster, *Center for Space Research Symposium*, Massachusetts Institute of Technology, 1968

Paintings
Hayden Gallery
Massachusetts Institute of Technology
September 19 through October 25, 1970
Preview September 18
8 to 10 pm
Artist will be present

The artist will discuss his work
in Hayden Gallery on
Thursday September 24 at 8 pm

Sponsored by the
MIT Committee on the Visual Arts

283

283
Poster, *Leon Golub Paintings*, Massachusetts Institute of Technology, 1970. "Golub used strong, sweeping, horizontal brushstrokes. I wanted the type to respond to his technique and the colors to his sober subject matter," expressed Casey in *Posters: Jacqueline S. Casey; Thirty Years of Design at MIT* (1992).

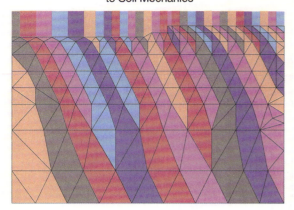

Massachusetts Institute of Technology
August 28 - September 1
Summer Session 1967

Application of Finite Elements
to Soil Mechanics

284

285

286

287

284
Summer session booklet cover, *Application of Finite Elements to Soil Mechanics*, Massachusetts Institute of Technology, 1967

285
Album cover, *Music at MIT* by MIT Choral Society, MIT Symphony Orchestra, and conductor Klaus Liepmann, Massachusetts Institute of Technology, originally designed before 1965. The curved lines of Eero Saarinen's Kresge Auditorium dome are fragmented and abstractly convey the music's energy and movement.

286
Poster, *The MIT Concert Jazz Band*, Massachusetts Institute of Technology, 1972. Under Casey's art direction, the MIT designers worked directly with their own clients. Casey saw the designers as equal members of the team. Ralph Coburn, who designed this poster, had a formal education in architecture and was a skilled designer and a well-established minimalist painter—a close friend and collaborator of Ellsworth Kelly.

287
Booklet cover, *Guide to MIT Libraries*, Massachusetts Institute of Technology, 1967. "All my life I have been intrigued by maps, both ancient and modern," Casey stated in *Posters: Jacqueline S. Casey; Thirty Years of Design at MIT* (1992). "I collect all kinds: the world, countries, cities, waterways, stellar and solar systems. I love geological survey maps and naval and oceanographic charts. There is so much beauty in the simplicity of presentation in spite of the very dense information content and need for fidelity. There is a very serious side to the responsibility inherent in maps. The Libraries Guide was a wonderful way to apply my interests to a real problem with the aim of helping students to find their way through a complex system."

Chermayeff & Geismar

Ivan Chermayeff: b. 1932; Thomas Geismar: b. 1931

Geismar and Chermayeff in New York, early 1960s

Ivan Chermayeff and Thomas Geismar: As duos go in the design world, they are as familiar as Lennon and McCartney, with almost as many greatest hits to their names. Chermayeff, born in London, studied at Harvard University and the Institute of Design in Chicago, and Geismar, born in Glen Ridge, New Jersey, studied at Brown University and the Rhode Island School of Design. Both met as students at Yale University's School of Art and Architecture in the midfifties. They started their dual partnership in 1960, following a three-year collaboration with Robert Brownjohn, and they established themselves as undisputed masters of late twentieth-century American Modernism, continuing the tradition of the Bauhaus and following in the footsteps of Lester Beall, Alvin Lustig, and Paul Rand, who practiced design, in part, as a curative for what ailed visual culture. "We believe that design is all about making order out of potential chaos," Chermayeff said with missionary zeal. For Chermayeff & Geismar, the quintessential bugaboo, chaos, lurks in the background hinting of something unexpected.

When the Chase Manhattan Bank logo was introduced in 1961, few American corporations dared to use abstract marks. Most corporations used letters, descriptive pictographs, or comic trade characters. But Chase served up a unique problem: It was an amalgam of two recently merged banks, Chase National Bank and Bank of the Manhattan Company, which were so large and omnipresent in the New York region that their newly forged identity demanded sophistication and simplicity, or else chaos would abound. Geismar was challenged to design a mark that at once expressed the essence of banking but transcended conventional financial symbolism. The octagon, which was influenced by traditional Japanese marks and crests, was selected "because it was a self-contained dynamic form that retained its integrity and legibility in a wide range of sizes and materials," explained Geismar. It also referenced the shape of certain ancient coins. Although such an unconventional mark was a gamble at the time, Geismar noted years later: "Basically, the original concept was correct. A very large organization with extensive media exposure can establish a more or less abstract mark as its identifier, and the mark will come to represent the institution." Since then, abstract marks are de rigueur.

Chermayeff & Geismar introduced methods throughout the early sixties that profoundly influenced the look and feel—and conceptual intelligence—of graphic design far beyond North America. Moreover, they were pioneers when it came to seamlessly combining two and three dimensions: Their educational and informative exhibitions for the U.S. Information Agency, which were shown behind the Iron Curtain, extolled the virtues of American practice and introduced Soviet designers to novel conceptual design thinking.

Their work ran the gamut from rational typography to abstract imagery, from traditional layout to hybrid composition, and from drawing to collage. One of their more subtle yet startling typographic solutions is the poster *Toward a Sane Nuclear Policy*, in which vibrating Gothic lettering metaphorically implies the impact of an underground atomic bomb test.

Modernism is "not a religion, it's a service," Chermayeff once said. Nor is his Modernism the ideological formulation it was for the post–World War II Swiss Style, known for prescribing graphic expression through strict formalist dictates. Although Chermayeff & Geismar came of age in the mid- to late fifties, a time when International Typographic Style standardization and gridlocked composition were ascendant, they resisted slavish adherence to the predigested rightness of form, preferring to follow what Paul Rand called the "play principle." Among their most playful work are the dozens of conceptual book covers they designed from the early to late sixties: These are outstanding examples of how clever visual puns enable readers to actually *tell a book by its cover.* Among the graphic toys that Chermayeff and Geismar played with were the complex shapes, signs, and symbols that were associated directly with their clients. For the annual reports designed for Perkin-Elmer, a corporation devoted to human health and medical safety, electronic patterns and scientific signs and symbols were brought together in collages that would have seemed merely abstract to the untutored eye yet easily deciphered by the recipients of the materials.

Inspiration came from early twentieth-century European avant-gardes, or in Chermayeff's words, "Our sources are art and artists, like Matisse, Picasso, Klee, de Kooning, Avery, Mondrian, Brancusi." This was channeled into the duo's graphic and exhibition design, but at times it was more directly quoted as well. But as respite from the rigors of professional design, Chermayeff also acknowledged the art of the outsiders and primitives, examples of which lined the shelves and walls of their spare, white-walled, light-filled offices. The duo's dynamic Modernist methodology was constantly being nurtured by their insatiable curiosity. One favored expressive technique—collage—enabled this curiosity and its cousin, serendipity, to flourish. Surprise should never be underestimated. Indeed, Chermayeff & Geismar's work employed contrasting (at times jarring) sensibilities to skew the viewer's expected perceptions: Harmonious typographies were wed to dissonant pictorial juxtapositions (and vice versa) for even the most staid of problems. Those with discerning eyes might readily recognize the hands of Chermayeff or Geismar in their respective works, but Geismar does not believe in a Chermayeff & Geismar style, "except that people say our work is strong and simple, and occasionally humorous. Our approach to design is idea-based, comprehensible, appropriate, and, if possible, original, if it is to be memorable and distinguished." Today, they are still fighting Modernism's fight. "Our design is more than valid in our time," said Chermayeff, "where mediocrity, ignorance, naiveté, not to mention stupidity run more rampant than ever and more and more voices insist on being heard." •

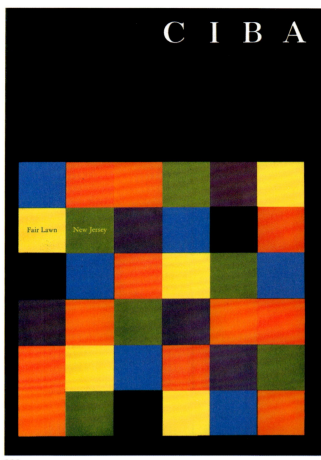

288

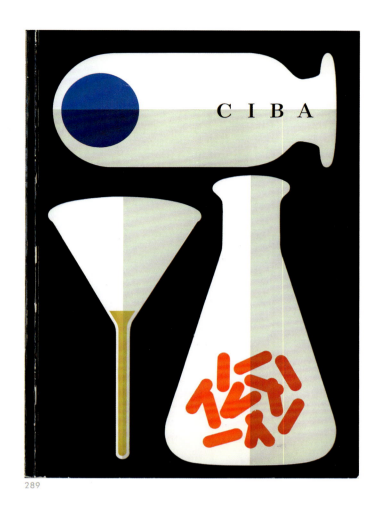

289

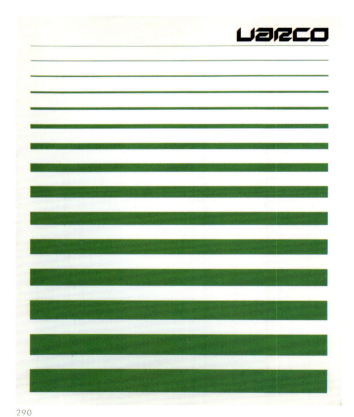

290

288
Booklet cover, *CIBA*, Fair Lawn, New Jersey, 1959

289
Booklet cover, *CIBA*, Fair Lawn, New Jersey, 1963

290
Folder cover, Uarco Incorporated, 1968

291

292

291
Booklet, Perkin-Elmer Corporation, 1966

292
Booklet, U.S. Pavilion, Expo 67, Montreal, 1967. Design: Chermayeff

293

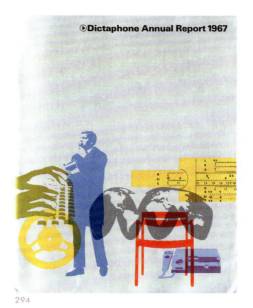

294

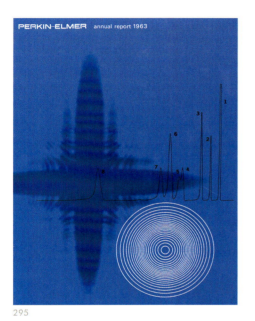

295

Interactive Data Corporation
The Data Utility

296

The General Fireproofing Company Annual Report 1969

297

293
Price list supplement, Edgewood
Furniture Company, September 1962

294
Annual report, Dictaphone
Corporation, 1967

295
Annual report, Perkin-Elmer
Corporation, 1963

296
Booklet, *The Data Utility*, Interactive
Data Corporation, c. 1969

297
Annual report, General Fireproofing
Company, 1969

Hermann Weyl

Philosophy of Mathematics and Natural Science

31   $1.65

Atheneum
ORIGINALLY PUBLISHED BY
PRINCETON UNIVERSITY PRESS

298

Jan de Hartog

The Hospital

300

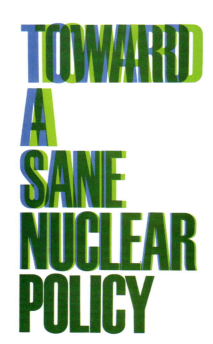

299

301

302

298
Book cover, *Philosophy of Mathematics and Natural Science*, by Hermann Weyl, Atheneum, 1963

299
Book cover, *Twelve Full Ounces*, by Milward W. Martin, Holt, Rinehart and Winston, 1962

300
Book jacket, *The Hospital*, by Jan de Hartog, Atheneum, 1964

301
Book cover, *Toward a Sane Nuclear Policy*, National Committee for a Sane Nuclear Policy, 1960. A conceptual idea is made to animate by gradually shifting and overprinting the type. Design: Ivan Chermayeff

302
Logo, General Fireproofing Company, 1968

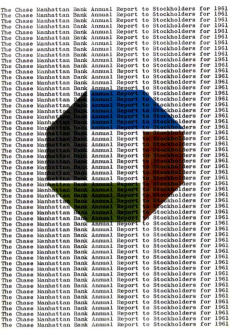

303

Mobil: the second century

304

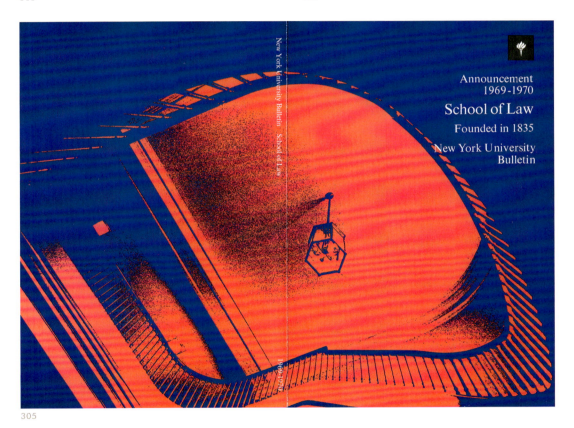

305

303
Cover, *Chase Manhattan Bank Annual Report to Stockholders*, 1961. From *Our New Symbol of Service*, ephemera introducing the new logo: "Chase Manhattan's symbol is a simple yet powerful geometric form embodying a strong feeling of motion and activity . . . It is divided in such a way as to suggest forward motion within a framework of control. Like the bank itself, the symbol is a single unit made up of separate parts. The activity is centered around the square, implying growth from a central foundation." Modern to be sure, "its octagonal shape is reminiscent of ancient coins, suggesting both banking and tradition."

304
Booklet, *Mobil: The Second Century*, Mobil Oil Corporation, 1966

305
Bulletin front and back covers, *Announcement 1969–1970*, School of Law, New York University

John and Mary Condon

John Condon: 1940–1996; Mary Condon: b. 1937

The Condons, New York, early 1960s

John and Mary Condon were devout practitioners of the International Typographic Style from the early sixties through the seventies, when they designed hundreds of paperback covers and hardcover book jackets. They worked for prominent publishers in science, mathematics, politics, philosophy, and other nonfiction genres. Today, their notable contributions are examples of how trade publishing was steeped in Modernist principles: sans serif typography, limited color palettes, and symbolic graphics gently representing the often-complex character of the book. This methodology was about "whittling everything down to the basic essence," said Mary.

Born in 1937 in Binghamton, New York, Mary Matias graduated from Cooper Union School of Art in 1959. She studied lettering with Paul Standard and Leo Manso, advertising design with Jerome Kuhl, and two-dimensional design with modern artist Neil Welliver. Influenced by classmates who studied with Rudolph de Harak, Mary cultivated a respect for grids, asymmetry, and tightly kerned, single-weight neutral typefaces like Akzidenz-Grotesk and Helvetica, along with the aesthetic philosophies these choices represented. She admired the purity of the examples found in issues of *Neue Grafik*.

Her first jobs included a short stint at *Vogue*, the American Heritage Publishing Company (1961–64), and the Madison Avenue advertising agencies L. W. Frohlich (1959–61) and William Douglas McAdams (1964–66), both of which specialized in pharmaceutical advertising. At Frohlich, Mary was a roving assistant designer, and she excelled at making precisely executed comps.

John Condon was born in 1940 in West Haven, Connecticut. Living close to Yale allowed him to sneak into Josef Albers's famed Color classes. In the late fifties, they developed a friendship and spent time talking about art, which fed into John's aspirations of becoming an artist. At the University of Bridgeport, in Connecticut, he studied painting with John Day, a former student of Albers's. Eventually, in late 1959, his interest turned to design. He also landed at L. W. Frohlich, where he met fellow designer Mary Matias. From 1961 to 1963, John worked for the Will Burtin design office with studio manager Peter Rauch and a small team of designers, focusing on IBM and the Upjohn Company projects.

Friendships at the office abounded. John and Mary became close to Donald Crews and his future wife, Ann Jonas, both graduates of Cooper Union. It was Ann, at the time working for Rudolph de Harak, her former teacher at Cooper Union, who introduced John to de Harak, a mentor to all of them. John freelanced with de Harak from 1963 to 1966 and had his own clients, the most important of which was Time Life Books, where he designed many interior graphic illustrations. Mary officially joined her husband in 1966 as John+Mary Condon (and later, in 1970, J+M Condon). For thirty years, they enjoyed the freedom and flexibility of working for themselves.

One of their first collaborations was a proposed map (unpublished) for the New York City Transit Authority Subway Map Competition. The Condons collected four thousand dollars as the winners of the 1964 contest (two years before the NYCTA commissioned Massimo Vignelli and Bob Noorda of Unimark International to undertake the same task). Of their map, John said, "As designers we were aware of existing flaws in the TA maps. As veteran subway riders, we always thought we could do better. The map boiled down to a pure problem of communication. The virtue of our map is clarity."

One of the Condons' first big clients was the educational publisher McGraw-Hill, for which they designed textbooks that notably rejected Times Roman as a primary typeface. John educated the client to entertain a more simplified approach to textbook design, best illustrated by the Condons' cover for *Human Relations at Work* (1967). Printed in black and white on ochre cloth, the title was set in Helvetica and paired with an abstract symbol; the interior included linear charts and other information graphics representing the dynamics of organizational behavior. Their reductive direction was a success: "It is with exceptional pleasure that I write to tell you that your design is not only strikingly handsome but is unquestionably the most beautifully and thoughtfully designed textbook in the subject," praised a book editor at McGraw-Hill in a letter to the Condons. "I wouldn't be a bit surprised if sales went up to a new high because of the good taste and appearance of your design." In 1966, John and Mary designed complete lines of prestige paperbacks—Clarion Books and Classic and Modern Film Scripts—for Simon & Schuster. One of their best-known jacket designs was for *Hitchcock/Truffaut*, an interview with Alfred Hitchcock by François Truffaut, which is a veritable bible for filmmakers. Their names, spelled out in tightly kerned Akzidenz-Grotesk and delicately printed in silver on a black background, offers a classic example of typographic symbolism: the celebrated directors going head-to-head. Upon being sent the design comp, Truffaut handwrote on the flap, "Très magnifique! —Truffaut."

The Condons played with techniques such as photographing type behind textured glass, photographing type on crumpled paper to create distortion, and experimenting with Kodalith film for a striking, high-contrast effect. Given the small budgets for book cover designs, they took many of their own photographs and, when possible, even modeled for the photos themselves. For Ed Koch, U.S. representative (1969–77) and then mayor of New York (1978–90), they designed posters, buttons, brochures, invitations to fundraisers and other events, and shopping bags. These exhibit a clean typographic honesty and objective aesthetics, a refreshing approach for political campaigns.

Born of a midcentury generation that was dedicated to use modern visual language, the Condons' minimalist functional aesthetic, neutral typography, and experimental imagery are reflective of the times. Yet their work has a sense of timelessness born of limitations, a quality that the moderns were so eager to achieve. No wonder that even today, Mary says about the Modernist ethos, "It's good to have parameters." •

306

306
Book cover, *Hitchcock: A Definitive Study of Alfred Hitchcock*, by François Truffaut, Touchstone, Simon & Schuster, 1967

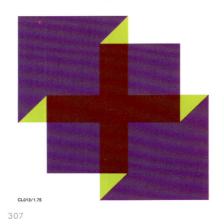

307

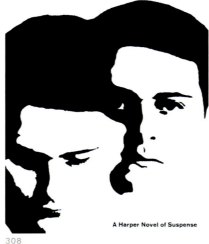

308

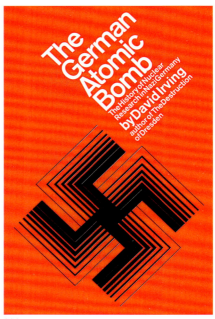

309

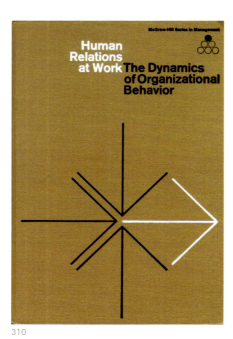

310

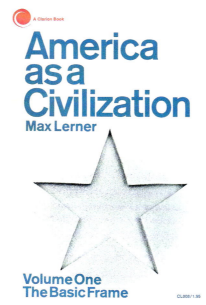

311

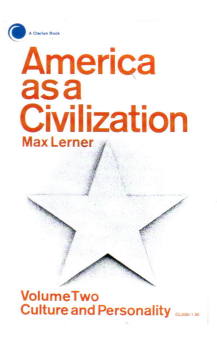

312

307
Book cover, *Why I Am Not a Christian*, by Bertrand Russell, Clarion, 1967

308
Book cover, *Trusted Like the Fox*, by Sara Woods, Harper & Row, 1964

309
Book cover, *The German Atomic Bomb*, by David Irving, Simon & Schuster, 1967

310
Book cover, *Human Relations at Work: The Dynamics of Organizational Behavior*, McGraw-Hill, 1967

311
Book covers, *America as a Civilization*, vols. 1–2, by Max Lerner, Clarion, 1962. Volume one shows the star as an impression and volume two as an extrusion.

312
Congressional pin, *Koch*, c. 1969. The Condons were among the first designers to address good design in political campaigns with their work for Ed Koch, U.S. Congressman and eventual mayor of New York City.

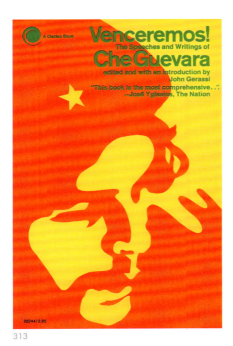

313

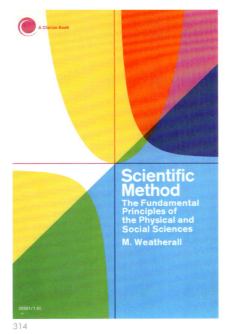

314

315

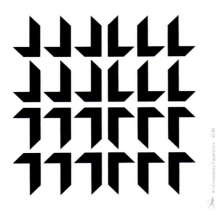

316

317

318

JOHN AND MARY CONDON

313
Book cover, *Venceremos! The Speeches and Writings of Che Guevara*, Clarion, 1968

314
Book cover, *Scientific Method*, by M. Weatherall, Clarion, 1968

315
Book cover, *Instant Vocabulary*, by Ida Ehrlich, Washington Square Press, 1968

316
Book cover, *The Heart of Our Cities*, by Victor Gruen, Simon & Schuster, 1964

317
Book cover, *The Responsibility of the Press*, edited by Gerald Gross, Clarion, 1969

318
Book cover, *The Conscience of the Revolution*, by Robert Vincent Daniels, Clarion, 1969

Donald and Ann Crews

Donald Crews: b. 1938; Ann Crews: 1932–2013

A self-portrait of Donald and Ann, Germany, 1963

The New York husband-and-wife design team of Donald and Ann (Jonas) Crews practiced a late Modernist visual language in their book covers, exhibition signage, posters, printed collateral, and congressional campaign material from the early sixties throughout the late seventies. Rooted in the International Typographic Style, their collaborative work included geometric, simplified abstract themes and modern, sans serif typefaces, yet overall, it was less exacting and more playful than the rigorous principles influencing corporate and institutional American design. "We always wanted to avoid the embellishments; sparseness was the way to make it work. We used symbols more than illustrative interpretations of the thing," said Donald.

The Crewses were an interracial couple when such marriages were rare. "We decided we had no problem with it and would avoid anyone who did," said Donald. But what made their partnership unique was a conscious decision to stay independent and work as a two-person studio for more than forty years. They never hired employees or expanded their offices. Yet they made a substantial practice designing hundreds of paperback covers and hardcover jackets for children, young adult, and adult audiences within a variety of categories, ranging from textbooks to mysteries. Like designers before them who embraced European Modernism, Donald and Ann Crews helped develop a distinct American modern look.

Ann Jonas, born in Flushing, Queens, in 1932, became interested in the arts through her family, who, she noted, "attached great importance to knowing how to do as many things as possible." Donald Crews was born in Newark, New Jersey, in 1938. His parents encouraged art making. He attended Newark Arts High School, the country's first public high school specializing in the visual and performing arts. After school, he worked at a retouching studio learning airbrush skills. Seymour Landsman, his mentor and teacher, "introduced us to art and culture," Crews recalled. "We read the *New Yorker* and designed covers for it. We copied art from books and posters. He got us into the habit of reading the *New York Times* and taking advantage of the Newark Museum." Landsman also insisted that he enroll in Cooper Union, New York's free art school. In fact, Donald and Ann met at Cooper Union, and both graduated in 1959. Both were heavily influenced by Rudolph de Harak. Donald recalled de Harak's classroom as "always instructive with useful critiques. He taught the importance of ideas and how to think and how that thinking leads you to find innovative directions."

In 1959, Donald landed his first job, with *Dance* magazine. While de Harak was the magazine's art director, he was so busy managing his recently opened design office that he "left everything to me," Donald recalled. This freedom to develop allowed him to sharpen his skills: choosing images, editing photographs, and creating page layouts. Despite working with a small budget, he enjoyed "making a silk purse of a sow's ear." Donald's one-year tenure kept him connected to de Harak—and allowed him to reconnect with Ann, de Harak's star pupil at Cooper and designer in the office.

In 1960, Donald moved to the Will Burtin office, where he worked with his lifelong friend John Condon, mostly redesigning and updating brochures included in the exhibition "The Brain" for Burtin's largest client, the Upjohn Company. Within a year he was drafted into the U.S. Army; he was stationed in Frankfurt, Germany. Ann followed him, and they were soon married. During his service, he wrote and designed his first book, a children's alphabet primer, *We Read: A to Z*, which was completed in 1963 as a portfolio piece to establish his Modernist credentials; it was published in 1967. *We Read: A to Z* and his subsequent book, *Ten Black Dots* (1968), paired the principles of clarity and function with abstract images to teach children how to read and count, an approach at odds with the more illustrative children's books published in the era. Meanwhile, Ann, who aspired to be exposed to the German and Swiss aesthetics, worked at a nondescript advertising agency for eight months but was let down by her experiences creating beer advertisements. Donald's favorite designers included Paul Rand, Charles and Ray Eames, and Bruno Munari, all of whom worked on children's books and projects. He never strayed far from de Harak's teachings and extensive library, where he first learned of Karl Gerstner and Swiss graphic design's Precisionist economy. "It's what we aspired to be," Donald said. He added that he and Ann "were two like-minded souls with the same interests—I'd have no achievements if it wasn't for her."

Both opted for the freelance life, working on their own terms. They worked with de Harak overseeing a small team that produced exhibition graphics for Expo 67 in Montreal. Ava Weiss, then art director at Greenwillow Books, provided some of their first assignments—it was their "bread and butter" during the sixties and beyond. "Freelance work is ephemeral," John Condon told the Crewses. "Find something that only you can do, and be the only one who can supply it." These words became significant and a pivotal point in their careers when, in 1978, Donald became a full-time children's book author and designer. He continued on his path of creating Modernist books, starting with *Freight Train* (1978), followed by *Truck* (1980), *Parade* (1983), *Bicycle Race* (1985), and many more. His distinctive visual language enabled him to bring his concepts to life with brilliant colors and myriad visual forms that inspire learning. In 2015, he received the prestigious (Laura Ingalls) Wilder Medal for his lifetime achievements and contributions in children's literature.

Soon Ann also began to write and design her own children's books, including *When You Were a Baby* (1982), followed by *Two Bears Cubs* (1982) and the imaginative *Round Trip* (1983). "I find myself drawn more and more often to designing books that involve some sort of visual play," she explained.

From their earliest book cover designs to their careers as celebrated children's book authors and designers, a preference for clear, functional, and visually impactful design reigned. Out of the panoply of Modernism, the Crewses found a niche that was uniquely and undeniably their own. •

Seymour

forCongress

319

Voting

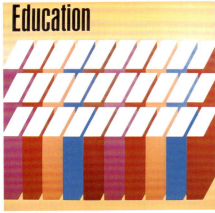

Education

320

Christmas Boutique/Film

To benefit
The West Village Nursery School
Saturday, December 9, 1967 at P.S. 41 11th St. and 6th Ave.
11 a.m. to 4 p.m.

DONALD AND ANN CREWS

Boutique: Hand crafted jewelry, clothing, Christmas gifts and decorations. Home baked goods. Books, records. Raffle. Texas Chili Parlor Snack Bar.

Admission free

Film: Two programs 11:30 a.m. and 2 p.m. "Hey There, It's Yogi Bear" preceeded by Bob Marcy singing folk songs for children.

Admission $1.00

321

Graphic symbols and forms (stars, voting levers, books and holiday ornaments) and vivid colors, illustrate ideas in a clear and distinct way.

319
Shopping bag graphic, *Seymour for Congress*, 1968

320
Signage, *Voting* and *Education*, New York World's Fair, Flushing Meadow, New York, 1964

321
Poster, *Christmas Boutique/Film*, West Village Nursery School, 1967

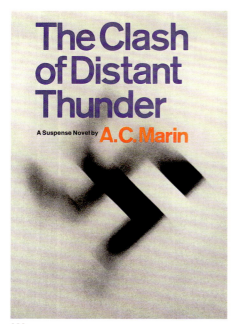

322

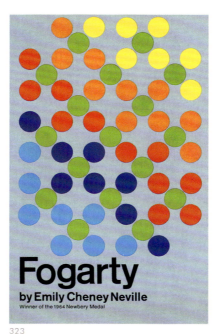

323

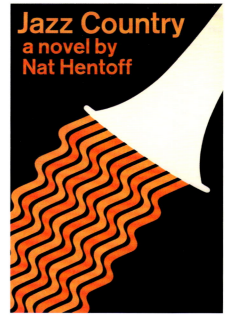

324

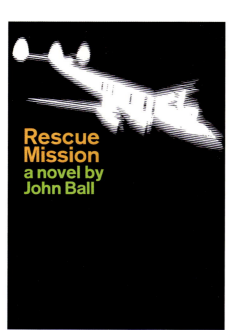

325

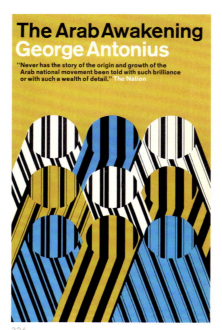

326

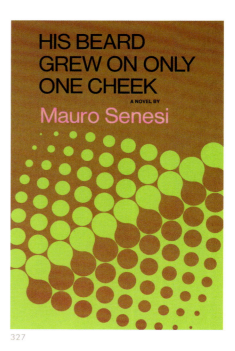

327

322
Book jacket, *The Clash of Distant Thunder*, by A. C. Marin, Harcourt, Brace, 1968

323
Book jacket, *Fogarty*, by Emily Cheney Neville, Harper & Row, 1969

324
Book jacket, *Jazz Country*, by Nat Hentoff, Harper & Row, 1965

325
Book jacket, *Rescue Mission*, by John Ball, Harper & Row, 1966

326
Book cover, *The Arab Awakening*, by George Antonius, Capricorn, 1965

327
Book cover, *His Beard Grew on Only One Cheek*, by Mauro Senesi, Charles Scribner's Sons, 1968

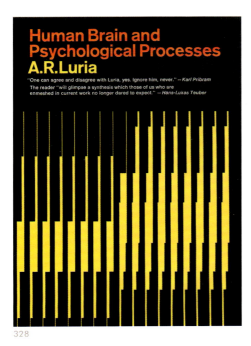

328

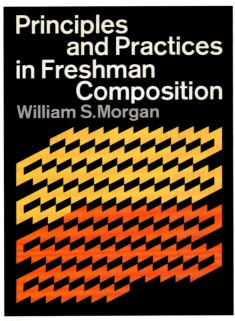

329

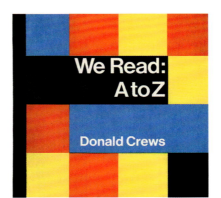

330

328
Book jacket, *Human Brain and Psychological Processes*, by A. R. Luria, Harper & Row, 1966

329
Book cover, *Principles and Practices in Freshman Composition*, by William S. Morgan, Macmillan, 1968

330
Book cover and interior spreads, *We Read: A to Z*, by Donald Crews, Harper & Row, 1967

Richard Danne

b. 1934

Danne in his Dallas studio, 1959,
Photo: Shel Hershorn

In 1975, Richard Danne and Bruce Blackburn of Danne & Blackburn introduced an expansive and coordinated design system for the National Aeronautics and Space Administration. It included a futuristic-looking logo, nicknamed the "worm": an interconnected serpentine word mark that radically modernized the agency's famous, illustrative "meatball" insignia. This major project propelled the emerging new firm, but it was not Danne's first design success. Years earlier, he had built a solo design career not only as a graphic communicator but as a leader of a new design discourse, a change maker in the corporate design world.

Born in Oklahoma during the Dust Bowl and Great Depression, he attended Oklahoma State University as an engineering major—and then, to the dismay of his parents, switched to art. "You'll need to eat!" they told him. So, during his college years, Danne played jazz trumpet to bring in extra money. In 1956, Danne set the trumpet aside and enrolled at the University of California, Los Angeles (UCLA) Graduate School of Design. Two years later, with a bank loan cosigned by his father, he packed up his 1956 Chevy convertible and headed for Dallas to begin his career. "Dallas was good to me, both professionally and personally," he recalled. "I was very fortunate to be in on the ground floor of an emerging design industry."

In 1959, he met Richard Coyne, the cofounder with Robert Blanchard of the California-based *CA: The Journal of Commercial Art*. Coyne invited Danne to design an April 1960 cover that was a transparent blend of oversize and outlined type and hand-drawn letters set in multiple colors in a linear arrangement against black. The type-only concept was one of the magazine's first modern compositions, and it earned Danne early recognition. Soon after, he was encouraged to join the design coalition Portfolio, where freelance designers shared space, expenses, ideas, and contacts. His clients included Fox & Jacobs, Ling-Temco-Vought, Dresser Industries, and Austin College, and he executed an intricate project for the theme park Six Flags Over Texas. He also met Barbara Wood, who eventually became his wife and business partner.

A pivotal moment in Danne's career occurred in 1961 when, as an officer in the newly founded Dallas/Fort Worth Art Directors Club, he organized a jury that brought design icons Saul Bass, Herb Lubalin, and Sam Scali, as well as illustrator Bob Peak, to Dallas. "Talking with judges at breaks and at evening dinners began to confirm my feelings that I wanted to be part of the larger picture," Danne recalled.

In 1962 he left Dallas. After a series of exploratory meetings in Los Angeles and San Francisco with Bass, Jim Cross, Lou Danziger, Margret Larsen, and Robert Miles Runyan, among other West Coast luminaries, he headed to New York, where he met Ivan Chermayeff, Lou Dorfsman, Milton Glaser, and Herb Lubalin. "One thing about New York in the early sixties, the graphic design community was a most welcoming bunch," he said. The Dannes moved there in early 1963. He sublet office space from the design partners Phil Gips and Lou Klein on East Forty-Fourth Street, and in short order, commissions came from Harper

& Row, Random House/Bantam Books, Harvard Business School, and Time. Robert Leslie of the Composing Room invited Danne to participate in its annual "Young Graphic Designers" exhibition, which launched a lasting friendship with Arnold Shaw.

When Klein left for London in 1964, Gips became partners with Danne, and their eponymous firm was launched. It lasted five years and included work for the State University of New York, the Ford Foundation, General Dynamics, Air India, Paramount Pictures, Beekman Downtown Hospital, and Westinghouse Broadcasting. In 1969, Danne went into a solo practice as Richard Danne—New Center, and he expanded his offerings to include film, television, and environmental graphics.

Increasingly dedicated to design education, Danne taught at the School of Visual Arts and became a leader of the American Institute of Graphic Arts (AIGA) during the mid- to late seventies, a period when the institute was on a downward slide. As president of AIGA, he proclaimed that "a business-as-usual attitude will no longer suffice." This meant that fiscal responsibility was critical to the institute's success. He called successfully for an expanded national approach and a focus on business and publishing opportunities. "It's not always a disadvantage to take over an enterprise when it's in trouble and in decline. 'Change' is possible when things are not right, when an organization is floundering," Danne said. Soon after, he organized and was founding president of the New York chapter (AIGA/NY).

This willingness to change was necessary for his design business too, as corporate design was quickly evolving into a highly competitive field. "Smaller firms and individuals were having a difficult go against the likes of Lippincott & Margulies, Anspach Grossman Portugal, Walter Landor, Saul Bass & Associates, and others," he recalled. That explains why in 1973 he joined forces with Blackburn to form Danne & Blackburn. Within ten months, they were awarded the NASA assignment, initiated through the National Endowment for the Arts (NEA), Federal Design Improvement Program.

The team (including designer Stephen Loges) worked laboriously to produce the *NASA Graphics Standards Manual*, which presented the new visual identity and described how the design program should be applied throughout the NASA network. Through detailed examples, it organized and communicated a system of design techniques and principles including logotype, color, typography, stationery, forms, publications, signage, vehicles, and more. For Danne, the nearly ten-year project was "a singular professional experience, loaded with struggle and success." A who's who of elite accounts soon followed: RCA, Bristol-Myers, Dow Jones, MasterCard, IBM, Memorial Sloan Kettering Cancer Center, Seagram Company, and the New York Power Authority, among others.

Danne has continued the modern ethic by making functional, elegant, and timeless work. His independent journey "from Dust Bowl to Gotham" is best described by the word "Onward!"—his guiding principle. •

331

332

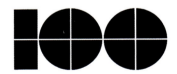

334

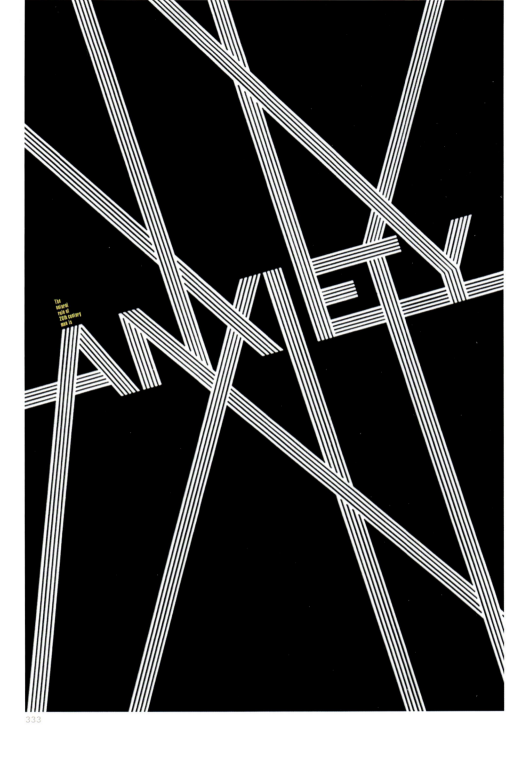

333

331
Quarterly magazine cover, *University Review,* "Adriatic Summer," State University of New York, Summer 1969. Design: Gips & Danne

332
Quarterly magazine cover, *University Review,* "Evolution," State University of New York, Autumn 1969. Design: Gips & Danne

333
Poster, *The Natural Role of 20th Century Man Is Anxiety,* Norman Mailer, University of Oklahoma, 1966. Design: Gips & Danne

334
Logo, Printing Industries of New York, 1964. Designed to mark its one hundredth anniversary

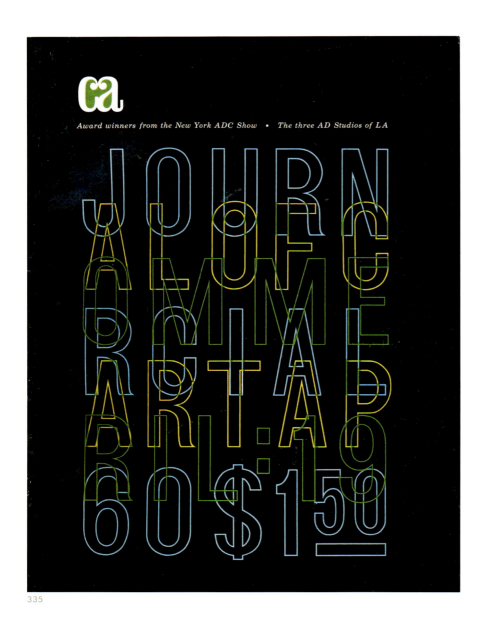

335

336

338

335
Magazine cover, *CA: The Journal of Commercial Art*, Coyne & Blanchard, Palo Alto, California, April 1960

336
Greeting card, *Christmas 1967*, Barbara and Richard Danne, 1967. Design: Gips & Danne

337
Album cover, *World War II*, Group W Westinghouse Broadcasting Company, 1967. Design: Gips & Danne

338
Promotional booklet insert, *Strathmore on Opaques*, Strathmore Paper Company, 1969. From the interior: "This booklet on opaques is the first in a series of demonstrations of out-of-the-ordinary techniques planned as a service to the graphic arts community by the Strathmore Paper Company." Design: Gips & Danne

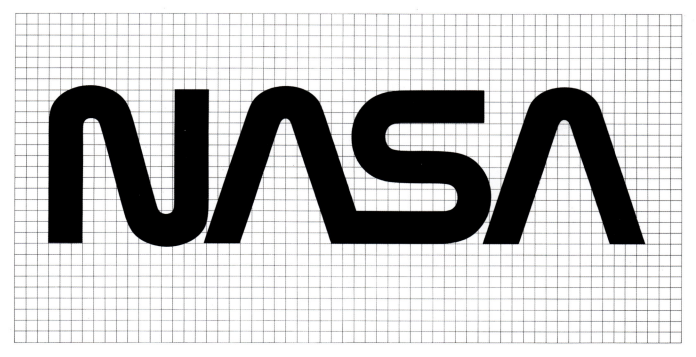

339

DALLAS

340

341

339
NASA logotype, 1975. The goal of the NASA logotype was to be reproduced photographically whenever possible. For large applications such as signage, the logo may be reproduced using this grid drawing as an accurate guide. Design: Darne & Blackburn

340
Book front and back covers, *Cyrano de Bergerac*, by Edmond Rostand, Bantam, 1964. Design: Gips & Danne

341
Dallas recruiting booklet, Ling-Temco-Vought, 1962

Louis Danziger

b. 1923

Danziger in his Hollywood, California, studio, c. 1970.
Photo: Roland Young

Louis Danziger belonged to the generation of fervent post-Bauhaus moderns who believed that the mission of graphic design was to provide order, beauty, and utility—cut with wit—to a chaotic commercial world. Reluctant to be tied to inflexible dogma, he insisted, "No matter what I do, I want to do it well"—a statement that for more than half a century exemplified the diversity of his practice and teaching. A "designer's designer and an educator's educator" is how Katherine McCoy, former cochair of the design department at Cranbrook Academy of Art, described the man who made an impact on many design genres—advertising, corporate identity, books, periodicals, museum catalogs, and exhibitions—and pedagogy. Hundreds of students who attended his classes at the Chouinard Art Institute, CalArts, Harvard University, and the Art Center College of Design came away with a greater appreciation for Modernist discipline and historical eclecticism, regardless of how they chose to design.

The institutional advertisements, brochures, catalogs, and posters that fill Danziger's extensive oeuvre express certain formal, architectonic, and conceptual virtues emblematic of their times, but they also stand as testaments to his personal sensibilities. He defined his method as employing "a minimal amount of material and a minimal amount of effort—nothing wasted—to achieve maximum impact."

Born in 1923 and raised in "the Coops," the "workers' paradise," a union-funded apartment complex in the Bronx, New York, Danziger was interested in letterforms from an early age. Like his friend Paul Rand, Danziger coveted copies of the German design magazine *Gebrauchsgraphik*: "I discovered that the Germans were doing the most interesting things with book jackets and posters," he recalled. "Although most Americans at the time were either hostile to or ignorant of modern art," he added, "in my high school [Evander Childs] all the art majors were given student memberships to the Museum of Modern Art." Commercial art was offered as a viable profession for the artistically inclined, and Danziger decided to follow this path. After serving in the U.S. Army in the Pacific from 1943 through 1945, designing the occasional poster, he moved to California and attended the Art Center School on the GI Bill.

Postwar California did not have the large number of industries to support modern graphic design that New York did, but it was nonetheless beginning to attract more creative talent. None of the transplants had a greater impact than Alvin Lustig, whose graphic and industrial design classes at Art Center changed Danziger's life in 1948. "I didn't like school at all, because it was very rigid at that time," he recalled. "But one day I heard this voice coming out of a classroom talking about social structure, religion, and the broadest implications of design. So I stuck my nose in the door and saw that it was Lustig. From then on I sat in on every class."

Danziger joined the Design Group, which included Lustig students "opposed to mindless, sentimental, nostalgic, commercial design." His cohorts—including Saul Bass, Rudolph de Harak, and Charles Eames (who introduced him to Buckminster Fuller's book *Nine Chains to the Moon*)—all became missionaries of progressive design. "But I don't think we talked about our work in the philosophical or theoretical terms," he recalled. "We were talking about very practical matters."

Danziger designed early identity and advertising for M. Flax Artists Materials (including a trademark that is still used), General Lighting, Steelbilt, and Fraymart Gallery, yet he was nonetheless disenchanted with the provincialism of Los Angeles—it was a "hick town," he said. He briefly returned to New York and worked with Alexander Ross, who specialized in designing pharmaceutical materials; he also had a job at *Esquire* magazine, where he sat in the art department next to Helmut Krone, who eventually became the chief art director for Doyle Dane Bernbach. At the time, Krone admired Paul Rand so much that his work area was covered with Rand's tear sheets. Danziger would later become a Rand confidant, but over his own desk he hung reproductions of Egyptian and Chinese artifacts, because, he told Krone, "If you want to be as good as Rand, don't look at Rand; look at what Rand looks at."

Danziger also attended Alexey Brodovitch's Graphic Journalism night class at the New School for Social Research in Greenwich Village in 1948. Brodovitch, he said, "instilled the idea that you cannot do good work unless you have guts to do something you have not seen before." From Brodovitch, Danziger learned to have "a proper disrespect for design." Contrary to Lustig's ministry of optimism, Brodovitch did not attach world-shaping significance to design. "I always felt that it was the contradictions between my two masters that allowed me to form my own point of view," Danziger explained.

He returned to Los Angeles in 1949 to study architecture. There, at the short-lived California School of the Arts, he resumed his studies with Lustig, as well as with architect Raphael Soriano and engineer Edgardo Contini. He embraced Buckminster Fuller's principle of "de-selfing," which challenged the prevailing notion that designers should be present in their work. "Bucky Fuller's idea was that you are invisible—everything is objective. And a very important thing was the idea of doing a great deal with very little—maximum performance with minimal means," Danziger said. He also found a kindred thinker when he read Paul Rand's book *Thoughts on Design*, "particularly where he talked about symbols and metaphors," he said. "Finding something that stands for something else."

Danziger might best be known for spreading his gospel through his pioneering design history lectures, which launched a design history movement of the eighties. Design literacy, he believed, was essential to the designer's main task of finding the essence of what needed to be communicated. Danziger routinely cautioned, "You can always find the appropriate symbol for the wrong message." •

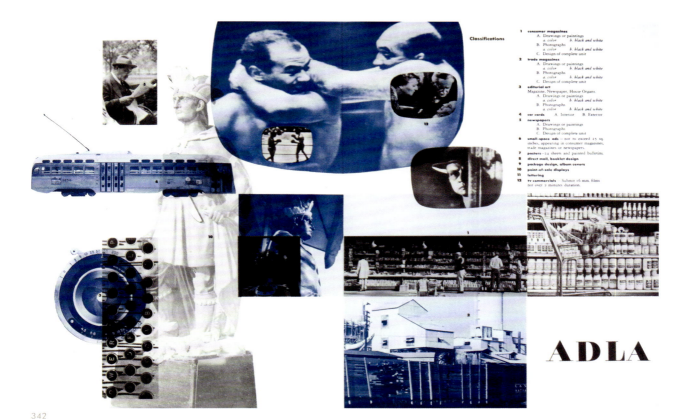

342

343

342
Call for entries spread, Art Directors Club of Los Angeles, 1952

343
Invitation, Lightrend Company, Los Angeles, 1952. Recognizing the design and cultural renaissance in Italy, Lightrend invited customers to its showroom to preview an exclusive line of imported lamps and lighting fixtures from Italy.

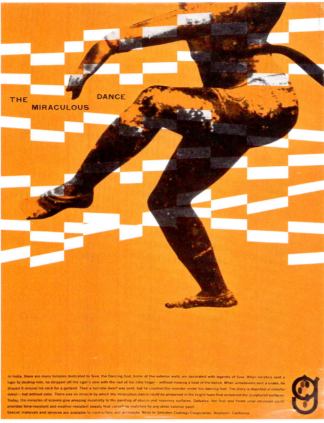

344

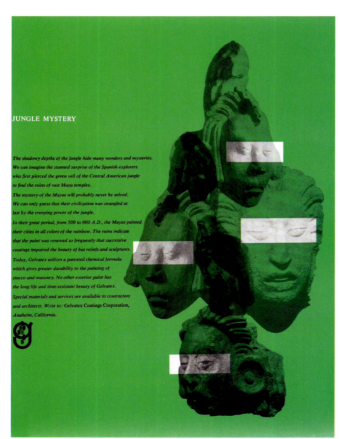

345

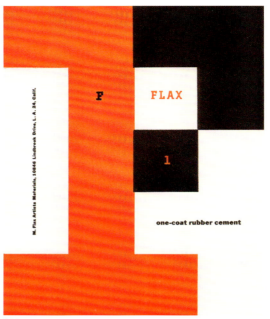

346

347

344
Advertisement, "The Miraculous Dance," Gelvatext Coatings Corporation, Anaheim, California, 1956

345
Advertisement, "Jungle Mystery," Gelvatext Coatings Corporation, Anaheim, California, 1956

346
Packaging label, "One-Coat Rubber Cement," M. Flax Artists Materials, 1949

347
Catalog cover for transcription players, Califone Corporation, Hollywood, California, 1953

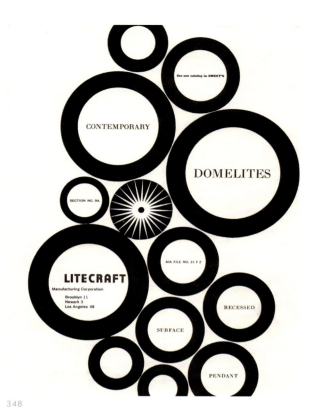

348

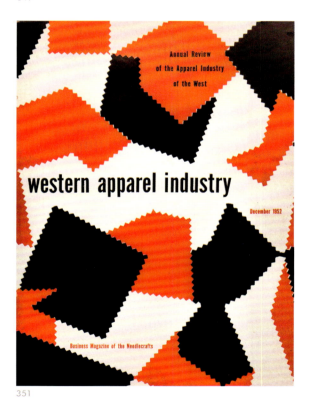

349

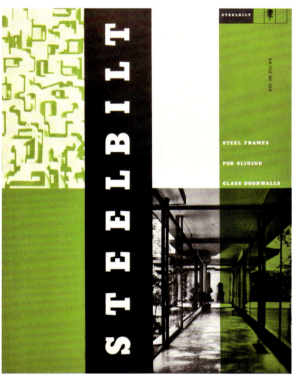

350

351

348
Catalog cover, *Contemporary Domelites*, Litecraft Manufacturing Corporation, 1950–51

349
Advertisement, "Samuel Taylor Coleridge on Language and the Mind," part of "Great Ideas of Western Man" campaign, Container Corporation of America, 1958

350
Catalog cover, *Steel Frames for Sliding Glass Doorwalls*, Steelbilt, 1950–51

351
Magazine cover, *Western Apparel Industry*, December 1952. In addition to being a self-styled historian of graphic design, Danziger is an essential player in the history of American modern practice.

Rudolph de Harak
1924–2002

De Harak in his New York studio, 1954. Photo: Norman Nishimura

Rudolph de Harak was consumed by the principles of classic Modernism and maintained a belief in the rightness of the modern methodology for efficient communication of information. Born in Culver City, California, de Harak soon moved with his family to New York, where he attended the New York City School of Industrial Arts and learned basic commercial art practices. Graduation coincided with World War II, and he was drafted into the infantry. But upon being discharged, he returned to Los Angeles, where he was encouraged by an employment counselor to accept an apprenticeship at a small art service/advertising agency.

De Harak's future course was profoundly influenced by two lectures that he attended at the Art Center School in the late forties: one by Will Burtin, the German master of information and exhibition design, titled "Integration: The New Discipline in Design," and the other by György Kepes, the Hungarian designer, on his book *Language of Vision*. Shortly after Kepes's lecture, de Harak and six other designers, including Saul Bass, Alvin Lustig, Lou Danziger, and John Follis, founded the Los Angeles Society for Contemporary Designers. De Harak explained that the reason for forming it was a matter of survival: "We were a young, very enthusiastic group trying to function in a desert, which is what Los Angeles was at that time."

De Harak moved back East in 1950. He became promotion art director of *Seventeen* magazine. *Seventeen* soon moved to 488 Madison Avenue—the Look Building—a hotbed of publishing and advertising activity, where Paul Rand, Henry Wolf, and Art Kane all worked.

De Harak's ideas about design were still being formulated, and the uneven quality of his *Seventeen* promotions revealed certain growing pains. Yet a personality was beginning to emerge: "Around 1950, I was particularly influenced by Alvin Lustig and Saul Bass, who were poles apart. Bass, who was a very content-conscious designer, would get a strong idea and put together a beautiful design based on that idea. Lustig, on the other hand, was a strong formalist, much less concerned with content, but deeply interested in developing forms and relating the type to them. I too went off in that direction and [became] dedicated to the concept of form. I was always looking for the *hidden order*, trying to somehow either develop new forms or manipulate existing form. Therefore, I think my work was more obscure, and certainly very abstract. Sometimes it was hard for me to understand why [my solutions] fell short. But one thing I did was to sharpen my design sensibilities to the point that my work generally fell into a purist category."

Purism was not, however, an extremely marketable methodology in the crassly commercial postwar culture. Frustrated by the limitations that business had placed on him, de Harak stayed at *Seventeen* for only eighteen months and then did a stint at an advertising agency for about four months. It was the last full-time job he would ever take.

De Harak's most public work in the early fifties was monthly illustrations for *Esquire*—"a kind of fifties Dada," as de Harak referred to them. They married conceptual and formal thinking and were collages composed of photographs, drawings, and found materials, which he juxtaposed in rebus-like compositions and then rendered as composite photographs. He saw these gems of abstract illustration as akin to jazz improvisations. At the same time, de Harak was improvising with various photographic processes, which he ultimately used for Columbia, Oxford, Circle, and Westminster record covers, all of which were also his labs for typographic experimentation. With one eye on the International Typographic Style and the other focused on pushing the boundaries of graphic composition, de Harak used abstract shapes, geometric forms, distinctive color, and photographic experiments, both in concert and in contrast.

Around 1958, he moved into an office on Lexington Avenue, hired a couple of students from Cooper Union (notably Ann Crews), and began seriously selling design under the name Rudolph de Harak Inc. His fifty album covers for Westminster Records were a warm-up for his book jackets for Meridian Books; New Directions; Holt, Rinehart and Winston; and Doubleday. And all the approaches that he developed during the late fifties led to his magnum opus: 350 paperback covers for McGraw-Hill that became laboratories for his experiments with color, type, optical illusion, photography, and other techniques.

De Harak's McGraw-Hill paperbacks were paradigms of purist visual communication based on the most contemporary design systems. At this time, the International Typographic Style and American Eclecticism were the two primary design methodologies at play in the United States. De Harak was profoundly influenced by the exquisite simplicity of the great Swiss Modernist Max Bill, but as an American he wanted to find a vehicle for somehow reconciling these two conflicting sensibilities. He worked with a limited number of sans serif typefaces, at first Franklin Gothic and News Gothic (preferring it over Futura), then Akzidenz-Grotesk, and ultimately Helvetica. Each element was fundamental, since de Harak did not allow for the extraneous. Yet, as economical as they were, each was also a marriage of expressionistic or illusionistic imagery and systematic typography, the same repertoire of elements that he would later use in other graphic work.

In the midsixties, as de Harak was building a solid reputation as a teacher and practitioner, a new facet to his career, exhibition design, began almost by accident. In 1965, a friend recommended de Harak to design the Man, His Planet, and Space Pavilion at Montreal's Expo 67. At the time, de Harak noted, there were simply not enough Canadian designers to handle the volume of work that went into making this milestone exposition. He spent two intensive years researching and developing information modules comprising light, sound, and text that presented complex information. It would become the cornerstone of his expanding practice. The confluence of de Harak's Modernism and personal vision is fully realized through his museum designs. •

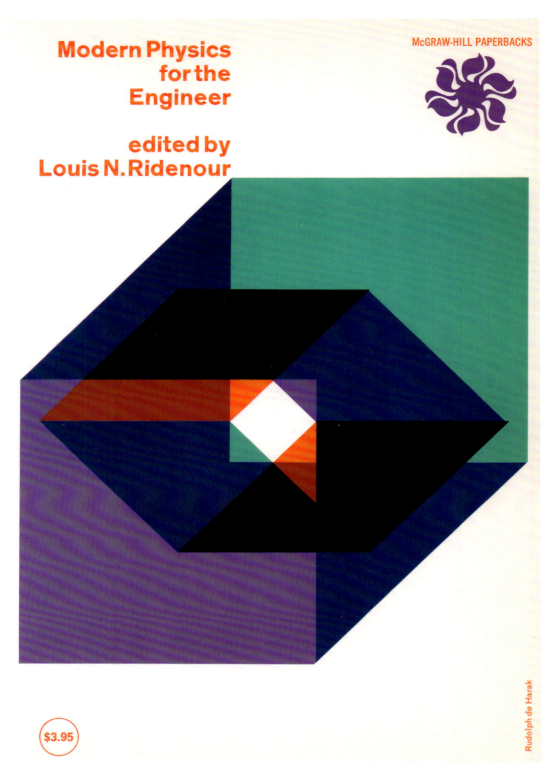

Modern Physics for the Engineer

edited by Louis N. Ridenour

RUDOLPH DE HARAK

Rudolph de Harak

$3.95

352

352
Book cover, *Modern Physics for the Engineer*, edited by Louis N. Ridenour, McGraw-Hill Paperbacks, 1961

Ivor Novello's
Music Hall Songs

WESTMINSTER

353

HERMANN SCHERCHEN
Conducts
TRUMPET CONCERTI
HAYDN/Vivaldi
Handel/Torelli

WESTMINSTER

354

LALO:
Symphonie Espagnole
WIENIAWSKI: Violin Concerto No. 2

WESTMINSTER

355

SHOSTAKOVITCH
Piano Concerto No.1 opus 35
& No.2 opus 102
Eugene List, Piano

WESTMINSTER

356

Vivaldi/Gloria

WESTMINSTER

357

SCHERCHEN CONDUCTS
the Bach Brandenburg Concertos Numbers: 5 & 6

WESTMINSTER

358

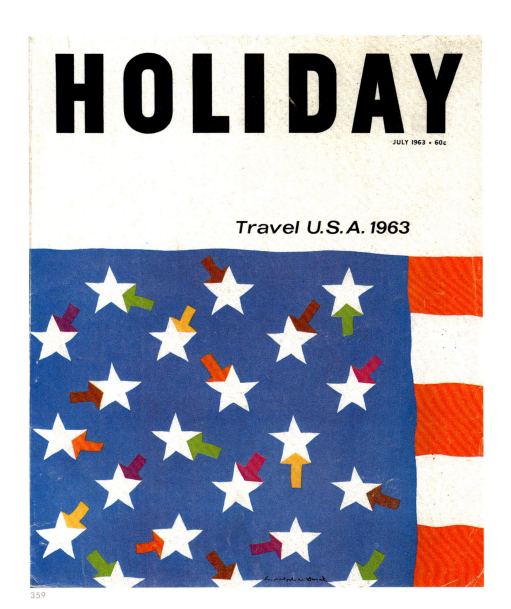

359

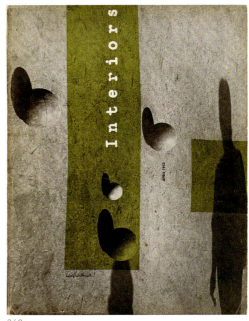

360

361

Industrial Algebra and Trigonometry
with Geometrical Applications

McGRAW-HILL PAPERBACKS

John H. Wolfe
William F. Mueller
Seibert D. Mullikin

$3.25

Rudolph de Harak

362

Statistical Treatment of Experimental Data
Hugh D. Young

McGRAW-HILL PAPERBACKS

$2.95

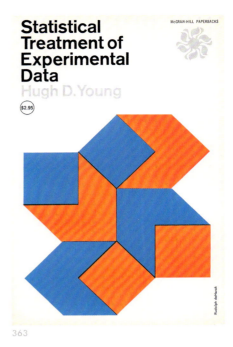

Rudolph deHarak

363

An introduction to Scientific Research
E. Bright Wilson, Jr.

McGRAW-HILL PAPERBACKS

$2.95

Rudolph deHarak

364

362
Book cover, *Industrial Algebra and Trigonometry with Geometrical Applications*, by John H. Wolfe, William F. Mueller, and Seibert D. Mullikin, McGraw-Hill Paperbacks, 1966

363
Book cover, *Statistical Treatment of Experimental Data*, by Hugh D. Young, McGraw-Hill Paperbacks, 1962

364
Book cover, *An Introduction to Scientific Research*, by E. Bright Wilson Jr., McGraw-Hill Paperbacks, c. 1962

365

366

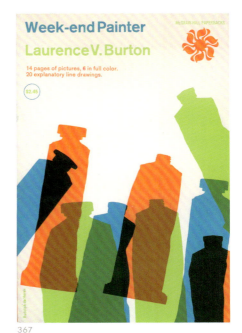

367

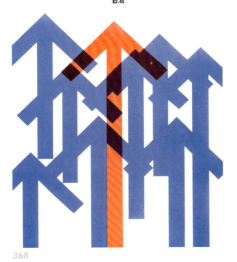

368

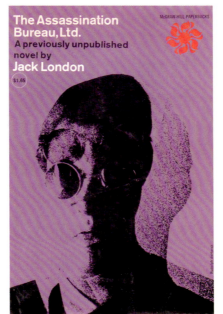

369

370

RUDOLPH DE HARAK

365
Book cover, *Men Under Stress*, by Roy R. Grinker and John P. Spiegel, McGraw-Hill Paperbacks, 1963

366
Book cover, *Monsieur Teste*, by Paul Valéry, McGraw-Hill Paperbacks, 1964

367
Book cover, *Week-end Painter*, by Laurence V. Burton, McGraw-Hill Paperbacks, c. 1960s

368
Book cover, *Techniques of Leadership*, by Auren Uris, McGraw-Hill Paperbacks, 1964

369
Book cover, *The Assassination Bureau, Ltd.*, by Jack London, McGraw-Hill Paperbacks, 1963. With an experimental photograph of de Harak's close friend John Condon.

370
Book cover, *Some Mathematical Methods of Physics*, by Gerald Goertzel and Nunzio Tralli, McGraw-Hill Paperbacks, 1960

Louis Dorfsman

1918–2008

Dorfsman in the CBS Building, New York, c. 1965

The Manhattan-born, Bronx-raised Louis Dorfsman wanted to be a bacteriologist but instead got a scholarship to Cooper Union, where he studied design until 1939. This set him on his l ife's trajectory with the Columbia Broadcasting System (CBS), the foremost American television network from the fifties through the early eighties. The "CBS Eye" was its proud emblem, which stood for the pinnacle of service and quality. Such inherently superb programming required an equally impressive corporate image, an identity born of memorable graphic design and compelling advertising. It can be argued that if not for the originality of its promotion, CBS would have had to slug it out much harder against ABC and NBC, whose advertising rarely reached the same heights.

CBS top management—William Paley, founder and CEO, and Frank Stanton, president of the network—understood the value of graphic design. In 1937, Paley hired William Golden as chief architect for the bold new graphic identity program for CBS, intended to distinguish the "Champagne Network" from the others, and Golden led the sophisticated program until his untimely death at age forty-eight in 1959. To assume the role of the seemingly irreplaceable Golden, Paley and Stanton named Dorfsman, then the promotion art director of the radio division, to take his place. Dorfsman earned the job through inspired trade advertising designed to sell advertisers on the viability of radio at a time when television was decidedly the more compelling market.

Dorfsman was the engine that drove CBS's most successful advertising campaigns and ultimately its entire graphic design program. He wrote much of his own copy and practiced the art of visual persuasion with distinctive wit. What his ads lacked in typical hyperbole was made up for in uncommon intelligence. He never lowered himself or his company to hard-sell tactics. He was a master of the Big Idea, a conceptual strategy characterized by understatement, self-mockery, and irony, and his ads were noted for clean design and strident copywriting wed to intelligent illustration and photography. In the more than forty years that Dorfsman managed the visual identity of CBS, there is not a single example where he used a typeface as novelty or decoration simply to grab attention or abused a photograph, painting, or drawing merely for shock value. Different designers take credit for the CBS Didot, originally designed by George Lois and Kurt Weihs under the direction of Golden, redefined by Freeman Craw and Tom Carnese under the direction of Dorfsman. The audience was never treated as visually illiterate, and by making the public feel good about CBS's intrusion into their lives, Dorfsman instilled a pride of viewing.

Dorfsman's ads still resonate as big ideas—indeed, many of them could be reprised today without changes. In one example, the words "Ha, Ha, Ha," in copy that reads "Ha, Ha, Ha: He laughs best who laughs last," grew larger according to the Nielsen ratings of the three television networks' comedy shows. The largest "Ha" represented the high standing of CBS: Without the benefit of a hard-sell slogan or sensational image,

Dorfsman, who had a deep understanding of the network and respect for its clients' intelligence, activated the persuasive force of statistics.

For an ad titled "Worth Repeating, CBS News," Dorfsman used enormous quotation marks as architectural elements framing a column of copy. These curiously abstract marks have greater shouting range than any single line of type or picture. "Dominate," a series of four advertisements used to convince potential advertisers that CBS enjoyed dominance in the ratings, was an example of "talking type": Once again, without the benefit of an image, Dorfsman used four words—"Captivate!" "Elucidate!" "Fascinate!" "Exhilarate!"—each set in a different typeface with an exclamation point dotted with the CBS Eye. The copy suggested the range of CBS programs in a market it totally controlled. Yet another exemplar was a soft-sell idea titled "A Glossary of Television Terms," an illustrated lexicon of words such as "fish bowl," "one shot," and "audio," that were introduced to the public through television. Cleverly illustrated, this compendium of trivia captured the interest of even the casual reader. After holding the reader's attention, it smartly climaxed with "Leadership: The quality invariably associated with the CBS Television Network."

Dorfsman injected a rare social urgency into some of his work for the network's public affairs programming. A full-page newspaper ad for *Of Black America*, the first network series on black history, showed a black man in black and white, with half his face painted with the stars and the stripes of the American flag—the image became a virtual emblem for race relations. Dorfsman also came up with the slogan "Re-elected the Most Trusted Man in America" to promote Walter Cronkite's coverage of the 1972 presidential election.

These ads did more than remind, inform, and persuade potential clients of the network's virtues; they increased the recognition of CBS by giving it a uniform identity, which in turn underscored the value of its corporate culture. Rarely did any of Dorfsman's designs, even the more decorative logos and trademarks, lack an idea. In fact, if an idea was not readily apparent, he went to great lengths to concoct one.

Advertisements were not his only métier. He created corporate annual reports and promotional commemorative volumes to bolster CBS's standing as the "Tiffany Network." To celebrate the first manned landing on the moon, Stanton proposed a limited-edition book, which Dorfsman designed with a special cover embossed to look and feel like the lunar surface. This and other promotional pieces set a standard for broadcast advertising. Without Dorfsman, CBS would have had its Eye, but with him the Eye became more than a mere logo—it was the jewel in a crown. •

371

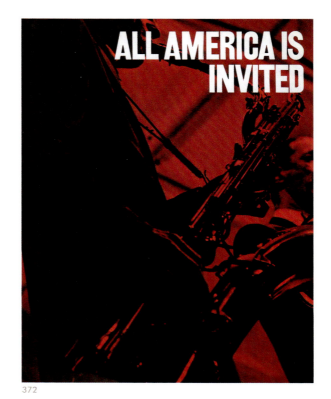

372

373

374

371
Annual report, *New Home of CBS*, Columbia Broadcasting System, 1962. Photograph by CBS employee Philip Mancino reveals the new CBS Headquarters building site.

372
Booklet cover, *All America Is Invited*, CBS Radio Network, c. 1960s. Dorfsman was the paradigm of a corporate design director. Nothing was allowed to have the CBS imprimatur without his approval, making certain it was indeed worthy.

373
Manual cover, *Charges for Facilities & Production Services*, Manual no. 7, CBS Television Network, 1952

374
Advertisement, "On the Spot, CBS News: Daniel Schorr Speaks to You from Moscow," CBS Radio Network, c. 1955–57

"I WAS 12. HAD MY FIRST PISTOL, A .38. STOLE IT. I SHOT ONE DUDE BEFORE, WASN'T NOTHIN'... DIDN'T THINK ABOUT IT. MOST I COULD HAVE GOT THEN WAS 18 MONTHS."

375

This Fall, the CBS Television Network will again chalk up the biggest attendance record in football. The same go-go-go spirit that first brought professional football home to a nationwide audience (the late National Football League Commissioner Bert Bell attributed the game's phenomenal rise to this network's pioneering coverage) is also responsible for many other CBS Television Network sports firsts. First to give the nation a front row seat at international competitions through exclusive coverage of the 1960 Winter and Summer Olympics. First to use video tape in sports, making it possible to rerun thoroughbred races, crucial golf rounds and scoring football plays as soon as they are over. First to televise the whole incredible range of sporting events from rugby to auto racing, from sky diving to figure skating—through the introduction of the weekly Sports Spectacular series. And throughout the year, this network continues to bring a hundred million television fans such major events of every season as the college bowl games, the Triple Crown, the UN Handicap, the PGA and Masters golf tournaments, and baseball's Major League Games of the Week. Sports play an exhilarating, exciting part in the powerful CBS Television Network line-up, which again this season has the balance, depth and quality to **DOMINATE**

376

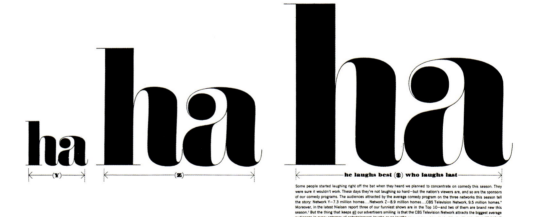

— he laughs best (👁) who laughs last —

Some people started laughing right off the bat when they heard we planned to concentrate on comedy this season. They were sure it wouldn't work. These days they're not laughing so hard—but the nation's viewers are, and so are the sponsors of our comedy programs. The audiences attracted by the average comedy program on the three networks this season tell the story: Network Y—7.3 million homes...Network Z—8.9 million homes...CBS Television Network, 9.5 million homes.* Moreover, in the latest Nielsen report three of our funniest shows are in the Top 10—and two of them are brand new this season.† But the thing that keeps all our advertisers smiling is that the CBS Television Network attracts the biggest average audiences in every category of entertainment, laughs or no laughs. * † ...

CBS Television Network

377

375
Booklet cover, *I was 12 . . .* , CBS Radio Network, c. 1960s

376
Advertisement, "ExHilarate!," CBS Television Network, 1961. The letter x serves dual purposes in a trade ad that reads: "Sports play an exhilarating, exciting part in the powerful CBS Television Network line-up, which again this season has the balance, depth and quality to dominate." Dorfsman used to claim "provocative words beat dull pictures any time!"

377
Trade advertisement, "Ha, Ha, Ha: He laughs best who laughs last," CBS Television Network, 1961. From the delightful typographic forms and elegant lettering to the intelligent copy, this ad is both economical and impactful; it communicates a lot with little means. Dorfsman had a deep understanding of the network and respect for its clients. He sold the importance of statistics and illustrated with each "ha, ha, ha" a side-by-side comparison of Nielsen ratings for comedy programs.

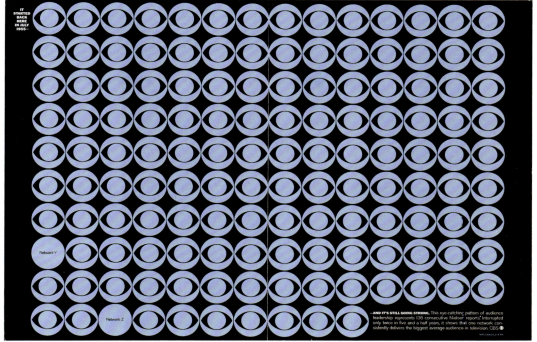

378

379

378
Advertisement, "It Started Back Here in July 1955—And It's Still Going Strong," Columbia Broadcasting System, c. 1960. "This eye-catching pattern of audience leadership represents 136 consecutive Nielsen reports. Interrupted only twice in five and a half years, it shows that one network consistently delivers the biggest average audience in television."

379
Advertisement, "Easy as PL1-2345," WCBS Radio, 1958

Ray Eames
1912–1988

Ray at her trestle desk in her Venice, California, Eames office, 1949

Charles and Ray Eames were a physically odd couple—he was tall, she was short—but despite their superficial disparities, they grew together in stature as the most highly esteemed designers of their generation—and for generations thereafter. It was, however, an era when women were aggressively rising through the design ranks but not yet given the fair and equal status that their achievements and numbers demand today, and although Ray was exclusively responsible for some of the iconic Midcentury Modern Eames textile designs, she sometimes did not get full credit for her furniture, toys, exhibitions, films, and sculpture. "The misplaced attention unfortunately confuses analysis of their early work. . . . Ray Kaiser, who enjoyed her own identity as an emerging artist in New York, nearly vanishes behind Charles," wrote Joseph Giovanni. Both Ray's collaborative and her singular contributions were essential to the Eameses' mammoth reputation.

Bernice Alexandra Kaiser, known as Ray-Ray to her parents, Alexander and Edna Burr Kaiser, was raised with her brother in Sacramento, California. She spent much of her life after high school in different locales with her widowed mother, ending up in Millbrook, New York, where she graduated in 1933 from Bennett College. Then she moved alone to New York, to study with the German-born Abstract Expressionist painter Hans Hofmann at the Art Students League and the Hans Hofmann School of Fine Arts. A serious painter, she was a founding member of the American Abstract Artists group, which included other modern designers. When her mother became ill, she returned home, and when Edna died in 1940, Ray left New York at twenty-eight to study at the Cranbrook Academy of Art in Bloomfield Hills, Michigan. There she met Charles Eames, then thirty-three, who was one of Ray's teachers. Ray worked as an assistant on one of his projects, and they were married in 1941. Ray channeled her passion for painting into design.

Together they opened an innovative design office in Los Angeles that came up with original concepts for furniture, houses, exhibitions, graphics, and their favorite, toys. They shared what Alice Rawsthorn called a "fluid and eclectic interpretation of design." They also had a sense of responsibility to function and developed several production processes that changed the look and feel of objects, starting with molded leg splints and stretchers for the U.S. Navy during World War II, which they later repurposed to produce their iconic chairs designed from molded plywood. They were pioneer design entrepreneurs, working for clients and on their own. Taking a page from the Bauhaus, the Eameses sought ways to engage with new materials and technologies so that everyday objects of high quality in both form and function could be produced at reasonable cost. Their furniture, made from molded plywood, fiberglass-reinforced plastic, bent and welded steel, and cast aluminum, and distributed by Herman Miller Furniture, sustained the studio financially and changed the way the consumer thought about and interacted with modern furniture.

Furthermore, the duo were pioneers of multimedia presentations; multiscreen slide shows for schools and corporations presented common objects in startling new ways. IBM commissioned them to produce ambitious films and exhibitions to educate the public about science and technology. The most famous of these, *Think*, their multiscreen film presentation on the future of information, in the IBM Pavilion at the 1964–65 New York World's Fair. Their exhibition work alone would have put them in any design pantheon—but it was only a fraction of their output.

"Ray knew what was art and Charles knew she knew it," said Deborah Sussman. Between 1942 and 1947, Ray designed twenty-six strikingly abstract collage and photomontage covers for the innovative art, design, and architecture magazine *Arts & Architecture* under editor John Entenza, who had rescued a moribund magazine and commissioned Alvin Lustig to do a new logo in 1942 to express its new energy and direction. These covers were mostly free from perspective, organic and loose, and they captured the modern spirit of Southern California. Her visual vocabulary showed an understanding of spatial compositions and dimensionality of forms and color, influenced by her accomplished studies with Hofmann. "Her splendid covers for *Arts & Architecture* show the influences of Miró, Arp, Calder, and Hofmann in their primary palettes, biomorphic shapes, ink splashes, irregular washes, and use of line," said Pat Kirkham, who wrote about the couple. The work was not done in solitude but rather with assistance and advice from colleagues, Entenza, Herbert Matter, and Charles, and many of his drawings and photographs were montaged into the design. She also designed early advertisements with Charles Kratka for Herman Miller Furniture, featuring Eames creations.

Charles was the public face, but photographs of the duo, which are iconic in their own right, reveal that this diminutive, energetic woman was ever present and playing a major role. By the seventies, Ray assumed a more public presence, but it is nonetheless difficult to pinpoint her oeuvre within the overall design process. Ray never really admitted to any one piece, but rather conceived details of the design in a million ways.

Charles died unexpectedly in 1978, and the Eames office was disbanded shortly afterward. Ray completed some existing projects, but she soon became chief archivist of their legacy and collaborated on a number of monographs. Ray Eames's extraordinary life was so totally intertwined her husband that it makes cosmic sense that she passed away on the exact day, only ten years later, as Charles. •

380

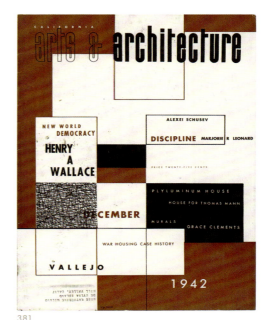

381

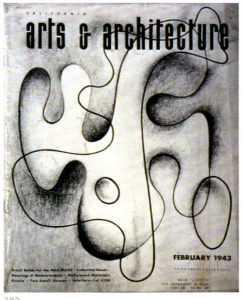

382

383

384

385

380
Magazine cover, *California Arts & Architecture*, April 1942

381
Magazine cover, *California Arts & Architecture*, December 1942

382
Magazine cover, *California Arts & Architecture*, February 1943

383
Magazine cover, *California Arts & Architecture*, January 1944

384
Magazine cover, *Arts & Architecture*, August 1944

385
Magazine cover, *Arts & Architecture*, October 1944

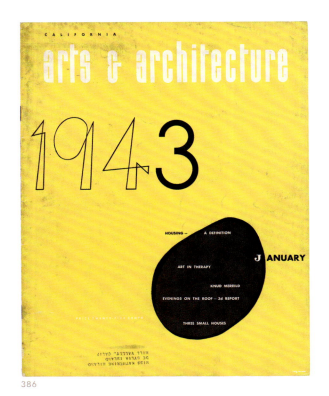

386

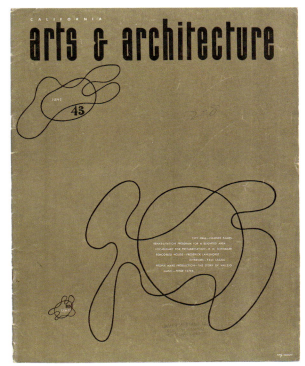

387

388

389

386
Magazine cover, *California Arts & Architecture,* January 1943

387
Magazine cover, *California Arts & Architecture,* June 1943

388
Magazine cover, *Arts & Architecture,* April 1944

389
Magazine cover, *California Arts & Architecture,* July 1943

390
Magazine cover, *Arts & Architecture,* July 1944

arts & architecture

PREFABRICATION

JULY 1944

PRICE 35 CENTS

Gene Federico

1918–1999

Federico in his home studio, Pound Ridge, New York, 1955

After an apprenticeship at an ad agency in the early forties, a tour of duty in the U.S. Army, and an unexceptional stint as a magazine art associate, Gene Federico realized that graphic design was his passion and advertising his métier. He became one of America's premier advertising art directors and designers, ultimately a principal of Lord Geller Federico Einstein.

Federico was born in New York's Greenwich Village, but the family soon moved to the Bronx, where he attended P.S. 89; in keeping with a New York City public school tradition, it held poster competitions for city-sponsored events. When the family moved to Coney Island a few years later, he enrolled at Abraham Lincoln High School and joined the Art Squad, led by the legendary teacher Leon Friend, who for more than fifty years taught intensive classes in commercial design and illustration.

He enrolled at Brooklyn's Pratt Institute for college, and in its voluminous library, Federico pored through European design magazines and American annuals, soaking up the work of Lester Beall and Paul Rand. At Pratt, "form" became an enduring watchword. A teacher recommended that Federico take a job with the Abbott Kimball Company, a small advertising agency in New York. Concurrently, he took a few weeknight classes with the commercial illustrator and type designer Howard Trafton at the Art Students League in Manhattan. One lesson was on the effects of so-called dumb light, in which, Federico recalled, "You just hang a naked lit bulb to see its effects on a model." On subway rides back to Brooklyn, he'd discuss the evening's lessons with Norman Geller, a younger classmate who later became his business partner.

In 1941, Federico accepted a job offer in the ad department of Bamberger's department store in Newark. Four months later, Uncle Sam offered less comfortable accommodations. From April 1941 to November 1945, Federico was a GI in North Africa and Europe, serving in a camouflage unit. He returned from the war to the job at Abbott Kimball.

Federico's pre- and postwar design was exhibited in 1946 at the prestigious A-D Gallery, in a show titled "The Four Veterans." Will Burtin, then art director of *Fortune* magazine, was impressed by what he saw and invited Federico to become his art associate. "I loved Will," recalled Federico, "but I couldn't follow the way he designed. So completely analytical, he could take the most complex subject and then build it into a dramatic structure. It was brilliant, but it wasn't my kind of design."

For a year and a half, Federico and his wife, Helen, who assisted Paul Rand at the Weintraub agency, struggled to make ends meet. Rand suggested that Federico take a job at Grey Advertising, where he met Bill Bernbach, Phyllis Robinson, Ned Doyle, and Bob Gage. His colleagues left in 1949 to open an agency with Mac Dane, called Doyle Dane Bernbach. Three years later, Gage invited Federico to join the new firm, and he was given the *Woman's Day* magazine account. This resulted in a series of ads that revealed Federico's deft picto-typographic sensibility. For Federico, the construction of the typographic image was extremely important. "Lester Beall opened my eyes to the idea that type could be used to emphasize the message," explained Federico. "One of his ads had the great line, 'To hell with eventually. Let's concentrate on now.' The 'e' in 'eventually' was very large and 'now' was the same size. The simple manipulation of these letter forms allowed the viewer to immediately comprehend the message." Federico's method was based on the integration of text and image, so he always worked intimately with a copywriter. He said, "I too look for those simple elements in copy," adding that "if the rhythm of the words is disregarded, the copy is likely to be laid out incorrectly."

Federico's most visible campaign for *Woman's Day* typifies this rhythmic sensitivity, with the catch line "She's got to go out to get Woman's Day," illustrated by a photo of a woman riding a bicycle with wheels made from two lowercase Futura o's in the headline. The aim of this ad was to explain to potential advertisers that more than three million devoted readers physically went to stores to buy this checkout-counter magazine.

Federico's love of and skill with type matured during the midfifties, and he remembered: "It was then that Aaron Burns at the Composing Room introduced me to a range of new typefaces." Burns developed a series of four sixteen-page booklets (written by Percy Seitlin) that allowed designers freedom to interpret a specific subject with type, photography, and illustration. Federico's was called *Love of Apples*. "I wanted to try something where I used metal type in extreme ways without having to cut it—without cutting up proofs or playing with stats," he explained. It was masterpiece of descriptive typography. "For some time, I had known that if you stacked Title Gothics they would have a different look than traditional types. So the whole book was based on that simple idea." But the aesthetics of type were not his only concern: "There's a line that reads 'When we, in business, industrial America began to get smart about apples, we packaged them and packaged them and packaged them until the apple itself became a package.' I illustrated that point with a photograph of an apple with a string tied around it."

After a few years at Benton & Bowles, Federico decided to form a partnership with copywriter Richard Lord and John Southard in 1967. Southard soon left, making it Lord Federico. One day, he ran into Norman Geller, his former classmate and subway companion, who had done quite well with his own agency. Wanting to take on a new challenge, Geller joined the fledgling firm. Soon the name of copywriter Arthur Einstein was added to the shingle. With two writers and two art people as principals, Lord Geller Federico Einstein was built on a solid creative foundation.

Federico retained a mild, self-effacing manner and a palpable concern for good design, but he showed that *passion* was paramount. He also professed that finding the best solution for a client's identity "is not a matter or a means of self-expression." By not underestimating the consumer's intelligence, and by recognizing the constraints of this persuasive art, Federico expanded advertising's boundaries and set its standards. •

391

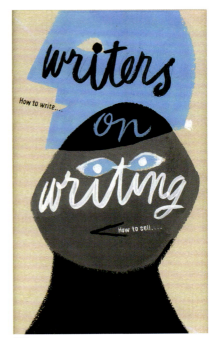

393

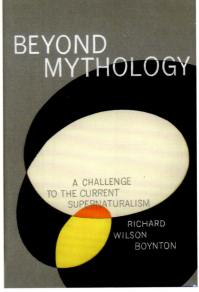

394

392

391
Folder, *Every Season Is a Jo Collins Season . . .* , Jo Collins, c. 1956–58

392
Accordion-fold brochure exterior, *1958 Graphics in Packaging*, a call for entries for the American Institute of Graphic Arts (AIGA), 1958

393
Comp, *Writers on Writing: How to Write . . . , How to Sell . . .* , c. 1950s

394
Comp, *Beyond Mythology: A Challenge to the Current Supernaturalism*, c. 1951

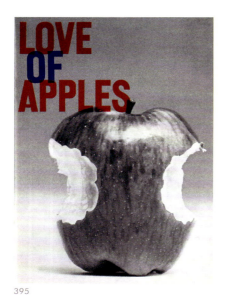

Of course not.
Nothing is.

395

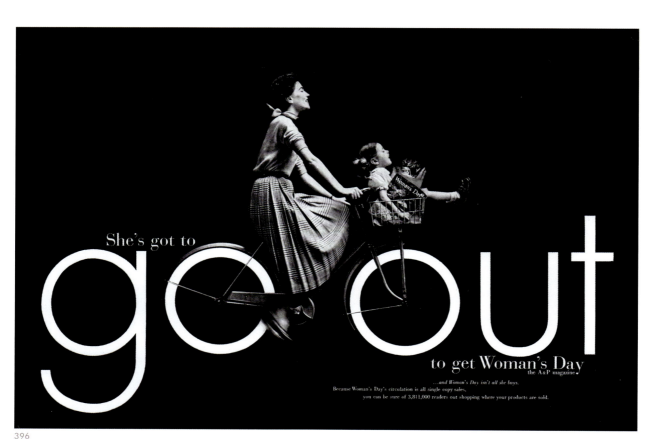

She's got to **go·out** to get Woman's Day
the A&P magazine.

...and Woman's Day isn't all she buys.

Because Woman's Day's circulation is all single copy sales,
you can be sure of 3,811,000 readers out shopping where your products are sold.

396

395
Booklet cover and interior spread, *Love of Apples*, Composing Room, 1960

396
Advertisement, "She's got to go out to get Woman's Day," 1953. A memorable visual pun and typographic solution, made by substituting the wheels of a woman's bicycle with two Futura letter Os.

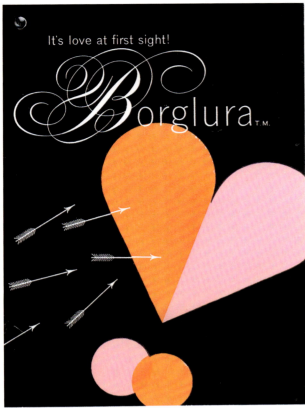

397

399

400

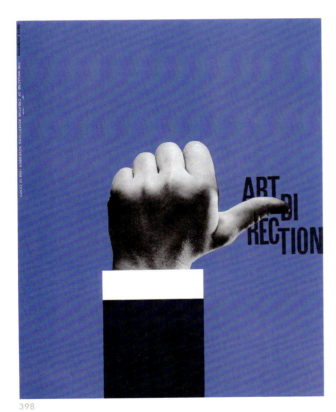

398

401

397
Hangtag, "It's Love at First Sight! Borglura," Borg Textiles, c. 1956

398
Magazine cover, *Art Direction: The Magazine of Creative Advertising*, November 1958. Advertising was traditionally a copywriter's domain. Federico was a key figure in the generation of art directors who made design endemic to the profession.

399
Brochure, *The 1953/1954 Season*, Cinema 16, New York, 1953

400
Brochure. *Now in Its Fifth Year . . . an Invitation to Join Cinema 16*, New York, 1952. A nonprofit film society for the adult moviegoer

401
Card, *Season's Greetings, Lisa, Helen and Gene Federico*, 1956

S. Neil Fujita
1921–2010

Fujita in New York, c. late 1950s

S. Neil Fujita may have been best known for his Columbia Records covers, which introduced abstract art to jazz packaging, and the iconic book jackets for *In Cold Blood* and *The Godfather*, but there was more to his modern portfolio. He was responsible for the *Today* show logo for NBC, the Shubert Organization logo, and the signature typeface for *Billboard* magazine, among a host of other key objects of design.

Sadamitsu Neil Fujita was born in Kauai, Hawaii, and raised on a sugar plantation in Waimea. He moved to Los Angeles when he was seventeen and attended the Chouinard Art Institute. At the outbreak of World War II, Fujita was imprisoned in a U.S. government internment camp in Wyoming; like other interned Japanese Americans, he volunteered for service in the all-Nisei 442nd Regimental Combat Team and fought in Italy and France. He also served with G-2 (Intelligence) as a translator in the Pacific.

Schooled in painting, Fujita moved to New York to find a more sustainable career, ultimately landing a job at N. W. Ayer in Philadelphia through the good offices of Bill Golden, the art director of CBS, who helped to launch many careers. Fujita worked at Ayer for around three years, and while there he won a gold medal from the Art Directors Club for designing an ad for Container Corporation of America. "That must have gotten people talking, because shortly after I left Ayer I got a call from Bill Golden, who says he is recommending me to run the art department at Columbia Records," Fujita recalled. Fujita would be starting from the ground up by building an internal graphic design staff, and he recalled Golden's warning: "'Neil, if you do this, you'll be taking work and income away from the two studios that have been working with us for many years, so you're going to meet up with a lot crap. First of all, you're Japanese and you're going to be called all sorts of names, from Nip to Jap and everything else. Do you still want to do it?'" The answer was a resounding affirmative.

Alex Steinweiss established the concept of album cover art. When Fujita arrived, he recalled that Columbia was doing album covers showing just type, a photo of the artist, and some shapes arranged in an interesting way. "Actually the first examples of album art that I can remember were on children's records, because they might have included a painting or something else to illustrate the idea." He believed that he was the first to use painters, photographers, and illustrators to do artwork on album covers. As head of the art department for Columbia Records, his responsibility involved designing album covers with commissioned artwork by Ben Shahn, Andy Warhol, and Roy DeCarava. His bold typography was Modernist in style, yet not strictly linked to the Swiss Style. He was not dogmatic but appreciated abstraction.

Many of his covers were for jazz albums, and Fujita noted that jazz called for abstraction, a certain kind of stylization using modern painters. Classical was different: He used more photography, hiring a photographer such as Dan Weiner and sending him to a Glenn Gould recording session, "because it was in the sessions that you could really catch the raw spirit of the performance," he said. Leonard Bernstein was going to do a jazz recording, and Fujita told him that "since we're doing a jazz album, don't be afraid to dress casually, even in a T-shirt." Bernstein replied, "'I'm not afraid of anything!'" It was not modern painting, but it was a modern approach. Fujita used his own abstract paintings as covers for the Dave Brubeck Quartet's *Time Out* and Charles Mingus's *Mingus Ah Um*.

Fujita left Columbia in 1957, because he wanted to do more than design record covers. He told the head of Columbia, Goddard Lieberson, "If I could sing or play the piano or any instrument, I might consider staying." Fujita recalled that "the New York designers' clique at the time spread the rumor that I had been canned, but that wasn't true." He opened a studio and was on his own for less than a year when Lieberson asked him to return temporarily; the art director who had replaced him was not working out. "This time the New York designers' clique took a different approach," he noted bitterly. "They spread the rumor that I was responsible for canning the guy that replaced me, which again wasn't true."

Fujita soon turned his attention to book jackets. He was not hamstrung by marketing people making suggestions, "but I did do a lot of reading," he said, adding, "I liked working with authors because it's usually the author that sells the book." That is why he always wanted to have the author's name as big as the title. One of his best known was Truman Capote's *In Cold Blood*, with a red hatpin stuck into the title to suggest death. According to Fujita, when Capote saw it, he said, "'It can't be red, because it wasn't a new death, it didn't just happen,' so I changed the color to purple and added a black border to suggest something more funereal. Capote loved that."

One of his most visible designs was the book jacket for *The Godfather*, for Putnam in 1969. By taking the G and extending it to the D, he created a house for God. When the first *Godfather* film opened in New York, Fujita saw a huge billboard going up in Times Square with his design on it. "I actually got them to stop work on it until we were able to come to an agreement," he said. •

402

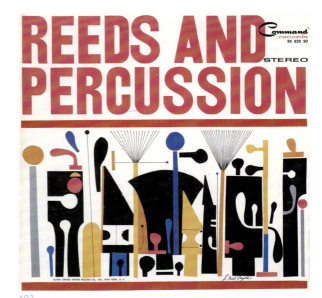

403

404

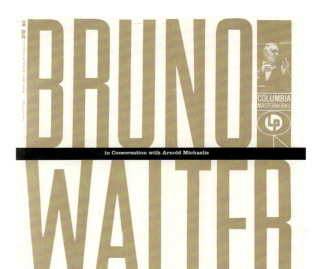

405

406

402

Album cover, *Tempestuous Trumpet* by Doc Severinsen and His Orchestra, Grand Award Record Company, New York, 1961

403

Album cover, *Reeds and Percussion* by The Command All-Stars, Grand Award Record Company, New York, 1961. When Fujita designed album covers, the field was suffering from too many cooks in the kitchen. He had vision, and it included making certain that art tells a musical story.

404

Album cover, *Billy Rowland Plays Boogie Woogie* by Billy Rowland, Grand Award Record Company, New York, 1961

405

Album cover, *Bruno Walter in Conversation with Arnold Michaelis* by Bruno Walter, Columbia Records, 1957

406

Album cover, *Ricardo Juarez and His Orchestra Play Happy Time Cha Chas* by Ricardo Juarez and His Orchestra, Grand Award Record Company, New York, 1960

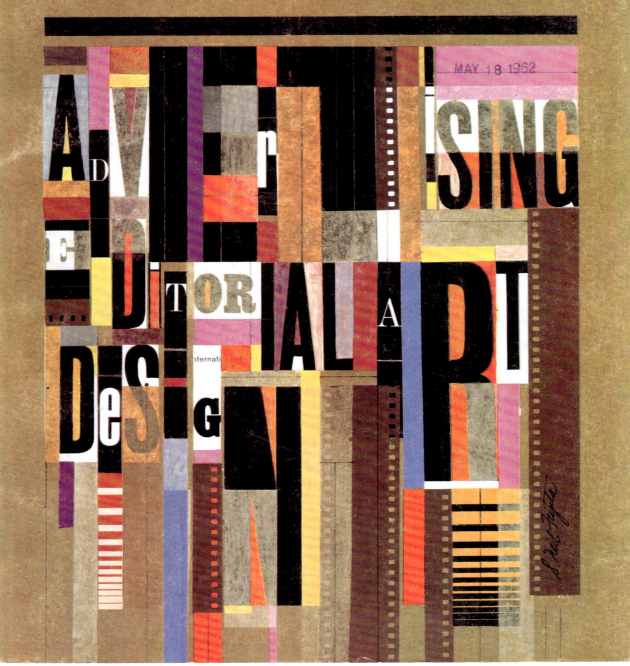

407

407
Magazine cover, CA: The Journal of Commercial Art, Coyne & Blanchard, Palo Alto, California, April 1962. Dominant vertical and horizontal rectangles are juxtaposed to create a mixed collage of color, pattern, and texture. The blended letters read "Advertising Editorial Art Design."

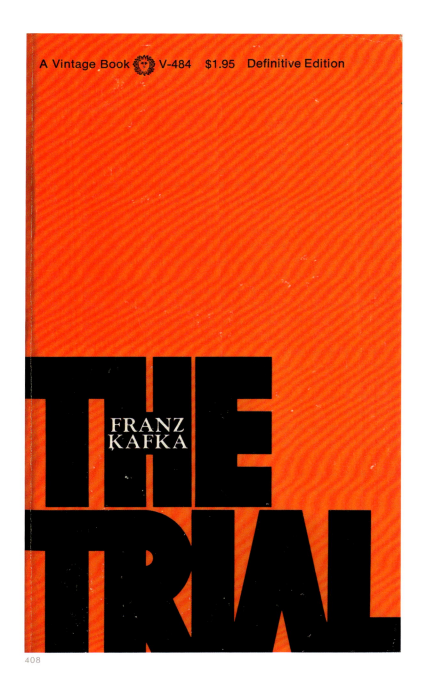

408

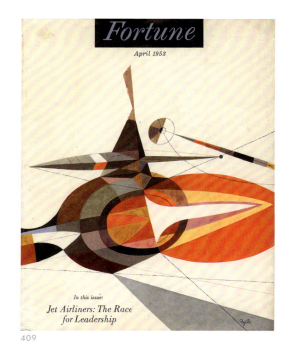

409

410

411

408
Book cover, *The Trial*, by Franz Kafka,
Vintage Books, Knopf, 1969

409
Magazine cover, *Fortune*, "Jet Airliners:
The Race for Leadership," April 1953

410
Magazine cover, *Modern Packaging*,
"Encyclopedia Issue," 1961

411
Logo, Modern Library, c. 1964

William Golden

1911–1959

Golden, c. 1958

Paging through the eye-boggling typography and advertisements reproduced in a long-out-of-print black-and-white monograph titled *The Visual Craft of William Golden*, published in 1962, reveals what television promotion was like before the age of flying logos and computer special effects. TV relied on print for promotion, and William Golden, who had been art director of the Columbia Broadcasting System since its radio days, oversaw the most exquisitely conceived and produced promotional advertising and visual identity of the three major American networks. He gave the network its graphic intelligence, panache, and, most important, the CBS Eye, which is as modern today as when it was introduced on November 19, 1951, overlaid on a photograph of a cloud-filled sky.

The logo was not just a mark of distinction; it symbolized the strength of all things ocular, or as Will Burtin wrote in *The Visual Craft*: "His designs hit the bull's eye of a target with that deceptive ease which only the strong can command."

Bill Golden was a corporate design czar, the archetypal master of a craft in which art solved design problems on a daily—almost hourly—basis for the largest-growing mass-communications medium of its time. Yet who could have predicted where the youngest of twelve children, born on Manhattan's Lower East Side, would end up? Golden did not go to prestigious art or design schools; his formal education began and ended at New York's Vocational School for Boys, where children of immigrant parents learned to earn their living, in this case photoengraving and commercial art.

Golden's earliest jobs were working in Los Angeles printing plants and then designing newspaper ads for the *Los Angeles Examiner*. Tiring of that city, he returned home to join the *New York Journal-American* promotion department, but his professional biography took a sharp turn when Condé Nast art director Dr. Mehemed Fehmy Agha—discoverer of talent and purveyor of innovation—hired Golden to design pages for *House & Garden*. Golden did so well that he was wooed over to CBS, where in 1940 he was appointed art director. In 1942, he married a fellow Agha protégé, Cipe Pineles, and the same year he took a leave of absence from CBS to work in the U.S. Office of War Information. Soon after, he joined the U.S. Army's Education and Information Division, as art director on training manuals. He returned to CBS in 1946 and became creative director of advertising and sales promotion five years later.

Golden was one of modern graphic and advertising design's most catalytic forces. The list of designers, photographers, and illustrators represented in *The Visual Craft* is a who's who of contemporary moderns (including Rudi Bass, Leo Lionni, George Lois, Ben Shahn, and Kurt Weihs). "His influence reached out to creative forces in graphics everywhere," Frank Stanton, president of CBS, wrote in *The Visual Craft*, "bringing them into new fields and, even more important, giving them new standards of excellence." Underscoring Stanton's words is the fact that a great designer or art director is measured not solely by the actual printed work but also by the ability to mentor and motivate others. Burtin wrote, "He distrusts a formula and respects only unreserved attention to a task, in which no detail is small or without significance."

The "Golden Rule" of CBS design was best stated in remarks he made in *Typography—U.S.A.*, the proceedings of the 1959 Type Directors Club conference: "It is sometimes frustrating to find," Golden wrote, "that hardly anyone knows that it is a very complicated job to produce something simple." This explains, to some extent, the work he brought to life. Visual nuance captured his audience, and he believed that modern design was possible because "more and more typography was designed on a layout pad rather than in metal. . . . The designer was able to bring a whole new background and a new set of influences to the printed page."

Golden's standing in the top ranks of art direction was founded on his thorough (and self-taught) understanding of how typography and art functioned in the modern world. In his talk before the Type Directors Club, he credited newspapers, magazines, and journalism with influencing typography: "Everyone knew instinctively what the journalists had reduced to a formula: that if you read a headline, a picture, and the first three paragraphs of any story you would know all the essential facts." It is clear that Golden embraced this kind of journalistic brevity and was opposed to what he called "the immature avant-garde designer" who hates the "hard-sell." He admonished, "Design for print is not Art. At best it is a highly skilled craft. A sensitive, inventive, interpretive craft."

Golden knew how to reach an audience. He was keenly aware that a corporation had to take ownership of its production in an honest and straightforward way. Before the "branding age," Golden understood, "A trademark does not in itself constitute a corporate image," as he wrote in *Print* magazine in June 1959. Nonetheless, the "service mark" that he designed for CBS is one of the most positively recognized of the world's graphic icons. So modern is it in its rendering, and so pristine in its representation, that this "symbol in motion" consisting of "several concentric 'eyes'" would by itself have made William Golden the master of his world. But as the artist Ben Shahn wrote, unlike so many other "publicity people," Golden was "incapable of cynicism toward the public. . . . His life-work was to bring something of highest quality into the public ken, to elevate public standards, never to be guilty of depressing them." •

412

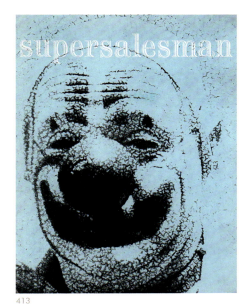

413

414

415

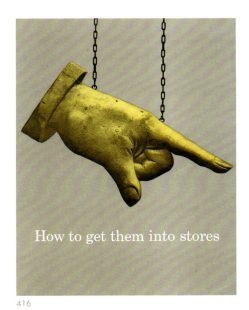

416

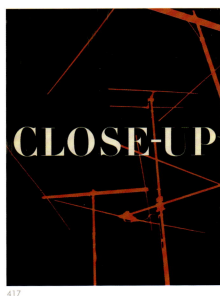

417

WILLIAM GOLDEN

412
Folded brochure cover, *The Empty Studio . . .*, Columbia Broadcasting System, 1948. Illustration: Ben Shahn

413
Folded brochure cover, *Supersalesman*, CBS Television Network, 1954. Photo: Don Briggs

414
Folded brochure cover, *The Pattern That Killed a Myth*, CBS Television Network, 1952. "Americans continue to find television as irresistible as easy money, as compelling as a thunderstorm. And the pattern of their devotion is as plain as the forest on the rooftops." Art: Robert Cato

415
Folded brochure cover, *The Orange Bowl Game*, CBS Television Network, 1947

416
Folded brochure cover, *How to Get Them into Stores*, CBS Television Network, 1950. "Of all the devices men have used to tell people what they have to sell, the most effective is the microphone." Photo: Ben Rose

417
Book cover, *Close-Up: A Picture of the Men and Methods That Make CBS Television*, Columbia Broadcasting System, 1949. Design associate: Mort Rubenstein

418
Booklet cover, *Eye Opener: CBS Television Program Promotion 1953–54*, CBS Television, 1954. Design: Kurt Weihs

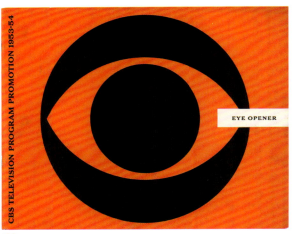

418

Morton Goldsholl
1911–1995

Goldsholl in his Northfield, Illinois, office, c. 1961

"There are many opinions about what design is and what design is not," declared Chicago designer Morton Goldsholl. "One thing for sure, meaning must be the measure of design." His contributions, as founder of Goldsholl Associates, are best represented by his commercial and industrial corporate identity programs, packaging designs, innovative experimental films and animations, and implementation of ethical industry practices and progressive hiring policies.

Born in Chicago, Goldsholl attended Carter H. Harrison Technical High School. From an early age, he had an affinity for drawing and an aspiration to become a painter. He regularly visited galleries at the Art Institute of Chicago and attended art classes at night. Throughout the Great Depression, he worked at various commercial art studios, including a paper-box manufacturer where he met his future wife, Mildred "Millie" Monat (1920–2012). It was here that, he said, "the Matisse, Renoir, Picasso world was soon forgotten for safe advertising art—for retouching, mat books, layouts, typesetting, engraving, and printing."

In 1939, Goldsholl and Millie took evening classes with László Moholy-Nagy and György Kepes at the Chicago School of Design (later, the Institute of Design). Moholy-Nagy, Goldsholl said, "changed my life, completely and totally . . . a man who was so vivid, so inspiring, so completely involved with the people that he touched. He was so completely warm and friendly, [yet] he could be as hard as nails, if he came on a problem that he felt was not solved in the very best way. He would walk into a class and he would find all of the things in a project that was being worked on that were not right and then he turned around and he found all the things that were right. He never left you feeling disappointed or insecure or without some sense of satisfaction in the work that you had done. He did this to everyone."

Each weekend, Moholy-Nagy would host film festivals where artists such as Fernand Léger, Luis Buñuel, and Salvador Dalí presented experimental films. "Film is the art of this century, it incorporates light, color, sound and image, writing, music," Goldsholl recalled Moholy-Nagy saying. Exposure to experimental film and photography helped bring an awareness of the technical, aesthetic, and social aspects of a project into his and Millie's own work and studio.

Goldsholl continued his day job, while Millie enrolled full-time in the architecture program, graduating in 1945. Millie was a filmmaker, designer, director, producer, and editor in her own right. She also designed their modern home and design studio. "It is better to be Utopic than myopic," she said. "It's not so much a matter of thinking big as thinking deep," she added. "We'd rather make films that have guts than gimmicks—and we don't equate gimmicks with honest experimentation and unorthodox techniques. Serendipity is something we are committed to."

In 1941, after finishing his studies, Goldsholl opened an office that offered graphic design, packaging, display, color consultation, and typography services. He was rewarded with a series of important design projects, including direct mail booklets for Egbert Jacobson, director of design for Container Corporation of America. With publisher Paul Theobald, Goldsholl designed *Rebuilding Our Communities* in 1945—the first in a series of books under the editorship of his mentor, Moholy-Nagy, "expounding the basic philosophy and creative approach of the Institute of Design, Chicago." Goldsholl's black-and-yellow covers are a synthesis of form and function, expressing Bauhausian ideals and European avant-garde aesthetics. An aerial view of new suburban sprawl on the cover represents Chicago's postwar building boom; this is juxtaposed against a torn image of a traditional house on the back cover. He also designed books and dust jackets by Jacobson, *Basic Color* (1948) and *Seven Designers Look at Trademark Design* (1952). For *Basic Color*, an interpretation of the Wilhelm Ostwald color system, Goldsholl presented the complex subject matter in a carefully planned, simplified and practical presentation.

In 1950, Robert Leslie invited Goldsholl to exhibit his work at the A-D Gallery, at the Composing Room in New York. Leslie "was, more than anyone, able to lift my sense of worth about my own work," Goldsholl recalled in *Inside Design, A Review: 40 Years of Work*. In 1950, he designed the iconic Good Design logo to represent a series of public exhibitions showing "the best new examples in modern design home furnishings," organized by Edgar Kaufmann Jr. for the Museum of Modern Art, New York, and the Merchandise Mart, Chicago.

In 1955, the Goldsholls expanded their design studio, opening Morton Goldsholl Design Associates. By this time, their client list included the Martin-Senour Company, the International Minerals and Chemical Corporation, Motorola, Abbott Laboratories, the Art Institute of Chicago, and the Society of Typographic Arts. In the late fifties, the Goldsholls broadened their scope by adding film to their list of design services, with a change in the name of the company to Goldsholl Design & Film Associates. Millie designed their new office facilities, which were equipped for filming, recording, and editing.

Goldsholl managed the graphic design services while Mille headed the film department, and the studio grew to thirty employees. Known for progressive hiring policies, the studio was one of the first in Chicago to hire minorities and women. Thomas Miller, an African American designer who worked with Goldsholl for thirty-five years, recalled a discussion about why Goldsholl hired him as a designer: "He said that he wasn't hiring me because I was black and he felt sorry for me. He said he was hiring me because he needed a designer. That turned a corner for me."

For Goldsholl, design meant more than winning awards, and a firm was more than its balance sheet; he believed that design should be evaluated by "how important it was in the world," and "what did it do for people." Design that served the public good was important. But, he said, "Write, draw, paint, design, film, compose, play. Do it your own way. Do it for others and for yourself. But do it." After forty years, the Goldsholls closed the office—but left a legacy. •

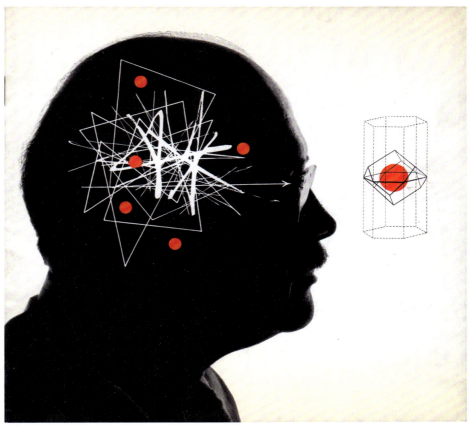

419

420

419
Exhibition keepsake cover, "The directors of A-D Gallery are pleased to present an exhibition of the work of Morton Goldsholl, designer, from February 7 to March 31, 1950 at A-D Gallery, Room 309, 130 West 46th Street, New York. Mondays through Fridays from 10:00 A.M. to 5:30 P.M." Sponsored by the Composing Room, with an introduction by Egbert Jacobson and exhibition execution by Millie Goldsholl and David Foster

420
Booklet cover and logo, *Good Design*, Museum of Modern Art, New York, 1953. Originating in January 1950, "Good Design" was a series of exhibitions of home furnishings, organized by Edgar Kaufmann Jr. (director, Good Design) from the Museum of Modern Art, New York, for the Merchandise Mart, Chicago. Furniture, floor and wall coverings, fabrics, lamps, tableware, appliances, and more were selected for their appearance, function, construction, and price.

421

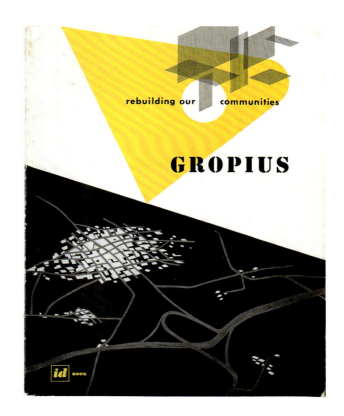

422

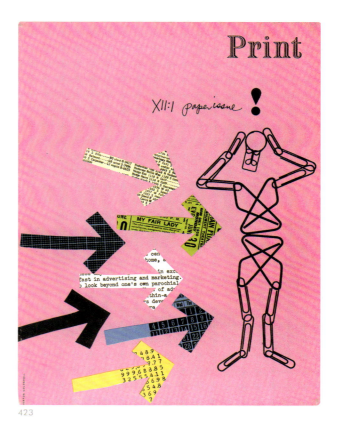

423

421
Back and front covers, *Rebuilding Our Communities*, by Walter Gropius with introduction by László Moholy-Nagy, Institute of Design Book, Paul Theobald, Chicago, 1945

422
Book cover, *Abstract and Surrealist American Art*, by Frederick A. Sweet and Katherine Kuh Sweet, Art Institute of Chicago, 1947

423
Magazine cover, *Print*, "Paper Issue," June-August 1958

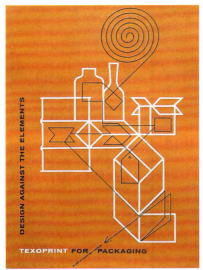

424

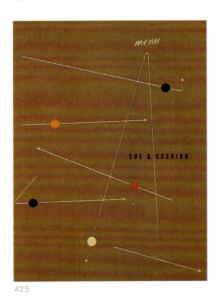

425

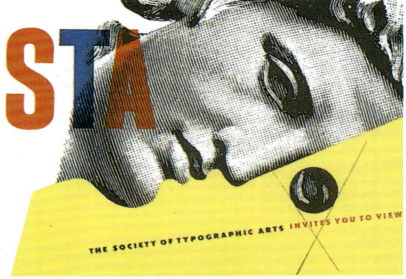

426

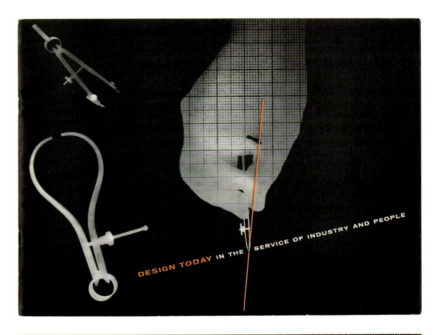

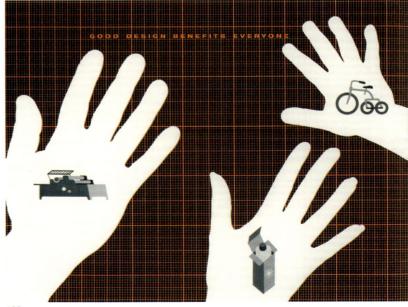

427

424
Sales sheet, "Design Against the Elements,"
Texoprint for Packaging, Kimberly-Clark,
c. 1959

425
Menu cover, *Cue & Cushion*, bowling alley,
Brunswick-Balke-Collender Company,
Springfield, Illinois, 1955

426
Exhibition invitation cover, "The Society of
Typographic Arts [STA] Invites You to View
the Twenty First Annual Exhibition of Design
in Chicago Printing as Selected by the
Society of Typographic Arts," 1948

427
Booklet cover and interior spread, *Design
Today in the Service of Industry and People*,
Institute of Design of the Illinois Institute of
Technology, c. 1954

Charles Goslin

1932–2007

Goslin in his Brooklyn, New York, home office, c. 1960s

In an article by former student Scott W. Santoro, Charles Goslin insisted that he "never bought into the 'less is more' Helvetica approach." Instead, his eclectic Modernism was a mix of individual expression and playful order that contrasted with Swiss austerity and the International Typographic Style prevalent in sixties New York. His work was a confident confluence of bold color, abstract shapes, and simplified symbols—conceptually clear and intriguing. "Visualizing ideas is the most important thing we do as graphic designers," he told Susan E. Davis in *Step-by-Step Graphics* magazine. "Without an idea, you've said nothing. But it's also not just expressing an idea. It's making a graceful idea, a beautiful idea."

Born in Attleboro, Massachusetts, Goslin graduated from the Rhode Island School of Design with a BFA in graphic design in 1954. His first job, from 1955 to 1958, was an apprenticeship at the Lester Beall Design Group, at Dumbarton Farm in rural Brookfield Center, Connecticut. "The minute I walked into Beall's studio," he told Santoro, "I knew it was the place for me. The studio wasn't decorated with utilitarian color charts or production materials; only framed photographs and paintings, carefully hung alongside choice design projects pinned to the walls. . . . The message was that design not only solved the client's problems, it also nourished the designer creating the work and the audience viewing the work." At Beall's studio, Goslin worked on a range of trademarks and packaging, editorial, and printed projects for International Paper, Labatt's of Canada, the U.S. Post Office Department, Davis & Geck, and one of Beall's landmark identity programs for Connecticut General Life Insurance, for which he drew the now-iconic, stylized, and elongated CG logo, with the G fitting snugly inside the C (see image 257). "The basic objectives were to graphically project the strength of the company," Beall said, "while also implying a feeling of warmth and friendliness and also provid[ing] a symbol that would lend itself to a multiplicity of uses."

From 1958 to 1961, Goslin was a staff designer at Lippincott & Margulies, industrial designers and marketing consultants, where his talent showed brightly through the issues he designed for *Design Sense*, Lippincott's house organ, focusing "on design as it affects marketing, merchandising, package and product planning, research and store planning." His economical cover designs are experiments in clarity using large reductive symbols and striking contrasts to playfully communicate the issue's theme. "Sometimes symbols don't belong together. They don't make any sense at all. However, if you stay at it long enough, you can make things come together aesthetically, he said in *Step-by-Step Graphics* magazine. Furthermore, "I love symbols," Goslin said. "They're the distillation of so much, and they need to work at the most basic level, which is black and white."

Preferring to work at home, Goslin opened his solo, independent practice in 1962 from a brownstone in Park Slope, Brooklyn. He remained a wide-ranging generalist who enthusiastically designed everything from symbols to printed collateral to record covers and book jackets. "I wanted to feel projects with my hands, and when they went out of my studio, I wanted them to have my signature, nobody else's," he told Davis.

Goslin worked for a variety of clients, ranging from small, independent businesses to such large companies as Abbott Laboratories, IBM, Columbia and Decca Records, Pfizer, RCA, Chase Manhattan Bank, the *New York Times*, *Harper's* magazine, to publishers such as American Heritage, Random House, Harper & Row, Atheneum, and Dutton. His covers for *Bedside Nurse: Official Journal of the National Federation of Licensed Practical Nurses* gave such an otherwise narrow theme compelling universality and exemplified his friendly tones. As consultant art director for *AORN Journal: Official Publication of the Association of Operating Room Nurses* his covers were controlled and functional, and illustrated complicated medical information with ease and style. It was a design philosophy rooted in economy. "I hate excess. It's vulgar. I'm a practical man. I love economy in all things," Goslin attested in *Graphis* magazine.

Goslin also had a strong reputation as a loyal and well-regarded teacher for nearly forty years. "The person who believes that applied art, commonly called commercial art, can rise only so far, and is intrinsically inferior to so-called fine art, is an uncomprehending figure." He first became a professor of graphic design and illustration at Pratt Institute's Brooklyn campus and later taught graphic design as continuing education at the School of Visual Arts, from about 1975 to 1985. In his teaching, he communicated deep convictions: "Push yourself to grow. If you're working, you're going to get better. . . . When you're climbing a hill with a rock on your back and it seems like you are never going to get anywhere, you're investing. You're building to something and then you harvest." •

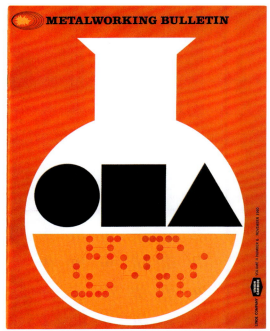

429

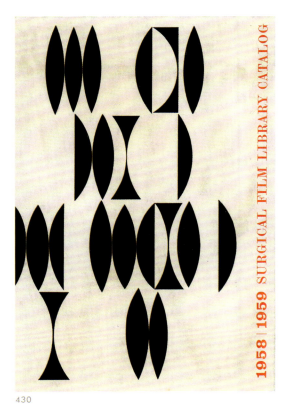

430

428

428
Cover, *Metalworking Bulletin*, Linde Company, Union Carbide Corporation, vol. 2, no. 6 (November 1960)

429
Catalog cover, *Surgical Film Library Catalog*, 1958/1959. Designed at Lester Beall Design Group

430
House organ cover, *ORS: For the Operating Room Supervisor and Nurse*, Surgical Products Division, American Cyanamid Company, Davis & Geck, no. 30, June 1957. Designed at Lester Beall Design Group

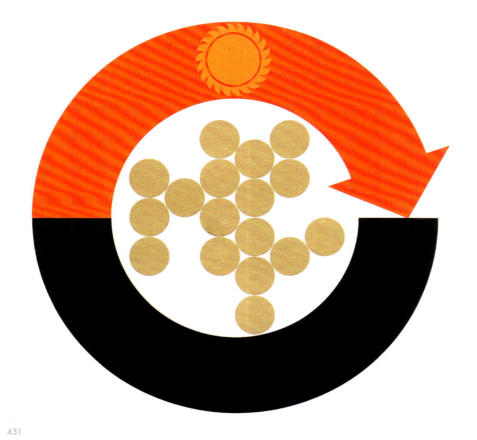

431
Promotional material, *Same Day Loan Service*, Chase Manhattan Bank, c. early 1960s

432
Journal cover, *Bedside Nurse: Official Journal of the National Federation of Licensed Practical Nurses*, May–June 1968. The cover graphically depicts the basic equipment of every bedside nurse including: bandage scissors, fountain pen, wristwatch, and the symbolic heart worn on the sleeve.

433
Journal cover, *Bedside Nurse: Official Journal of the National Federation of Licensed Practical Nurses*, January–February 1969

434

435

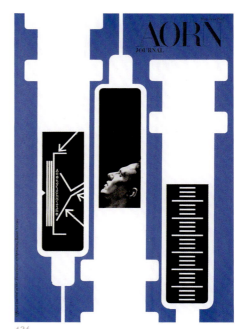

436

437

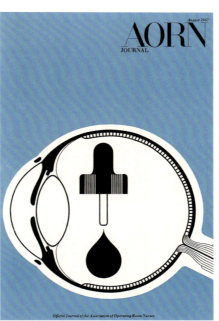

438

434
Journal cover, *AORN Journal: Official Journal of the Association of Operating Room Nurses*, January–February 1963. Illustrating an article on the surgical treatment of chronic sinusitis

435
Journal cover, *AORN Journal: Official Journal of the Association of Operating Room Nurses*, March–April 1965

436
Journal cover, *AORN Journal: Official Journal of the Association of Operating Room Nurses*, May–June 1965

437
Journal cover, *AORN Journal: Official Journal of the Association of Operating Room Nurses*, February 1967. Illustrating an article on total laryngectomy

438
Journal cover, *AORN Journal: Official Journal of the Association of Operating Room Nurses*, August 1967

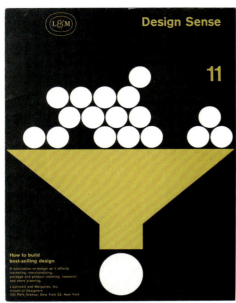

439

440

441

442

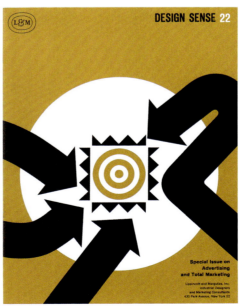

443

444

439–445

House organ covers, *Design Sense*, nos.
11, 13, 16, and 20–22, Lippincott and
Margulies, Industrial Designers, New York,
c. 1958–1961. A house organ on design
as it affects marketing, merchandising,
package and product planning, research,
and store planning

Design Sense

12

How much is
good design worth?

A publication on design as it affects
marketing, merchandising,
package and product planning, research
and store planning.

Lippincott and Margulies, Inc.
Industrial Designers
430 Park Avenue, New York 22, N.Y.

CHARLES GOSLIN

Irving Harper

1916–2015

Irving portrait (perhaps a passport photo), c. 1950s

Irving Harper was best known as design director for George Nelson & Associates from 1947 to 1963; he was associated with the studio's most notable furniture, industrial, exhibition, and graphic projects. Although never formally trained as a graphic designer, Harper crafted a uniquely American graphic approach for advertising, promotion, and identity, principally for the Herman Miller Furniture Company. He borrowed forms developed from modern furniture and architecture and reworked them into his graphic communications as abstract, organic, and compositional elements. His distinct aesthetic spirit was characterized by spatial harmonies, perspective, transparency, texture, contrast, saturated color, and collage, all with minimal typography.

Irving Hoffzimer, who changed his name to Harper in 1939, was born to Jewish immigrant parents in the tenements of New York's Lower East Side. From 1932 to 1937, he attended Brooklyn College and evening classes at the Cooper Union for the Advancement of Science and Art, where he studied architecture. After graduating, he was hired by the architect and industrial designer Morris B. Sanders to work on displays for the Arkansas Pavilion at the 1939–40 New York World's Fair. Shortly after, he became a draftsman for the industrial designer Gilbert Rohde and contributed to exhibits that Rohde designed for the fair. Architectural jobs were at a premium, and these experiences swayed his decision to focus on graphic and industrial design.

During World War II, Harper served in both the U.S. Army Corps of Engineers and the U.S. Navy. Following the war, he went to work at the New York office of industrial designer Raymond Loewy, designing department store interiors. Working with Loewy was a valuable experience, but being hired to design graphics for Herman Miller under George Nelson, the industrial designer, writer, educator, and a leader of the American Modernist movement, was a lifelong career move.

Nelson, who had just opened a small office in the Empire State Building, was on the verge of starting George Nelson & Associates and had been recently hired by D. J. De Pree, president of Herman Miller, to design a line of furniture. His earliest collaborator was Ernest Farmer, a German émigré cabinetmaker and former Gilbert Rohde associate, who had also worked with Harper. It was Farmer who persuaded Nelson to hire Harper as the graphic designer for the Miller project; Nelson had said he wanted a designer and typographer comparable to Paul Rand. In an interview by Paul Makovsky in *Metropolis*, Harper recalled how he was given that mantle and offered the job: "One day after work George Nelson showed up in the drafting room [at Loewy Associates] with his only employee at the time, my close friend Ernest Farmer. We went down to a local coffee shop, and George told me that he was going to form an office and asked if I would be willing to quit my Loewy job and join him. I jumped at the chance. At the time, George had only the Herman Miller account, and he needed somebody to do graphics for them. I'd mentioned that I had never done graphics but was willing to try. What

the hell? I turned out the first ad for Herman Miller and designed the logo that became their trademark. I did one ad a month for years."

His most influential graphic work for Herman Miller started in 1947, with what Harper admitted was "probably the cheapest logo campaign in advertising history." The stylized, abstract M trademark that he designed was "made with a French curve. The top was done with one part of the French curve, the bottom with another part. Two straight lines and that was it," recalled Harper to Julie Lasky. This visual device and signature is an early example of a versatile American identity program loosely developed across all of a company's collateral—stationery, forms, mailing and furniture labels, advertisements, brochures, books, promotional materials, and more.

In 1953, Harper hired George Tscherny as his assistant, and Tscherny eventually assumed the graphic and advertising responsibilities for Herman Miller. Tscherny was later replaced first by Don Ervin and ultimately, in 1963, by Tomoko Miho. Harper moved on to design an important Nelson project for the Chrysler Corporation's imaginative pavilion at the 1964–65 New York World's Fair: "a wonderful project . . . that almost drove [himself] to knit," he told Lasky. During this prolific period of creating graphics, interiors, textiles, and exhibitions, Harper also designed iconic, midcentury furniture and other products for Nelson, including the Marshmallow Sofa, Howard Miller Ball and Sunburst clocks, Schiffer China Shop and Pavement fabrics, Piccard and Walker china, Prolon dinnerware, and numerous end tables, lighting fixtures and lamps, and fireplace accessories.

In 1963, after seventeen years working for George Nelson & Associates, he teamed up with Philip George (a former Nelson associate) and opened Harper & George, a design company well known for its inventive and lively environments for clients such as Jack Lenor Larsen, Continental Airlines, the city of Bangkok, Hallmark Cards, Herman Miller, and Braniff International Airways, for which the company designed airplane interiors and American passenger terminals. Harper retired in 1983.

A solitary man, Harper spent more than forty years of his life coping with the stress of his office job and crafting painstakingly detailed paperboard sculptures, which became his métier during his last years. "He scouted Manhattan art galleries and the Metropolitan Museum of Art for inspiration and fashioned Egyptian cats and stylized antelope heads, Byzantine towers, African masks, a Renaissance Florentine church in relief. He built constructions stacked like molecules, and abstractions that peeled off the picture planes like a grid of flames. He worked in the styles of Surrealism and De Stijl and made study after study of Picasso, the artist he admired above all others," Lasky explained.

However, his graphic and furniture design is what he will be remembered most for. Harper's commitment to total design and eclectic style broadened George Nelson's and Herman Miller's reach and reshaped how the American public interacted with modern design. •

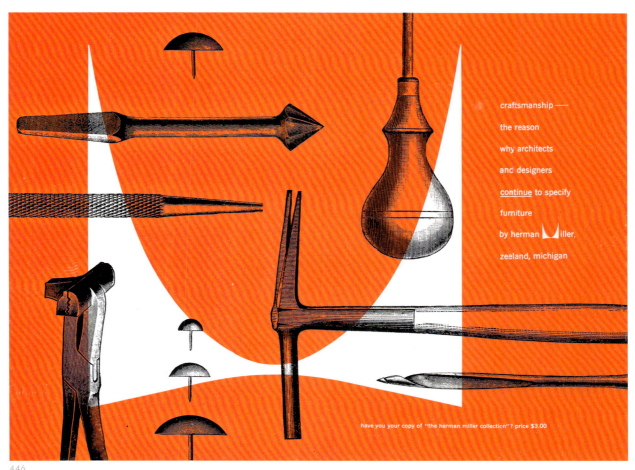

446

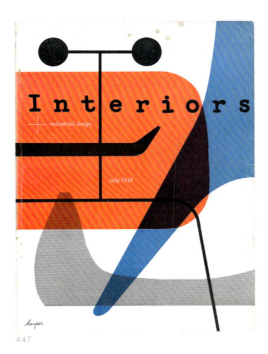

447

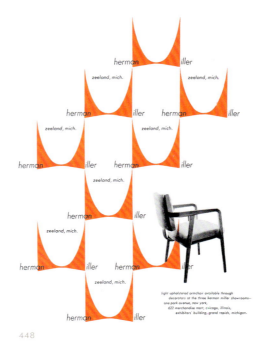

448

446
Advertisement, "Craftsmanship—The
Reason Why Architects and Designers
Continue to Specify Furniture by Herman
Miller," Herman Miller, 1949

447
Magazine cover, *Interiors*, Whitney
Publications, vol. 108, no. 12 (July 1949)

448
Advertisement, "Herman Miller, Zeeland,
Mich.," with multiple logos, Herman Miller,
c. 1950

449

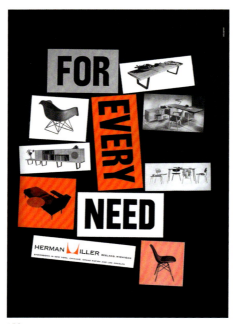

450

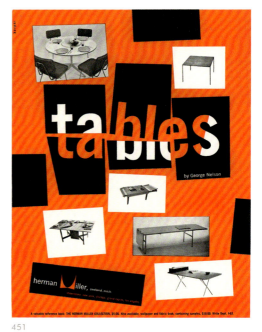

451

452

453

449
Advertisement, "Home Entertainment,"
Herman Miller, 1952

450
Advertisement, "For Every Need," Herman
Miller, 1952

451
Advertisement, "Tables by George Nelson,"
Herman Miller, 1953

452
Advertisement, "Herman Miller's
Comprehensive Storage System," Herman
Miller, 1960

453
Advertisement, "EOG (Executive Office
Group)," Herman Miller, 1951

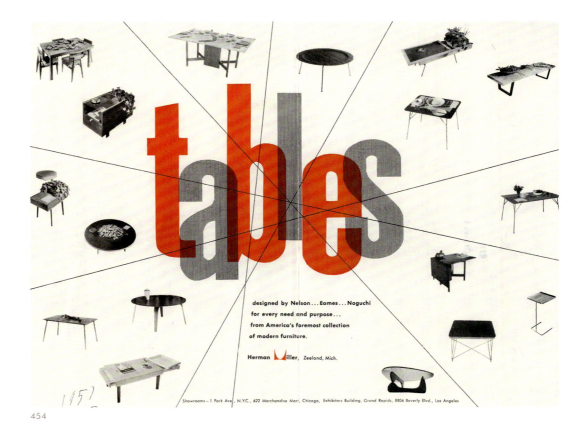

454

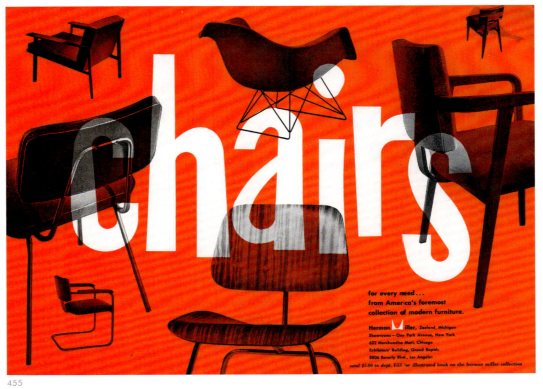

455

454
Advertisement, "Tables Designed by Nelson
. . . Eames . . . Noguchi," Herman Miller,
1951

455
Advertisement, "Chairs for Every Need . . .
from America's Foremost Collection of
Modern Furniture," Herman Miller, 1951

From a collection of new Nelson designs to be shown in April

HERMAN MILLER
Zeeland, Micl

456

456
Advertisement, [Coconut Chair,] "From a Collection of New Nelson Designs to Be Shown in April," Herman Miller, 1956

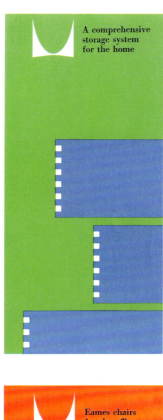

A comprehensive storage system for the home

Steelframe Seating

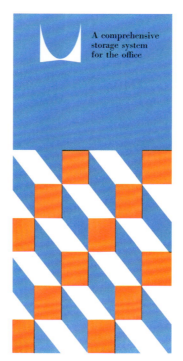

A comprehensive storage system for the office

Eames lounge chair and aluminum group

Eames chairs for the office

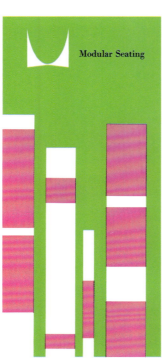

Modular Seating

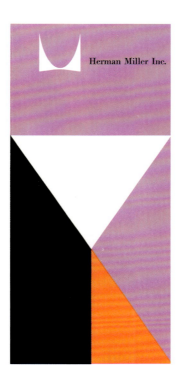

Herman Miller Inc.

Eames chairs for the home

457

457

Trifold product brochures, *A Comprehensive Storage System for the Home, Steelframe Seating, A Comprehensive Storage System for the Office, Eames Lounge Chair and Aluminum Group, Eames Chairs for the* Office, *Modular Seating, Herman Miller, and Eames Chairs for the Home*, 1960. Art direction: Irving Harper with Don Ervin, Tony Zamora, and Dick Schiffer

E. McKnight Kauffer

1890–1954

E. McKnight Kauffer in New York, 1948. Photo: George Platt Lynes

Edward "Ted" McKnight Kauffer was a versatile Montana-born American designer who, during the twenties and thirties, was one of the most influential advertising artists in England. As an expatriate living in London, Kauffer invested advertising art with twentieth-century pizzazz. Unable to fight for Britain during World War II, he returned to New York, where he settled into doing posters, advertisements, textiles, and book covers for many American companies. According to his friend Frank Zachary, America did not trigger the same avant-garde originality from this exemplar of Vorticism and modern art.

Kauffer had gone abroad when Joseph McKnight, a customer at a San Francisco bookstore where he was working, loaned him the money to study in Paris—he appropriated his patron's name in gratitude. He attended the Académie Moderne in Paris and, in Munich, was introduced to Ludwig Hohlwein's poster masterpieces. Before crossing the Atlantic, Kauffer took a detour to Chicago, where he visited the 1913 Armory Show, the exhibition that gave Americans their first exposure to the European avant-garde. Kauffer was perplexed by the works by Picasso, Cézanne, Duchamp, and Matisse on view: "I didn't understand it. But I certainly couldn't dismiss it," he wrote some years later.

The art capitals of Europe beckoned, but clouds of war loomed, and Kauffer earned refugee status. Yet instead of sailing back to America then, he discovered that England had a tranquillity he had not experienced in the States. "I felt at home for the first time," he wrote, and although he volunteered to serve in the British army, his American citizenship made him ineligible. Instead, he volunteered for a variety of menial jobs while waiting for painting commissions.

Through John Hassall, an English poster artist, Kauffer met with Frank Pick, the creative director responsible for the most progressive advertising campaign and corporate identity program in England. Pick had the vision both to unify the London Underground's graphic system and to diversify its publicity, thus making it more efficient and appealing. He commissioned Edward Johnston to design an exclusive sans serif typeface and logo for the Underground; his selection of the finest artists in England to design posters for its stations was foresighted. Kauffer's first Underground posters, produced in late 1915, were landscapes; his subsequent 145 posters, spanning twenty-five years, showed his remarkable turn toward Modernism, and particularly Cubism.

Kauffer was influenced by the machine-worshiping Vorticists, the movement of British Futurists led by Wyndham Lewis. Kauffer's benchmark work, a woodcut of 1916 titled *Flight*, echoed the Vorticists' obsession with speed as a metaphor for the machine age. It was not American, but the image departed just enough from direct quotation of Cubist form to become the basis for a personal visual language. "He had a childlike wonder" for nature and based this image not on imagination but on his firsthand observation of birds in flight, wrote author Mark Haworth-Booth. However, if Kauffer had not submitted it in 1919 to *Colour* magazine, which regularly featured a "Poster Page" in which unpublished maquettes

were reproduced free of charge as an inducement for advertising agents to employ talented poster artists, *Flight* might not have become an icon of modern graphic design. *Flight* was bought by Francis Meynell, a respected English book publisher and printer who organized a poster campaign for the Labour newspaper, the *Daily Herald*, where a version of the image adapted to a poster format was published with the title *Soaring to Success!—The Early Bird*. For Meynell, Kauffer's novel design somehow suggested hope.

Despite an affinity for painting, Kauffer never abandoned his advertising career. He questioned the growing schism between fine and applied art. "He could see no reason for conflict between good art work and good salesmanship," wrote Frank Zachary in the short-lived American design journal *Portfolio* no. 1. Designs incorporating geometric patterns and forms, Kauffer asserted, "can effect a sledge hammer blow if handled by a sensitive designer possessing a knowledge of the action of color on the average man or woman." It was the artist's job to foster an appreciation of diverse visual stimuli that transcended the conventional marketing tricks. His own productivity is evidence that certain businessmen appreciated the power of unconventional form, but even in such a receptive milieu (particularly compared to turgid American advertising), there were hostile critics who referred to Kauffer's abstract designs as "McKnightmares."

Despite the criticism, Kauffer made significant inroads in the applied arts, first in the application of Cubist form, and then, after 1923, using his so-called jazz style. He later introduced Modernist photomontage, influenced by German and Russian advertising of the time; replaced diagonal layouts with rectilinear ones; crushed his type into parallelograms; favored positive/negative lettering; and, most important, took up the airbrush to achieve the streamlined effect that characterized his work of the thirties. Kauffer was further involved with the popular new medium of photomurals, and he developed the "space frame" to give an illusion of multiple vantage points on a single picture plane.

In the Museum of Modern Art's 1937 exhibition catalog on Kauffer's posters, Aldous Huxley wrote: "Most advertising artists spend their time elaborating symbols that stand for something different from the commodity they are advertising. Soap and refrigerators, scent and automobiles, stockings, holiday resorts, sanitary plumbing . . . are advertised by means of representations of young females disporting themselves in opulent surroundings. Sex and money—these would seem to be the two main interests of civilised human beings. . . . McKnight Kauffer prefers the more difficult task of advertising products in terms of forms that are symbolic only of these particular products."

England inspired him; America depressed him—but there were nonetheless great spurts of unbridled energy that gave his multifaceted design work a European flair that American industry desperately needed. •

458

459

460

458–459
Posters, *American Airlines: All Europe* and
American Airlines: To Europe, c. 1946–49

460
Poster, *American Airlines: To Washington,
Night and Day*, c. 1947

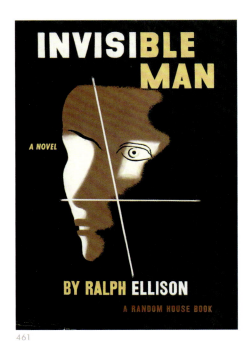

461

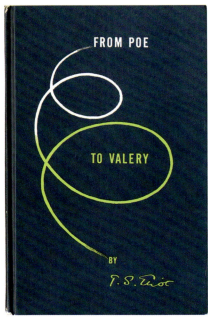

462

463

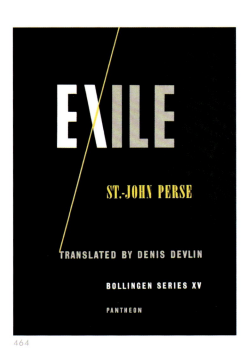

464

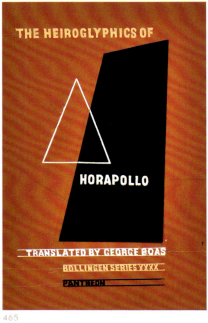

465

461
Book jacket, *Invisible Man*, by Ralph Ellison, Random House, 1952

462
Book cover, *From Poe to Valery*, by T. S. Eliot, Harcourt, Brace, 1948

463
Journal cover, *A-D: An Intimate Journal for Production Managers, Art Directors, and Their Associates* 8, no. 2 (December–January 1941–42)

464
Book jacket, *Exile*, by St.-John Perse, Pantheon Books, 1949

465
Book jacket comp, *The Heiroglyphics of Horapollo*, Bollingen Series 23, Pantheon Books, 1950

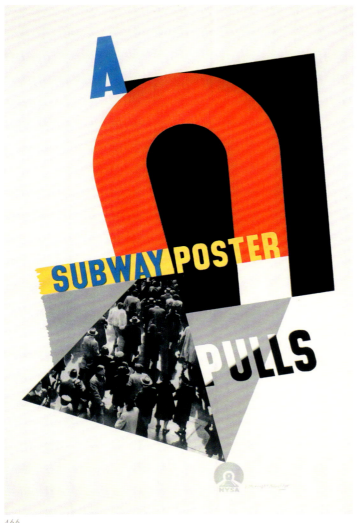

466

467

468

466
Poster, *A Subway Poster Pulls*, Subway
Advertising Company, 1949

467
Point of purchase poster, *Give*, American
Red Cross, 1945

468
Book cover, *Organic Design in Home
Furnishings*, by Eliot F. Noyes, Museum of
Modern Art, New York, 1941

E. MCKNIGHT KAUFFER

Ray Komai
1918–2010

Komai in New York, c. 1944

Ray Komai was known for his iconic plywood chair, tables, upholstered seating, and textile and wallpaper designs. Yet Komai's contributions to the Modernist graphic design landscape were also significant. From the late forties to the early sixties, he ranged from the organic and expressive to the minimal and abstract, while always activating a keen sense of color. His commissions included covers for architectural, craft, and interior design periodicals; exhibition posters; institutional booklets; trade advertising; and, later in his career, book design, as well as exhibitions and supergraphics. Komai's rejection of specialization provided a freshness to his work during a period of American innovation and helped pioneer the transdisciplinary design ethos of today.

Komai was born in Los Angeles. From about 1936 to 1941, he took interior, industrial, and commercial art courses at the Art Center School, founded in 1931. The faculty included Richard Neutra, Frank Lloyd Wright, Kem Weber, R. M. Schindler, and former student Alvin Lustig, who taught master classes. For eight months in 1942, Komai, a Japanese American, was interned at the Manzanar War Relocation Center, California, one of the ten internment camps in the United States during World War II. There he worked in the industrial division, designing children's toys. In 1944, he and his wife, Harumi Kawahara, moved to New York, where Komai pursued a career in advertising design and commercial art.

In 1946, Komai was hired by Irving Miller at CBS and worked "back-to-back in a tiny space" with Lou Dorfsman on illustrations, trade periodicals, advertisements, and brochures. He contributed to CBS projects as late as 1962, under the direction of William Golden and Dorfsman, notably the 1953 CBS Radio promotional kit *Summertime . . . and the Listening Is Easy!*; with illustrations by Joseph Low, a 1952 recording of a CBS Radio special titled *The Nation's Nightmare*, with album cover illustrations by Andy Warhol; and on-air television graphics courtesy of Dorfsman.

Komai opened an office on West Forty-Sixth Street starting in 1948. He shared the space with industrial designer and art director Carter Winter, and occasionally they collaborated on projects. Komai's practice specialized in commercial, exhibition, and furniture design, working for both emerging and established businesses in furniture and industrial design, including J. G. Furniture, Century Lighting, Laverne Originals, L. Anton Maix, and Gotham Lighting, a leading manufacturer of advanced architectural lighting fixtures. He was commissioned by textile producers Erwine and Estelle Laverne (of Laverne Originals), who worked with Alvin Lustig, Paul Rand, and Juliet and György Kepes, to design wallpaper and matching fabrics. In *The Big Catch* (1948), green fish floated in a field of blue behind a black fishing net. *Masks* (1949) was influenced by African archetypes as filtered through modern art. Two of his chairs were selected by the Museum of Modern Art for one of the Good Design award exhibitions that the museum presented with the Chicago Merchandise Mart of Chicago, in 1950. One was the streamlined chair of molded plywood and steel that he became best known for. Its slit seat and hollow-chrome tubular legs gave it a lightness and comfort.

Komai's drawing was looser and more playful than the hard-edged style of the period. Of a line drawing for an *Interiors* magazine cover in May 1948, Komai said, "I just sat down and doodled, developing a favorite scratch pad motif to its logical conclusion." However, a note in the magazine stated, "Nothing could give a more misleading impression about Komai's methods. He is a serious artist who works hard and systematically at industrial and graphic design."

From 1953 to 1961, Komai was an associate art director for *Architectural Forum*. Under the German émigré Modernist architect and photographer Paul Grotz, who served as art director and later managing editor, Komai designed more than thirty covers that offered conceptual takes on the magazine's featured stories. Komai worked with Charlotte Winter (Carter's wife) and later, in 1960, with Peter Bradford, whom he hired and who became a lifelong friend. Even after Komai left the magazine in 1961, Grotz occasionally turned to him to design covers to maintain the magazine's unique look. Komai's cover for a July 1962 special airports issue featured multicolored paper airplanes that Komai hand-folded from airline timetables.

In 1963, through a relationship with Chester Bowles, Komai broke away from the mainstream of commercial design and left the United States for more than twenty years to work for the U.S. Information Agency (USIA), serving in India, Japan, Austria, Germany, the Soviet Union, and Communist bloc countries designing brochures, installations, exhibitions, and supergraphics. He contributed to the government's well-designed mission to promote American values overseas.

In the late sixties, Komai worked on the exhibition designs for the United States Pavilion at Expo '70 in Osaka, Japan. He also overhauled the design of USIA libraries. His library interiors in Osaka "gave it a bright, contemporary uncluttered feeling, conducive to free conversation and communication," said Alan Carter, public affairs officer at the U.S. Embassy in Japan. He further noted, "Komai tore out false ceilings, splashed the empty white walls with huge clean-edged black letters, installed spotlights in the lecture room and controlled selection of every ashtray and pencil holder on the premises. A revolving collection of American prints was hung on the walls. The library's main reading room was sectioned off into thematic areas by white canvas stretched between shiny white tubing." Komai worked closely with Dennis Askey, a Foreign Service officer who created magazines for the USIA, on *Trends*, an upscale monthly Japanese-language magazine featuring modern American art and architecture. After he returned to the United States in 1989, he went on to design books for Harry N. Abrams, including a monograph on Russian émigré designer Alexey Brodovitch for the Masters of American Design series. •

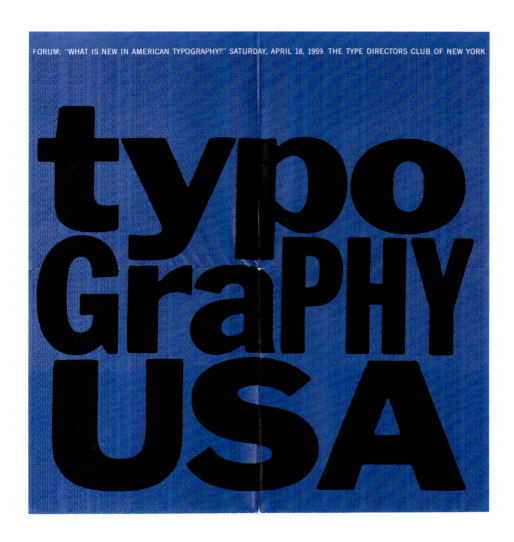

FORUM: "WHAT IS NEW IN AMERICAN TYPOGRAPHY?" SATURDAY, APRIL 18, 1959. THE TYPE DIRECTORS CLUB OF NEW YORK

typoGraPHY USA

470

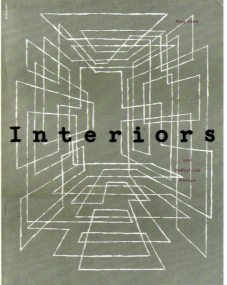

Interiors

RAY KOMAI

471

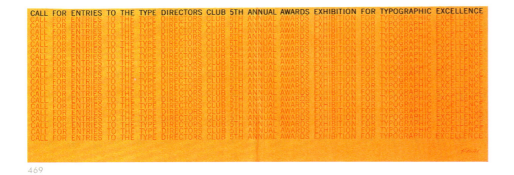

CALL FOR ENTRIES TO THE TYPE DIRECTORS CLUB 5TH ANNUAL AWARDS EXHIBITION FOR TYPOGRAPHIC EXCELLENCE

469

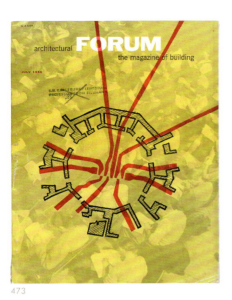

473

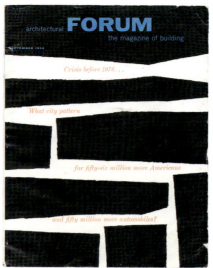

474

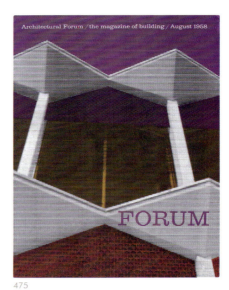

475

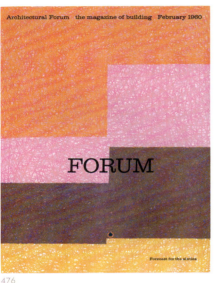

476

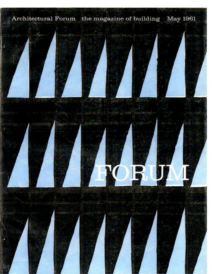

477

478

479

472
Magazine cover, *Architectural Forum*, April 1960. Based on a photograph of the President's Palace in Brasilia designed by architect Oscar Niemeyer.

473–476
Magazine covers, *Architectural Forum*, July 1956, September 1956, August 1958, February 1960

477
Magazine cover, *Architectural Forum*, May 1961. Based on a photograph of the Sacramento Municipal Utility District building and its vertical aluminum louvers.

478
Magazine cover, *Architectural Forum*, January 1961. The abstract design illustrates how transportation is radically changing the character of the suburbs, and how the suburbs, in turn, are radically changing the needs of transportation.

479
Magazine cover, *Architectural Forum*, July 1962. For this airports issue, Komai constructed multicolored paper planes from folded airline timetables.

Burton Kramer

b. 1932

Kramer at his Geigy office, 1960

"To be a Modernist is to not rely on the solutions and stylistic quirkiness of the past, but to become part of creating an idiom of today and tomorrow," said graphic designer Burton Kramer. He added, "Modernism . . . is a way to improve what exists, and to be part of an ongoing process that does not, without understanding, revere or accept what has come before." For the Bronx-born Kramer, Modernism was a design fusion inspired by American boldness and Swiss Style restraint. His more-than-fifty-year career as a designer, educator, and painter took him from New York to Zurich and ultimately to Toronto, where he practiced an uncompromising and functional modern design.

Kramer matriculated in the industrial arts program at the State University of New York at Oswego, where he was introduced to László Moholy-Nagy's *Vision in Motion* and *The New Vision*, the architecture of Frank Lloyd Wright, wood turning by James Prestini, and the wood sculptures of Henry Moore—he even considered a career as a sculptor. Next, he attended Chicago's Institute of Design, with Ivan Chermayeff and Deborah Sussman, where he experimented with etching, lithography, woodcut, and wood sculpture. In 1954, he attended the Yale School of Art and Architecture's graduate program in graphic design, studying with Josef Albers, Alexey Brodovitch, Herbert Matter, Paul Rand, and Bradbury Thompson. After a one-year Fulbright Scholarship at the Royal College of Art in London, he graduated from Yale in 1957 with his MFA in graphic design—his master's thesis tackled the photogram.

At his first job in New York, at the Will Burtin office, Kramer worked with Betty Broadwater, George Klauber, and Swiss graphic designer Yves Zimmermann on projects for IBM and the U.S. Information Agency. For the Upjohn Company, Burtin's most significant client, he helped develop large-scale models for the 1958 exhibition "The Cell." After his work with Burtin, Mildred Schmertz, his classmate at Yale, brought him to *Architectural Record* magazine, where he prepared camera-ready art, worked on the layout, and designed a few covers. He designed *Infinity* magazine for the American Society of Magazine Photographers, and in 1959 he worked briefly as assistant art director for the New York Life Insurance Company on a variety of printed collateral.

Kramer's most significant modern work in the United States was done for Geigy Chemical Corporation in Ardsley, New York, in 1960–61. "Geigy was the first opportunity I had to do what I was proud of, and pursue the design direction that interested me," Kramer explained. Geigy art director Jürg Schaub hired Kramer partly due to his experiences with photography, which weighed heavily in his design approach. The Geigy art department in Ardsley included Swiss designers Gottfried Honegger, Markus Low, August Maurer, Fred Troller, Theo Welti, and Yves Zimmermann, as well as American designers Betty Broadwater, Harold Pattek, and Barbara Stauffacher Solomon. The department established a clear, functional visual vocabulary known as the "Geigy style." Kramer worked for the Dyestuffs and Industrial Chemicals divisions, creating trade advertising, sample packaging, traveling exhibitions, and covers and inserts for Geigy's in-house journal *Catalyst*. He experimented with an expressive and less austere approach, following a general design ethos characterized by white space, sans serif type, abstract graphics, intense use of color, photography, visual metaphors, geometric shapes, contrasts, and the support of a grid. It was this Geigy approach to pharmaceutical design that differed from other companies' text-heavy, concept-driven aesthetics.

In 1961, Kramer relocated to Zurich with his Swiss wife, Irène Marguerite Thérèse Mayer, whom he met at Geigy. He became art director at the Erwin Halpern advertising agency in Zurich, where he designed advertisements, packaging, and posters. "I made use of grids," Kramer wrote in *Burton Kramer Identities*, "but never followed one slavishly, discovering that things 'came to life' when a consistent system was suddenly broken." He "came to an interest in multiple or variable grids, which allowed for heightened drama, where required." In Zurich, he was increasingly interested in the optical art of Albers, Franco Grignani, and Victor Vasarely.

In 1965, he was invited by Armin Hofmann to teach at the Allgemeine Gewerbeschule Basel, but he had already accepted a job in Toronto. His American and Swiss Modernist legacy fostered a new Canadian sensibility, also practiced by Stuart Ash, Jacques Charette, Allan Fleming, Fritz Gottschalk, Rolf Harder, and Ernst Roch, among others. As art director for Paul Arthur & Associates, he designed maps, directory systems, pictograms, point-of-sale graphics, and signage for Montreal's Expo 67. By year's end, he became director of corporate design for the Clairtone Sound Corporation and developed a fully integrated identity program.

Kramer ultimately opened Kramer Design Associates in 1967 and offered research-driven design systems, corporate identification programs, and successful logotypes to Canadian companies and cultural institutions. For the Canadian Broadcasting Corporation, one of his most important clients, he developed a striking symbol in which he animated elements of the letter C, for Canada, as the centerpiece of an extensive overall graphic identity program.

Kramer has been recognized as a dedicated educator for twenty-one years at the Ontario College of Art and Design. He became a leader in Canadian corporate identity and research-driven design systems, earning an international reputation built on steadfast principles and consistently high standards. "Graphic design," he said, "is the conscious, intelligent, visible result of addressing and solving a visual problem." •

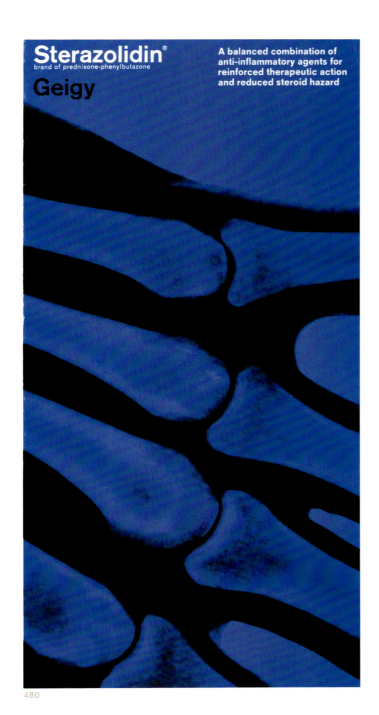

BURTON KRAMER

Brochure covers, *Sterazolidin*, an anti-inflammatory pharmaceutical, Geigy, 1961

481

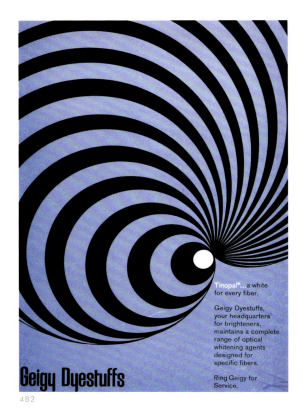

482

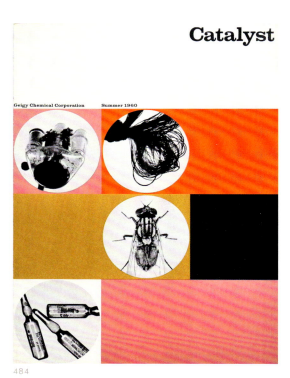

483

484

481
Advertisement, "Automotive Fabric Color Dyes,"
Geigy, 1960

482
Advertisement, "Tinopal," Geigy, 1960

483
Magazine cover, *Catalyst*, Geigy, no. 6, 1960

484
Magazine cover, *Catalyst*, Geigy, Summer 1960

Consult Geigy Research
Development and Technical
Laboratory Service about
your dyestuff problems.

Geigy products are
carried in all important
tanning centers.

Geigy Dyestuffs, Division of Geigy Chemical Corporation
Branches in Charlotte, Chattanooga, Chicago,
Los Angeles, Newton Upper Falls, Mass., Philadelphia,
Portland, Ore., Canada-Toronto.

Geigy Dyestuffs

485

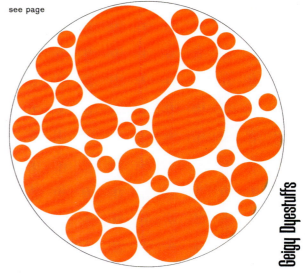

Sequestrene* and Chel*...
names that speak for themselves.

see page

Geigy Dyestuffs

486

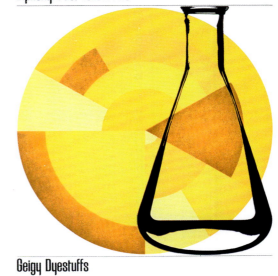

A companion color for Diphenyl Fast Yellow GP, being greener in shade with neutral build-up in depth, a minimum of two-sidedness and easily bleachable.	Suggested for canary shades as a self color or in combinations with Chinoline Yellow P Conc or Auramine 000. For green shades, in combination with Solophenyl Bond Blue 8GP and Solophenyl Turquoise Blue GTL Extra.	Fastness Properties:		May we demonstrate the efficiency of this product of Geigy research and know-how. Ring Geigy for service.
		light	very good	
		alkali	very good	
		acid	excellent	
		bleachability	good	
		appr. sol ozs/gal	4.0	
		affinity for clay	good	

high in quality-low in cost
Diphenyl Fast Yellow P2G

Geigy Dyestuffs

487

BURTON KRAMER

HOMEGROWN

488

Tinuvin P
ultraviolet absorber

**protects
against
ultraviolet
radiation**

Tinuvin P combines superior light, heat
and chemical stability with maximum
ultraviolet absorption without yellowing;
has heat stabilizing properties, too.
Write for sample and new bulletin.

**Geigy Industrial Chemicals
Division of Geigy Chemical Corporation
Ardsley, New York**

for protecting
and formulating:
Polyesters
Polystyrene
Acrylates
Polyvinyl Chloride
Polyvinylidene Chloride
Polyvinyl Butyral
Alkyds
Polyamides
Cellulose Esters
Ethyl Cellulose
Packaging Film
Oil Extended Rubber
Polypropylene
Nitrocellulose
Plastic and
Silicone Coated Glass
Synthetic Fibers
Rayon

Polyethylene
Polyurethanes
Lacquers, Varnishes
Polishes
Paint
Colors
Adhesives
Photographic Materials
Paper, Leather,
Textile Finishes
Sun Screens
Cosmetics
Liquid Detergents
Optical Goods

489

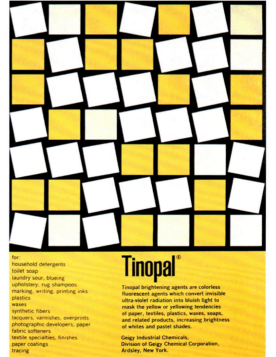

for:
household detergents
toilet soap
laundry sour, blueing
upholstery, rug shampoos
marking, writing, printing inks
plastics
waxes
synthetic fibers
lacquers, varnishes, overprints
photographic developers, paper
fabric softeners
textile specialties, finishes
paper coatings
tracing

Tinopal®

Tinopal brightening agents are colorless
fluorescent agents which convert invisible
ultra-violet radiation into bluish light to
mask the yellow or yellowing tendencies
of paper, textiles, plastics, waxes, soaps,
and related products, increasing brightness
of whites and pastel shades.

Geigy Industrial Chemicals,
Division of Geigy Chemical Corporation,
Ardsley, New York.

490

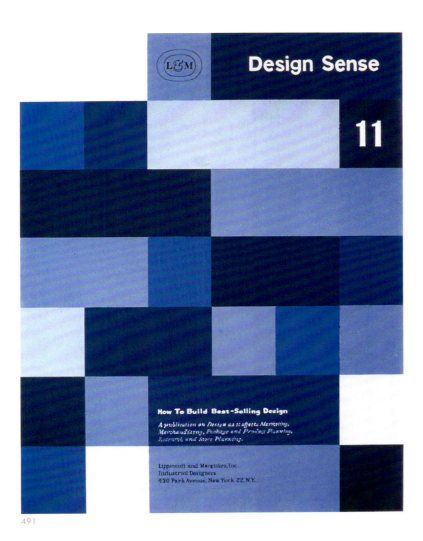

491

492

Roy Kuhlman

1923–2007

Kuhlman in New York, c. late 1950s

Roy Kuhlman's jazzy improvisational paintings and expressive typographic designs for book jackets and covers, mainly for Grove Press throughout the fifties and sixties, injected an Abstract Expressionist's spontaneity into editorial design, altering the conventions, particularly of paperbacks, with "the strong, simple" style influenced by the painter Franz Kline. He further evolved his own array of colorful painted and drawn abstract and geometric forms, which he combined with either crisp Gothic typefaces or roughly sketched letterforms. Although this work echoed the prevailing Modernist methods of Paul Rand and Alvin Lustig, his own minimalist graphic style was distinct. Setting his work apart was a free-form painterly swirl, as well as carefree splotches that gave personality to visual ideas.

He eschewed literal representation because, he modestly opined, he "couldn't really draw well." His random color patterns and amorphous shapes seemed totally independent from the texts they were illustrating. In fact, he admitted to rarely reading the manuscripts for books before designing their covers—yet every one was a provocative, eye-catching mini poster, as book covers and jackets had to draw attention on the shelves.

Robert Alexander Kuhlman, who called himself Roy, was three years old when his family moved from Fort Worth, Texas, to Glendale, California, so his father, a mechanic, could find work. Kuhlman was a so-called blue baby, born with a hole in his heart, and since his treatment required staying indoors for much of his early life, he naturally pursued art. Throughout his years at Glendale High School, he enrolled in adult drawing classes, "doing caricatures of friends, airplanes, Roscoe Turner types, cars, low-slung Model A's." In 1946, he received a scholarship to the Chouinard Art Institute in Los Angeles, and then he moved on to the Art Students League in New York. There, like other designers of his generation, he was drawn to Abstract Expressionism.

Making a living as a painter in New York was not easy, so Kuhlman sought out commercial work, and in 1951 he showed a portfolio to Barney Rosset, the controversial publisher of Grove Press, a small yet daring literary imprint, whose authors included the often-banned Samuel Beckett and Henry Miller. Rosset was looking for a distinctive style to upgrade his lackluster book jackets. Kuhlman's portfolio did not excite him, but by happenstance Rosset glanced at some abstract sketches tucked inside the case that Kuhlman had prepared for his next interview, at a jazz record label. The expressively dissonant abstract designs were exactly what Rosset wanted for a new line of avant-garde literature.

Rosset described Kuhlman's designs as an attempt to "go between being a purely creative act and a commercial one." These included covers for Beckett's *Krapp's Last Tape*, Hubert Selby Jr.'s *Last Exit to Brooklyn*, and Jean Genet's *The Balcony*; for the latter, Kuhlman filled minimalist black brush shapes with bright red and purple. "Kuhlman's work for Grove fell into three main categories: abstract, typographic, and photographic," wrote Steven Brower for an as-yet-unpublished monograph. "Within these, he would experiment and explore, and the categories themselves would

blur and cross. Upon closer examination often his abstract paintings were actually more representational than expected. . . . Likewise the geometric solutions for the myriad psychology texts, one red square among the many black for *The Compulsion to Confess: On the Psychoanalysis of Crime and of Punishment* by Theodor Reik."

Kuhlman used everything, including African patterning, photo collage, photograms, vintage engravings, stats, stencils, hole punches, halftone sheets, cut paper, and wood type. Kuhlman experimented with photographic techniques, including photograms, à la Man Ray. He combined these and other photos with painting elements to achieve layers of image and color. When printed on glossy cover paper, this achieved a fresh vibrancy. Ultimately, he produced about sixty covers a year, at fifty dollars per cover until the midsixties, when his rate was raised to one hundred dollars.

Starting in 1957, Kuhlman also designed the original format for Grove's progressive arts and politics journal, *Evergreen Review*, conceived by Rosset and Donald Allen as an edgy, quarterly literary magazine. Originally quarto sized, it featured many up-and-coming authors who were being published for the first time, such as Jack Kerouac and Gregory Corso, as well as Allen Ginsberg's famous poem *Howl*. The work of New York artists was there, too: Jackson Pollock and Larry Rivers, along with photographers Richard Avedon, Robert Frank, and Mary Ellen Mark.

Although best known for covers and jackets, Kuhlman had a varied career throughout the fifties and sixties. He said, "I guess you'd say I was a job jumper. When I learned what I wanted to know, I quit. I have been known to reach that point in as short a time as one day." He was commissioned to do advertisements by art director Herb Lubalin at Sudler & Hennessey, and he was an art director and designer for Columbia Records. Eventually, he was hired by the public relations firm Ruder & Finn to run an in-house art department, until he joined Benton & Bowles, where he designed the award-winning IBM "Mathematics Serving Man" campaign. IBM also commissioned him to produce 700 slides and 52 live-action and animated shorts to promote computer sales. In 1962, he joined Electra Films to work on motion graphics and title sequences. Two years later, he launched Kuhlman Associates to create advertising, promotion, audiovisual, and studio photography. Clients included AT&T, Hertz, CIBA, Chemstrand, and the United States Plywood Corporation, where he freelanced as creative director for five years. When United States Plywood merged with Champion Paper, Kuhlman designed the annual report's cover that showed their two logos carved in two entwined hearts on the bark of a tree. Brower noted that it humanized the cold takeover of one corporation by another. Kuhlman had the knack. •

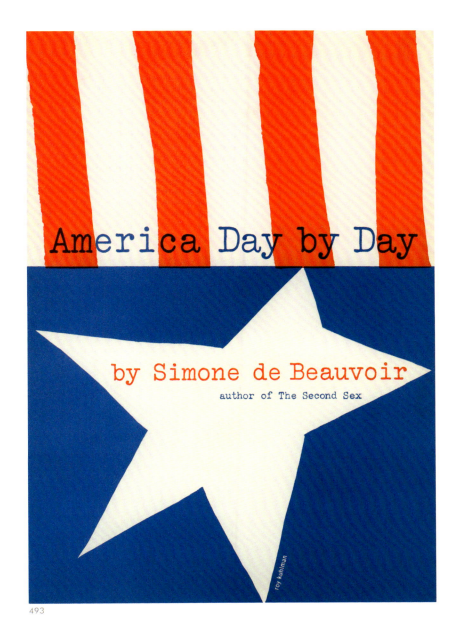

493

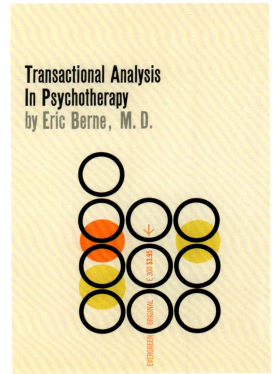

494

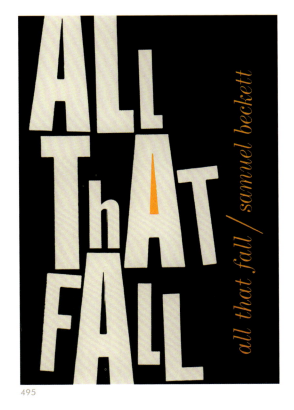

495

493
Book jacket, *America Day by Day,* by
Simone de Beauvoir, Grove Press, 1953

494
Book cover, *Transactional Analysis in
Psychotherapy,* by Eric Berne, Evergreen,
Grove Press, 1961

495
Book jacket, *All That Fall,* by Samuel
Beckett, Grove Press, 1957

496

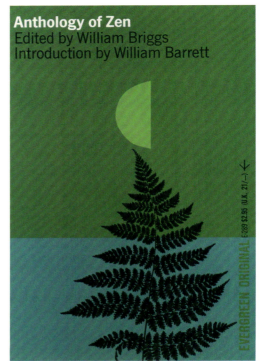

497

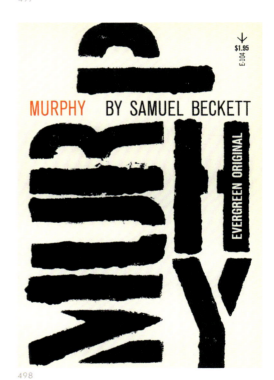

498

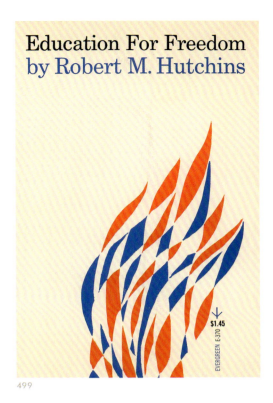

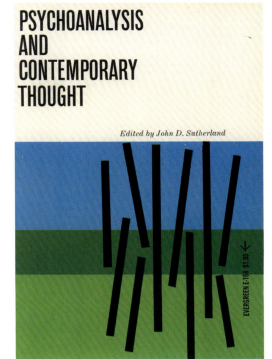

499
Book cover, *Education for Freedom*, by Robert M. Hutchins, Evergreen, Grove Press, 1963

500
Book cover, *Psychoanalysis and Contemporary Thought*, edited by John D. Sutherland, Grove Press, Evergreen, 1959

501
Book cover, *Lorca: The Poet and His People*, by Arturo Barea, Evergreen, Grove Press, 1960

502
Book cover, *A Walker in the City*, by Alfred Kazin, Evergreen, Grove Press, 1958

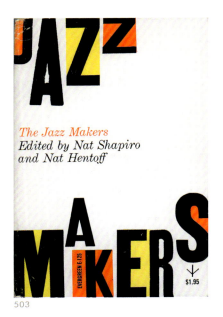

503

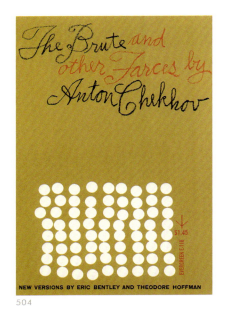

504

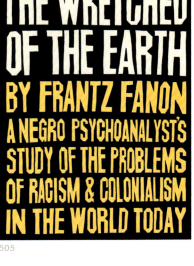

505

506

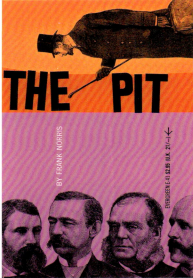

507

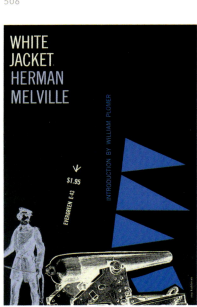

508

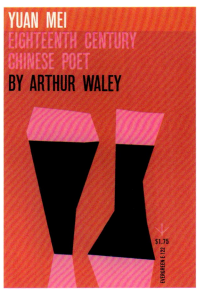

509

503

Book cover, *The Jazz Makers*, edited by Nat Shapiro and Nat Hentoff, Evergreen, Grove Press, 1957

504

Book cover, *The Brute and Other Farces*, by Anton Chekhov, Evergreen, Grove Press, 1958

505

Book cover, *The Wretched of the Earth*, by Frantz Fanon, Evergreen, Grove Press, 1966

506

Book cover, *The Art of Jazz: Essays on the Nature and Development of Jazz*, edited by Martin T. Williams, Evergreen, Grove Press, 1960

507

Book cover, *The Pit*, by Frank Norris, Evergreen, Grove Press, 1956

508

Book cover, *White Jacket*, by Herman Melville, Evergreen, Grove Press, 1956

509

Book cover, *Yuan Mei: Eighteenth Century Chinese Poet*, by Arthur Waley, Evergreen, Grove Press, 1956

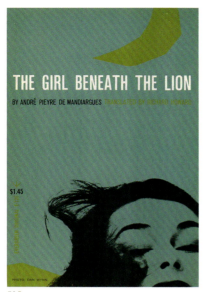

510

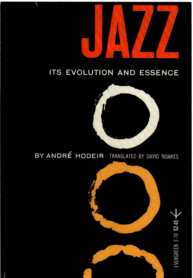

511

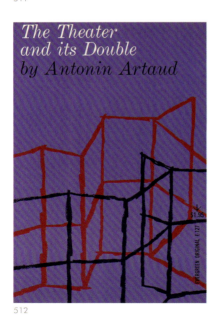

512

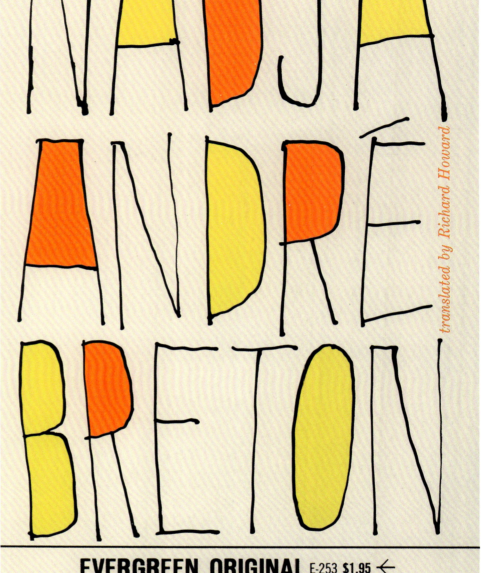

513

510
Book cover, *The Girl Beneath the Lion*, by André Pieyre de Mandiargues, Evergreen, Grove Press, 1958

511
Book cover, *Jazz: Its Evolution and Essence*, by André Hodeir, Evergreen, Grove Press, 1958

512
Book cover, *The Theater and Its Double*, by Antonin Artaud, Evergreen, Grove Press, 1958

513
Book cover, *Nadja*, by André Breton, Evergreen, Grove Press, 1960
To look at Kuhlman's book covers and jackets is to see the future of design. Even those he did in the sixties look as though they were done yesterday. His sense of space, color, and form was not a period style but a personal attitude.

Matthew Leibowitz

1918–1974

Leibowitz in his home office, Rydal, Pennsylvania, c. 1952

"The Europeans pioneered in the modern vogue, but Leibowitz has surpassed them in his distinctly American manner. His montages and collages are worthy of a gallery showing," wrote Robert Leslie, editor of *A-D* magazine, in the late forties. Matthew Leibowitz was a visual communicator with a gift for creating inspired ideas from modern art with clarity in the service of the client, revealing Dada, Constructivist, De Stijl, and Surrealist influences. Although Leibowitz may be less celebrated than his contemporaries Saul Bass, Lou Dorfsman, Herb Lubalin, Alvin Lustig, and Paul Rand, he advanced the development of an ambitious postwar American graphic design ethos.

Born in Philadelphia to Romanian immigrant parents, Leibowitz took evening classes from 1936 to 1939 at the Philadelphia Museum School of Industrial Art, where Alexey Brodovitch first arrived in 1930 and initiated a program to introduce European advertising design to American students. The evening school emphasized the principles of color, design, and modeling, with studio and lecture classes offered in drawing, illustration, advertising design, lettering, painting, art appreciation, art history, and more. His advertising design teacher was Raymond A. Ballinger, who authored books on design, including *Lettering Art in Modern Use* in 1952 and *Layout* in 1956.

While studying in Philadelphia, Leibowitz worked during the day at one of the city's most esteemed agencies, Gray & Rogers. After graduation, he spent a short summer in Paris before World War II compelled him to return home, where he worked as an art director for the next two years. He was a conscientious objector, and although he never served, he did provide alternative service. One project was his billboard-size, twenty-four-sheet poster for the International Red Cross. The problem, Leibowitz said, was "how to resolve the well-known symbol into a dynamic, living form?" He placed a hand at each end of the iconic symbol's red, horizontal crossbar; superimposed the familiar form of the globe over the cross; and stenciled "GIVE" on one of the hands, "expressing the universal gesture of appeal, the outstretched arms." Of the design, he said, "The poster can only be successful when the advertiser, in conjunction with the designer, harnesses the medium, to express one idea only: and that to be conveyed simply, forcefully."

For Leibowitz, personal expression was important. In 1942, he established an independent practice, first in the Lincoln-Liberty Building in Philadelphia, and by 1949 in a custom-built studio in the modern home he designed in Rydal, Pennsylvania—where he continued to work throughout his lifetime. His distance and independence from New York and routine agency work allowed him to nurture his own style, influenced by European Modernism and American Eclecticism.

"The work reflected clearly the progress and hope of America in the post-war period. His was the era of aerodynamics, the atomic bomb, first computers, satellite communications and space travel, long playing records, electric typewriters and big business," wrote Sid Sachs. Leibowitz employed a playful combination of woodcut illustrations and vintage Victorian engravings, and his use of pure, flat color palettes and schematic compositions was strikingly modern and intelligent. He expressed a passion for minimalist, geometric shapes and pure form: "Whether precise as geometry or sculptural as stone, [a design] must declare a clear, direct, and strong visual statement, complete as such," he said in *ID* magazine in 1957. His typography was skillfully crafted and functional. "The complete integration of typography with the graphic image is indicative of the maturity attained by the contemporary designer," he wrote in *Typography—U.S.A.* in 1959.

Leibowitz was friendly with Lester Beall, who helped him get commissions. Along the way, he made connections with Alexey Brodovitch, Jean Carlu, Charles Coiner, Herbert Matter, and Raymond Savignac, as well as Man Ray, whom he met via Naomi Savage, Man Ray's niece. Leibowitz also met A. M. Cassandre and was deeply moved; *Normandie*, Cassandre's best-known poster, hung in his office. Leibowitz may have apprenticed under the legendary artist and designer on one of his summer trips to Paris or through N. W. Ayer's Charles Coiner, who commissioned Cassandre to design Container Corporation of America's first series of advertisements in 1936.

From his Philadelphia base, Leibowitz maintained a healthy practice as art director and adviser for agencies and titans of American industry, designing everything from logos to annual reports for IBM, RCA, CBS, ITT, TWA, Otis Elevator, Fortune, General Dynamics, Container Corporation of America, and Reichhold Chemicals, along with pharmaceutical giants White Laboratories, Sharp & Dohme, and Geigy. Leibowitz "is today one of the most representative and successful as well as one of the youngest of the new generation of American designers who have profited by the teachings of modern painting and the new theory of art," stated Walter Allner in *Graphis* (1947). Leibowitz turned commercial design into a calling, and his approach was influential abroad, where his work was featured in *Graphis* (1946), *Idea* (1957), *Gebrauchsgraphik* (1960), and *Graphic Design Japan* (1962).

Leibowitz was in constant pursuit of a new functional and symbolic language to help further his ideas. He summed up his design ideas best in *Typography—U.S.A.* in 1959: "The translation can communicate well only if expressed in clear, concise terminology to the audience for whom it was intended. Ideas and content are expressed with the designer's imagination and awareness. Synchronized, these qualities are his tools of creativity." Leibowitz's own abstract paintings, said Sachs, "attained a purity that was universal and beyond the commercial function of his design work." •

a new CAREY-McFALL service

514

514
Brochure cover, *Precision Tools: A New Carey-McFall Service*, Carey-McFall Company, Tool Division, Philadelphia, c. 1945

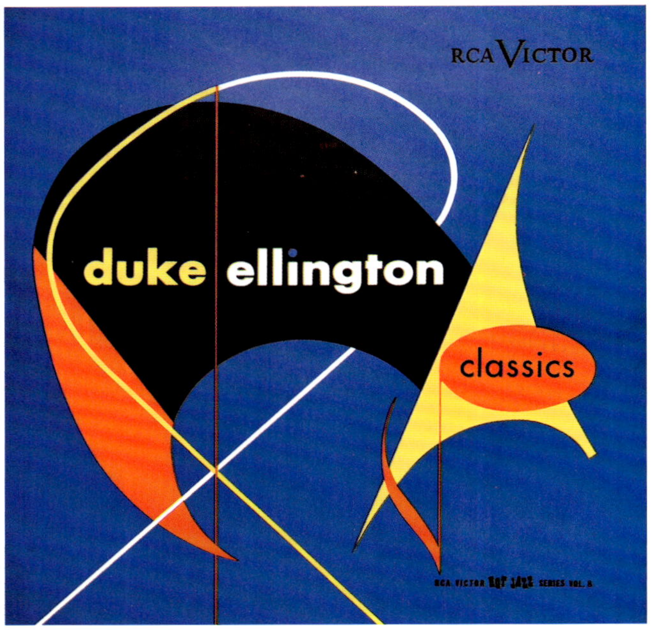

515

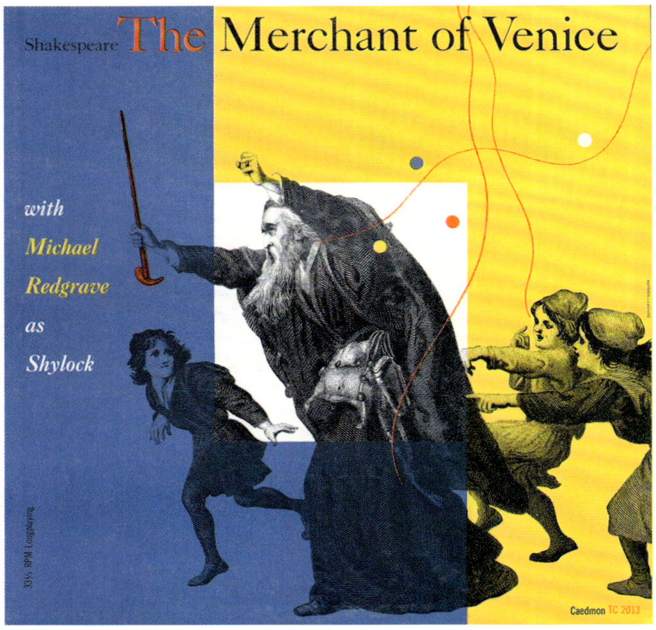

516

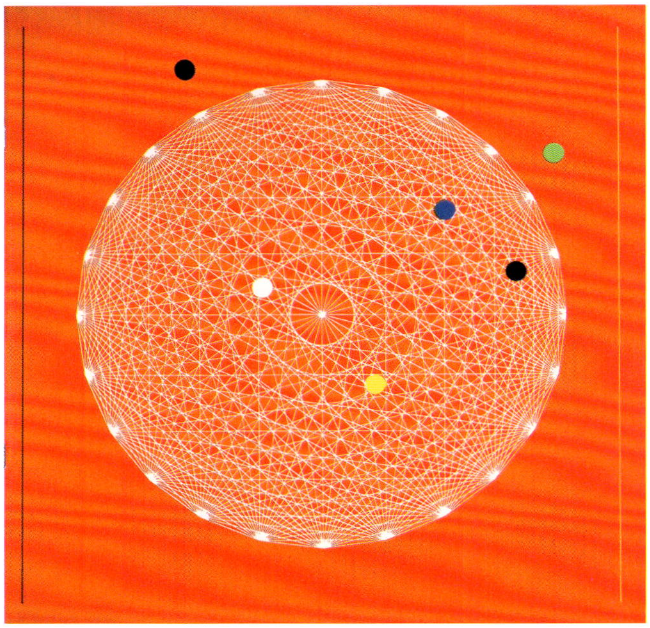

517

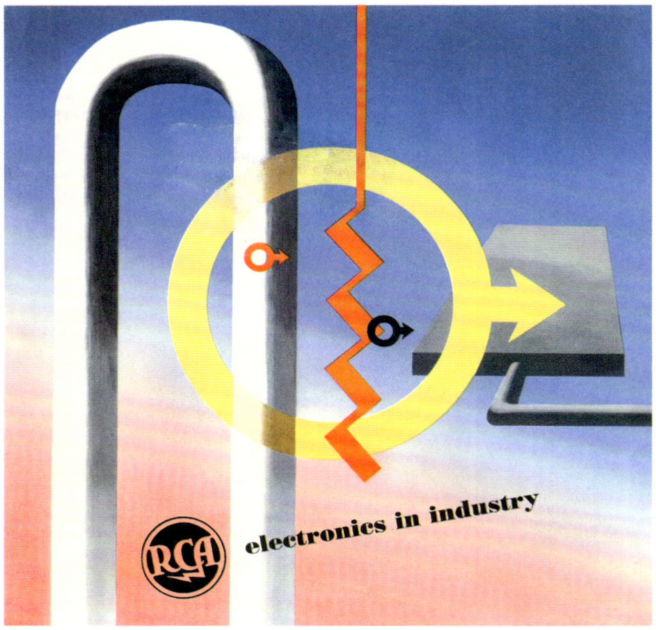

518

515
Album cover (possibly unpublished), *Duke Ellington Classics* by Duke Ellington, Hot Jazz Series, vol. 8, RCA Victor, c. 1946

516
Album cover, *The Merchant of Venice with Michael Redgrave as Shylock*, Caedmon Records, 1957

517
Booklet cover, *Philco Model 212 Computer*, Philco, c. 1962

518
Booklet cover, *Electronics in Industry*, Radio Corporation of America, RCA Victor Division, Camden, New Jersey, 1943

519
Advertisement, "Anacin: To Relieve Regular Pain," Whitehall Pharmacal Company, New York, undated

520
Brochure front and back covers, Matthew Leibowitz, D&C Black & White, Mead Papers, c. 1945. Leibowitz skillfully juggles the ornamental past with new Modernist ideas. His playful and dynamic montage unites pattern and perspectives, vintage nineteenth-century engravings, photography, and a mix of type, resulting in a balance of form and function.

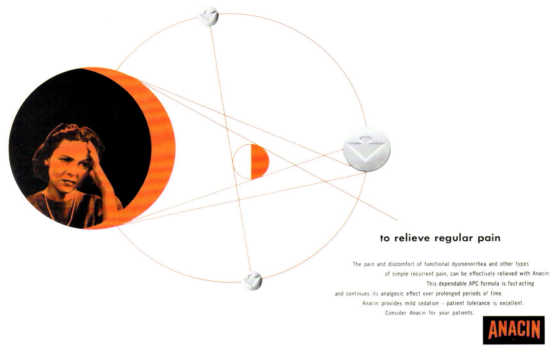

to relieve regular pain

The pain and discomfort of functional dysmenorrhea and other types
of simple recurrent pain, can be effectively relieved with Anacin.
This dependable APC formula is fast-acting
and continues its analgesic effect over prolonged periods of time.
Anacin provides mild sedation — patient tolerance is excellent.
Consider Anacin for your patients.

ANACIN

Whitehall Pharmacal Company, New York 16, N. Y.

519

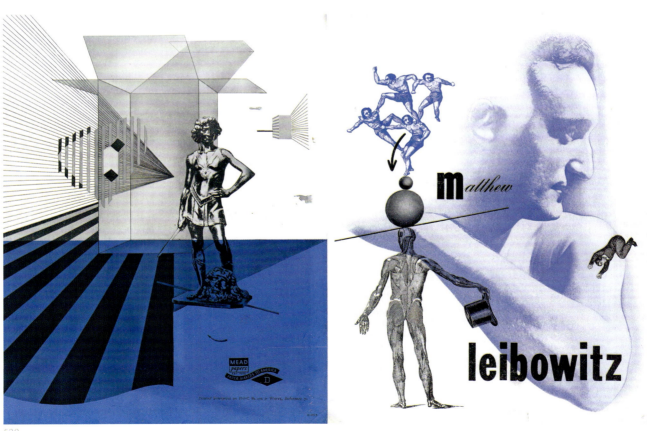

520

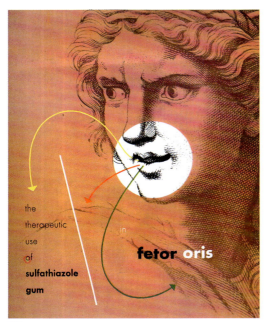

521

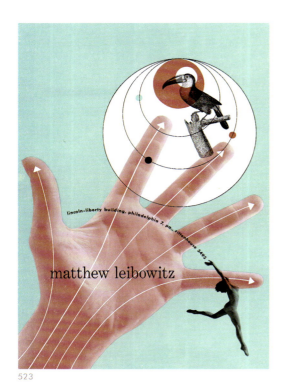

523

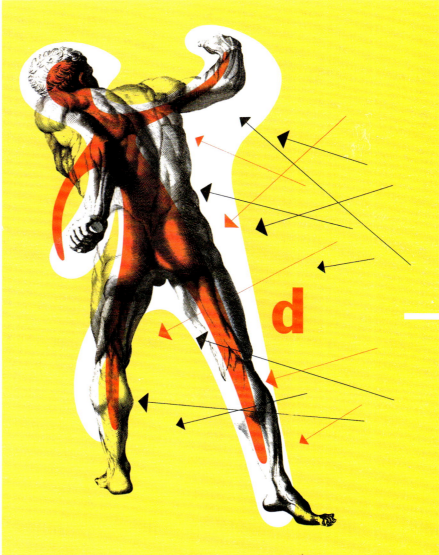

522

521
Brochure cover, *The Therapeutic Use of Sulfathiazole Gum in Fetor Oris*, White Laboratories, Newark, New Jersey, 1946

522
Brochure cover, *Delcos Granules, Protein Carbohydrate Granules—for the Treatment of Protein Nutritional Deficiency States*, Sharp & Dohme, 1946

523
Self-promotional advertisement, Matthew Leibowitz, Lincoln-Liberty Building, Philadelphia, 1946

524
Advertisements, "Partners in Precision," IBM Supplies, c. 1956–59

525
Advertisement, "Today It's Unlimited Elevator Automation," Otis Elevator Company, c. 1963

526
Interior page, *First Annual Report*, Reichhold Chemicals, 1955. The red globe is printed on a clear acetate overlay.

527
Poster mechanical, *Anywhere*, TWA, c. 1947

528
Poster, *Give*, International Red Cross, before 1949

524

525

526

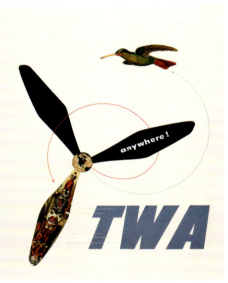

527

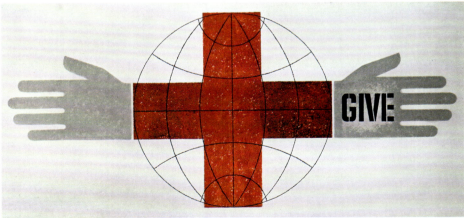

528

George Lois

b. 1931

Lois in his Seagram Building office, New York, 1960

"You can't research a big idea. The only ideas that truly research well are mediocre, 'acceptable' ideas. In research great ideas are always suspect," said George Lois, proponent of a creative revolution in the fifties and instigator of the Big Idea in American advertising during the sixties. Papert Koenig Lois (PKL), his first agency, founded in 1960, was, in Lois's words, the "second creative agency," challenging Doyle Dane Bernbach's hegemony. Looking back, Lois could plausibly claim victory: His iconoclastic campaigns for Xerox, Wolfschmidt Vodka, Coldene, Maypo, Braniff International Airways, and scores of other products were among the most modern of their era.

Lois is a critical mass of culture, art, and left-wing causes. The son of Greek immigrants, he has shown an enduring sympathy for the working class and the poor and has used his propaganda skills in the service of promoting social causes and political candidates. He has a street-smart manner of no-nonsense communication seasoned with humor, including biting satire. Lois's advertising has been both a revolution in his profession and, in its own way, a commentary on its hypocrisy. Advertising, he believes, is not about forcing people to acquire unnecessary merchandise. Rather, it is a medium that informs, entertains, and, if executed with intelligence, has the power to alter behavior—even change the world.

Among his most lasting contributions was a series of design ideas for ninety-two *Esquire* magazine covers produced from the sixties to the early seventies—graphic commentaries that are among the most memorable icons of an unsettling social and political era. One cover shows the former heavyweight champion Muhammad Ali, who had been stripped of his title for refusing to fight in the Vietnam War, posing as the martyr Saint Sebastian pierced with arrows; another has Lieutenant William Calley, the officer who led the infamous My Lai massacre in South Vietnam, flanked by smiling Vietnamese children—what irony. Lois also introduced the first black Santa Claus—Sonny Liston—ever to appear on a magazine cover.

Lois's Modernism began in elementary school in the Bronx, where "I was more excited looking at a Cassandre poster than a Stuart Davis painting. Also I could draw very well, and I was very precocious about the history of art." He attended New York's High School of Music and Art. He said that he would design with a Bauhaus sensibility, "but always put *words* into my work. I really had a designer's mentality." Paul Rand was God to him then.

Then he went to Pratt Institute in Brooklyn. The first year was terrible, but in the second year he took a class with Herschel Levit. "Mr. Levit would give an assignment and I'd come in with six finished ones while everybody in the class was struggling to get one done. However, I didn't go to other classes except for the life drawing class." From there, he went to work with Reba Sochis, the first woman in New York to run a major design studio. "She was a wonderful designer and a great typographer with a light touch," Lois recalled. Sochis and some of her friends were big influences on Lois. "I hate the unfairness of the system and the continuing injustices in America. I cared about the working class, about the working man. I've always had that thing in me. . . . Reba crystallised it for me, and many of her pals—Paul Robeson, W.E.B. Du Bois, and Alger Hiss—became my friends."

Lois did not see a contradiction in being an advertising designer and selling capitalist goods. "It was always communicating, designing, convincing." But in those days, advertising was basically a schlock industry. CBS, where Lois went next, was a dream job for a graphic designer. That started those balls rolling. "I like to do things that change people's minds," he noted. "It's the power of a hungry mind and a hungry eye. Back then I was hungering to work on selling bread or cars, or an airline. I was hungering to get my face into changing the culture, my way."

The Big Idea was advertising's Modernist signpost. It was a shift from formulaic pitch to creative thinking. Bill Bernbach of Doyle Dane Bernbach, where Lois plied his trade for a year before launching PKL, was instrumental in shaping the idea that copy and graphic imagery could work in harmony. PKL's offices were in the Seagram Building, a citadel of Modernism, and it was there that Lois developed ads for the Seagram brand Wolfschmidt Vodka. They were witty, irreverent, and a little bit racy, as well as Modernist in design and conception. Lois's idea was to position Wolfschmidt subtly as a vodka that is almost tasteless ("the touch of taste"), easily covered in drinks by the flavor of tomato, lemon, or orange juice: "Since it left no after-taste you can drink it at lunch and not be found out. When I did those ads with the talking fruits and vegetables, everybody talked about them. Sales exploded."

Lois was once asked, "How do you know that you have the big idea that will change the world?" He responded, "You try to epitomise the uniqueness of the product by doing it in a way that's incredibly memorable. The first rule is theatre. Attract attention by doing something absolutely fresh and dramatic. What most people in advertising don't understand is, great advertising, in and of itself, becomes a *benefit* of the product." There is so much bad advertising that stays in the brain because it's so insidious. "I don't do campaigns where you spend zillions of dollars. I do campaigns where they don't spend much money and I don't have much time to make it famous, and I make it work, pronto."

With Lois, the Big Idea, almost always, had to come from him: "I'm never satisfied with somebody else's idea. . . . Once I feel I have all the input I need, I totally concentrate and nail the idea. If I have trouble coming up with what I consider to be a thrilling concept, it's because I didn't really understand all the input. But when I nail the idea . . . I love to work things out with a great writer. Boy, is that great fun." •

529

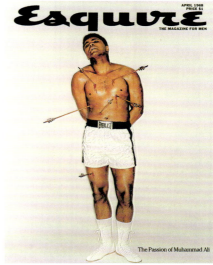

530

531

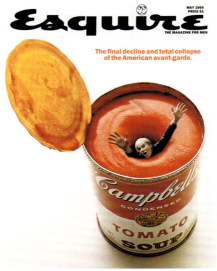

532

529–532
Magazine covers, *Esquire*, August 1966,
April 1968, June 1964, May 1969

533

Dansk stainless (not shown: 11 museums, 4 medals, 22 fairs)

DANSK

534

First you thought small.

Now think a little bigger.

PEUGEOT 403

535

Lois's rebelliousness came through in his aggressive attacks on the conventions of design. What he called "the big idea" was more than a good layout; it was a strong message that moved an audience to laugh, cry, or yell in anger.

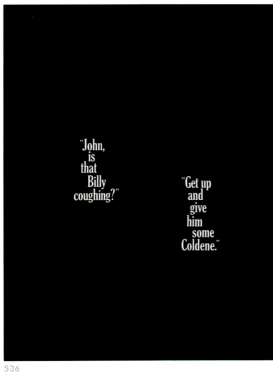

536

537

538

539

536
Advertisement, "John, Is That Billy Coughing? Get Up and Give Him Some Coldene," Pharmacraft Laboratories, 1960. This clever ad does not show the product, ingredients, or logo and shocked the advertising industry. Design: Papert Koenig Lois

537
Advertisement, "Ronson 'Talks,'" Ronson Corporation, 1960–61. This onomatopoeia is both visual and audible and communicates the sound of whiskers being removed. Design: Papert Koenig Lois

538
Advertisement, "Renault Runs Rings Inside Other Cars," Renault–Peugeot (Eastern Distributor), 1960–61. Design: Papert Koenig Lois

539
Advertisement, "Wolfschmidt Vodka," Joseph E. Seagram & Sons, General Wine & Spirits Company, 1962. Design: Papert Koenig Lois

Herb Lubalin

1918–1981

Lubalin in his Sudler & Hennessey, New York, office, c. 1957

Herbert Frederick Lubalin had two disabilities for an artist designer: He was color-blind and left-handed. Yet years later, few graphic designers would embody the aesthetics of their time as completely as he did.

He was born in New York with a twin brother named Irwin to German and Russian parents. At the age of seventeen, Lubalin enrolled in Cooper Union, where he transformed from poor student to master calligrapher. From the late fifties through the early seventies, he epitomized innovative American graphic design. His eclectic modern sensibility pervaded advertising, editorial, and package design so thoroughly that the era may best be called "Lubalinesque." He defined the art of illustrative typography and photocomposition in one fell swoop. His work was a window on how new technologies would alter typographic expression. Lubalin's type exploded off the printed page and into the consciousness of the popular culture.

Lubalin was the father of conceptual typography. This was the bridge between Midcentury Modern and late Modernist schools. Letters were not merely vessels but objects of meaning; he made words emote and liberated white space, refusing to follow the edict that "less is more." He believed that "more" was better if it enlivened the page. Lubalin tirelessly experimented, yet his radical approaches became so thoroughly embraced, first in advertising and then in publication design, that it's hard to remember how impressive these advances were.

He was one of the type experimenters invited to contribute to the About U.S. series published by the Composing Room in 1960. This was the period when the constraints of hot-metal composition made it difficult to achieve such now-common effects as tight spacing, touching, or overlapping letters without the designer cutting repro with a razor blade, repositioning it on the proofs, and then making an engraving of the mechanical. Lubalin's *Come Home to Jazz*, a pictorial jam of jazz instruments photographed in high contrast with dropout type in different sizes and weights running in and out of the images, suggested the discordance of the music itself. This was a moment when Lubalin was beginning to influence contemporary typography with visual puns and type-pictures by busting through the confines of hot metal (which he would later do with phototype).

Lubalin became known for innovative pictorial and humorous advertising typography created while working at the agency Sudler & Hennessey, which specialized in pharmaceuticals. But by the midsixties, he had also changed the course of editorial design through two remarkable magazines, each a benchmark of American culture.

Both were published by Ralph Ginzburg. *Eros* was America's first sophisticated magazine of erotica between hard covers. In addition to its content, it demonstrated the most elegant magazine pacing and composition since Alexey Brodovitch's design for *Portfolio* held that honor. *Avant Garde* was an expression of the social and cultural flux within American society, as affected by the antiwar movement and alternative culture. It was a hybrid: It crossed a magazine with a literary journal;

it was square, the size of a long-playing record album; its illustration and photography evoked the revolutionary spirit of the times. *Avant Garde* lived up to its own name, and *Eros* gave sex an exotic allure. Both publications offered alternatives to mainstream design conventions, but without the raucous anarchy of the youth culture's underground graphics.

Later, as art director of *Fact*, an "investigative" periodical that included a diet of consumer advocacy, liberal rhetoric, and conspiracy theorizing, Lubalin reinvented the notion of quietude. What Lubalin did with this ostensibly black-and-white, text-dominated periodical was give new meaning to the word "classical." All the visual elements were toned down—one single illustrator and one typeface per issue—yet it was the most eye-catching minimalism anyone had seen.

Even when Lubalin's typography was subdued, it was never neutral. Maybe it was compensation, because Lubalin himself was soft-spoken; through typography, he spoke loudly. His headlines for articles and advertisements were signs that forced the reader to halt, read, and experience. He would tweak story titles until he had just the right combination of letters to make a striking composition. "No More War," originally an advertisement for *Avant Garde* that featured block letters forming the pattern of an American flag, with a bold black exclamation point at the end, was one of the strongest graphic statements issued during the Vietnam War era.

Lubalin used type in the ways a sculptor uses clay or stone. Although his bashing, smashing, and overlapping of letters was contrived at times, Lubalin was the inventor of the form. Not all his experiments worked. The Avant Garde typeface, for example, was beautiful as a magazine logo, but as a commercial typeface it contained an excessive number of ligatures, which were misused by designers who had no understanding of how to employ these typographic forms. Avant Garde was Lubalin's typographic signature, and in his hands it had character; in others', it was almost always flawed.

Lubalin was on the Modernist fence. He was too eclectic to follow rules. In 1971, he cofounded the International Typeface Corporation, and two years later he launched the tabloid magazine *U&lc* as a sales tool that doubled as an outlet for his eclectic interests. Under his editorship, eclectic typography overpowered the Swiss Style.

He died before digital typography took a sharper turn toward distressed and illegible letterforms. But the revolution might not have happened if Lubalin had not pushed against the limits imposed by the marketplace, which at once provided certain safeguards and made taking liberties all the more difficult. Lubalin's work was not "design for design," but design for communication. Even his most radical ideas never strayed far from Modernism, just enough to keep them surprising. •

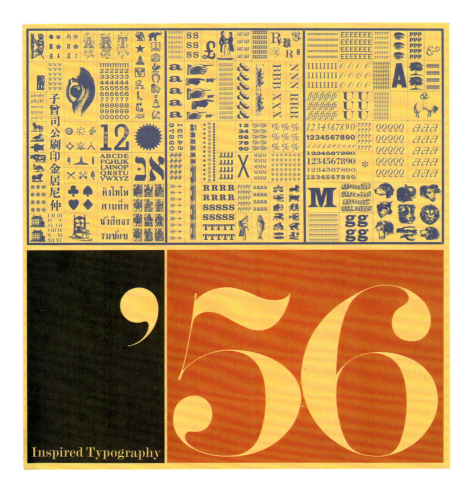

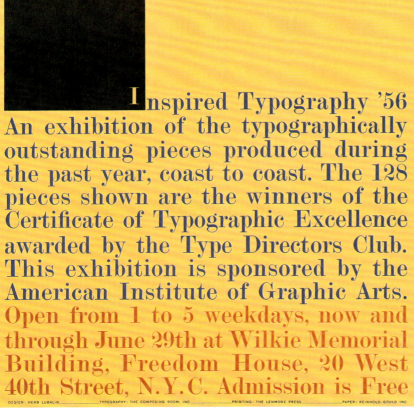

542

HERB LUBALIN

540
Promotional, *Inspired Typography '56*,
Type Directors Club, 1956

541
Business cards, "Anthony Hyde, Jr.,
Photography," and "Li-lian Oh,
Representative," New York, 1968.
Lettering: Tom Carnase

542
Logo, World Trade Center, 1968

543

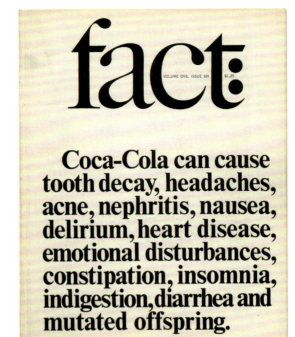

544

let's talk type let type talk

545

546

543
Magazine cover, *Holiday*, October 1959. *Holiday*'s editors decided that no one pictorial view could possibly encompass the multifarious aspects of New York, so they hired Herb Lubalin to create a special type design, stating simply the theme of the issue. It took sixteen tries before he came up with a "New York" in the *Holiday* mood. Art direction: Frank Zachary

544
Magazine cover, *Fact*, "The Case Against Coca-Cola," vol. 1, no. 6 (December 1964). Lubalin's skillfully crafted, type-only cover mirrors the magazine's distinct and authentic approach to journalism.

545
Advertisement, "Let's Talk Type, Let Type Talk," Sudler & Hennessey, 1958. "Some ads must whisper, some must shout. But whatever the tone of voice, creative typography speaks with a distinction that sets your advertising above the clamor of competing messages. If you share our interest in good typography, and the other creative tools that work with it, we would welcome the opportunity to show you how we at Sudler & Hennessey . . . let type talk." Lettering: John Pistilli

546
Advertisement, "Sudler & Hennessey: The Language of Communication through Design Needs No Translation," 1957

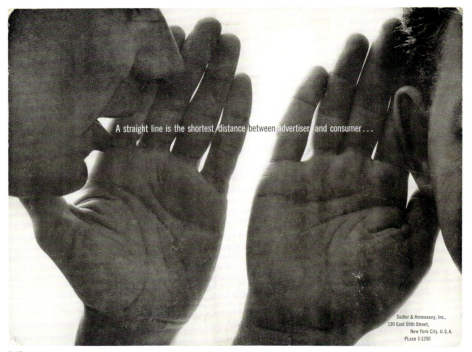

547

548

549

547
Advertisement, "A Straight Line Is the Shortest Distance Between Advertiser and Consumer . . . ," Sudler & Hennessey, 1956. Photo: Carl Fischer

548
Advertisement, Sudler, Hennessey & Lubalin, 1959. "SH&L Expanded—redesign of a familiar face. A more flexible version of S&H, long a favorite of people who work with fine design. You can specify SH&L for a wide range of uses from small space campaigns to large corporate image projects. We offer a Bold Face (for impact), Oblique (new ways of viewing old problems), and Casual (no straining for mere effect)." Lettering: John Pistilli

549
Booklet cover, "TDC '26–'66," Type Directors Club, New York, 1966

Alvin Lustig
1915–1955

Lustig in his Los Angeles office, 9126 Sunset Boulevard, 1949.
Photo: Ann Rosener

Harry Houdini and Alvin Lustig had one thing in common: Each escaped straitjackets. "The words 'graphic designer,' 'architect,' or 'industrial designer' stick in my throat giving me a sense of limitation, of specialization within the specialty, or a relationship to society that is unsatisfactory and incomplete. This inadequate set of terms to describe an active life reveals only partially the still undefined nature of a designer." He wrote this in a September 1946 *Interiors* magazine article about his brief yet variegated career as master of many design forms. By age thirty-nine, he was totally blinded by early onset diabetes, and within a year he died, but not before packing a lifetime of experience into half a life span.

Lustig proclaimed membership in a group "that was born modern." Design was not a job but a calling, and he held a messianic belief that anything a modern designer laid hands on—from book cover to room interior—could make the world better. So whenever one of his clients or friends innocently requested his advice about, say, what lamp to purchase for an office or home, he replied, "I won't recommend a lamp, but I will redo the entire room."

He attended the Art Center School in Los Angeles in 1934; the following year, he leaped into the depths of Modernism with Frank Lloyd Wright at Taliesin East in Wisconsin. Yet he grew weary of kowtowing and doing menial jobs, so he returned to Los Angeles, where California architect Richard Neutra gave Lustig unlimited access to a library of remarkable design books and magazines that influenced his practice. Although graphic design was his métier, he was inspired by Italian furniture designer Franco Albini and later by Philip Johnson, who responded to Lustig's natural affinity for architecture and innate ability to conceive in three-dimensional space. With native instinct, Lustig showed a high degree of self-taught proficiency in decorating his own studios.

Lack of work in California forced Lustig to move to New York, where he became visual research director of *Look* magazine's design department in 1944. Two years later, he returned to Los Angeles, where for five years he ran an office specializing in architectural, furniture, and fabric design, while continuing his book and editorial jobs. He became a charter member of the seminal group of intrepid Angelenos, including Saul Bass, Louis Danziger, Rudolph de Harak, and John Follis, called the Los Angeles Society for Contemporary Designers, whose members were frustrated by the surrounding dearth of creative vision.

Lustig's practice seamlessly integrated everything from record albums to textiles. He designed a helicopter for Roteron, a pioneering aerospace company; signage for J. L. Hudson's Northland Center in Detroit, one of the first American shopping malls; the opening sequence for the popular animated UPA cartoon series *Mr. Magoo*; and print materials for the Girl Scouts of America, transforming aspects of their graphic identity from homespun quaintness to sophisticated Modernism. He was passionate about design education, and at Joseph Albers's request he conceived design courses and workshops for Black Mountain College in North Carolina and the design department at Yale University.

Lustig was pioneering in his graphic design, especially for book jackets. He began designing them in the early forties, when they were ephemeral wrappers that protected bindings from dust, removed and discarded as routinely as gift paper. Lustig turned book jackets, and paperback book covers, into a minor art genre, influenced by abstract art and projecting impressions and moods. His jackets for New Directions suggested a book's content with nuanced graphic gestures. "His method was to read a text and get the feel of the author's creative drive, then to restate it in his own graphic terms," James Laughlin, New Directions' publisher, wrote in *Print* magazine in 1956.

Laughlin hired Lustig and gave him license (within bounds) to experiment with the house's list of classic reprints, which featured such authors as Henry Miller, Gertrude Stein, D. H. Lawrence, and James Joyce. Basing his work on Abstract Expressionist painting, Surrealist drawing, and pre-Columbian ceramics, among other disparate art influences, Lustig sketched his imagery in light and dark lines, sometimes with pen and brush, other times including an eclectic yet recurring selection of cryptic glyphs and signs. From running his own printing shop, Lustig had acquired an interest in compositions made from metal type slugs that resembled Russian Constructivist experiments from the early twenties and Frank Lloyd Wright's graphics of the same period, and for his first New Directions assignment, Henry Miller's *Wisdom of the Heart* of 1941, he eclipsed the "conservative" and "booky" designs of the house's previous books.

Laughlin allowed Lustig to create styles when appropriate. His cover for *Lorca: 3 Tragedies* in 1949 was unique in its day, comprising a grid of five symbolic photographs linked through poetic disharmony yet bound together by the confines of the book itself. The book's title is incorporated into the photographs. In his own way, Lustig pioneered this otherwise realistic medium as a tool for creating abstractions through reticulated negatives, photograms, and still lifes.

In 1950, diabetes began to erode his vision, and by 1954 he was blind. His wife, Elaine Lustig (later, Cohen), recalled that he fulfilled his obligations by directing her and his assistants in every meticulous detail to complete the work he could no longer see. He specced color by referring to the color of a chair or sofa in their house, and he used simple geometries to express his faded vision.

Before his death, Lustig proposed immigrating to Israel because he believed that in its infant state, good design could have a significant impact on the society. Design was a potent force, he insisted, and if wed to fine art, painting, and sculpture, it could also be used for the collective good. But he died before he had the chance to test his theory. He left behind a body of work that stands up to the scrutiny of time, but more important serves as a model for how a personal vision and modern form can be a potent cure for what ails the visual landscape. •

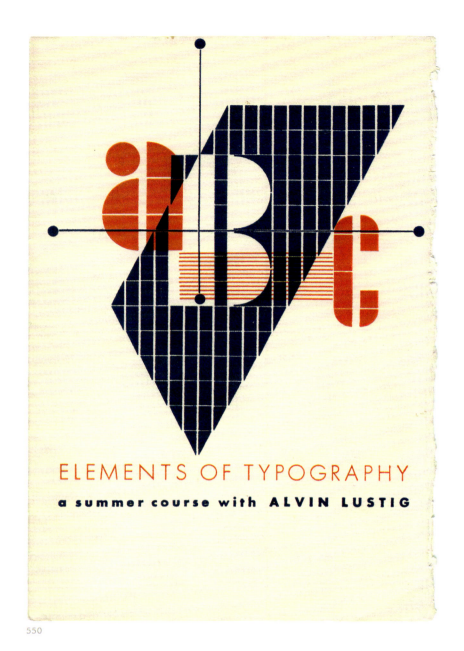

550
Brochure cover, *Elements of Typography: A Summer Course with Alvin Lustig*, late 1930s. From the interior: "A summer workshop course in typography is offered to a limited number of students seeking advanced, concentrated instruction in the elements of book, periodical, and general printing design. Problems will be carried out completely, including planning, setting of type, choice of paper, mixing of ink and final printing. The workshop will be augmented by the discussion of the principles of contemporary design, examination of the work of leading practitioners and a comparative study of traditional and modern typography."

551
Cover, *Robinson's 58*, late 1930s

552
Catalog cover, *Ski Alta*, 1946

553

553
House organ cover, *Look,* "Staff,"
March 28, 1944

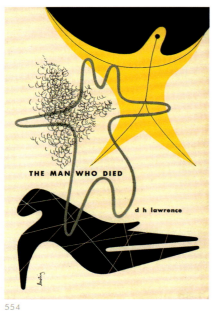

554

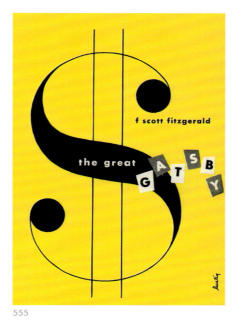

555

556

557

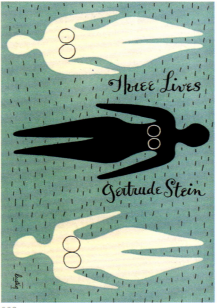

558

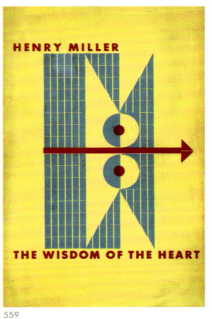

559

554
Book jacket, *The Man Who Died*, by
D. H. Lawrence, New Directions, New
Classics, 1946

555
Book jacket, *The Great Gatsby*, by F.
Scott Fitzgerald, New Directions, New
Classics, 1945

556
Book jacket, *3 Tragedies*, by Federico
Garcia Lorca, New Directions, 1948.
Photo: J. Connor

557
Book jacket, *Amerika*, by Franz Kafka, New
Directions, New Classics, 1946

558
Book jacket, *Three Lives*, by Gertrude Stein,
New Directions, New Classics, 1945

559
Book jacket, *The Wisdom of the Heart*, by
Henry Miller, New Directions, 1941

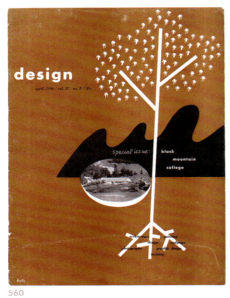

560

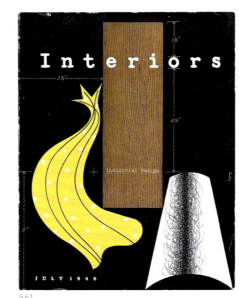

561

562

563

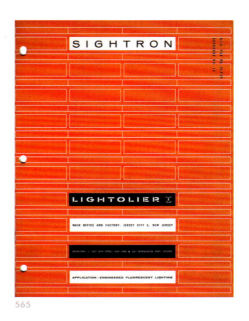

564

565

560
Magazine cover, *Design*, "Special Issue," Black Mountain College, North Carolina, vol. 47, no. 8 (April 1946)

561
Magazine cover, *Interiors*, Whitney Publications, July 1946

562
Magazine cover, *Industrial Design*, Whitney Publications, no. 2 (April 1954)

563
Catalog cover, *Jim Lansing Signature Speakers*, James B. Lansing Sound, 1949

564–565
Catalog covers, *Optiplex* and *Sightron*, Lightolier, New Jersey, 1952

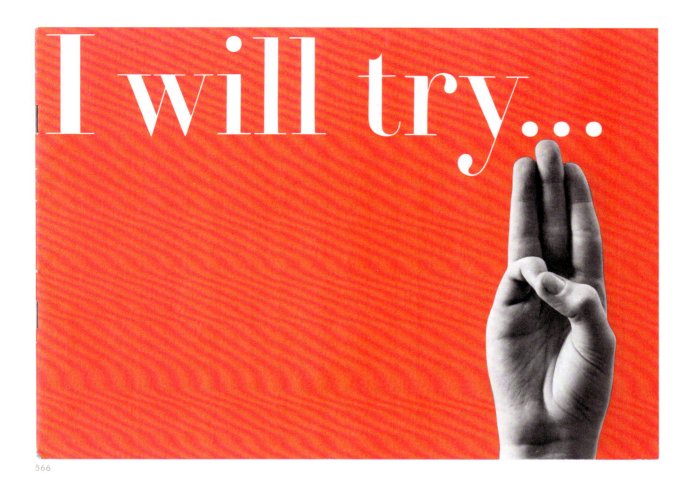

566

form

Clarity of form is a basic element of good contemporary furniture.
The rocker, designed by Ralph Rapson, exemplifies
the honest design characteristic of all H. G. Knoll products.

H. G. KNOLL associates
601 MADISON AVENUE, NEW YORK 22, NEW YORK

form
structure
economy

to improve design
to perfect craftsmanship
and to lower costs is our constant aim

H. G. KNOLL associates, 601 MADISON AVENUE, NEW YORK 22, N. Y.

567   568

566
Brochure cover, *I Will Try*, Girl Scouts of America, 1954

567
Advertisement, "Form," Knoll Associates, New York, February 1945. Advertisement reads: "Clarity of form is a basic element of good contemporary furniture. The rocker, designed by Ralph Rapson, exemplifies the honest design characteristic of all H. G. Knoll products."

568
Advertisement, "Form Structure Economy," Knoll Associates, New York, July 1945. Advertisement reads: "To improve design, to perfect craftsmanship and to lower costs is our constant aim."

Elaine Lustig Cohen
1927–2016

Lustig Cohen at home, New York, 1966. Photo: Ugo Mulas

From 1948 to 1955, Elaine Lustig Cohen was, in her own words, "a blind disciple" of her then husband, Alvin Lustig. When she took over the practice after his death in 1955, most of his clients expected her to complete his unfinished commissions. They did not know that he had never included her in his projects.

It was a man's world, and few women graphic designers owned their own studios in the early fifties. Nonetheless, the twenty-eight-year-old widow rose to the challenge and emerged as a savvy Modernist in her own right, eventually specializing in books, catalogs, and signage. "My gender may have been an issue for other designers, but not for my clients," she said. Simply running the operation posed unanticipated challenges, but getting work was not a problem. Her client roster included TWA, the Federal Aviation Administration, and General Motors, among others. And up to the day in 1962 when she closed the studio, Cohen continued to garner commissions from museums, architecture firms, and book publishers, including Noonday Press, whose cofounder, Arthur Cohen, she later married.

The daughter of a plumber and a bookkeeper, Elaine Firstenberg was fifteen when she wandered into a Kandinsky exhibition at Peggy Guggenheim's influential Art of This Century Gallery in New York City, across the river from her home in Jersey City. That visit ignited a lifelong passion for modern art. Soon, she enrolled in Newcomb College at Tulane University, where she studied art. One of her classes was based on basic Bauhausian fundamentals. In those days, women were not encouraged to pursue art as a profession, so art education courses at the University of Southern California prepared her for a teaching career.

Elaine was twenty when she met thirty-two-year-old Alvin at an art opening in 1948. A whirlwind courtship was followed by marriage—and a job as the "office slave," she recalled. "Teaching me was not even an issue. It was, after all, a different time." He did, however, encourage Elaine to research materials for interior design projects, and she made collages for prospective children's books and sketches of fantasy furniture.

About a week after Alvin's funeral, Philip Johnson, who had earlier commissioned him to design the Seagram Building signage, called Elaine to tell her that the job was hers. He then asked her when the official alphabet would be complete. "When Alvin died nothing had been done on Seagram," she said. "Eventually my schedule of the lettering and signs were incorporated into the architectural working drawings." In addition to signs, she designed *New York Times* ads for the building. Johnson recognized her remarkable efforts, which helped to forge an important bond between them.

Soon she moved the studio into her apartment, and publisher Arthur Cohen asked her to design Meridian Books' new line of paperbacks. Alvin had designed the first twenty-five—and Elaine went on to do more than one hundred. Those jackets helped to distinguish her more free-form style from Lustig's late-period Precisionist approach. In 1956, she married Cohen, who convinced her that having a real office could earn her more ambitious and remunerative commissions. She opened Lustig & Reich, with former Lustig studio member Jack Reich. After a year, however, the business was disbanded, and she returned to her sole proprietorship at home.

Cohen designed lobby signs and catalogs for the Jewish Museum, the Museum of Primitive Art, Rio de Janeiro's Museum of Modern Art, Lincoln Center (with Chermayeff & Geismar, on signage that was never adopted), and the 1964–65 New York World's Fair, creating graphic design for the architectural firm Harrison & Abramovitz. For Johnson, she designed signs for two Yale buildings. "Much work came from Philip," she reported, "as he would recommend me to people he was working for, like John de Menil and his Schlumberger oil company." Further commissions came by way of other architect friends. Cohen designed building interiors and, with Richard Meier, created the graphics for Sona, an Indian government-sponsored handicrafts store on New York's East Fifty-Fifth Street. In 1963, she launched a longer relationship with the Jewish Museum, designing catalogs, invitations, bags, and exhibition installations for such groundbreaking artists as Jasper Johns, Yves Klein, and Robert Rauschenberg.

Cohen once said she was "brainwashed" into wanting to design everything. Her approach was based on fluency with forgotten twentieth-century avant-garde typography. A knowing eye might notice telltale signs of the New Typography and Modernist painting, curiously meshed together but interpreted separately. She developed her own palette, type preferences, and personal glyphs, and she savored the meditative pleasure of assembling pasteups and refining the details. Her work depended on accidents. Her design was akin to creating a painting or collage. Books' title pages extended over spreads, unconventional at the time. The pages were modeled on film, building up speed and motion as type stretched over pages.

In 1969, she decided to turn her attention almost exclusively to painting. Coincidentally, Cohen's husband left the publishing world, which triggered some financial woes. So together they founded Ex Libris, a rare-book dealership that became a wellspring of newly appreciated European avant-garde documents and a boon to the burgeoning design history movement. Although she still accepted the occasional client, Cohen primarily designed the Ex Libris catalogs, in an appropriate historical manner.

By 1970, she turned to collage and printmaking, combining type and image where possible. Beginning in Alvin Lustig's shadow, Cohen emerged among her male counterparts as an exemplar of contemporary graphic design and typography. Ex Libris became a fount of design history and a generous resource for scholars and students of design. She was a vital link between design's Modernist past and its changing present. •

569

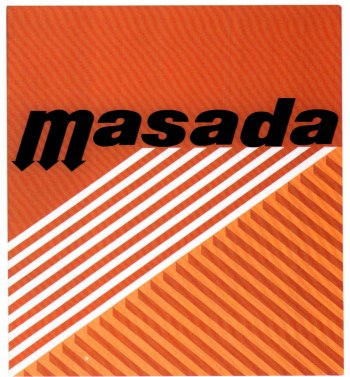

570

A Program for the New Whitney Museum of American Art

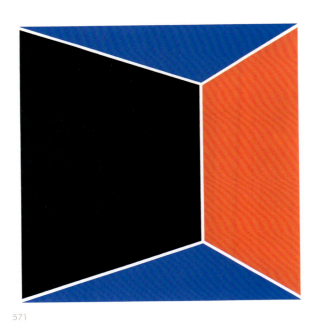

571

572

569
Catalog cover, *A New Aesthetic*, Washington Gallery of Modern Art, 1967

570
Catalog cover, *Masada*, Jewish Museum, New York, 1966

571
Catalog cover, *A Program for the New Whitney Museum of American Art*, Whitney Museum, 1964

572
Catalog cover, *Primary Structures*, Jewish Museum, New York, 1966

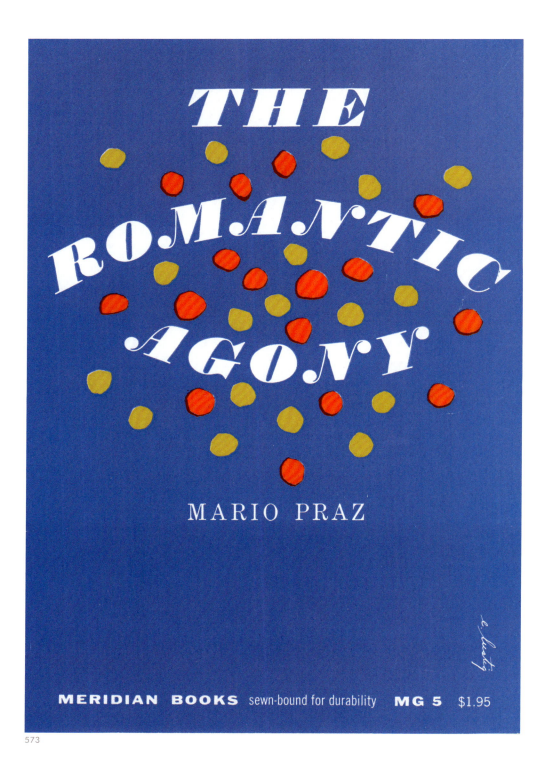

573

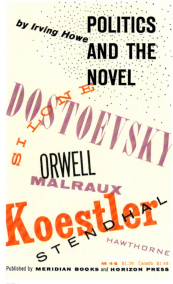

574

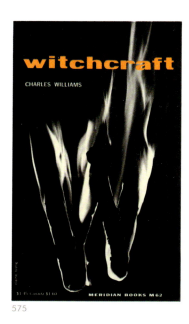

575

573
Book cover, *The Romantic Agony*, by Mario Praz, Meridian Giants, 1956

574
Book cover, *Politics and the Novel*, by Irving Howe, Meridian Books, 1958

575
Book cover, *Witchcraft*, by Charles Williams, Meridian Books, 1958

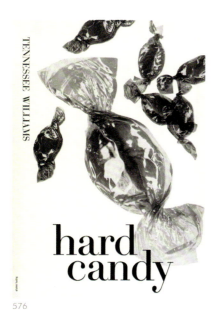

576

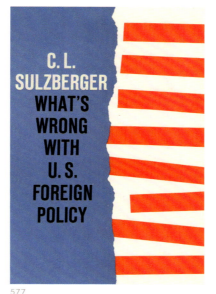

577

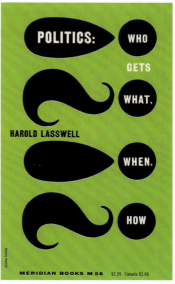

578

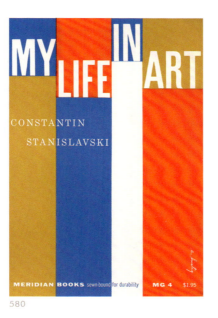

580

581

582

576
Book cover, *Hard Candy*, by Tennessee Williams, New Directions, 1959

577
Book cover, *What's Wrong with U.S. Foreign Policy*, by C. L. Sulzberger, Harcourt, Brace, 1959

578
Book cover, *Politics: Who Gets What, When, How*, Meridian Books, 1958

579
Book cover, *The Philosophy of Spinoza*, by Harry Austryn Wolfson, Meridian Giants, 1958

580
Book cover, *My Life in Art*, by Constantin Stanislavski, Meridian Giants, 1956

581
Book cover, *The Book of Jazz*, by Leonard Feather, Meridian Books, 1958

582
Book cover, *General, Marchese Usted*, by Salvador de Madariaga, Iberica, 1959

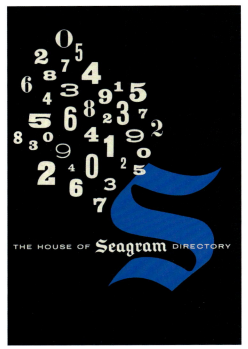

583

584

585

583
Cover, *The House of Seagram Directory*,
1961

584
Catalog cover, *Lightolier*, "Recent Additions
to Lightolier's 50th Anniversary Lighting
Collection," 1955

585
Logo, Frederik Lunning, A Division of Georg
Jensen Inc., 1960

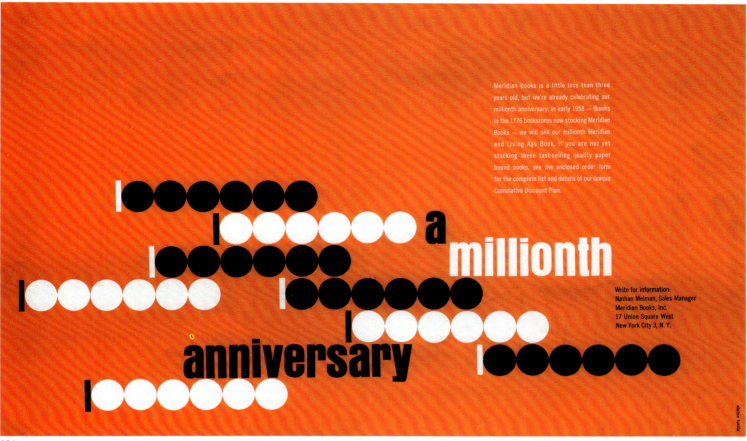

586

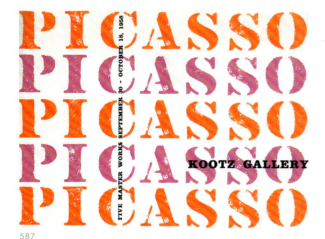

587

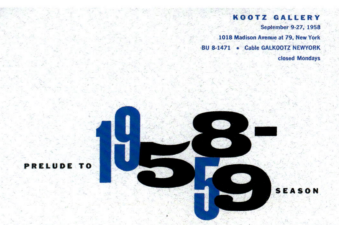

588

Promotional announcement, "A Millionth Anniversary," Meridian Books, 1958

Exhibition announcement, "Picasso: Five Master Works," Kootz Gallery, 1958

Gallery announcement, "Prelude to 1958–59 Season," Kootz Gallery, 1958

John Massey

b. 1931

Massey in New York, 1968. Photo: Warren Uzzle, *New York Herald Tribune*

John Massey played a principal role in bringing European Modernism to Chicago. Through his work for Container Corporation of America from 1957 to 1983, and as founder of the Center for Advanced Research in Design (CARD), he consulted with some of America's largest and most forward-thinking companies on the role of design and its impact. "By definition, graphic design should encompass the visual organization, clarification, and strengthening of ideas expressed through the two dimensions of the printed page," Massey said about his contributions. "Furthermore, if this defined job is done creatively, logically, and economically, it can be of great service in helping industry to widen the now constricting profit margins."

Born in Chicago, Massey graduated with a BFA from the University of Illinois at Urbana-Champaign. His early exposure to the young, Basel-based Armin Hofmann and Zurich-based Josef Müller-Brockmann, whom he met as a student intern at the International Design Conference in Aspen in 1953, deeply influenced his minimalist modern designs and approach to geometry, abstraction, scale, asymmetry, texture, white space, and the restrained use of modern, sans serif typography. Equally inspired by the masters of modern art, Massey produced work that combined mathematics and play. It was both practical and artful. "Massey thinks as artist and designer simultaneously," wrote Victor Margolin.

Massey's first job out of school in 1956 was at the University of Illinois Press, where he worked under the direction of Ralph Eckerstrom, associate professor of industrial design at the University of Illinois and later cofounder of Unimark International. Eckerstrom became director of design at Container Corporation of America, and he invited Massey to join him there in 1957. After Eckerstrom's departure in 1964, Massey assumed the position of director of design, advertising, and public relations. As a designer and manager at Container Corporation of America, he helped guide decision making related to the impact of design on advertising, policy, marketing, management, and communications. In *Print* magazine, Massey stated, "Graphic design is in a position to influence industry in greater depth than ever before. . . . It is necessary that people concerned with design do not concern themselves solely with the organization, placement of elements and color within the confines of two dimensions. . . . Increasing the designer's responsibilities is the only way that he can be in a position to evaluate the purposes and objectives of everything he works on. This kind of approach, I believe will help reduce the superficial and trite solutions that are often superimposed unthinkingly in many printed messages and will contribute to a greater efficiency in communication between product and consumer."

Prior to 1964, Massey ran his own design firm in Chicago in addition to his work for Container Corporation of America; when he took over for Eckerstrom, the corporation bought Massey's practice, which became a separate corporate division called the Center for Advanced Research in Design. Massey's small team included Giulio Cittato, Karen Kutner, Tomoko Miho, Peter Teubner, and others. Commissions included an iconic cultural program for the city of Chicago, beginning in 1967, for which Massey designed bold abstract and geometric graphics in primary colors for banners and posters. He had been impressed by the public graphics he spotted in Zurich (and other cities), and he conceived the idea of a "planned civic graphics program" for Chicago. "America's first civic cultural communications program seeks to express through graphic design the virtues and diversity of the city's cultural life," Massey announced in *Graphis* magazine. The program would be "a graphic expression of the city as a place of cultural and human enrichment."

Massey also worked for Inland Steel, the Atlantic Richfield Company, and Herman Miller Furniture, and he made a significant contribution with his 1974 graphic system for the U.S. Department of Labor, including a recognizable logo mark, visual identity, and the *Graphic Communication Standards Manual*; this was part of Richard Nixon's Federal Design Improvement Program, directed and coordinated by the National Endowment for the Arts. Massey made bureaucratic life a little bit better by providing the Labor Department with a high-quality graphic scheme that set the standard for future publication designs.

In 1983, Massey left Container Corporation of America and started a practice under his own name, doing extensive work especially for Herman Miller. "Massey's credo as a designer holds as one of its basic tenets that all of the environment should be an expression of a higher, well-ordered and completed dedication to the well-designed," stated Yustin Wallrapp in *Graphis* in 1968. "And by the environment Massey means all that surrounds us. Trains and roads, packages and toys, buildings, doorways, clothing and refrigerators. The overwhelming enlarged surroundings of the total environment." As a painter, Massey's homage to Herbert Bayer comes through his embrace of bright color, fascination with space, and evocation of mystery through the stillness of his abstract forms. But throughout his career, he always had his own voice. Rooted in art and design, Massey's contribution was summed up by this belief: "Design is nothing in itself. It is only significant when it serves a worthy purpose." •

chicago has a great lake

589

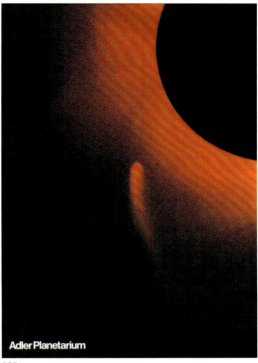

Adler Planetarium

590

lincoln park

run jump play look think dream

591

589
Poster, *Chicago Has a Great Lake*, Chicago
Cultural Program, 1968

590
Poster, *Adler Planetarium*, Chicago Cultural
Program, 1968

591
Poster, *Lincoln Park*, Chicago Cultural
Program, 1968

592

Catalog cover, *Facilities, Products, Services,*
Container Corporation of America,
1967. A uniquely modern design of pure
rectilinear and angular forms, thick rules,
and primary colors.

Our country calls not for the life of ease, but for the life of strenuous endeavor. The twentieth century looms before us big with the fate of many nations. If we stand idly by, if we seek merely swollen, slothful, ease, and ignoble peace, if we shrink from the hard contests where men must win at hazard of their lives and at the risk of all they hold dear, then the bolder and stronger peoples will pass us by and will win for themselves the domination of the world. Let us therefore boldly face the life of strife, resolute to do our duty well and manfully; resolute to uphold righteousness by deed and by word; resolute to be both honest and brave, to serve high ideals, yet to use practical methods.

Theodore Roosevelt: *from a speech, "The Strenuous Life," delivered in Chicago in 1891*

Great Ideas of Western Man ... one of a series. CONTAINER CORPORATION OF AMERICA

designer: John Massey

593

---

the very essence of a free government consists in considering offices as public trusts, bestowed for the good of the country and not for the benefit of an individual or a party.

John C. Calhoun, speech July 13, 1835, Great Ideas of Western Man, one of a series. CONTAINER CORPORATION OF AMERICA

594

593
Advertisement, "The Strenuous Life," part of "Great Ideas of Western Man" campaign, Container Corporation of America, c. 1965

594
Advertisement, "The Very Essence of a Free Government . . . ," part of "Great Ideas of Western Man" campaign, Container Corporation of America, c. 1967

595
Logo, U.S. Department of Labor, 1974. This identifies and unifies the multitude of components produced by the DOL. The mark consists of interlocking L's positioned on their point, surrounding a five-pointed star. The use of the official red and blue colors, along with the stripe effect and star, evoke the American flag. Massey provided the DOL with a quality, uniform identification and one that set the standard for future publication designs.

595

596

597

598

596

January and May monthly calendar posters produced as gifts for clients of Container Corporation of America's South American subsidiary. Massey's minimal, abstract designs illustrate the company's square and triangular cardboard boxes. Calendar Poster, *Enero*, "Carton de Venezuela," Container Corporation of American subsidiary, 1962

597

Calendar Poster, *Enero*, "Carton de Venezuela," Container Corporation of American subsidiary, 1962

598

Calendar Poster, *Mayo*, "Carton de Venezuela," Container Corporation of American subsidiary, 1962

The New World

International
Design Conference
Aspen

June 20–25
1965

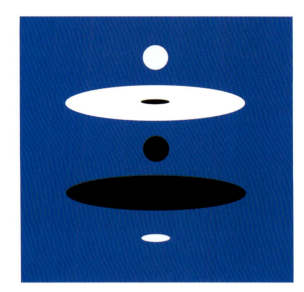

599

Aspen Institute for Humanistic Studies

600

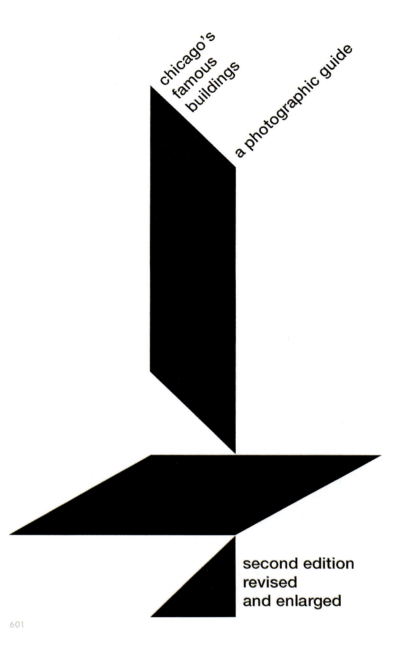

chicago's famous buildings a photographic guide

second edition revised and enlarged

JOHN MASSEY

601

599
Poster with symbol, *The New World*, 15th Annual International Design Conference, Aspen, Colorado, June 20–25, 1965

600
Collage, Aspen Institute for Humanistic Studies, 1964

601
Book cover, *Chicago's Famous Buildings: A Photographic Guide*, by Arthur Siegel, University of Chicago Press, 1969

Tomoko Miho

1931–2012

Miho at the Center for Advanced Research in Design (CARD) office, Chicago, 1967

Tomoko Miho's graphic design was a composite of many cultures and disciplines. She was a multidimensional designer in both the literal and the spiritual sense. The convergence of experiences, from her Japanese ancestry to her travels throughout Europe and America to friendships with modern design pioneers, contributed to her brand of reductive modern design. "I don't feel as though I'm attached to a particular style or fashion," she said in an interview in *Hall of Femmes*. "That's when things are more likely to become dated. I try to do the simple statement, to make it relevant and clean . . . and impart information."

Tomoko Kawakami was born in 1931 in Los Angeles, where her family was in the flower business. They instilled in Tomoko her earliest concept of space as a design element. The Japanese traditions of flower arranging and gardening, with an emphasis on shape, form, harmony, and the combining of foregrounds and backgrounds in totality, were visible in her posters, logotypes, and books. "I always look at a sheet of paper or cardboard as potentially three-dimensional, so a design exists in space, not just on the drawing board. That's how I see things," she told *Hall of Femmes*.

During World War II, the Kawakami family spent three years in an internment camp in Gila River, Arizona. This experience motivated Tomoko, like many Japanese Americans, to seek out new opportunities once her family had relocated to Minneapolis. Through her high school art teacher, she received a summer scholarship to the Minneapolis School of Art (now Minneapolis College of Art and Design), where she took college classes in advertising and graphic design. During college, she worked part-time at the U.S. Bureau of Engraving and Printing. Having received a full scholarship at the Art Center School in Los Angeles, she learned hand lettering and took classes in "structural design," drawing, graphics, and art history, graduating in 1958 with a degree in industrial design. Around that time, she met fellow designer James Miho, whom she later married.

The Mihos settled in Philadelphia, where Tomoko worked as a graphic designer and James landed his first job, at N. W. Ayer, where he worked on Container Corporation of America's "Great Ideas of Western Man" advertising campaign. When James was transferred to Detroit, Tomoko worked as a packaging designer for Harley Earl Associates, the automotive design consultancy.

In 1960, the Mihos embarked on a life-changing, six-month tour of Europe with Bob and Vicky McClain, friends from the Art Center School. The couples traveled throughout Europe in a silver Porsche and met with notable designers of the period: Giovanni Pintori at the Olivetti plant in Milan, Hans Erni in Lausanne, Josef Müller-Brockmann in Zurich, and Herbert Leupin in Basel. At the Hochschule für Gestaltung in Ulm, Germany, they met Tomás Gonda, and in Helsinki, Finland, they connected with Tapio Wirkkala and Armi Ratia, founder of Marimekko. The trip left an indelible mark. "Swiss design became very influential when we were

there," Tomoko told *Hall of Femmes*. "Traveling through Europe opened my eyes to design work that was both freer and more structured than what we'd learned at Art Center."

Back in the States in 1960, she was hired in New York as a graphic designer at George Nelson & Associates, under the direction of Irving Harper. "Perfection was Tomoko's very own mandate," Harper told Veronique Vienne. "Her work was remarkably clean, beautiful pristine." Harper became her mentor.

"It was a memorable learning experience to work with Irving, who was an architect crossing over different disciplines to participate in the design of important projects like the Herman Miller furniture, the Howard Miller clocks and Bubble lamps, exhibitions, graphics, a beautiful series of advertisements with photography by Art Kane and copy by Mary Welles," she told Paul Makovsky at *Metropolis* magazine. Tomoko worked on visual identities, brochures, and the iconic, immense, loose-leaf binder for the furniture manufacturer Herman Miller. In 1963, she replaced Don Ervin as director of graphic design for Herman Miller.

The Mihos moved to Chicago in 1967. Tomoko worked with a small team at John Massey's Center for Advanced Research in Design (CARD) and later opened the New York office of CARD, working on corporate identities for the Atlantic Richfield Company and Herman Miller projects. At CARD, she designed a *Great Architecture in Chicago* poster (1967), silkscreened on aluminized, silver paper, that captured the essence of the city. Her *65 Bridges to New York* poster, from the "Aspects of New York City" campaign sponsored by Container Corporation of America in 1967–68, features a dominating, tightly cropped and high-contrast photograph of the recently built Verrazano-Narrows Bridge. This unique point of view is further dramatized by her choice of a red-and-black palette and discreet, vertically aligned, lowercase Helvetica.

This was not the only time Tomoko referenced architecture in her work. Her brother Mikio, was an architect and influenced her greatly. She also credited Frank Gehry, Buckminster Fuller, and Isamu Noguchi as inspirations. For a client, Harrell & Hamilton Architects, Tomoko renamed the company to the much simpler and more contemporary Omniplan. The geometric logo consists of unified geometric shapes representing the versatility of the company in engineering, architecture, and interior design. It was scaled for different uses and even became a three-dimensional sculpture.

From 1974 to 1982, James and Tomoko were partners in the company named Miho. In 1982, they divorced. She then founded Tomoko Miho Design to work on corporate identities, book and brochure design, office environments, and architectural signage, often collaborating with George Nelson alumnus Lance Wyman. Tomoko kept the Modernist faith, never yielding to fashion while staying loyal to the principles of clarity. •

65 bridges   to new york

602

602
Poster, *65 Bridges to New York*, Aspects of
New York City series, Center for Advanced
Research in Design, 1967

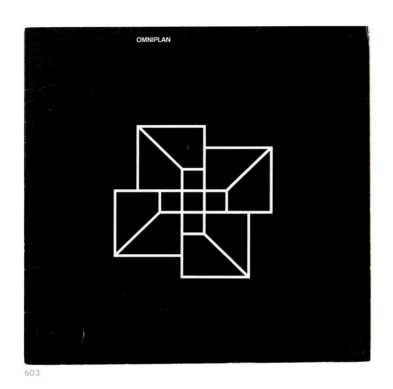

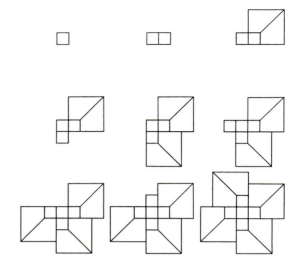

603

604

603
Booklet cover and interior page, *Omniplan*, Dallas, 1970. Miho designed the 1967 logo—a dynamic and flexible symbol for an environmental development corporation offering services in architecture, design, engineering, and planning.

604
New logo announcement, Hardwood House, Rochester, New York, Center for Advanced Research in Design, c. 1971

great architecture in chicago

605

HERMAN MILLER LOUNGE SEATING

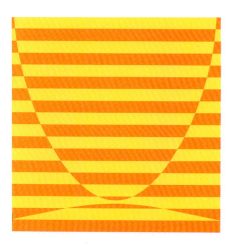

HERMAN MILLER SEATING SYSTEMS

606

607

608

605
Poster, *Great Architecture in Chicago*,
Center for Advanced Research in Design,
1967

606
Booklet covers, *Herman Miller Lounge
Seating* and *Herman Miller Seating
Systems*, Herman Miller, George Nelson &
Associates, 1961. The Herman Miller logo
illustrated as an optical vibration.

607
Logo, Everbrite Electric Signs, George
Nelson & Associates, 1961

608
Logo, Atlantic Richfield Company (ARCO),
Center for Advanced Research in Design,
c. 1967

Reid Miles
1927–1993

Miles in New York, c. late 1950s

If Alex Steinweiss was the father of the modern record album cover, then arguably, Reid Miles was the father of the modern jazz album cover. Working mostly for the inventive Blue Note Records, founded in 1939 by German émigré Alfred Lion and a Berlin childhood friend, photographer Francis Wolff, as well as for Prestige Records and other labels, Miles helped set in motion innovative Modernist approaches to album cover design. During a roughly eleven-year period in New York, from the midfifties to 1967, Miles designed nearly five hundred covers at "fifty bucks an album," as he recalled. These designs matched the music with a spirited visual language. His improvised and spontaneous way of gestating ideas allowed him at times to design as many as three covers in one sitting. Wolff said about the label, "We established a style including recording, pressing, and covers. The details made the difference."

Miles grew up in Long Beach, California, where his mother moved the family after splitting from his father in Chicago. After high school and World War II service in the U.S. Navy, he enrolled in the Chouinard Art Institute, a small, professional art school in downtown Los Angeles that later merged and became the California Institute of the Arts, or CalArts. Miles was to credit his earliest influences as William Moore, who taught at Chouinard, and Saul Bass, for his use of type and design.

In the early fifties, after a breakup with his fiancée, a fellow student at Chouinard, he dropped out and moved to New York, portfolio in hand. There he got a job as assistant to the Abstract Expressionist painter, graphic designer, and jazz aficionado John Hermansader. As a freelance designer, Hermansader had designed iconic record covers for his client Blue Note as early as 1951, working alongside Paul Bacon, Tom Hannan, Bill Hughes, and Gil Mellé, all credited as early influences who set in motion the work on which Miles and others continued to build. Hermansader had studied at the New Bauhaus in Chicago, and later at the New School for Social Research in New York, with Robert Motherwell. Around 1955, Miles began to design his own covers for Blue Note, and even though he left the Hermansader studio in 1956 for a job at *Esquire* magazine, he continued as Blue Note's art director, creating innovative twelve-inch record covers aimed at attracting broader audiences.

Personally, Miles was more interested in classical music than jazz, and he depended on Blue Note founder Lion "to describe the mood and intent of each album." His approach to covers ranged from classic Swiss Style design with restrained typography to more expressive gestures signifying energy and motion, evoking the feeling of the music. Miles found his style early. For *Thelonious Monk: Genius of Modern Music* (1956), one of his first efforts for the label, a tightly cropped photograph by Wolff floats on a bright red field above a staggered "Thelonious Monk" set in a sans serif typeface. This seemingly effortless design was unconventional when compared to other American covers issued during the same time; it embraced the melody, harmony, and rhythms of Monk.

One of Miles's favorite album cover designs was for Freddie Hubbard's *Here to Stay*. His energized and attention-getting typography uses repetition, cut letters, and alternating color to convey the intensity and confident sounds of Hubbard's trumpet. He also occasionally worked with Andy Warhol, and he used Warhol's mother's unique script handwriting for *Monk: Thelonious Monk with Sonny Rollins and Frank Foster* in 1954 and *The Story of Moondog* in 1957.

Miles's lasting contribution to record design was his ability to improvise with conviction. His mostly two-color, economical design solutions employed both objective and expressive elements, and his covers were always inventive. His use of large, flat areas of color; contrast; negative space; cropping to activate photographs; and asymmetry was masterful. He sometimes used his own blurred, dreamy photographs (which he would take when Wolff's were not right), but he relied mostly on soulful, graphic, black-and-white studio session photos taken by Wolff. In either case, he always found a synergy between image and text. Wayne Adams, his studio assistant in the seventies, said of Miles: "He was happiest when he had his sleeves rolled up, pushing the pieces around to create a design."

Throughout his years in New York, Miles worked for diverse clients, including Columbia Records, the *New York Herald Tribune*, and *Gentlemen's Quarterly*. Warhol once pleaded on his behalf with Margaret Hockaday, the pioneering founder of Hockaday Associates, a Madison Avenue advertising agency with a reputation for inventive, playful, and stylish work. Miles got the gig, which lasted until he "slipped off in a client meeting." He recalled: "I'm no politician. New York taught me to scream, that's its claim to fame."

Eventually, Miles left New York and ended his design practice, maintaining a healthy commercial photography studio until his death in Los Angeles in 1993. In his heyday, he had an instinctive understanding of how design could be used to communicate (and sell) the music. And he was lucky to have a generous client who allowed him the freedom to explore his ideas and generate a striking visual identity for modern jazz. •

609

610

611

612

609
Album cover, *In 'N Out* by Joe Henderson,
Blue Note Records, New York, 1964. Photo:
Francis Wolff

610
Album cover, *The Rumproller* by Lee Morgan,
Blue Note Records, New York, 1965. Photo:
Francis Wolff

611
Album cover, *Jutta Hipp with Zoot Sims* by
Jutta Hipp, Blue Note Records, New York,
1956

612
Album cover, *It's Time!* by Jackie McLean,
Blue Note Records, New York, 1965.
Photo: Francis Wolff

HERBIE NICHOLS TRIO
HERBIE NICHOLS TRIO
HERBIE NICHOLS TRIO
HERBIE NICHOLS TRIO
HERBIE NICHOLS TRIO
HERBIE NICHOLS TRIO
HERBIE NICHOLS TRIO

BLUE NOTE 1519

613

james spaulding/herbie hancock/reginald workman/clifford jarvis

STEREO
84115 BLUE NOTE.

hub-tones
freddie
hubbard

614

volume two *blue note 1511*

THELO-
NIOUS
genius of modern music
MONK

615

TIME
WAITS
THE
AMAZING
BLUE NOTE 1598
BUD
POWELL

616

Thelonious Monk with
MO
NK
Sonny Rollins and Frank Foster
Prestige 7053

617

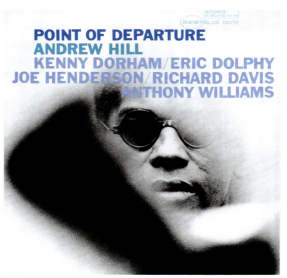

STEREO
84167 BLUE NOTE

POINT OF DEPARTURE
ANDREW HILL
KENNY DORHAM/ERIC DOLPHY
JOE HENDERSON/RICHARD DAVIS
ANTHONY WILLIAMS

618

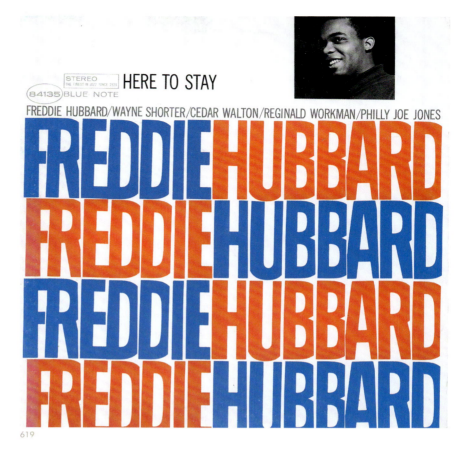

619

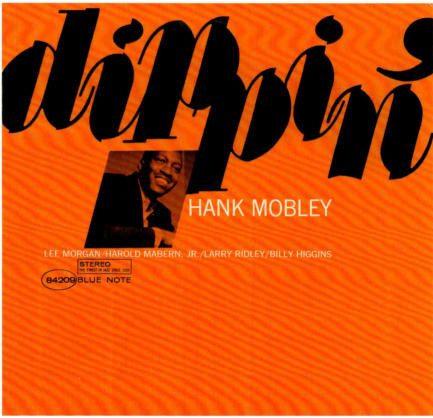

620

613
Album cover, *Herbie Nichols Trio* by Herbie Nichols Trio, Blue Note Records, New York, 1956. Photo: Francis Wolff

614
Album cover, *Hub-Tones* by Freddie Hubbard, Blue Note Records, New York, 1962. Photo: Francis Wolff

615
Album cover, *Genius of Modern Music* by Thelonious Monk, *Volume Two*, Blue Note Records, New York, 1956. Photo: Francis Wolff

616
Album cover, *Time Waits: The Amazing Bud Powell* by Buddy Powell, *Volume 4*, Blue Note Records, New York, 1958. Photo: Francis Wolff

617
Album cover, *Monk* by Thelonious Monk, Prestige, 1954. Decorative handwritten lettering by Andy Warhol's mother, Julia Warhola

618
Album cover, *Point of Departure* by Andrew Hill, Blue Note Records, New York, 1964. Photo: Reid Miles

619
Album cover, *Here to Stay* by Freddie Hubbard, Blue Note Records, New York, 1963. Photo: Francis Wolff

620
Album cover, *Dippin'* by Hank Mobley, Blue Note Records, New York, 1966. Photo: Francis Wolff

Charles E. Murphy
1933–2005

Murphy routinely applied his signature to his more painterly album covers from 1963 on.

Best remembered for his rhythmically inspired record album covers, Charles E. Murphy was a prominent New York art director and graphic designer from the late fifties to the early seventies. His most significant work was for Command Records, the legendarily innovative label "for discriminating people who desire the finest in sound," which was recognized for engineering a superior sound for jazz, big band, folk, easy listening, popular, and classical music. Murphy was responsible for more than eighty-five covers. His imagery is noteworthy for its lively experimentation, resulting in a playful artistic and geometric graphic orchestration, which gave visual timbre to the first-rate recordings. As art director, he commissioned a who's who of midcentury designers and artists to handle specific cover art, including Josef Albers; Paul Bacon; Brownjohn, Chermayeff & Geismar; Neil Fujita; George Giusti; and pioneering women Barbara Brown Peters and Gerry Olin, among others. But Murphy's own designs helped set a cool tone and intense style that defied the conventions of the day.

Born in New York, Murphy graduated with a BFA in 1958 from the Yale School of Art and Architecture, where he took drawing and color classes with Albers. He later served in the U.S. Army during the Korean War. In 1959, Enoch Light hired Murphy as the art director of his new company, Command Records. Light sought to give the adventurous listener a selection of young, relatively obscure musicians. Thanks to Murphy's art direction and expressive visual style, the label produced its own brand of covers that conveyed the avant-garde spirit of the recordings while seizing the attention of new audiences. Many of the albums were packaged in high-quality glossy gatefold jackets, with interiors that featured detailed information for audiophiles. Murphy's lively graphic language, concepts of symbolism, and sensitivity to color, shape, and composition gave Command its distinctive American style, which not only set it apart from competitors and imitators, but also challenged the recording industry's marketing standards.

Initially, distributors resisted Command's higher prices and Albers's black-and-white abstract covers of dots and squares, but resistance broke down when early releases turned out to be chart toppers. During Murphy's tenure, geometric abstraction was Command's signature style. He favored a more expressive approach than Albers's, to help evoke the energy and motion of the music. His personal preference was for energetic and loose graphic representations of diverse sounds: trumpet, woodwinds, trombone, piano, guitar, bass, and percussion. For an album such as *Provocative Percussion Volume 4* (1962), Murphy's simplified, collage-like shapes paired well with his condensed sans serif typography that signaled modernity.

Unlike his Modernist peers Reid Miles and Ronald Clyne, Murphy rarely featured photographs of musicians, choosing instead to use abstract imagery in a contrapuntal, rhythmic manner. *The Persuasive Trombone of Urbie Green and His Orchestra* (1960), for example, relies on simple red-and-black circles pulsating from the center. Pattern and repetition convey the tempo of the young virtuoso's smooth and seductive trombone—or, as the liner notes explain, "the glorious, butter-smooth, big, rhythmic sound of the dancers' dance band of the 'Sixties."

As an experienced art director and an artist himself, Murphy rarely overdirected others' work. Instead, he established a visual tone for others to follow. For *The Pertinent Percussion Cha Cha's* (1960), "the most challenging record you have ever put on your turntable," he commissioned female artist Gerry Olin. Her enigmatic abstract shapes, in an unusual color combination of hot pink, purple, and gold, must have made for startling sales displays for distributors and retail stores.

Murphy also created a decades-long painting series, New York Impressions, but he was best known for his work for Command Records, which introduced a generation of innovative musicians to the world and had the good sense to let Murphy design in a modern idiom that is as fresh today as it ever was. •

RS 33 • 815

THE PERSUASIVE TROMBONE OF URBIE GREEN
AND HIS ORCHESTRA

Command
records

© 1960 GRAND AWARD RECORD CO. INC., New York, N. Y.

DESIGNED BY CHARLES E. MURPHY

621

CHARLES E. MURPHY

621
Album cover, *The Persuasive Trombone of
Urbie Green and His Orchestra* by Urbie
Green, Command Records, Grand Award
Record Company, New York, 1960

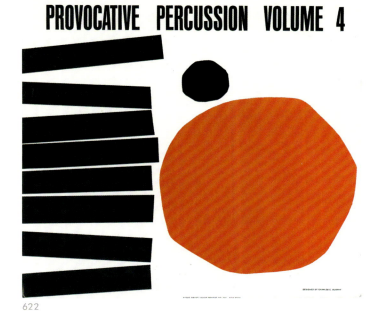

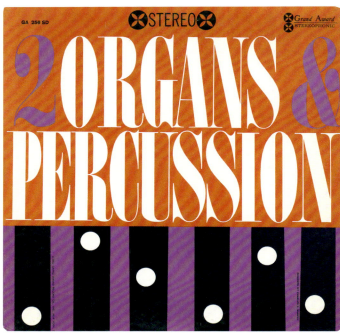

622

623

624

625

622

Album cover, *Provocative Percussion Volume 4* by Enoch Light and the Light Brigade, Command Records, Grand Award Record Company, New York, 1962

623

Album cover, *The Persuasive Trombone of Urbie Green Volume 2* by Urbie Green, Command Records, Grand Award Record Company, New York, 1962

624

Album cover, *Two Pianos & Twenty Voices* by Lew Davies and His Orchestra, Command Records, Grand Award Record Company, New York, 1960

625

Album cover, *2 Organs & Percussion* by Sy Mann & Nick Tagg, Grand Award Record Company, New York, 1961

627

628

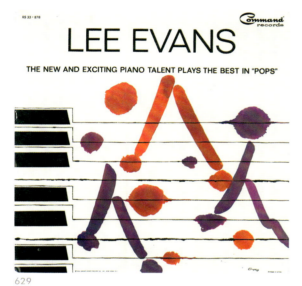

629

630

626

626
Album cover, *High—Wide & Wonderful* by Doc Severinsen, His Trumpet & Orchestra, Command Records, Grand Award Record Company, New York, 1965

627
Album cover, *Roman Guitar* by Tony Mottola and His Orchestra, Command Records, Grand Award Record Company, New York, 1960. Art direction: Charles E. Murphy; Cover art: Paul Bacon

628
Album cover, *Lee Evans: The New and Exciting Piano Talent Plays the Best in "Pops"* by Lee Evans, Command Records, Grand Award Record Company, New York, 1964

629
Album cover, *Pertinent Percussion Cha Cha's* by Enoch Light and the Light Brigade, Command Records, Grand Award Record Company, New York, 1960. Art direction: Charles E. Murphy; Cover art: Gerry Olin

630
Album cover, *Provocative Piano Volume II* by Dick Hyman and His Orchestra, Command Records, Grand Award Record Company, New York, 1961. Art direction: Charles E. Murphy; Cover art: Barbara Brown Peters

Georg Olden

1920–1975

Olden in his McCann Erickson office, New York, c. 1965

Georg Olden was head of network on-air promotions for the Columbia Broadcasting System (CBS) from 1945 to 1960. The visual acuity and conceptual verve he brought to designing promotional title cards, which had been little more than afterthoughts at other networks, was unparalleled on television at the time. Appealing for their playful pictographs and witty typography, Olden's titles transformed the space between programs and commercials into happy respites for the eye that whetted the viewer's appetite for upcoming programming. He and his staff designed imagery for leading ratings magnets such as *I Love Lucy*, *Ed Sullivan*, *Burns and Allen*, *Lassie*, *Gunsmoke*, and so many more. His on-air duties also shaped news broadcasts, and he helped produce the vote-tallying scoreboard for the first televised presidential election returns: the 1952 race between Dwight D. Eisenhower and Adlai E. Stevenson. He was "undoubtedly the first person to design news graphics for CBS," wrote Julie Lasky in *Print* magazine in 1994.

Georg Elliott Olden was born in Birmingham, Alabama, the son of a Baptist minister whose own father had escaped slavery and fought in a black regiment of the Union Army during the Civil War. His mother, from New Orleans, was a classically trained singer; his sister, Sylvia, coached some of the great performers of the day and was the first person of color to work at New York's Metropolitan Opera. Olden attended Virginia State College before dropping out shortly after the attack on Pearl Harbor to serve as a graphic designer for the Office of Strategic Services (OSS), where he worked alongside Will Burtin and Eero Saarinen, among other Modernist designers. The OSS job introduced him to a range of art options, including cartoons, which he sold to publications including the *New Yorker*. In fact, when he was in his early twenties, Olden choose to drop the final "e" from his given name in order, he told *Advertising Age*, to attract the attention of magazine editors. In 1945, Secretary of State Edward R. Stettinius Jr. hired Olden to work as a graphic designer with the fledgling United Nations Secretariat, designing presentation records, maps, and charts. Shortly thereafter, Hu Barton, his OSS supervisor, recommended him to the agency's communications director, Colonel Lawrence W. Lowman, who in civilian life was vice president of CBS's TV division. Working under CBS art director William Golden, Olden eventually headed a staff of fourteen in charge of sixty CBS weekly shows.

As one of the few African Americans to be successful in the advertising and design fields, Olden was in the "precarious role of being a black man in a field that had only recently admitted ethnic whites to positions of power," Lasky noted. During the fifties, issues of race, ethnicity, gender, and sexual orientation were handicaps, yet Olden was a visible presence. His name frequently appeared in annuals, and in 1970 he won seven Clio Awards. Olden was an undisputed innovator for the nascent TV industry. But it was far from easy. In 1954, of the 72,400 people employed full-time in television, fewer than 200 were black.

"Olden's attitude towards his race," Lasky explained, "was one of the most ambiguous aspects of his life." In the fifties, he was a member of the National Urban League and designed its powerful mark—a black equal sign in a white circle. However, Olden's friends told Lasky that he acted "whiter than a lot of white people," and Olden was quoted in an *Ebony* magazine article as saying, "In my work I've never felt like a Negro. Maybe I've been lucky."

When Olden started in television, the quality of broadcast transmission was poor. Home receivers rarely received a perfect signal. So Olden avoided tonal nuances in his work, and since his job was to create four-by-five-inch cards that were flashed in front of the huge cameras for a few seconds, he found ways to make gold from the static on screen. He designed vignettes with iconic imagery or relevant metaphors, usually combined with crisp typographic treatments. Some he designed on his own; others were farmed out to a repertory troupe including Alex Steinweiss, David Stone Martin, and Bob Gill.

After fifteen years at CBS, Olden left in 1960 so he could "work on cigarettes, beer and automobiles." For that he needed to be at an ad agency, and he landed at the TV division of BBDO. Three years later, he joined McCann Erickson, where he was placed on the Professional Advisory Council, a creative task force that offered consultation on various campaigns throughout the agency. That same year, he was selected as the first African American to design a U.S. postage stamp—a broken chain, commemorating the one hundredth anniversary of the Emancipation Proclamation. It earned a commendation from President John F. Kennedy, who said the stamp was "a reminder of the extraordinary actions in the past as well as the business of the future."

Olden was laid off from McCann in 1970, starting a personal slide. "The ostensible reason was economic—a recession," wrote Lasky. But he was devastated by "what he clearly saw as a betrayal" after playing by the rules of white society. "He believed that the real reason for his dismissal was McCann's reluctance to promote him to the top executive ranks." Charges of racial discrimination were filed with the Equal Employment Opportunity Commission and the New York State Division of Human Rights. However, the case was never resolved to Olden's satisfaction. He had his share of additional misfortunes, and as Lasky reported, although he had earned the equivalent of a six-figure salary at McCann, Olden ended his life in poverty. •

631

631
On-air title cards promoting CBS television series and specials from the golden age of the network, c. 1953–57. When Olden began on-air graphics for television, it was not enough to make something readable on a cathode-ray screen; it had to pique the viewer's imagination too.

Tony Palladino

1930–2014

Palladino in New York, c. 1950s

Saul Bass created the dramatic opening title sequence for Alfred Hitchcock's chilling thriller *Psycho*, but it was Tony Palladino, a street-smart, Italian American, New York graphic designer and illustrator, who designed the violently slashed, psychotically inspired block-letter word that is decidedly one of the most recognizable logos in publishing, advertising, and even film history. Palladino's stark book jacket design for Robert Bloch's 1959 thriller, published by Simon & Schuster, was so emblematic that two years after Hitchcock acquired the movie rights, J. Walter Thompson, Universal Pictures' advertising agency, bought the original typographic collage for use as the film's graphic identity. Palladino explained that the austere white letters, torn and disturbingly and unsteadily reassembled against a black background, was intended to express the homicidal madness of the novel's protagonist, Norman Bates. "How do you do a better image of 'Psycho' than the word itself?" he asked. "Subliminal as it may be, Palladino's initial design helped make *Psycho* a motion picture classic," stated the Art Directors Club 1987 Hall of Fame induction précis.

Anthony Americo Palladino, raised on the mean streets of East Harlem by non-English-speaking Italian parents, was a contradiction: With his New York accent, he was a roughneck with a good right hook, but rather than join a street gang, he became a charter member of an influential band of savvy, creatively gifted children of immigrants who swooped down en masse to dominate New York's post–World War II advertising and graphic design fields. This urban army of artists, writers, and designers launched a creative advertising revolution to challenge the staid, WASP, "white shoe" propriety of Madison Avenue.

Art cut with humor was the best way for Palladino show his mettle and communicate with others. He attended the storied High School of Music and Art and "was light-years ahead of the world," recalled George Lois, Palladino's classmate and lifelong friend. "Not the world of art students, but the world of artists! He adored Dada and drew like a Fra Angelico. He digested Man Ray, Mondrian, Malevich, Magritte, and Matisse, and it came out pure Palladino."

As an artist, Palladino had a flowing linear and amorphous style that also emulated two of the founding fathers of Abstract Expressionism, Mark Rothko and Robert Motherwell, whom he admired. Although a stint in the U.S. Army from 1950 to 1953 forced him to put art on hiatus, Palladino joined the creative mainstream from the midfifties on. His keen sense of the absurd resulted in evocative visual puns, as he employed illustrative typographic concepts to give voice to words. Among his favorite examples was a promotional piece for package designer Irving Werbin: a brown paper bag with Werbin's name visually incorporating the word "packaging." Among other projects, he later illustrated posters for the Mobil-supported *Masterpiece Theater* series on PBS and, in 1976, designed the propulsive blue-and-white logo for Conrail.

Although advertising was his bread and butter, his art was closer to his heart, and bringing the two together was bliss: "Everything he touched became art," said Lois. Always freelance, he consulted for various Madison Avenue agencies, including Papert Koenig Lois, bringing with him a modern aesthetic and less-is-more style combined with the visual language of Abstract Expressionism. Palladino collaborated with some of the most renowned art directors and designers of the day, including Push Pin Studios cofounder Milton Glaser and illustrator-animator R. O. Blechman, briefly his partner until 1960, who recalled that "he did a lot of his most interesting work"—what Blechman refers to as poetry—"when he was doing his own, and not corporate, work."

Teaching was also a particular passion. Palladino's close association with the School of Visual Arts began in 1958, when designer-illustrator Bob Gill introduced him to the school's founder, Silas Rhodes. Palladino taught a class with Ivan Chermayeff, whose own modern ethos he shared. The school commissioned him to work on a few of its notable subway posters, which inspired Palladino to trek around New York's more curious neighborhoods in search of unusual vintage signs and other graphic artifacts that he could use for conceptual projects. Of his many recruitment posters for the school, one depicted two smashed automobile hubcaps that had been repainted and transformed into women's hats, suggesting the transformative power of the artist. Everything had to have an idea.

Palladino further developed a penchant for making quirky associations between everyday objects and common letterforms. In a newspaper ad for the antiwar organization Women Strike for Peace, the headline read, "Did you hear the one about the third world war?" Under it he positioned three square panels: The first said, "Knock knock." The second said, "Who's there?" The third was empty. Voilà! The message was clear, concise, and spot-on. Pure image worked for him too: In an ad conceived for the restaurant Positano, which was briefly located at Park Avenue South and East Twentieth Street, he photographed glass salt-and-pepper shakers of various sizes as opposing pieces on a chessboard.

He saw advertising as a means to reach a higher artistic level. "People don't want to look at advertising," Palladino told an interviewer in *Graphis* magazine. "People want to get entertained intellectually." And this he was very happy to oblige. •

632

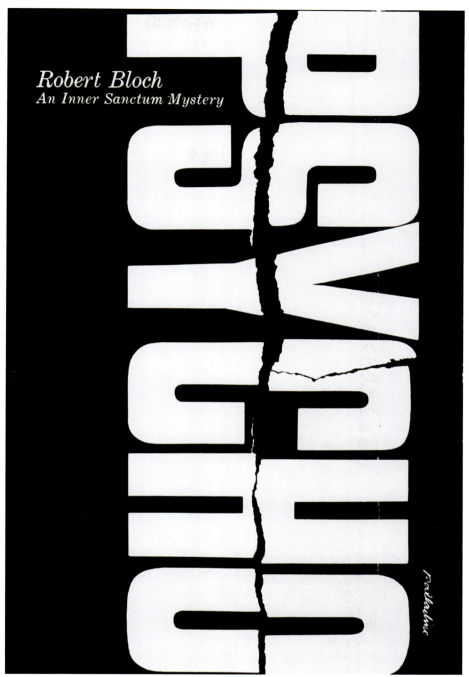

633

632
Promotional paper bag mailer, *Irving Werbin Packaging*, 1957

633
Book jacket, *Psycho*, by Robert Bloch, Simon & Schuster, 1959. The unique graphic quality of the torn title and crisp black-and-white design chillingly illustrates the main character's deranged state of mind.

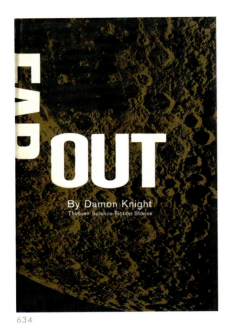

634

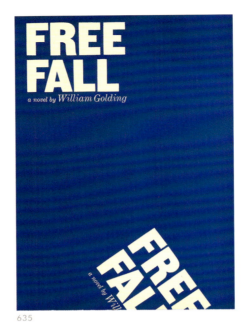

635

636

637

638

639

634
Book jacket, *Far Out: Thirteen Science-Fiction Stories*, by Damon Knight, Simon & Schuster, 1961

635
Book jacket, *Free Fall*, by William Golding, Harcourt, Brace, 1960. Palladino was a New York street kid with a sense of wit and gift of irony. These and a natural sense of order and balance contributed to beautiful book jacket designs.

636
Book jacket, *Funeral of Figaro*, by Ellis Peters, William Morrow, 1964

637
Book jacket, *A Thief in the Night*, by Thomas Walsh, Simon & Schuster, 1962

638
Book jacket, *How Hard to Kill*, by Thomas Dewey, Simon & Schuster, 1962

639
Book jacket, *Vein of Violence*, by William Campbell Gault, Simon & Schuster, 1961

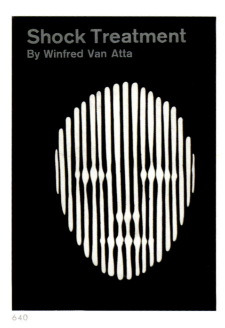

640

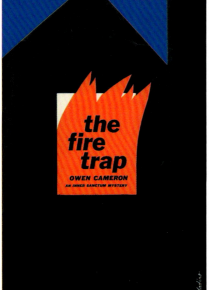

641

642

TONY PALLADINO

640
Book jacket, *Shock Treatment*, by Winfred Van Atta, Doubleday, 1961

641
Book jacket, *The Fire Trap*, by Owen Cameron, Simon & Schuster, 1957

642
Magazine covers, *Architectural & Engineering News* 5, no. 12 (December 1963), 5, no. 7 (July 1963), and 5, no. 8 (August 1963). All were executed while Tony Palladino and R. O. Blechman worked together as *Blechman Palladino* from 1958 through the early 1960s.

Paul Rand
1914–1996

Rand in his Weston, Connecticut, studio, 1970. Photo: Milton Ackoff

When Paul Rand died at eighty-two, his career had spanned six decades and numerous chapters of design history. In the late thirties, he contributed to the transformation of commercial art from craft to profession. By the early forties, he influenced the look and tone of advertising, book, and magazine cover design. Later in that decade, he was proffering a graphic design vocabulary based on form, where once only style prevailed. By the midfifties, he altered the ways that major corporations employed design for graphic identity. And by the midsixties, he had created some of the world's most enduring corporate logos. He was a main channel through which European modern art and design were introduced to American designers. In later years, he was a design teacher, theorist, and philosopher.

Rand understood how American commercial requisites were different from those in Europe, where image-based advertising reigned. While he admired the Bauhaus, he was not utopian. He had modest goals but made bold experiments that helped alter American practice. From the outset, Rand had an instinctive understanding of modern painting and a passion for the popular arts. He was critical of the lack of quality in American commercial art and believed that even the most common engagement in everyday life could be enriched by an artist's touch.

Rand grew up in East New York, Brooklyn, a tough neighborhood and the stomping grounds of the infamous Murder Inc., where his father owned a grocery store. He attended night classes at Pratt Institute in Brooklyn and the Art Students League in Manhattan, but his real education came from perusing foreign design magazines, such as the German *Gebrauchsgraphik*, in which he was introduced to the masters of the modern. After high school, he got his first job with the package, product, and graphic design firm George Switzer Agency, designing lettering and packages for Squibb and Hormel meats, among other clients. In 1935, he opened his own "closet-sized" studio on East Thirty-Eighth Street and worked in the manner of the reductive German poster artist Lucian Bernhard and the Swedish industrial designer Gustav Jensen. At twenty-two, he was offered a job as art director for the New York office of Esquire-Coronet—but he refused, insisting that he was not ready. A year later, however, he accepted the job and was given responsibility for the special fashion sections in *Esquire*.

By 1938, Rand had produced enough noteworthy work that *PM* included him in its pantheon of luminaries. The magazine found its way to Marguerite Tjader Harris, the daughter of a wealthy Connecticut munitions manufacturer, who was intent on having Rand design covers for *Direction*, a left-wing arts and culture magazine. Rand was not paid but given plenty of freedom—and eventually a few original Le Corbusier drawings as recompense. The *Direction* covers exemplify the timelessness that Rand attributed to the most significant art and design. "Good work has a universal and timeless character," he often said.

In 1941, William Weintraub, a former partner at Esquire-Coronet, started an advertising agency, and Rand joined it as art director from 1941 to 1954. He collaborated with Bill Bernbach on Dubonnet, Lee hats, Autocar Company, and other projects. He also worked for Smith, Kline and French, a pharmaceutical company, and Ohrbach's department store, creating weekly newspaper advertisements. In his work, Rand modernized advertising design. Before the forties, very little American advertising was really designed; rather, it was simply composed or laid out, as if by a printer or board man. Rand saw the entire process as a design problem that required intelligent solutions, and the best are worthy of being signed.

When he was thirty-two, he wrote *Thoughts on Design*, an annotated portfolio published by Wittenborn. With typical sarcasm, he once admitted, "God forbid, there would ever be a fire, at least I'd have all my samples in one place." In the preface, he wrote: "This book attempts to arrange in some logical order certain principles governing advertising design. The pictorial examples used to illustrate these principles are taken from work in which I was directly engaged. This choice was made deliberately, and with no intention to imply that it represents the best translation of these principles into visual terms. There are artists and designers of great talent whose work would be perhaps more suitable. But I do not feel justified in speaking for them, nor secure in attempting to explain their work without any possibility of misrepresentation."

Book jackets were a large part of Rand's oeuvre. One of his favorites was for *The Tables of the Law* (1945) by Thomas Mann, which defied the standard of fussy, calligraphy-laden jackets. Its bold typographic statement and poster-like simplicity earned him a letter of praise from Mann himself. For another innovation, *Leave Cancelled* (1945), a novel by Nicholas Monsarrat about war's ravages and loves lost, he used die-cut circles as bullet holes piercing a silhouetted picture of an angel against a pale red background. Rand's interpretations were sometimes more eloquent than the manuscripts.

In 1956, he was hired by Eliot Noyes as the graphic design consultant for IBM and designed the identity system and logo still used today. IBM became a paradigm of corporate identity. Soon afterward, logos followed for Westinghouse (1961), United Parcel Service (1961), ABC (1962), and Cummins Engine (1979). All but the one for UPS are still in use.

In 1946, Rand wrote an essay titled "The Designer's Role" that serves as a fitting epitaph: The designer "improvises, invents new techniques and combinations. He coordinates and integrates his material so that he may restate his problem in terms of ideas, pictures, forms, and shapes. He unifies, simplifies, and eliminates superfluities. He symbolizes . . . by association and analogy. He intensifies and reinforces his symbol with appropriate accessories to achieve clarity and interest. He draws upon instinct and intuition. He considers the spectator, his feelings and predilections." •

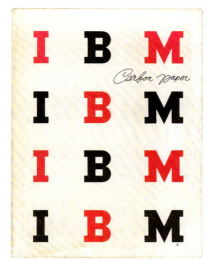

644

645

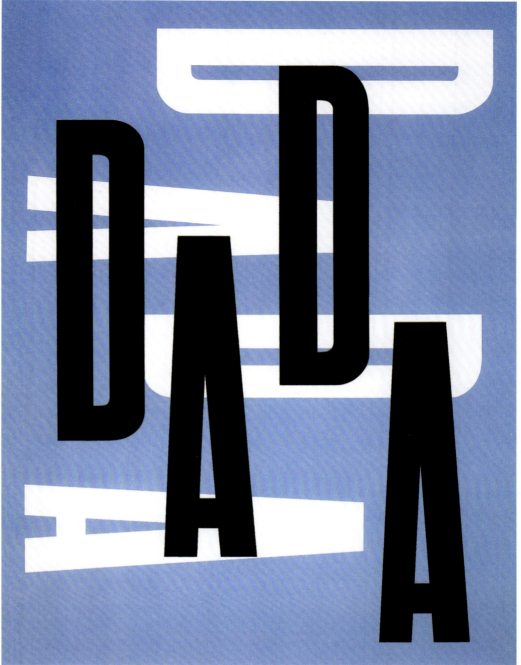

643

643
Product packaging (box top), Carbon Paper,
IBM, c. 1957

644
Journal cover, *PM: An Intimate Journal
for Production Managers, Art Directors,
and Their Associates* 4, no. 9 (October–
November 1938)

645
Book cover, *Dada Painters and Poets: An
Anthology*, edited by Robert Motherwell,
Wittenborn Schulz, 1951. This cover is not
a copy or pastiche of the unconventional
and chaotic Dada typography but is an
interpretation. Modern movements, and
Rand in particular, built upon rather than
mimicked one another.

646

647

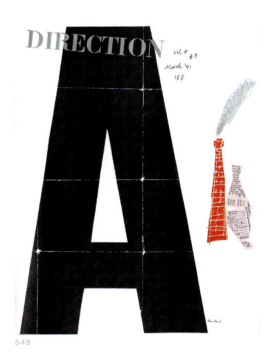

648

649

646
Journal cover, *Journal of the American Institute of Graphic Arts (AIGA)*, no. 6 (1968). Rand often worked with abstract shapes that leave the deciphering to the viewer. Among his favorite forms, this could be interpreted as a clown face that reveals a jumble of the AIGA letters.

647
Magazine cover, *Direction*, "Summer Fiction Number," vol. 5, no. 3 (1942)

648
Magazine cover, *Direction* 4, no. 3 (March 1941)

649
Logo, Westinghouse, 1960

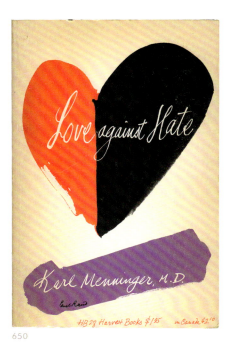

650

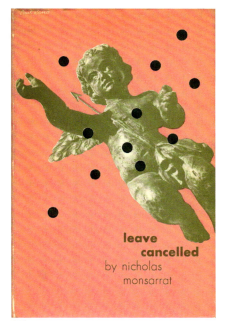

651

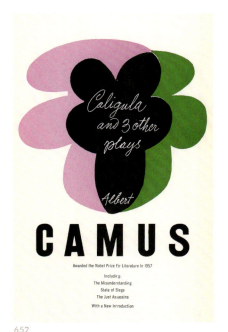

652

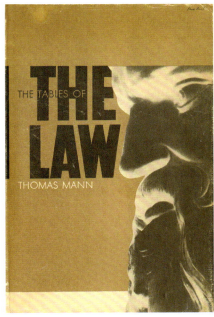

653

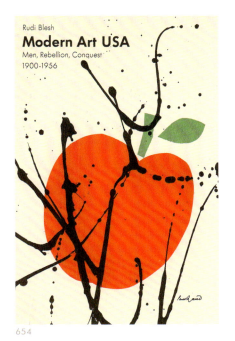

654

655

Rand was master of the play principle, the idea that graphic design did not have to be serious to be taken seriously. His sense of play, which ensured memorability, ran the gamut from photographic to typographic to illustrative book jacket and paperback cover designs.

650
Book cover, *Love Against Hate*, by Karl Menninger, Harvest Books, 1959

651
Book jacket, *Leave Cancelled*, by Nicholas Monsarrat, Knopf, 1945, with die-cut bullet holes over a floating image of Eros

652
Book jacket, *Caligula and Three Other Plays*, by Albert Camus, Knopf, 1958

653
Book jacket, *The Tables of the Law*, by Thomas Mann, Knopf, 1946. Rand's first book jacket (and book) designed for Knopf

654
Book jacket, *Modern Art USA: Men, Rebellion, Conquest 1900–1956*, by Rudi Blesh, Knopf, 1956

655
Book cover, *The Anatomy of Revolution*, by Crane Brinton, Vintage Books, Random House, 1956

Alexander Ross

1914–1950

Ross studio portrait, New York, c. 1948

"The modern designer is one who makes efficient blueprints for various craftsmen to follow. . . . He is more the architect, dealing with perspectives and ideas." These are the words of Alexander Ross, a name rarely mentioned and often overlooked in graphic design histories. Yet he played an important role in New York's modern design community, particularly within the burgeoning pharmaceutical industry. His pharmaceutical designs between 1944 and 1947 are equal to (and sometimes eclipse) the work of such contemporaries as Lester Beall, Will Burtin, Matthew Leibowitz, Paul Rand, Alex Steinweiss, and Bradbury Thompson. His work routinely employed modern techniques, including grids, experimental printing, photomontage, photograms, asymmetry, white space, modern type, and dramatic shifts in scale. Throughout the 1940s, his name appeared frequently in lists of award-winning advertising designers (Art Directors Club, AIGA, *Financial World*, Direct Mail Advertising Association, Pharmaceutical Advertising Club, and more). Represented by the well-respected Stephan Lion agency, his studio specialized in publication design, direct mail booklets, industrial design, and packaging. He was a skilled furniture and industrial designer. His professional practice and contributions were varied and valuable and on the cusp of maturing when he died in 1950, at only thirty-six years of age.

Born Alexander Rosenzweig in New York and raised in Brooklyn, Ross graduated from Pratt Institute in about 1934. At some point, he changed his surname, and he used "Alex" on many of his designs. Early in his career, he worked at Rosenbaum Studios in Manhattan, doing projects for the packaging giant American Coating Mills, and later at the Reiss Advertising Agency and Diamond Press. From about 1942 to 1945, Ross worked as an associate art director under the direction of Tobias Moss, for Bradbury Thompson, the associate chief at the U.S. Office of War Information's Bureau of Overseas Publications, designing printed materials for both New York and London.

After his time there, he opened his own practice at 141 East Twenty-Fifth Street, in the same building as New York's leading commercial printer, Davis, Delaney, to which he provided design services. The studio was small. Louis Danziger worked for Ross for two weeks in the summer of 1948; Aaron Burns, for two years, from about 1946 to 1948—and called it "the biggest break of his life." The office also employed a female illustrator. Ross executed the designs, or "roughs," while Burns produced well-crafted comps. Commercial clients included General Electric, the Barrett Company, Daystrom Corporation, Corn Products, General Foods, Beech-Nut Packing, Coca-Cola, Sheffield Farms, Manhattan Shirt, and Schenley Distillers. Starting about 1947, Ross was the associate art director of the little-known *Musical Digest,* which describes itself as *"An Independent Magazine Devoted to All Types of Good Music,"* under European émigré art director Jean Carlu. Ross designed the interiors and covers for some of the issues not signed by Carlu.

Ross's most engaging contributions were his booklets and advertising projects for pharmaceutical clients Sharp & Dohme, A. H. Robins,

Squibb, and his award-winning direct mailers for White Laboratories (where Alex Steinweiss also worked), a job he held in high regard and acquired through Asher Aron, vice president of Davis, Delaney. Designing for selected audiences such as doctors (who, pharmaceutical companies felt, were intelligent enough to appreciate the modern art and design being used), Ross succeeded in presenting conventional medical products and services with innovative graphic solutions. Sylvia Brown, in a remembrance in the *AIGA Journal*, said of Ross: "Always he would take his original copy draft to a physician for explanation, so that his design elements were not only appropriate—they were inspired."

For his pharmaceutical work, Ross experimented with photographs and photograms, Victorian engravings, and transparent color overlays, skillfully mixing function and form. His dynamic page compositions were composed with thick and thin angular lines, bleeds, unusual color palettes, and modern typography. Brown said, "He seemed to have a passion for functionalism and a gift of being both practical and creative in his projects and often lamented the need 'for things doing a job.'"

In the May 1947 issue of *Friem's Four Pages* (the free monthly bulletin-newsletter for A. I. Friedman, New York), editor P. K. Thomajan spoke of Ross: "He has no toleration for embroidered niceties, frills that give only secondary thrills in place of primary ones—that of connecting directly with dollars. When summoned into a situation, Ross doesn't dip into old bags of tricks, putting on a one-man-show of his whole repertoire; rather he immediately pits his wits against a problem and whittles out a solution with the minimum means. He has a strict approach, wherein he precisely ascertains: 1) character of audience 2) time allotted 3) appropriation and 4) objective. Ross places great stress on the necessity of knowing physical limitations and working creatively within them. Before a designer can proceed, he must know how far equipment to be used can cooperate."

Ross was a sharp critic of design education, and in a lecture he gave at Pratt Institute, he stated, "In our business, the knowledge consists of the standards of graphic trades, typography, engraving, printing process, paper, ink, photographs and paints. . . . Schools leave a great deal to be afraid of by not showing the breadth, width or depth of the arena which the student is going to operate. . . . Fear of one's lack of knowledge is the greatest deterrent to successful practice." Described by Sylvia Brown as "a warm, magnetic individual," Ross believed that designers should form professional associations to help "inform the public about good design and have them demand more of it." •

656

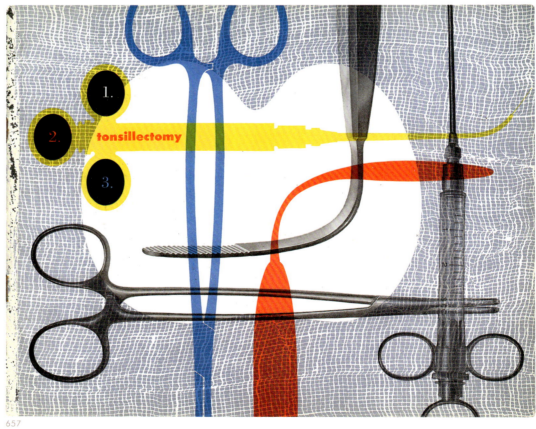

657

ALEXANDER ROSS

656
Booklet cover, *Authoritative Thought on Multiple Vitamin Therapy*, White Laboratories, Newark, New Jersey, 1945. The cover design is an adaptation from a cast of *The Thinker* by Auguste Rodin.

657
Booklet cover, *Tonsillectomy*, White Laboratories, Newark, New Jersey, 1946. This publication for the medical profession pictorially and diagrammatically communicates the conditions commonly considered indications for tonsillectomy, as well as operative techniques and management of post-tonsillectomy complications.

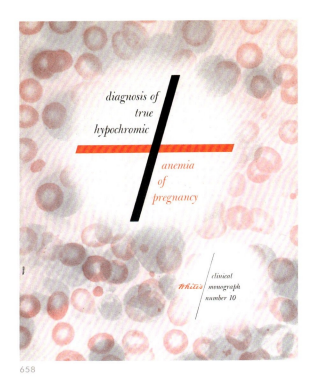

658

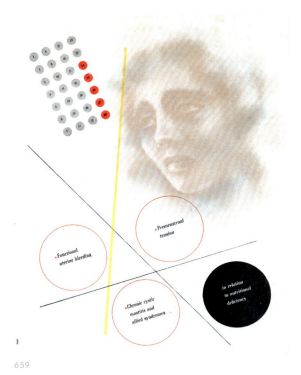

659

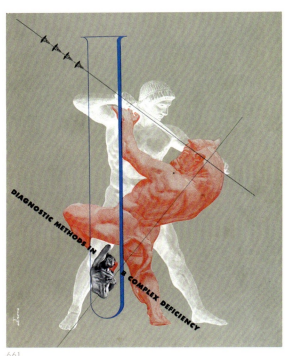

660

661

658
Booklet cover, *Diagnosis of True Hypochromic Anemia of Pregnancy*, Clinical Monograph no. 10, White Laboratories, Newark, New Jersey, 1947

659
Trifold booklet cover, *Common Gynecologic Syndromes Associated with Excess of Body Estrogen and Nutritional Deficiency*, White Laboratories, Newark, New Jersey, 1946

660
Booklet cover, *Common Lesions of the Nursing Nipple: Pathology, Etiology, and Therapy*, Clinical Monograph no. 9, White Laboratories, Newark, New Jersey, 1946

661
Booklet cover, *Diagnostic Methods in B Complex Deficiency*, White Laboratories, Newark, New Jersey, 1944. From the interior: "Cover design is an adaptation from the cast Theseus Battling with the Minotaur symbolic, here, of the triumph of medicine over disease."

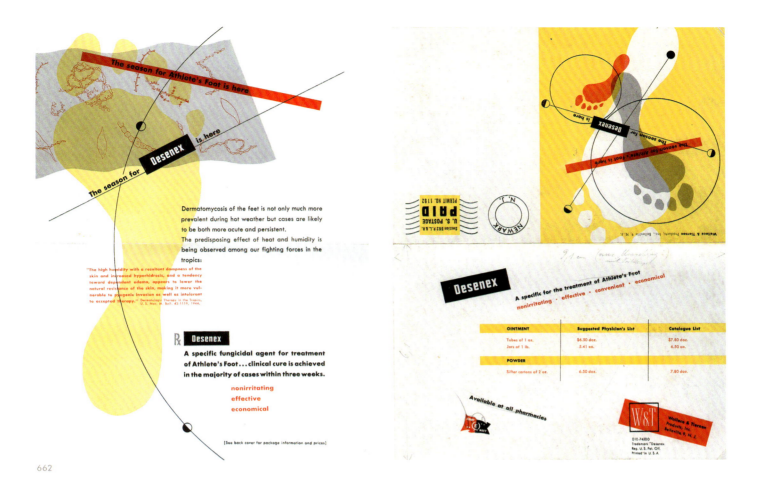

662
Direct mail front and back, *Desenex*,
Wallace & Tiernan Products, Belleville,
New Jersey, c. 1945

663
Self-promotional direct mail, *Plan*, *Skill*,
Craftsmanship, Davis, Delaney, New
York, 1945

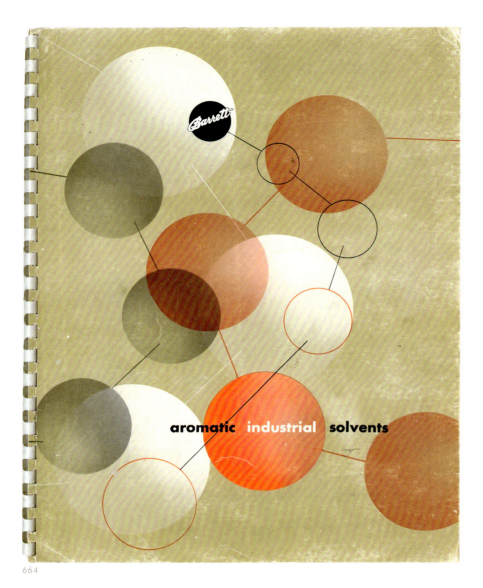

664

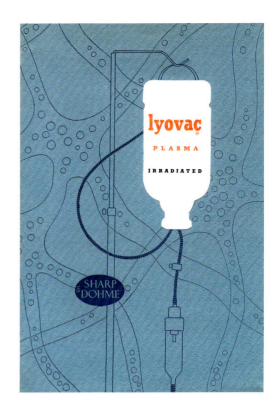

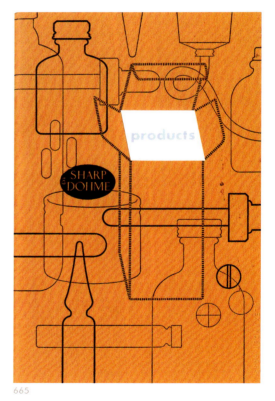

665

664
Catalog cover, *Aromatic Industrial Solvents*, Allied Chemical and Dye Corporation, New York, 1949

665
Booklet covers, *Lyovac, Normal Human Plasma, Irradiated* and *Products*, Sharp & Dohme, Philadelphia, 1949, both with die-cut covers revealing the title pages

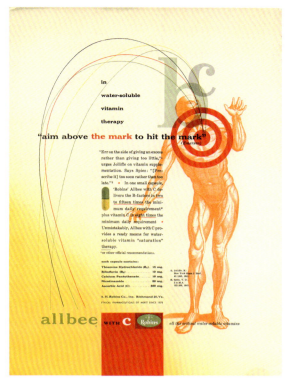

666

667

668

669

Advertisements, "Allbee," "Donnatal,"
"Phenaphen," and "Pabalate," A. H. Robins
Company, Richmond, Virginia, 1947–49

ALEXANDER ROSS

Arnold Saks

b. 1931

Saks in his New York studio, in front of his Laverne Furniture logo, c. 1962

Since he first opened Ward & Saks in the late fifties, and later in his solo practice, Arnold Saks has distinguished himself by his graphic clarity, deeply influenced by Swiss objectivity. His accomplishment is especially evident in his "less subjective, more analytical" work, including trademarks, exhibition design, and corporate communications and annual reports for clients ranging from small textile companies to major American industries. Saks's practice was uniquely positioned in a space where American requirements intersected with the International Typographic Style that he and others, including Chermayeff & Geismar, Rudolph de Harak, Unimark, Massimo Vignelli, and MIT, helped create and cultivate.

From a young age, Saks was inspired by the early work of Lester Beall and George Giusti, and, he recalled, "I just knew what I wanted to do, I didn't have to search hard to find a path that made sense to me." Raised in Brooklyn with grandparents who emigrated from Eastern Europe, Saks attended the High School of Music and Art and then entered Syracuse University on a scholarship. In 1954, he joined the Yale School of Art and Architecture's graduate program for graphic design, although his father's death forced him to leave before receiving his master's degree. Saks credits Herbert Matter and Alvin Lustig as influences, as well as designer and painter Norman Ives, who, said Saks, "showed me another way to look at graphics" and "how to think about design."

As the Korean War was ending, Saks was assigned to the U.S. Army Exhibition Unit in Alexandria, Virginia, an assignment also held by designers Tom Geismar and Bob Gill. While in the army, Saks also worked in Albuquerque, New Mexico, designing an exhibit to help teach members of Congress about the evolution of atomic weapons. When his service ended in 1956, he got married in Albuquerque and returned to New York, where he worked as an exhibition and graphics designer at the American Museum of Natural History under Lothar Witteborg, director of the exhibition department. When that work ended, he became the art director for *Interiors* magazine, responsible for the layouts and covers. Given a small budget, he made do with distinction.

An *Interiors* cover for September 1959, codesigned by Saks with Yale graduate Lou Klein, symbolized the architectural vigor of the interior design firm Welton Becket & Associates, whose work was featured in the issue. In a statement in the magazine about the cover, the editor explained, "The artwork consists of tint blocks laid over a photogram. The latter was made by slipping two pieces of perforated metal and one piece of an Erector Set into an enlarger and projecting them onto a tilted easel covered with photographic paper." In 1960, Saks summed up his design approach in the magazine *CA: The Journal of Commercial Art*: "Conceptually I try to make *Interiors* look clean and somewhat formal. Letting the material come forth as the most important element. I use very few tricks. I believe in the anonymous quality of design. A designer's demonstration of muscle flexing can become dull and tiresome. Also, it interferes."

That same year, Saks and James Ward, a Cranbrook Academy of Art graduate, art director for *Industrial Design*, and friend whom Saks had met at the U.S. Army Exhibition Unit, joined forces to open their eponymous partnership on West Fifty-Third Street in New York, directly across the street from the Museum of Modern Art. The duo's similar interests and backgrounds (Ward trained as an industrial designer and Saks as a graphic designer) complemented each other, and they quickly earned a reputable list of clients: Jack Lenor Larsen, a fellow Cranbrook graduate; Laverne Furniture; Charles Stendig Furniture; IBM; and Burlington Industries. Particularly notable was their early use of neon in a showroom exhibition that they designed to introduce the new IBM System/360 computer in 1965. After an eight-year run, the studio was dissolved.

In 1968, Saks opened Arnold Saks Associates. Karl Katz, director of the Jewish Museum, introduced him to Cornell Capa, who was in the process of launching the International Center of Photography (ICP). One of Saks's earliest projects in his solo practice was the ICP's first logo. He also added the Jewish Museum to his client roster, thanks to Elaine Lustig Cohen, who had been designing exhibition catalogs and graphics for the museum. Saks's monthly calendar of the museum's programs and events was an economical "series" using only black ink and a variety of handsome colored papers. This less-is-more approach arranged and connected the pieces, a result of his being "very heavily influenced" by the Swiss journal *Neue Grafik*, which he subscribed to early on. For Saks, "*Neue Grafik* was more important to me than any American design publication."

Along the way, his studio transitioned into being a leader in designing corporate annual reports. In 1977, he said of this genre: "The annual report is the record of a company's life for a specific year—and being so, becomes almost self-consciously important to corporate top management and their respective peer groups." For this purpose, Saks was an early American adopter of modern sans serif typefaces, notably Helvetica. For three years, beginning in 1965, he designed annual reports for Eastern Air Lines, and this business expanded to Time, Colt Industries, Chase Manhattan Bank, and eventually General Dynamics, where he followed in the footsteps of, and was influenced by, Erik Nitsche. Other clients included Goldman Sachs, Squibb, Bristol-Meyers, Pfizer, and American Home Products. At the height of his business career, Saks recalled "designing eighteen annual reports at one time, in one year."

Saks was adept at finding seemingly simple solutions for design problems, as his thinking was rooted in clarity, aesthetics, and a philosophy of design that benefited his clients. "Design should be anonymous to ensure that the solution is the problem's solution rather than the designer's," he told *Graphis* in 1977. •

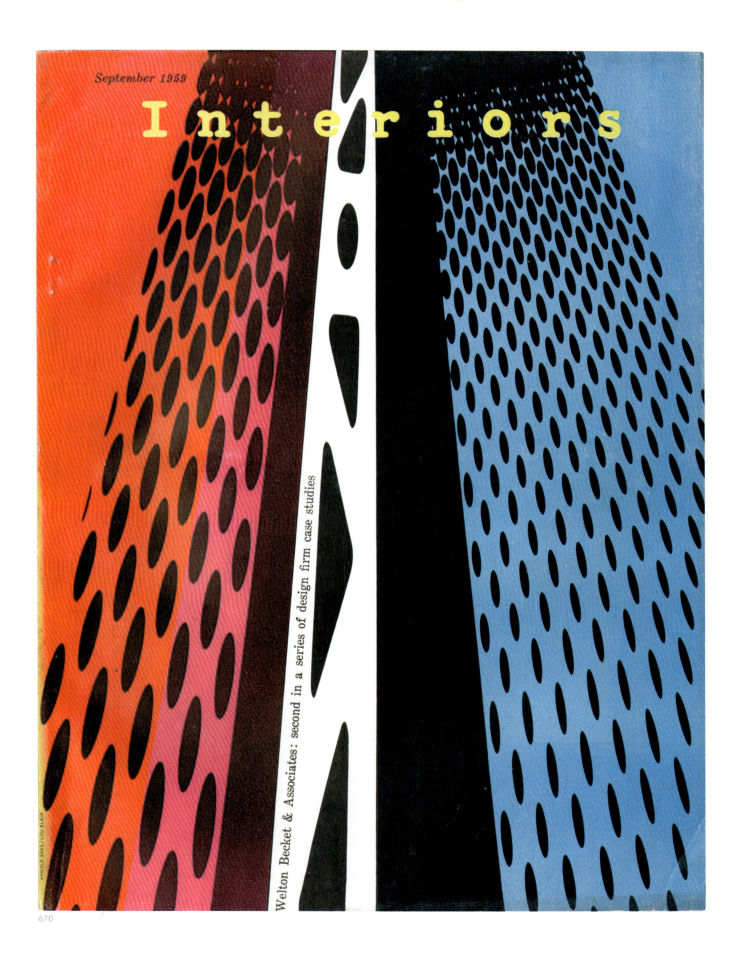

September 1959

Interiors

Welton Becket & Associates: second in a series of design firm case studies

ARNOLD SAKS/LOU KLEIN

670

670
Magazine cover, *Interiors*, Whitney
Publications, September 1959.
Codesigned with Yale graduate Lou Klein

671

672

675

676

673

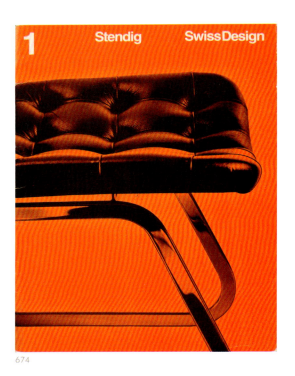

674

671
Magazine cover, *Art Direction: The Magazine of Visual Communication*, October 1968

672
Annual report cover, Eastern Air Lines, 1966

673
Magazine cover, *CA: The Journal of Commercial Art*, Coyne & Blanchard, Palo Alto, California, January 1960. Design: Ward & Saks

674
Product catalog cover, *Swiss Design*, Stendig, New York, 1972. The catalog illustrates the work of three Swiss designers: Hans Eichenberger, Robert Haussmann, and Kurt Thut.

675
Logo, Cultural Presentations U.S.A., U.S. Information Agency, 1967

676
Logo, Transammonia, 1969. A mark for a chemical importer-exporter

The Jewish Museum: March 1969

The Jewish Museum: January 1969

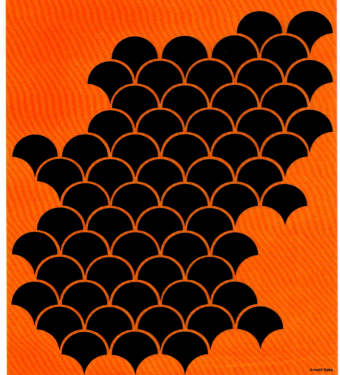

677

678

677–678
Calendar pages, programs, and events
at the Jewish Museum, New York, shown
with only black ink and a variety of
colored papers

679

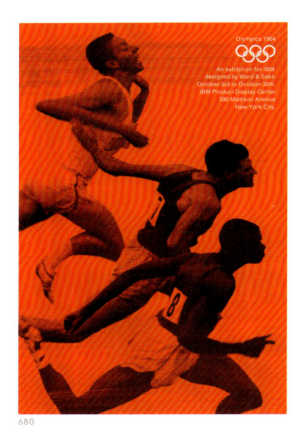

680

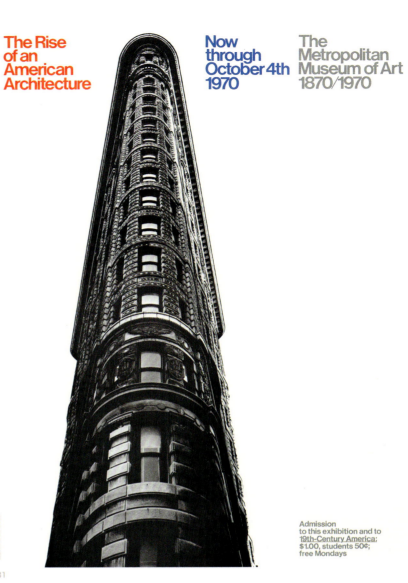

The Rise
of an
American
Architecture

Now
through
October 4th
1970

The
Metropolitan
Museum of Art
1870/1970

Admission
to this exhibition and to
19th-Century America:
$1.00, students 50¢;
free Mondays

681

679
Poster, *Laverne Furniture*, 1960. This poster
designed by Ward & Saks announces the new
Laverne logo and address. The mark signifies
designed space with its complementary
Laverne furniture, textiles, and wallcoverings.

680
Mailing announcement, *Olympics 1964*,
IBM. For the opening of the display windows
held at the IBM Product Display Center in
New York, Oct. 3–30, 1964. IBM reported
and recorded real-time electronic sports
results for the 1964 Tokyo Olympic Games.

681
Poster, *The Rise of an American Architecture*,
Metropolitan Museum of Art, New York,
1970. Photo: Elliott Erwin

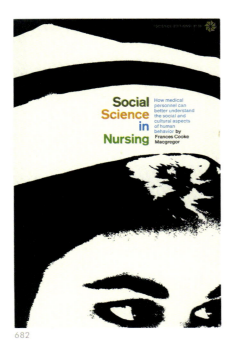

682

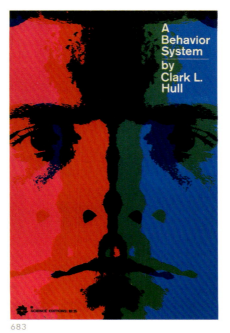

683

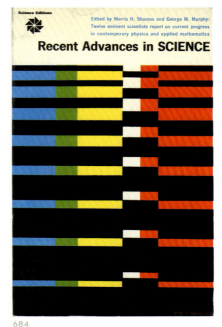

684

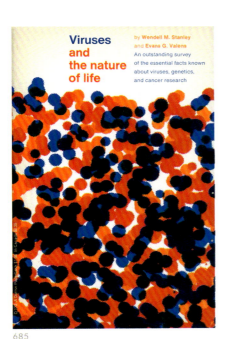

685

686

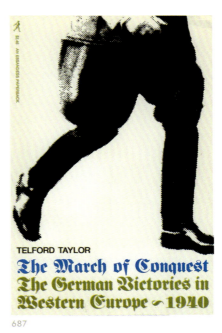

687

682

Book cover, *Social Science in Nursing*, by Frances Cooke Macgregor, Science Editions, John Wiley & Sons, 1965. Design: Ward & Saks

683

Book cover, *A Behavior System*, by Clark L. Hull, Science Editions, John Wiley & Sons, 1965

684

Book cover, *Recent Advances in Science*, edited by Morris H. Shamos and George M. Murphy, Science Editions, 1961. Design: Ward & Saks

685

Book cover, *Viruses and the Nature of Life*, by Wendell M. Stanley and Evans G. Valens, Dutton, 1965. Design: Ward & Saks

686

Book cover, *Mathematics: The Man-Made Universe*, c. 1960s

687

Book cover, *The March of Conquest: The German Victories in Western Europe, 1940*, by Telford Taylor, Simon & Schuster, 1958. Design: Ward & Saks

Arnold Shaw

1922–1967

Shaw in his New York studio, 19 East Forty-Eighth Street, c. 1950

Designer, typography consultant, and educator Arnold Shaw was a catalyst of communication in the New York modern design scene between 1946 and 1967. For seven years, he organized and designed landmark exhibitions and lectures at the Composing Room, the city's premier type house, and its Gallery 303, promoting modern practice to designers far beyond its New York hub. His immersive educational curricula at New York University and the School of Visual Arts were designed to advance the art and profession.

Born in New York, Shaw attended Straubenmuller Textile High School, one of the city's highly esteemed vocational schools. At eighteen, he worked during the day in the promotion department at RKO Radio Pictures, the studio responsible for such classics as *King Kong* and *Citizen Kane*. In the evening, he attended advertising design classes at the Cooper Union School of Art, graduating in 1946. He also took György Kepes's sought-after design class in visual fundamentals at Brooklyn College (with twenty-four-year-old classmate Saul Bass) and classes at the Art Students League with commercial illustrator and type designer Howard Trafton. In addition, Shaw was accepted into Alexey Brodovitch's workshop at the New School for Social Research. Early exposure to modern methods had an epic influence on the twenty-four-year-old Shaw.

In 1948, he opened Arnold Shaw & Associates, specializing in direct mail, advertisements, logotypes, book jackets, and posters. He built a notable list of national clients, including Squibb and Sandoz Pharmaceuticals, Doubleday, International Paper, *Interiors* magazine, Hu-Art Studios, *Modern Lamps*, *Time* and *Sports Illustrated* magazines, Time International, the Custom Shop, Educational Facilities Laboratories, the Ford Foundation, Kiplinger, and Bankers Trust Company.

"It takes terrific nerve to put a black line on a sheet of white paper, yet I prefer to start on black paper with white ink first," Shaw told *Interiors* magazine in 1949. The magazine reported that "he gets many design ideas from microscopic slides," presumably a reference to his pharmaceutical work. Shaw found inspiration in the world of science. This ability to find unusual graphic forms was similar to that of his peers Alexander Ross, Matthew Leibowitz, and Lester Beall, who were also involved in progressive pharmaceutical projects at this time.

In 1950, Shaw acquired the ideal client for his experimental approaches: the quarterly *Modern Lamps* magazine, for which he designed visually dynamic covers with fluid gestures that explore light and form using expressive and angled lines juxtaposed with bold colors and thick sans serif type. He believed that "excitement and interest are a necessary part of the design but only if they do not interfere with the simplest expression of the idea." This organic, abstract design was a direct result of ideas developed in Kepes's course.

In 1961, Shaw was hired by typophile luminary Robert Leslie and joined the Composing Room as a design and typographic consultant. The Composing Room was known for its commitment to promoting intellectual and educational ventures related to the graphics industry,

through journals, educational courses, lecture series, and rotating gallery exhibitions. As design director, Shaw organized and designed gallery exhibitions, lectures, and events featuring a bounty of local, national, and international designers. Its annual "Young Graphic Designers" exhibitions explored and promoted the work of up-and-coming professionals, including the Daly & Max Studio, Richard Danne, Nicholas Fasciano, Phil Gips, Charles Goslin, Richard Hess, Lou Klein, Andrew Kner, Mo Lebowitz, Clarence Lee, Alan Peckolick, and Bernie Zlotnick. Through this work, Shaw helped network and nurture young designers into the mainstream, an endeavor he found extremely rewarding. During the same time period, he produced two comprehensive type-specimen books, smaller type-specimen booklets, printed collateral, holiday cards, promotional materials, and exhibition announcements.

Shaw taught at New York University's Center for the Graphic Industries and Publishing from 1959 to 1967 and began teaching typography at the School of Visual Arts in 1961. His course at NYU, Typography in Visual Communications, was geared toward professionals, advanced students, and art teachers, with participants having basic knowledge of typography, typefaces, and reproductive processes. Shaw believed, "A designer . . . must be aware that his education does not end with the termination of formal training," but rather it is a constant process where the designer "must continually seek to grow in awareness and challenge his powers of perception and ingenuity."

In 1961, he became program chairman for the cooperation between NYU's Center for the Graphic Industries and Publishing and the American Institute of Graphic Arts, organizing a series of design clinics, including "Graphics at the New Frontier, Design and Responsibility"; "On Color Photography," by the acclaimed Viennese émigré Ernst Haas; and "The Organization Image as Graphic Invention," with notable guest lecturers Henry Wolf, Milton Glaser, Ralph Eckerstrom, Lou Dorfsman, and Herb Lubalin. Shaw and design assistant Steven Richter designed the promotional materials, including posters, course announcements, and catalogs. The aim of his 1963 course New Concepts in Design and Typography was "to encourage the designer to develop his typographic perspicacity and pursue a vigorous point of view." Topics covered included analysis of typographic appeals, the importance of innovation, expressive typography and international influences, letters and type as structural parts of design, and a thorough examination of rules that govern typography. Shaw believed, "Typography is more than a tool in the hands of a sensitive designer. It's an art form."

Shaw's philosophy is best summed up as, "Design is a very large aspect of our culture: it is a conveyor or betrayer of our standards and values and our thinking. It is the image through which we speak not only to each other but to all peoples." •

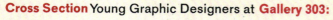

Cross Section Young Graphic Designers at Gallery 303:
Sponsored by The Composing Room, Inc., typographers
130 West 46th Street, New York. Gallery hours—10 am to 5.30 pm.
December 13, 1962 through January 30, 1963
Alan Fleisler, Phil Gips, Lou Klein, Mo Lebowitz,
Jack Lesko, Harry Redler, Herb Rosenthal, Bernie Zlotnik.

Preview Wednesday, December 12,
Refreshments 5 to 7 pm.
R.S.V.P. Mrs. Bayer JU 2.0100

Design: Arnold Shaw

688

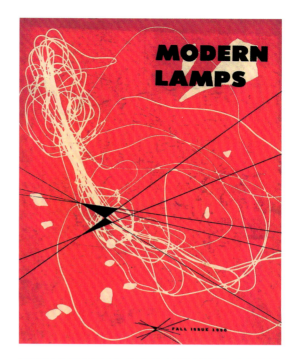

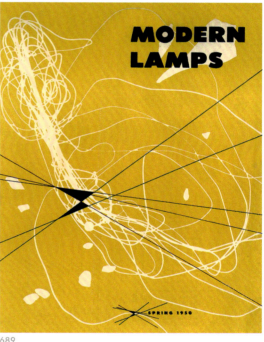

689

ARNOLD SHAW

688
Exhibition announcement, "Cross Section,
Young Graphic Designers," Gallery 303,
Composing Room, New York, 1962,
exhibiting the work of Alan Fleisler, Phil Gips,
Lou Klein, Mo Lebowitz, Jack Lesko, Harry
Redler, Herb Rosenthal, and Bernie Zlotnik

689
Magazine covers, *Modern Lamps*, Krieger
Publications, New York, vol. 1, no. 2
(Fall 1950). This experimental cover is a
photographic rendering of light, refraction,
and reflection.

690

691

692

693

694

690
Direct mail, *One Man's Fish Is Another Man's Poisson, Time* magazine, 1958, a promotional mailer sent to agencies and advertisers using die-cut fish gills.
Art direction: Fritz Brosius

691
Holiday card, "Happy Holidays and Best Wishes for '65," Composing Room and Photo-Composing Room, 1965

692
Magazine cover, *Interiors*, Whitney Publications, New York, November 1948

693
Logo, Arnold Shaw, Design and Typographic Consultant, Composing Room, 1961

694
Logo, Kiplinger Book Club, 1960

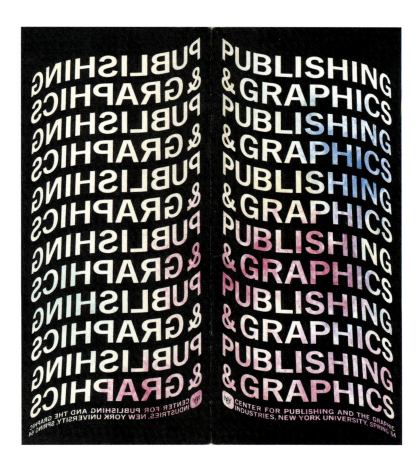

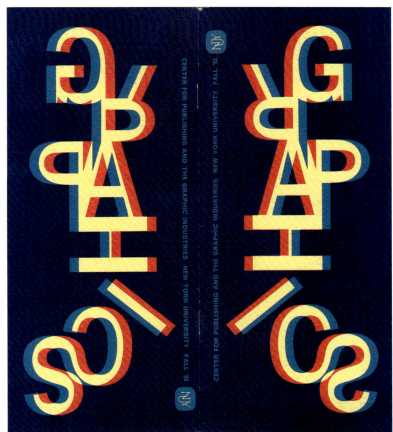

695
Course catalog covers, *Graphics* (Design, Publishing, Advertising, Printing), Center for Publishing and the Graphic Industries, New York University, Division of General Education and Extension Services, Spring 1964, Spring 1961, and Fall 1963. Design and typography: Steven Richter and Arnold Shaw

Louis Silverstein
1919–2011

Silverstein, New York City, c. 1948

Louis Silverstein was the godfather of modern newspaper design. After joining the *New York Times* in 1952, he rose through the creative ranks as promotion art director in 1953, corporate art director in 1969, and ultimately the first assistant managing editor for design in 1976. He retired in 1985 but continued to design newspapers for the Times Company and others. Silverstein revolutionized the *Times*'s design when he shifted from a tight eight-column format to a more breathable six-column grid on the front page and throughout the interior; introduced feature sections that were magazine-like newsprint broadsheets; expanded the strategic use of white space as a design element; took the vintage period off the *Times*'s nameplate; and generally transformed the *Times* from the "the Old Gray Lady" into an epitome of modernity.

Silverstein's mission was to attract a younger audience to a dwindling newspaper base. That included assuming a key role in developing visual content, such as the pioneering use of allegorical and metaphorical illustration rather than traditional editorial cartoons on the Op-Ed page. He also perfected conceptual data-driven graphics (what he called "sides of beef") that prefigured computer-age information graphics, which remain signatures of the *Times*'s visual character today. He hired a slew of significant art director–designers and built a creative ecosystem like no other.

Silverstein imparted more about visual journalism, dramatic presentation, storytelling, conceptual thinking, headline writing, and simply ways of getting untested ideas through a gauntlet of editors than any class in any school. Put a tracing pad in front of him and he could sketch out an entire newspaper. Give him a black litho crayon and he'd produce award-winning and newsworthy pages in minutes. His love for the *New York Times* was infectious. He instilled an esprit de corps in his designers, inspiring them to move beyond the everyday, even for a daily paper. But his newspaper accomplishments can easily overshadow his prodigious advertising work, which involved often self-motivated conceptual campaigns that combined Modernist formalism with aesthetic instincts.

Born in Brooklyn, Silverstein received a BFA degree from Pratt Institute, then began a short career in the advertising industry. For three years while serving in the military, he designed graphics for the U.S. Army Air Corps (the pre–World War II forerunner of the U.S. Air Force). He later earned an MFA at the Institute of Design in Chicago, where his thesis concerned individual responses to tactile experiences. He turned his talents to abstract painting, joining the American Abstract Artists group, and continued painting as time allowed. Meanwhile, as the 1984 précis to his induction into the Art Directors Club Hall of Fame mentions, he had an epiphany after listening to György Kepes lecture on design as a bridge between man and society, after which Silverstein "had business cards printed up that read, 'Designs for People.'" He worked for various institutions that had a social impact, including the Cooperative League of the United States of America, the American Federation of Labor, and the U.S. Department of State publications branch, where he served as art director of *Amerika*, a Russian-language magazine distributed in the Soviet Union and satellite nations.

As the *Times*'s promotion art director, Silverstein was in charge of promotion both for the newspaper and for the company's radio station, WQXR. According to *Graphis* magazine, his huge output of posters, mailing pieces, educational booklets, and ads promoting the *Times* "raised current graphic standards." Many of his *Times* ads played off one another, either thematically or visually, in series, such as those in which he engaged the then-struggling photographer Robert Frank to do the pictures. Likewise, his "I got my job through the *New York Times*" series of posters for the paper's classified section, with casual in situ photography of people at work and straightforward typography, was one of the most influential campaigns ever. His first redesign of the paper, in 1967, changed the reading typeface from 8-point Ideal to 8 1/2-point Imperial. This was also the year that he had Ed Benguiat redraw and enlarge the *Times*'s Old English logotype, dropping the period. ("Its removal saved the paper $45 a year in ink," noted his obituary.) As corporate art director, he oversaw design of the annual reports and the "piano keys," as the paper's corporate logo—Gothic initials positioned inside dimensional rectangles that looked like keys—was called.

To keep up with its shifting readership, the *Times* needed even more modernization. Section by section, Silverman redesigned almost the entire Sunday paper. In 1970, he entered the hallowed editorial halls with the launch of the Op-Ed (opposite the editorial) page, under the direction of John Oakes, editorial page editor, and Harrison Salisbury, editor of the Op-Ed page. Silverstein commissioned art from an international roster of artists and illustrators that did not literally depict the articles, but rather suggested emotions and ideas. Although there was no master plan for the news sections of the paper, Silverstein, with editors A. M. Rosenthal, Seymour Topping, and Arthur Gelb, succeeded in producing brand-new sections—Sports Monday, Weekend, Style, Home, and Science among them—that captured a wider audience. Gelb, a former managing editor, said in the *Times* obituary by Douglas Martin that Silverstein "responded with a vision for opening up the design, making more creative use of typefaces, enlarging photographs, adding explanatory graphics and running fewer stories on a page." Gelb added, "'He wanted the paper to breathe.'" Yet for every innovation, Silverstein battled stubborn, hard-boiled editors. Traditionalists complained that the newly designed "soft news" sections trivialized the meaty "hard news," but this proved to be untrue.

When Silverstein was inducted into the Art Directors Club Hall of Fame in 1984, the designer Massimo Vignelli said, "By changing the *Times* and so many newspapers in other cities, we are indebted to him for improving the quality of our lives." •

696

697

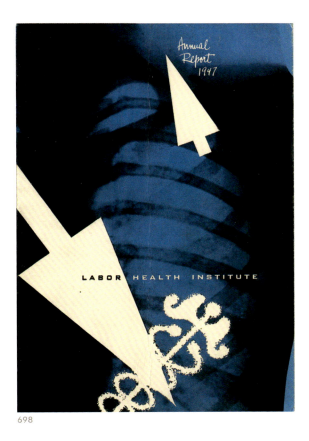

698

699

696
Advertisement, Action In Agate, New York Times, c. 1960s

697
Advertisement comprehensive, (unpublished), "The Listener with Three Ears (listener, advertiser, and critic)," Columbia Broadcasting System, 1948

698
Annual report cover, Labor Health Institute, St. Louis, 1947

699
Promotional booklet cover, Winner!, Annual Motor Boat Show Feature, New York Times, c. early 1960s

700

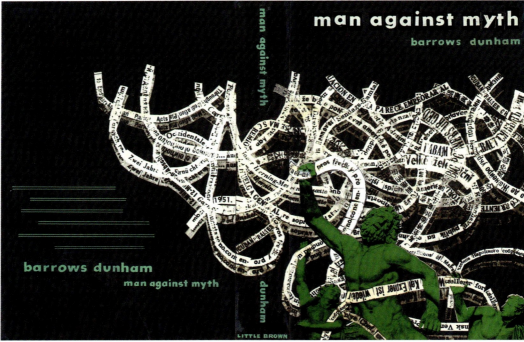

701

Commercial Banks and
Their Trust Activities:
Emerging Influence on the American Economy

Introduction by
Adolf A. Berle

700
Brochure comprehensive (possibly
unpublished), *CINEMART Schedule of Rates
and Service*, c. late 1940s

701
Book jacket comprehensive (possibly
unpublished), *Man Against Myth*, by
Barrows Dunham, Little, Brown, Boston,
1947

702
Book jacket, *Commercial Banks and Their
Trust Activities: Emerging Influence on the
American Economy*, Staff Report by the
House Subcommittee on Domestic Finance,
Arno Press, 1969

702

703

The New York Times Company

704

Corporate Advertising Manager

705

703
Direct mail promotionals covers (folded and flat), *New York Times*, 1967

704
Logo, New York Times Company, 1971. Before Silverstein became art director of the *New York Times*, it was despairingly called the Old Gray Lady. Once he got his hands on its advertising and editorial pages, the designs of newspapers were never the same again.

705
Advertisement, "I Got My Job through the New York Times," c. mid- to late 1960s

706
Advertisement, "A Bach Cantata. A Beethoven Sonata. This Is Good Music," WQXR, Radio Station of the New York Times, c. 1957

A Bach cantata. A Beethoven sonata. This is good music.

This is WQXR...whenever you tune in.

706

Barbara Stauffacher Solomon

b. 1928

Solomon at the Sea Ranch, Sonoma County, California, 1967

"Learn some rules," Armin Hofmann said. "Follow them. Later, if you're brilliant enough, you can break all the rules. Fine. If not, you will be competent at your profession." Barbara Stauffacher Solomon mastered the rules. Under the tutelage of modern Swiss masters in Basel, she became an early and devout practitioner of Swiss Style design starting in the late fifties. In the early sixties, she brought these ideas to America, merging them with a bold, expressive, and enthusiastic California spirit and pioneering the world of large-scale forms, murals, and signage—supergraphics.

Born in San Francisco, Solomon was a trained ballet and flamenco dancer at just sixteen. She attended the California School of Fine Arts (now San Francisco Art Institute), where she studied painting under American artist David Park and lithography with Nathan Oliveira, both of the Bay Area Figurative Movement. In 1948, she married Frank Stauffacher, the experimental filmmaker and director of the important Art in Cinema series at the San Francisco Museum of Art (now Museum of Modern Art), which introduced avant-garde cinema from American and émigré filmmakers. In 1949, she enrolled at the University of California, Berkeley, where she graduated with a bachelor's degree in history. "Taking art classes seems too self-indulgent, so I took history and philosophy," she said. Restless, Solomon moved to New York. There, she took classes at the Art Students League, studying painting with Reginald Marsh and Hans Hofmann, and enrolled as a student at the School of American Ballet. However, she missed Frank and soon returned to California. They had a child, but Frank died in 1955.

That year, Solomon became interested in design. With her portfolio in hand, the twenty-six-year-old, her three-year-old daughter, and her mother boarded a plane for Switzerland. From 1956 to 1959, Solomon studied eight hours a day under Armin Hofmann at the influential Basel Allgemeine Gewerbeschule. For her first assignment, she took six months to paint a complete Latin alphabet in Helvetica. "Our design tools were minimal: white boards, pencils, black and white paint, brushes, T-squares, a straightedge, scissors, our hands and eyes . . . but no compass, no French curves. Curved lines were drawn by eye," she recalled. This intense exercise would prove crucial to her career. "Experimentation or self-expression wasn't what we were there to do," she recalled. "We learned to reduce objects to their simplest form, forms representing information, ideas, and ideals: how to give messages, events, and values a visible form." These ideals were at odds with Solomon's hometown, San Francisco, where "breaking rules was supposed to be fun."

Solomon then moved to New York, where she worked for George Nelson & Associates and then, in 1961, under consultant Gottfried Honegger at J. R. Geigy. The art department was small. There, Solomon drew an "alphabet based on Helvetica . . . tall, thin, and bold" for pharmaceutical packaging. The Geigy office established a clear, functional visual vocabulary known as the "Geigy style," an approach that differed from the text-heavy, concept-driven American aesthetic.

In 1962, Solomon returned to San Francisco and rented a small office in a warehouse building from landscape artist Lawrence Halprin. Business was good. "I was a Californian. I went back to San Francisco and I broke all the rules. My designs were bigger and bolder than my Swiss classmates' solutions had been. Give me a big white wall and I covered it with big red stripes," she recalled. She may have been the first American designer to use Helvetica. In San Francisco, "local typesetters used Times Roman, Baskerville, Garamond, Caslon, Bodoni or Wild West-style typefaces," she said, and "hippies painted squiggles, free, loose, and sexy." For her own letterhead, she typed and specced the text as 10-point Helvetica Medium and mailed it to a friend in Switzerland, as no American typesetters had the typeface. When she received the proofs from Basel, she cut and pasted the type and prepared a mechanical, which she sent to the printer. "My designs were the antithesis of the psychedelic hippy posters made in the Haight-Ashbury," she said.

Solomon met architect Al Boeke, who was developing a new kind of self-governed, cohesive community—he called it Sea Ranch. This was her first big job; she designed the logo and all printed matter with Helvetica. She used pure colors to paint simple geometric and energetic shapes on the weathered wood of the buildings—giant waves, vertical and angled stripes, circle, arrows, and red hearts—along with signage in large, all-capital letters. "In this superworld . . . I combined the super-sized enthusiasm of California Abstract Expressionism with hard-edge Swiss graphics, and ended up with . . . supergraphics," she said. The Sea Ranch opened in 1967, and Solomon's work was received with fanfare.

From 1964 to 1972, Solomon designed monthly San Francisco Museum of Art program guides. The project, which had a small budget, was printed economically on inexpensive paper in a square format (nine by nine inches) with one-color printing (except for the occasional holiday colors) and enhanced by simplified covers and exaggerated forms—the synthesis of her clear Swiss Style and bold California sensibility. She had a steady stream of clients. But by the early seventies, Solomon became disillusioned with design: "It's hard to hate hypocrisy and work as a designer."

In 1973, she closed her office and returned to the University of California, Berkeley, for more studies in history, philosophy, and architecture: "what I hadn't learned in Basel; the myths and misinterpretations behind the messages of the Modern Movement," she said. Soon after, she earned a master's degree in architecture. Since 1963, Solomon has taught at various institutions: San Francisco Art Institute; University of California, Berkeley; Yale University; University of Washington; Kent State University; and Harvard University.

Solomon's designs, in which "intuition merged with geometry" and "fantasy mixed with order," have become part of the American landscape. According to Solomon, "designers make the invisible visible," and this spirit has taught her how to see. •

707

708 Oct o ber °

709

710

711

712

707–712
Monthly program guides, San Francisco
Museum of Art, January 1967, October
1967, February 1968, April 1968, August
1968, and June 1969

BARBARA STAUFFACHER SOLOMON

713

714

715

716

713–716
Monthly program guides, San Francisco
Museum of Art, September 1969, May
1964, April 1966, and May 1966

SeaRanch
Design
Brochure

The Sea Ranch
Sonoma County
California

720

San Francisco
Review
Annual

1

New Directions—San Francisco Review

721

717–719
Monthly program guides, San Francisco
Museum of Art, March 1964, November
1966, and August 1965

720
Brochure cover, *Sea Ranch Design
Brochure*, The Sea Ranch, Sonoma County,
California, c. 1965

721
Book cover, *San Francisco Review Annual 1*,
New Directions, 1963

Alex Steinweiss
1917–2011

Steinweiss in his home studio, Brooklyn, New York, 1947

Alex Steinweiss, a.k.a. Piedra Blanca (the name, Spanish for "white stone," that he used for art other than Columbia albums), defined the look of recorded music in its nascent years. He designed the first illustrated 78 rpm album package in 1940, and by 1948 he had invented the paperboard 33 1/3 LP jacket.

Steinweiss's father was a ladies' shoe designer from Warsaw, and his mother, a seamstress from Riga, Latvia. They eventually settled in Brighton Beach, Brooklyn, where Steinweiss was raised. His high school teacher Leon Friend, founder of the Art Squad at Abraham Lincoln High School, inspired his graphic arts side. On the strength of his high school portfolio, Steinweiss earned a scholarship to attend Parsons School of Design in New York. After graduating, he worked for three years for the Austrian poster designer Joseph Binder, whose iconic flat color and simplified poster figurations were quite popular at the time. Binder recommended Steinweiss to CBS.

He stumbled into an industry without a graphics tradition when he was hired in late 1939 to design promotional displays for the Columbia Broadcasting System's newly acquired record company, the brainchild of Ted Wallerstein. In those days, shellac 78 rpm records, which played for four or five minutes per side, were packaged in albums of three or four records in separate sleeves bound between pasteboard covers. They were differentiated only by variously colored spines with embossed titles.

The record cover was a tabula rasa waiting for Steinweiss to come along and make design history. CBS Records was headquartered in the gloomy industrial city of Bridgeport, Connecticut, without graphic arts suppliers, typographers, or designers anywhere. Steinweiss was given space in the corner of a huge, barn-like room that he called "the ballroom," with a drawing table and an airbrush. He designed promotional pieces for the classical, pop, and international lines. "I put some style into it," he said about the difference between his modern influences and the design conventions of the competing record companies. For the first six months, he was the entire art department and pasteup staff.

The plain paper wrappers common to the record industry lacked sales appeal, so Steinweiss offered to design a few covers and was given a chance. The first album was a Rodgers and Hart collection, for which he used a theater marquee with the album title rendered in lights. Other covers treatments followed, and sales dramatically increased for the albums with the Steinweiss designs. Shortly after the first covers were issued, *Newsweek* reported that sales of Bruno Walter's recording of Beethoven's Symphony no. 3 had surged, with an 895 percent increase over the same release with an unadorned package.

Steinweiss's most memorable covers maximized the limited image area by treating it as if it were a large poster—strong central image, eye-catching type, and distinctive color combinations. Some of his designs are viewed as ham-fisted today, but they helped to push an industry into the modern era.

Without a type shop nearby, he was pressured by time and financial constraints to use hand lettering, which developed into a trademark script, and the Steinweiss Scrawl was licensed to Photo-Lettering in the early fifties. Moreover, the local engravers worked only in black and white—process color was not an option: "They didn't know what to do with color," quipped Steinweiss. "Everything was printed as a solid. When they made color proofs they didn't even know how to remove the guidelines. I had to teach them to do it all."

During one of Steinweiss's meetings at Columbia, around 1948, Wallerstein mysteriously took a disc out of his drawer and went over to the record player. Steinweiss started listening to the music as they talked. He recalled, "In those days you got into the habit of waiting for the record to change every four or five minutes. But this one didn't change. It played for ten, fifteen, possibly twenty minutes, so I asked, 'What the hell is this?' And he said, 'you're listening to the first pressing of an LP record.' But he said, 'we've got a packaging problem.'" Apparently they had tried using kraft paper envelopes, but owing to the heaviness of the folded paper it left marks on the vinyl microgrooves when they were stacked up. "'We've got to solve this,' he said, 'or we're up the creek.'"

Trial and error surrounded the development of the LP jacket. In the end, the physical package turned out to be easy; more difficult was finding a manufacturer willing to invest about 250,000 dollars in new equipment. Steinweiss enlisted his brother-in-law to locate a manufacturer, and he admits that the two of them made some money on the deal, independent of Columbia. Although Steinweiss held the original patent, his contract with Columbia obligated him to waive all rights.

Steinweiss's LP package, a thin board covered with printed paper, became the standard for the industry. The invention was not merely an effective protection for LPs; it allowed more artistic variety, since it was easy to print in color on the paper that covered the board—but this proved to be a mixed blessing for its inventor. More advanced printing encouraged the use of photographs, and conceptual photography was soon in vogue, with live models posing for dramatic mood portraits and clever setups. Although Steinweiss preferred the more personal illustrative and typographic approaches, he art directed and designed photographic shoots for London and Decca records and worked for most of the major labels during the period, sometimes changing his style or adding a pseudonym. But by the late fifties, the pop labels wanted only photography. "It was the beginning of a lousy time in my life," Steinweiss lamented.

At age of fifty-five, Steinweiss reluctantly opted to bow out of graphic design. Today, the best of his record work should be judged for how it revolutionized music packaging, and how it influenced and reflected the styles and trends in the music industry, during that curiously adolescent period of American culture. •

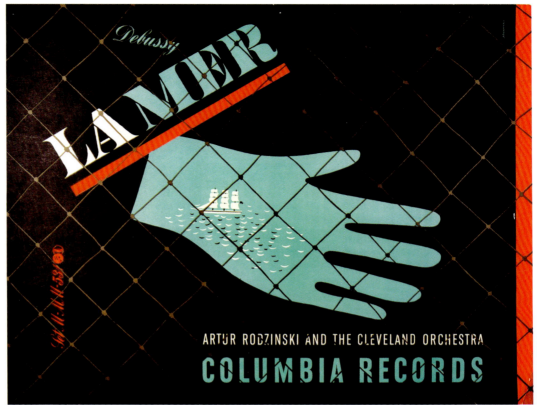

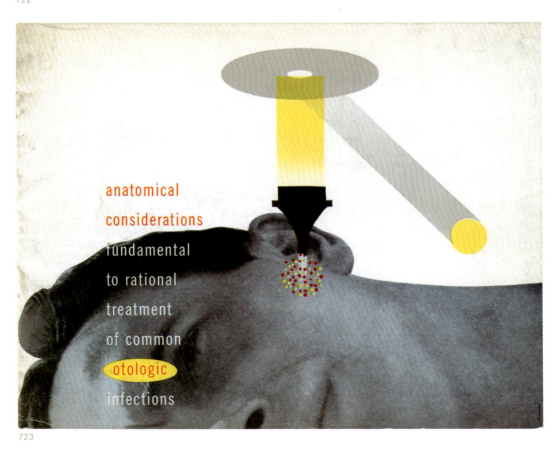

722
Poster, *La Mer*, Columbia Records, 1942

723
Brochure cover, *Anatomical Considerations Fundamental to Rational Treatment of Common Otologic Infections*, White Laboratories, Newark, New Jersey, 1946

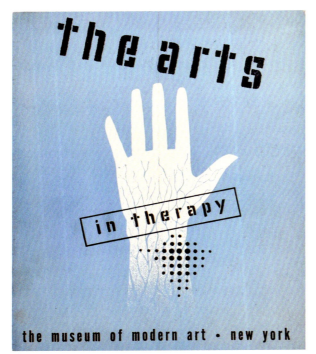

724

725

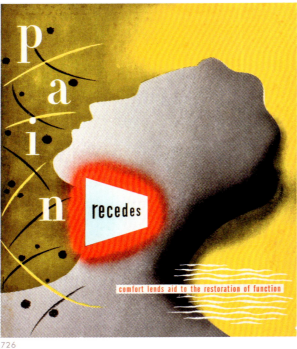

726

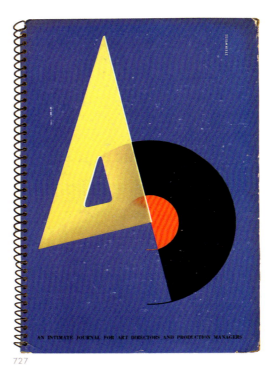

727

724
Brochure cover, *The Arts in Therapy*,
Museum of Modern Art, New York, 1943

725
Booklet cover, *Camouflage*, Training
Circular no. 4, U.S. Department of War,
1943

726
Folder, *Pain Recedes, Comfort Lends
Aid to the Restoration of Function*, White
Laboratories, Newark, New Jersey, 1945

727
Journal cover, *A-D: An Intimate Journal for
Production Managers, Art Directors, and
Their Associates*, "Design for Music," 2,
no. 5 (June–July 1941)

728

729

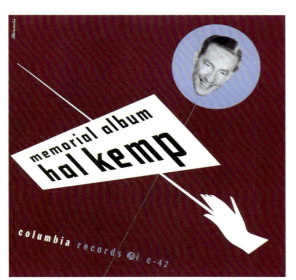

730

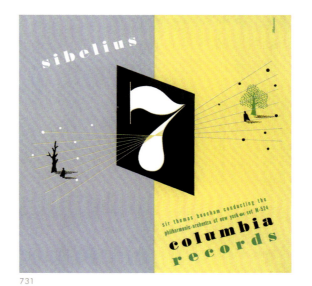

731

732

728
Album cover, *Contrasts in Hi-Fi*, London
Records, c. 1959

729
Album cover, *Verdi Requiem*, Decca
Records, 1961. Design: Piedra Blanca

730
Album cover, *Hal Kemp Memorial Album*,
Columbia Masterworks, c. 1941. The
first time Steinweiss printed his own
original artwork on a Columbia record
album, its sales increased greatly. He
created the symbiosis of art and music
that continues today.

731
Album cover, *Sibelius Symphony no. 7*,
Columbia Records, 1942

732
Album cover, *Beethoven Concerto no. 1 in
C Major for Piano and Orchestra, op. 15*,
Columbia Masterworks, 1950

Sussman at the Eames office, 901 Washington Boulevard, Venice, California, c. 1964

Deborah Sussman

1931–2014

The 1984 Summer Olympics in Los Angeles made a huge splash—of color, that is—on the world stage when it chromatically exploded through the graphic pyrotechnics of Deborah Sussman and her husband, architect Paul Prejza, working with the Jerde Partnership and a collaborative team of 150 architects and designers. They called this award-winning spectacle "graphic architecture," and they were certainly its pioneers. Sussman's eclectic, carnivalesque Pacific Basin color system was applied to an outdoor environmental kit that included tents, scaffolding, fence graphics, banners, uniforms, signage, Sonotubes, and a myriad of details, including even the flowers that the winners received. The celebratory spirit filled the Olympic Stadium and the twenty-five other sports venues and sixty-seven arts festival sites with sun-drenched exuberance that powered a post-Modernist charge throughout the California graphic design world—although that was not really Sussman's intention.

The Brooklyn-born Sussman, whose father was a commercial artist, did not identify as a post-Modernist (a term that has too many conflicting connotations and a style that evokes numerous aesthetics), but rather she was a modern spirit. In the summer of 1948, she attended summer school at storied Black Mountain College, an enclave of avant-garde ideas in North Carolina. There she was taught performance by Merce Cunningham and John Cage and painting by Franz Kline. Later she studied painting and acting at the progressive Bard College in New York, eventually focusing more intently on graphic design at the Institute of Design in Chicago—the heir to the Bauhaus.

At the Institute of Design, Sussman met many people who became friends for life. Among them was Konrad Wachsmann, a faculty member who was friendly with Charles and Ray Eames; this led to an invitation for Deborah to join their office as a summer intern. She stayed five years. In 1958, she was awarded a Fulbright Scholarship to study at the Hochschule für Gestaltung in Ulm, Germany. Max Bill, rector of the school, had been ousted, departing the day she arrived. After the freedom of the Eames office, she rejected the rigid and restrictive curriculum of the new regime and spent most of her time photographing the villages around Ulm.

Returning to America imbued with the modern spirit short of Swiss Style austerity, she settled in Manhattan. The impetus for Sussman's esoteric Modernism was doubtless derived mainly from her experiences at the Eames office and her mentoring by Charles and Ray, at a time when the office was small and she was treated as a family member. But another major force in her life was Alexander Girard, who had been close to the Eameses. "Deborah was very friendly with the Girards, especially after working with them on the *Day of the Dead* film in Mexico, and was very influenced by his color sense," noted Prejza.

A self-mailer for a sale that Sussman designed for Textiles & Objects, a New York store that sold Girard's Herman Miller fabrics, as well as folk art and accessories, exemplifies her vision, combining plenitude with precision. Prejza described it as an extension of the work Sussman was doing for Galeries Lafayette in Paris: "Similar use of color (pink & aqua), similar wry use of typography . . . a jack-in-the-box constrained in its box and waiting for it to be opened to reveal its surprises."

In 1961, Sussman was lured back to the Eames office, where she worked on the 1964–65 New York World's Fair exhibits for IBM, projects for the government of India, and Herman Miller Furniture showrooms. The Eameses' cross-disciplinary vision and their eccentric aesthetics had a demonstrable impact on Sussman's future. When she started her own firm in 1968, she carved out a métier that she came to call "urban enhancement." According to the announcement for her 1995 "Masters Series" exhibition at the School of Visual Arts in New York, her "passion for the marriage of graphics and the built environment has led to collaborations with planners, architects, developers and other designers on multi-dimensional corporate, commercial and civic programs."

In an interview not long before she died in 2014, Sussman defined her own place in the modern design firmament, acknowledging that her greatest accomplishment was becoming more conceptual, with ideas coming faster and more easily. "Learning from the young," she added. "Exploring new territory. Conceptualizing out of the box. Collaborating with people in real time and physical presence. . . . Those moments when I can 'fly' despite the enormous constraints of budget, program, and client preferences—those are what keep me going."

About her fealty to Modernism, she defined herself as a guerrilla, "constantly showing up in unexpected places at strange times; versus a phalanx, which is a planned, controlled disciplined linear singular force. The language of the communal speaks to me in louder voices than theory or doctrine." After a little more thought, she added, "Context, for me, is a major determinant in designing. One size fits none. Which doesn't mean that design solutions have to 'fit in'; they just need to be educated. To accomplish the most effective result within a minimum of time and means is a worthwhile goal. That's modern, isn't it? But also eternal!" Sussman was an eclectic: "messy, intuitive and emotional," she proudly announced. Although "modern" was part of her whole journey, "actually, I am not sure I ever was an 'ist' of any kind," she concluded. "Besides—less can be more and more can be less. But less can actually be less. And more can be more!" •

733

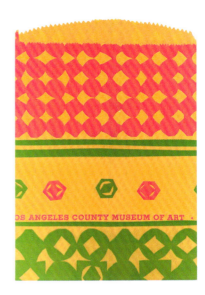

734

735

733
Self-mailer and poster, *Textiles and Objects Sale* (T&O), Herman Miller, New York, c. early 1960s

734
Exhibition catalog front and back covers, *6 More*, Los Angeles County Museum of Art, 1965

735
Gift shop bags, Los Angeles County Museum of Art, c. 1965

309

736

Best wishes from
Deborah Sussman and office
Steve Stuck
Ron Rezek
Alice Sherman
Philip Schwartz

737

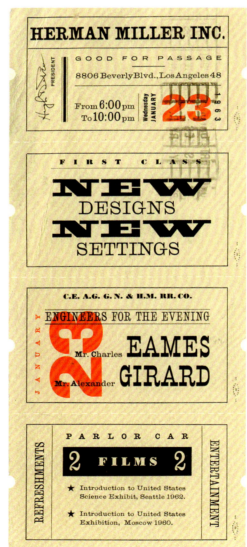

738

736
Holiday card, "Best wishes from Deborah Sussman and office, 69–70," 1969

737
Film credits poster, *Day of the Dead*, Museum of International Folk Art, Santa Fe, New Mexico. Design: Charles and Ray Eames, 1957

738
Showroom invitation, "New Designs New Settings," Herman Miller, 1963

739

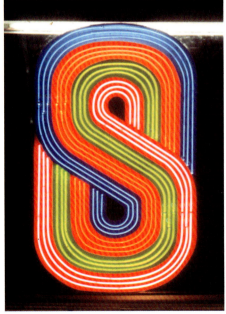

740

739
Signage detail, Joseph Magnin
Department Store, California, 1968–69

740
Signage and store graphics, Standard
Shoes, Los Angeles, c. late 1960s

Bradbury Thompson

1911–1995

Thompson in his New York City apartment, c. 1949

If a young economics major from Topeka, Kansas, by the name of Bradbury Thompson had not left his job designing high school yearbooks, and had not come to New York in the late thirties, would a significant chapter of American graphic design history have ever been written? It is certain that the one of the essential design publications that he edited and designed, *Westvaco Inspirations*, would not have been such an influence on the design field, and it would not have become such a vital historical record of American Modernism. However, in 1938 Thompson did leave the American heartland and did come East to work for one of those fabled art directors in the big city he had read about in the design magazines he pored through in the Topeka library. That was also the year he began the collaboration with the West Virginia Pulp and Paper Company (Westvaco) that cemented his legacy as an American modern. From the outset, he had a progressive but elegant bent.

Westvaco Inspirations, which during the early twenties and thirties was the paper company's spiritless promotional brochure, became the bible of graphic design and a textbook for a generation, thanks to Thompson. He went on to design and edit sixty issues—including special issues devoted to such themes as "Type as a Toy," "Primitive Art as Modern Design," and the phonetic "Monalphabet" (which eliminated the need for separate upper- and lowercase letters). *Westvaco Inspirations* was a compendium of what Thompson believed to be the best of contemporary practice. There he promoted a vision that wed the European modern spirit of simplicity and economy to a respect for classical golden rules. "My early interest in type came from the humanist typographers," explained Thompson, "the classic types of Europe from the fifteenth, sixteenth, and seventeenth centuries. Later, *Vanity Fair* [art directed by M. F. Agha] influenced me in the use of sans serif type—especially Futura." When he was inducted into the New York Art Directors Club's Hall of Fame, he said, "I believe an avid interest in type necessarily includes a zest for everyday life."

His appreciation for unadorned layout further evolved from studying the behemoth fashion magazines of the thirties, while his graphic adventurism came from an intimate knowledge of printing and its potential. He was admittedly smitten by French and German poster art of the thirties, which integrated type and image as one entity. Thompson practiced a similar kind of illustrative design, using an airbrush for *More Business* and for a catalog cover for the 1939–40 New York World's Fair. He also believed that these word-and-picture compositions would lead him to future design options that were at once avant-garde and classical.

"In working on *Westvaco Inspirations* I just naturally applied all these forms," he explained, and he borrowed liberally from many arts and styles—painting and sculpture, photography and drawing, realistic and abstract. One of his best-known designs, a *Westvaco Inspirations* spread titled "Kerr-choo-oo," presents type that is not read as a word but as sound. Although inspired by Apollinaire's *Calligrammes* and Filipo Tommaso Marinetti's *Parole in Libertà*, it was decidedly American in its wit.

Thompson was a fiery designer whose magazines were his manifestos—not the rabble-rousing kind that emanated from Futurism or Dada, but a soft-spoken kind that sought to teach rather than preach. Thompson was not radical but modern in the catholic sense: Anything was possible within his aesthetic parameters; anything was doable as long as quality was the goal. His experiments were, moreover, rooted in terra firma. Everything presented in the publication (including that convention-busting Monalphabet and Alphabet 26, designed to make English easier to learn) was appropriate within the convention of visual communications.

He loved constraints and reveled in those aspects of letterpress printing and hot-metal composition that stymied creative activity; he capitalized on the limitations, testing the resilience of design against them, and pushed the boundaries. One of the single most important lessons he taught to his students at Yale was that type could be made expressive, emotive, personal, and still be part of a tasteful composition. "There is no creative aspect of graphic design more enjoyable or rewarding than the indulgence in play," he once wrote.

Thompson had a large practice outside his work for Westvaco. As an art director for the U.S. Office of War Information, he designed *U.S.A.*, a magazine aimed at Americans and allies (there were Arabic and French editions), as well as the occasional enemy. The U.S. government produced a lot of low- and high-impact propaganda. *U.S.A.* fell somewhere in between: It was classically designed while vociferously propagating American values. After World War II, he art directed *Mademoiselle*, *Art News*, and other magazines. His work at *Mademoiselle*, in particular, was incredibly artful and playful. He steered this magazine for young women into the calm waters of economical typography, while emphasizing smartly shot and cropped visuals. His signature mix of old and contemporary graphic elements was nicely presented on the cover and interior spreads at a time before color for the run-of-the-book was economically feasible. He was also a book and advertising designer and even created U.S. postage stamps. He never possessed a fixed style per se, but rather an attitude. His magazine layouts were devoid of artifice but decidedly modern. His modern book design was based on classical models. He reconciled the two sensibilities with this simple word: "Appropriateness."

He also proclaimed: "You can't get away from tradition, if you want to bridge past, present, and future." •

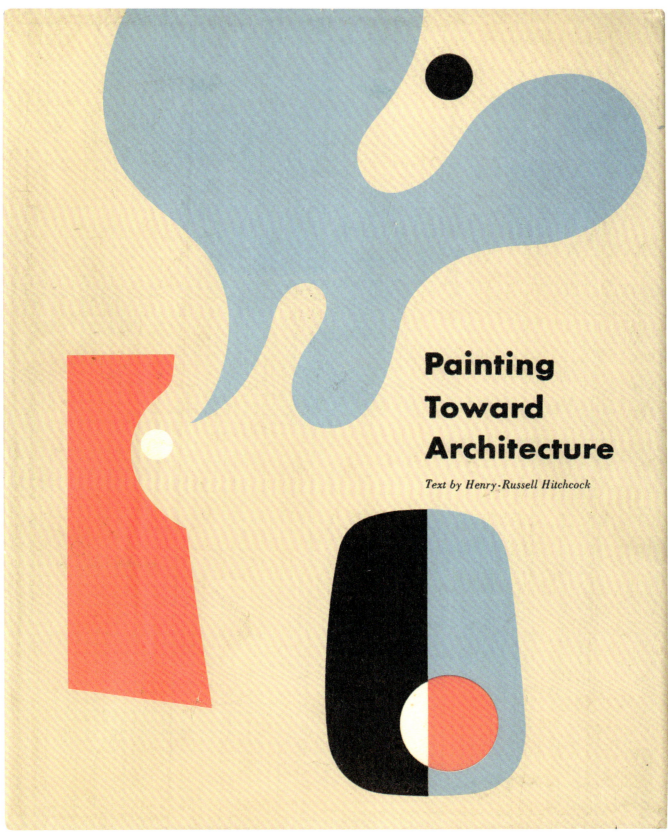

Painting Toward Architecture

Text by Henry-Russell Hitchcock

741

741
Book jacket, *Painting Toward Architecture*,
by Henry-Russell Hitchcock, Miller
Company collection of abstract art, Duell,
Sloan and Pearce, 1948. This new collage
uses Futura type and repurposed abstract
shapes borrowed from the artwork in the
book by Jean (Hans) Arp, Paul Klee, John
Tunnard, and Ben Nicholson.

742

743

742
Magazine cover, *This Week*, Sunday Supplement, *Portland Oregonian*, October 11, 1964. To illustrate the magazine's feature about new cars from 1965, the design relates automobile parts, traffic signs, and signals to an engraving of a horse.

743
Magazine cover, *Mademoiselle*, January 1950. Photo: Ben Somoroff

744–751
Double page spreads, *Westvaco Inspirations for Printers*, West Virginia Pulp and Paper Company

Boom, Bang, no. 216, 1961

Inspirations from Contemporary Advertising Art, no. 156, 1945

Westvaco, no. 149, 1944

Keep Your Eye on the Ball, no. 210, 1958

Combining Abstract Painting and Modern Typefaces, no. 172, 1948

Inspirations, no. 186, 1951

Clarendon, no. 210, 1958

Victory, no. 194, 1953

744

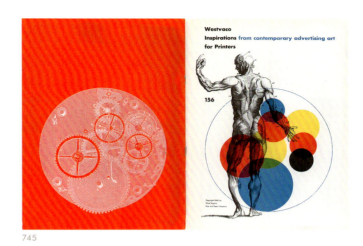

745

746

747

748

750

749

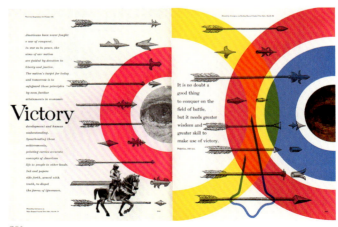

751

Lance Wyman

b. 1937

Wyman at the George Nelson office, 1965

For more than five decades, Lance Wyman has created environmental designs, branding campaigns, identity programs, and way-finding systems for cities, events, institutions, and transit systems, blending systematic modernity with personal flair. Yet he has received the majority of his accolades for one monumental work: the identity system for the controversial 1968 Olympic Games in Mexico City—the one where two African American sprinters raised the Black Power salute on the awards podium—that put Wyman's name on the international map.

While a designer at the George Nelson office in New York, Wyman had discovered that a competition was scheduled to determine the design of the logo for the Summer Olympics; he was granted permission to participate. When he left for Mexico City in November 1966, he asked a friend, British industrial designer Peter Murdoch, to collaborate on the project with him. After a grueling two-week trial, Wyman designed the winning mark.

The graphics had to integrate well with the architectural scheme that was overseen by Mexican architect Pedro Ramírez Vázquez, who had also been appointed chairman of the nation's Olympic organizing committee. Fortunately, he was as design savvy about graphics as he was about buildings. Yet, as expected, the overall coordination of the event was destined to be difficult, because the games were not confined to one stadium in a single district but rather spread throughout a sprawling, not always hospitable, Mexico City. "The problem," wrote *New York Times* art critic John Canaday, "went beyond the business of posters, programs, advertisements and other self-contained visual material and impinged on the area of urban logistics." To ensure order out of potential chaos, Ramírez created a team of directors that included Wyman heading the graphic team, with Murdoch directing special projects.

Wyman's fundamental graphic solution was to build on Baron Pierre de Coubertin's original 1913 symbol of five interconnected circles representing the five major continents: "Wielding compasses and ruling pens, Wyman introduced numbers into the lockup by adjusting line widths and counter spacing," wrote designer Juanita Dugdale about the contoured linear mark. Wyman "recalls an epiphany: 'Discovering that the geometry of those five rings could be expanded into the 68 was like a miracle!'" Building on rows of contoured radiating lines, the word "Mexico" in all-capital letters was added to the mix. "Wyman relates the pattern to sound waves spreading outward but its concentricity also resembles a target focusing attention at the center," Dugdale wrote about the multidimensional integration of logos, typography, and color developed to communicate to a multilingual audience.

Wyman noted that his influence derived from the Museum of Modern Art's 1965 "Responsive Eye" exhibition, including dazzling Op Art works by Richard Anuszkiewicz, Bridget Riley, and Victor Vasarely. He also credited pre-Columbian Mayan art, with its linear patterns, for contributing to what designer Michael Bierut, writing on the website *Design Observer* in 1994, called "a geometric fantasia of concentric stripe patterns that expanded into a custom alphabet, groovy minidresses, and eventually entire stadia." Philip B. Meggs, in *A History of Graphic Design*, called the system "one of the most successful in the evolution of visual identification."

Wyman learned many design lessons on his own. He came from a working-class family in Newark, New Jersey, and always had his heart set on designing. In 1960, he graduated from Pratt Institute in Brooklyn with a degree in industrial design. "When I met a student who studied logo design with Paul Rand at Yale, I knew I wanted to design logos," he told an interviewer. Jump ahead to the start of his career in Detroit, first with General Motors and later with the office of William Schmidt. At the former, he helped design the Delco automotive parts packaging system that unified 1,200 different packages. At the latter, he designed the graphics for the 1962 U.S. Pavilion at the Zagreb International Trade Fair in Yugoslavia, with the theme of "Leisure Time." Wyman was somehow blessed with the logo gene and instinctively devised an hourglass-shaped form with a sun-and-moon image in the upper half that was used as a gateway to the entire exhibit. "It was my first experience integrating logo design into a three-dimensional environment," he proudly recalled.

In 1963, Wyman joined the George Nelson office, where he worked on graphics for the Chrysler Pavilion at the 1964–65 New York World's Fair in Flushing Meadows, designing a "pointing hand" device that he adapted as the site's directional signs. He said it convinced him "that logos could play a more important role in an overall design program."

Wyman's role in the turmoil of 1968 went beyond the Olympics. To mark the assassination of Dr. Martin Luther King Jr., he designed the first commemorative stamp issued by Mexico. After the Olympics were over, Wyman stayed on in Mexico for two years to develop graphic programs for the Mexico City Metro and the 1970 World Cup. "Like the Olympics, these urban programs were integral to the vitality of the city streets," he explained. He returned to New York determined to continue working in the way-finding disciplines. In 1971, he opened Wyman & Cannan with environmental and exhibit designer Bill Cannan, and he established his own firm, Lance Wyman, in 1979. Since the outset of his career, Wyman has developed work that "can be easily coordinated with new-media platforms," he told the website *Design Boom* in 2014. "Well-conceived representative images have longevity and can adapt easily to new media platforms as well as to standard formats such as static signs and maps." So while Mexico may be a large part of his legacy, he is still doing what he set out to do. •

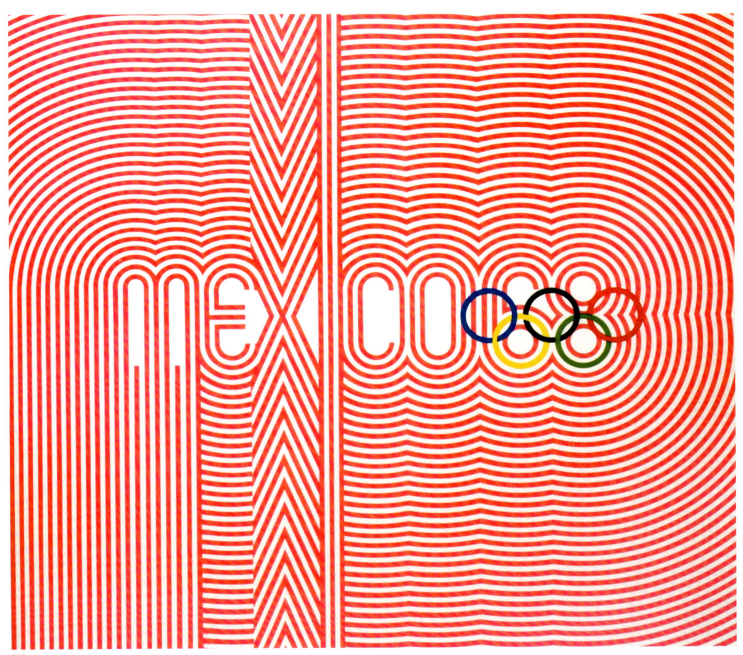

752

752
Logo and poster, Mexico 68, Organizing
Committee of the Games of the XIX
Olympiad, 1968. The 1968 Mexico
Olympics identity not only branded the
event for all times but inspired a generation
of designers to free themselves from chains
of simplicity.

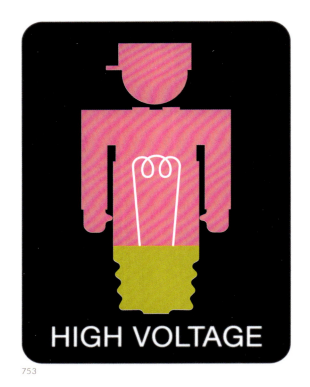

HIGH VOLTAGE

753

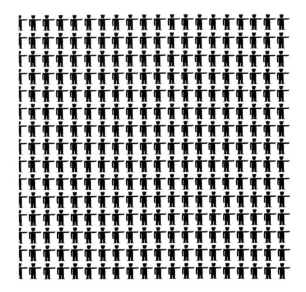

HOWARD ⊕ MILLER
PRONTO POSTERS

754

ПРОМЫШЛЕННАЯ
ЭСТЕТИКА США

755

756

753
Poster, *High Voltage*, Pronto Posters, Howard Miller, 1964. One in a series of safety posters originally designed for the USA Pavilion. "Pronto Posters say what has to be said quickly and deftly," noted the direct mailer selling the posters. "Just a word or two with illustration doing the rest. They add flair and humor to the surroundings, improve morale, reduce accidents, and aid efficiency."

754
Direct mail cover, Pronto Posters, Howard Miller, 1964. Design: George Nelson office

755
Logo and booklet cover, U.S. Information Agency (USIA) Exhibition on American Industrial Design, 1966. Design: George Nelson & Associates

756
Graphic mural, Chrysler Pavilion, New York World's Fair, Chrysler Parts Division, 1964

SEASON'S GREETINGS
PETER MURDOCH INC

757

758

759

760

761

762

763

765

764

LANCE WYMAN

757
Holiday card, "Season's Greetings," Peter Murdoch, c. 1965

758
Logo, Contemporary Records, 1960

759
Logo, Hyatt Roller Bearings, 1958

760
Logo, Ford Vinyl, 1961

761
Logo, Guide Lamp, 1959

762
Logo, Challenger Sales, 1962

763
Logo, Delco, General Motors, 1960

764
Logo, Bicentennial, USA Bicentennial Commission, 1971

765
Logo, McLouth Steel, 1962

a journal for art directors and production people

Journal cover, *PM: An Intimate Journal for Production Managers, Art Directors, and Their Associates* 4, no. 7 (June–July 1938). Design: M. Peter Piening

04 THE BAUHAUS TRADITION AND THE NEW TYPOGRAPHY

By L. Sandusky

1

In September of last year the Association of Arts and Industries announced the establishment in Chicago of a "new" Bauhaus, with L. Moholy-Nagy as Director. The following month its doors opened to a group of American students, who began, a little uncertain, one would imagine, to grope their way toward a new philosophy of art and industry. It has now completed its first year. In the minds of many who had been interested in the Bauhaus as a cultural and historical phenomenon its re-establishment suggests far-reaching implications. Among other things, it brings to the fore again the problem of Continental modernism, which in printing and advertising design has made uneven progress in America.

The bodily presence of an American version of the internationally famous German school, which played so conspicuous a part in the development of the "New Typography," makes it timely and worthwhile to re-examine the set of circumstances which made it what it was. For the story of the Bauhaus is the story of how a considerable body of contemporary American printing and advertising came to be what it is.

The thing of first interest is that the Bauhaus stood resolutely for the "new" as against the "old." In the eternal battle (in all the arts and crafts through which men have sought in different ways and with differing practical aims to express themselves) between "tradition and individual talent"—between the authority of the past and the needs of today—it threw its weight persistently on the side of individual talent. It was the converging point of everything that was alive with burgeoning possibilities.

Established at Weimar, in 1919, by Walter Gropius, a young architect dissatisfied with the sterile imitation of outworn styles and irrelevant forms, the Bauhaus began with the avowed object, "not to propagate any style, system, dogma, formula, or vogue, but simply to exert a revitalizing influence on design." Denying the traditional distinction between the "fine" and the "applied" arts and conceiving of mass production as the greatest single reality of the day, it sought to come to terms with the "machine." It rejected at once the utopian "handicraft" idealism, which would save men's souls through the creative work of their hands, and the sterile aestheticism of "Art for Art's Sake," which would preserve art from the slightest taint of usefulness. It sought, in short, "to eliminate every drawback of the machine without sacrificing any one of its real advantages." This "machine aesthetic" it applied (though the first emphasis was on architecture) to almost every branch of design, including furniture, interior decoration, typography, and advertising design.

Such a working philosophy, with the sociological goal of averting "mankind's enslavement by the machine by giving its products a content of reality and significance," had much to do with making the Bauhaus, within the fourteen years of its existence, a world-wide influence. But the more important thing was that it offered, in a way unparalleled in history, the right conditions for the birth of the "new." It came at the right time, established itself in the right place, and attracted the right men.

2

The Bauhaus was born amid a welter of war and post-war "isms"—belligerent movements, many of them, with evangelical leaders and followers who armed themselves for the fray with elaborate theories and a set of manifestoes. It was a time of tumult and shouting. But it was, more than anything else, a time of general trading of ideas and men among the arts, of the attempt to give form in one art to ideas and impressions imported from another.

The Russian painter Wassily Kandinsky (among the first to join the Bauhaus staff) was thinking of his work in terms of music and putting on canvas mystical Debussy-like compositions to which he gave the name "improvisations." Though they were (in his own words) painted "rather subconsciously in a state of strong inner tension," he was not unaware of the specific influences that played a part in determining them—the poetry of Maeterlinck and the music, not alone of Debussy, but as well of Wagner, Mussorgsky, Scriabine, and Schönberg. Of these men Scriabine had already composed music in terms of painting; and Debussy had, because of the obvious analogy of his work with the current school of French painting, earned the title "Impressionist."

Kandinsky belonged to a group known as the "Blaue Reiter," which included painters, poets, musicians, and dramatists. At the same time that he was discovering the *soul*—the *innerer Klang*—of nature and humanity as the goal of abstract painting, he was rediscovering music as the perennial methodological ideal of all the arts. His ideas were set forth in *The Art of Spiritual Harmony*, originally published, in 1912, as *Uber das Geistige in der Kunst*:

> They [the arts] are finding in Music the best teacher. With few exceptions music has been for some centuries the art which has devoted itself, not to the reproduction of natural phenomenon, but rather to the expression of the artist's soul, in musical sound.

> A painter, who finds no satisfaction in mere representation, however artistic, in his longing to express his inner life, cannot but envy the ease with which music, the most non-material of the arts today, achieves this end. He naturally seeks to apply the methods of music to his own art. And from this results that modern desire for rhythm in painting, for mathematical, abstract construction, for repeated notes of color, for setting color in motion.

While Kandinsky, preoccupied with music and painting, was unconsciously laying the "spiritual" foundation for many of the things being done today in advertising art (such, for instance, as the work of "Desha" for New York's *Lord & Taylor*); Alexander Archipenko (now a member of the staff of the New Bauhaus) was combining sculpture and painting as one art and experimenting with constructions in glass, wood, and metal, which were a kind of cross between sculpture and industrial design. In his emphasis on elements of form and rhythm he was, like Kandinsky, moving swiftly away from the traditional conception of art as imitation of the surface characteristics of nature and life. In the same year that saw the publication of *Uber das Geistige in der Kunst* he produced his "Médrano" juggler—the first clear example of "machine age" sculpture—which gave impetus to "constructivist" tendencies in Germany, Russia, and Hungary and was the prototype for such contemporary American "constructivist" advertising art as that of L. L. Balcom and Warren G. Thomas.

What Kandinsky and Archipenko were doing others were doing. It was a time of breaking down the fences which tradition had so carefully built up about each art and craft and of the artificial distinction between what was useful and what was good-in-itself. It was a time of discovering "the interdependence of painting, sculpture, and the technique of modern industry" and of the underlying unity of all creative work.

For typography here was the beginning of what Paul Renner (designer of the type face which acted in America as a kind of press agent for the New Typography) was later, with the perspective of time on his side, to regard as "a great cleansing process." It remained for the creator of "Futura," in the same year that the Bauhaus closed, to summarize it as a creative phenomenon:

> We are always inclined to regard our own sphere of work as strictly fenced in on all sides against all other spheres; and the more thoroughly we farm our own field, the more do we incline to the intellectual attitude peculiar to the expert, to whom the past of his own particular craft is nearer and more familiar than the present aspect of any neighboring craft. We need not, therefore, be astonished to find that the renaissance of style which we have experienced in all regions of creative work . . . during the past decade should often have been imported into the several crafts by non-professionals from the outside.

It has, of course, always been true that new forms and new expressive idioms arise only as a result of influences from other fields than the one in which they obtain—for they are necessarily non-traditional. The point here is that the creative process which gives birth to the "new" was intensified during the period in which the Bauhaus took shape.

3

Because of their liberating force and because of their incidental suggestions for a new kind of typography, three influences of the period deserve special mention. They are a man, a movement, and a program for destruction.

The man was Guillaume Apollinaire (pseudonym of Wilhelm von Kostrowitzki), a poet with Montmartre proclivities and a penchant for adventure. He was, as one commentator has put it, the "Marco Polo of the new spirit." He reversed the time-honored platitude that "there is nothing new under the sun" by declaring that for the poet and the artist everything under the sun *must* be new. As self-appointed interpreter and aesthetician of the new movement in art and literature, he was always on the alert for the unusual and the startling. In Paris he struck up a close friendship with the men who were doing what was then a new and strange kind of painting—Matisse, Picasso, Braque, and Rousseau. He was among the first to champion the cause of Cubism, publishing, in 1912, a volume of appreciative essays entitled *Les Cubistes*. It was he who invented the word *Surrealism*.

In *Caligrammes*, a volume of poems about peace and war written between 1913 and 1916 and published a few months before his death in 1918, he ventured upon some experiments in typography, of which the poem *La Cravate et la Montre* is an example. In having it set in the actual form of a necktie and a watch he sought, not too seriously, an

organic relation between the inside and the outside of the poem and something of that element of surprise which he regarded as a fundamental difference between the "new spirit" and all preceding artistic and literary movements. There was nothing very new or startling about this: yet, historically, it had a thrust in the direction of a new typography.

The movement was Futurism—a hotheaded revolt against the tyranny of the past in poetry, drama, literature, music, painting, sculpture, architecture, and the graphic arts. Beyond that it had social and political ramifications. Its Italian founder, Filippo Tommaso Marinetti, was the champion manifesto-maker of the whole period of tumult and shouting. "We want to free our country [Italy] from the fetid gangrene· of professors, archaeologists, guides, and antique shops," read the first *Futurist Manifesto*, published, in 1909, by a Paris newspaper. Among other things, the Futurists proposed that every artist should he banished at the age of forty from the art world, and his works along with him, so that with each generation a new cultural growth could spring from the root and not from the previous season's hardened wood.

The city of Venice was to them "a magnificent wound of the past." With 200,000 gayly colored manifestoes they exhorted its inhabitants "to fill its small fetid canals with the ruins of its tumbling leprous palaces." They would abolish everywhere "the languishing curve of the old architectures . . . and erect up to the sky the rigid geometry of large metallic bridges and factories." In painting they wanted to put the spectator in the midst of the picture. In sculpture they would destroy the "nobility of bronze and marble" by using every non-traditional material they could think of. Their poetry, for the most part, looked like a page from a book on symbolical logic. Their idea of the drama was that it should consist of things happening to the audience. And so it was on one occasion when Marinetti hurled back at the audience the missiles flung upon the stage in protest against the meaninglessness of a Futurist performance.

A good Futurist believed that "we must make a clean sweep of all hackneyed subjects and express henceforth the whirlwind life of our day, dominated by steel, egotism, feverish activity, and speed." His total aesthetic was nicely summed up in the feeling that a speeding automobile was more beautiful than the Victory of Samothrace. This aesthetic was carried into the sphere of printing under the head of *Typographical Revolution*:

> Our revolution is directed against the so-called typographical harmony of the page, which is opposed to the flux and reflux, the jerks and bursts of style that are represented in it. We shall use, therefore, on the same page three or four different colors of ink and, if necessary, even twenty different forms of type.

"Nouvelle conception de la page" Marinetti called it. The "SCRABrrR-rraaNNG" composition, from *Les Mots en liberté futuristes*, 1919, is a frequently reproduced example. However indiscreet and extravagant, here was an organic relation between the inside and the outside plus a kind of deliberate design for unrest.

The program for destruction was Dadaism. Some have preferred to think of it as an organized program for spoofing, others as war hysteria in the grand style. At all events, it was created in the war period, 1916, by a group of disillusioned writers and artists, who set about to confront one madness with another. The name of the "movement" was simply the first word that turned up in the dictionary on the insertion of a pen knife; it was launched from the Cabaret Voltaire, a literary night club in Zurich. The first official Dada publication was an indication of the network of influences that played upon it. Within its covers were brought together, among others, the names of Picasso, Apollinaire, Kandinsky, and Marinetti. Later publications, of which there were many, added such other names as Archipenko, Bergson, and Charlie Chaplin.

Though ostensibly bent on destroying all art tendencies by laughing them out of existence, the Dadaists could not escape the powerful influence of Picasso. They seized upon that part of his work which looked to them least like art—his *papiers collés*, pasteup compositions using newspaper, imitation wood, and other materials for their texture values. Working half-seriously with anti-art materials and experimenting with accidental compositions, they developed a medium of expression which was to enter the New Typography first as "composite photography" and later as "photomontage."

Within the short lifetime of Dada (for it was soon to grow into Surrealism) there were demonstrations, performances, and exhibitions in Zurich, Berlin, Cologne, Hanover, and Paris. A journalist of the period describes one of them:

> With characteristic bad taste the Dadaists make their appeal this time to the human instinct of fear. The scene is a cellar with all lights in the shop extinguished. Moanings are heard through a trap door. Another wag, hidden behind a cupboard, insults the more important visitors. . . . The Dadaists, with no neckties and wearing white gloves, walk around the place. Breton crunches matches. G. Ribemont-Dessaignes keeps on remarking at the top of his voice, 'It's raining on a skull.' Aragon mews like a cat. Ph. Soupault plays hide and seek with Tzara; Benjamin Péret and Charchoune never stop shaking hands. On the threshold, Jacques Rigaut counts out loud the cars and the pearls of the lady visitors.

It is not surprising that the announcements of such premeditated antics should take the form of the "Theatre Michel" handbill. These handbills, and other publications of the Dadaists, were, thinks Jan Tschichold, "the earliest documents of the New Typography."

4

It was a part of the Bauhaus philosophy that life was not rigidly departmentalized and that, since all branches of design were knit together by an underlying unity, each had something of value to give to the other. It was, therefore, psychologically prepared to be receptive to the rivulets of influence which crossed and re-crossed one another. It probably drew something from all the "isms" then current. But the more enduring elements in its typography derived primarily from two of them—Neo-Plasticism (or the *de Stijl* influence) in Holland and Constructivism (used here in a sense broad enough to include the allied movements of Suprematism and Non-Objectivism) in Russia and Hungary.

The activities of the *de Stijl* group—founded in 1917 by Théo van Doesburg, who has been described as a painter, sculptor, architect, typographer, poet, novelist, critic, lecturer, and theorist—covered almost as broad a field as the talents of its founder. The group made itself felt first through the abstract geometrical paintings of Van Doesburg and Mondrian. Seen through the prism of a "machine aesthetic" their simplicity in form and color—their "purified tonal and plane harmonies"—seemed right and appropriate for architecture, furniture, interior decoration, and typography which would be in consonance with the time. When Van Doesburg went to Germany in 1921, to divide his time between Berlin and the Bauhaus, the influence of the group had already been at work for two years.

The Constructivist influence on the Bauhaus followed close upon that of the *de Stijl* group. The movement—influenced, like every other tendency of the time, by Cubist art—had been initiated, in 1913, as Suprematism by Kasimir Malevich, who, in his effort "to free art from the ballast of the objective world," fled to the form of the square. To a startled public he exhibited as a work of art a plain black square against a white background. For him it was a direct rendering of "the experience of non-objectivity." From this point onward he combined simple formal elements—the square, the circle, the parallelogram, the trapezoid, and others—achieving in some of his compositions, inspired by aeroplane views of cities, the first intimation of the diagonal axis and the internal tensions so prominent later in the New Typography.

The *Suprematist Composition* of 1914 is perhaps his nearest approach to practical design. Done in solid tone of black, white, blue, red, and yellow it gave the "new typographer" almost his whole range of color preferences. The diagonal Futura advertisement, from an old issue of *Gebrauchsgraphik*, is the classic example of a similar plastic conception and treatment applied to typography. It may seem an interesting commentary on the timidity of human nature that it took the audacity of a Malevich to suggest that there was plastic value in such simple geometrical element as a square, a circle, and a line. Whatever may be the intrinsic value of his work as art, it had much the same kind of historical thrust in the direction of practical design as the work of the Cubists, the Futurists, and the Dadaists. It was a part of the cleansing process.

Malevich was followed by Alexander Rodchenko, who in 1922 deserted "art" for the more practical pursuits of theatre art, furniture design, photography, and typography, creating in a new field the design prototype of one of the most striking of the newer American magazines [*Cue* magazine]. The tendency toward utilitarian design was carried still further by El Lissitzky, for whom it was an easy step from his own abstract paintings, which he called "prouns," to a built-up architectural typography with plastic values.

The Hungarian wing of the Constructivist movement was represented by L. Moholy-Nagy, whose chief contributions to the New Typography were to be made as a member of the staff of the Bauhaus and as co-editor of the *Bauhausbücher* and the *Bauhaus* magazine.

Both *de Stijl* and Constructivist painting showed a marked architectural sense; but it was for Constructivism actually to invade the domain of architecture. It is significant that El Lissitzky regarded his "prouns" as a transition from painting to architecture and that Malevich had earlier done sculpture that looked very much like a building in the abstract. Modern architecture was recently defined by J. M. Richards, of the London *Architectural Review*, as Constructivist art applied to the science of building and Constructivist art, correspondingly, as architecture liberated from the dictatorship of function. As the he best illustration of the close relationship he points to the London Zoo buildings, of which Moholy-Nagy, in 1936, made a film for the Museum of Modern Art and Harvard's Department of Architecture.

What Richards had in mind, though, was not painting, but a species of art, influenced by the "machine-age" sculpture of Archipenko, midway between painting and sculpture, on the one hand, and engineering mechanics and industrial design on the other. It was an art in which "the school concepts of mechanics, dynamics, statics, kinetics, the problem of stability, of equilibrium were tested in plastic form." The quotation is from Moholy-Nagy's *The New Vision, from Material to Architecture*, in which he describes the basic training at the Bauhaus. By way of commenting on the exhibition of the Russian Constructivists in Moscow, 1921, he appraises the tendency:

> The constructivists reveled in industrial forms, so much so that a technical monomania governed them. As a transitional stage this interest was surely sound, for thereby the former dry musty conceptions of 'art' were given a new measuring rod from a different angle.

The whole Constructivist preoccupation with materials, abstract form, and mechanical stress-relations was put to work at the Bauhaus by

Moholy-Nagy as an educational method; and it has ever since been in process of filtering into the industrial art schools throughout the world as a fundamental technique. Under his direction Bauhaus students experimented freely with old and new materials for textural contrasts, surface treatment, and massing effects. Their serious "play activity"–for which they drew upon the collages of Picasso and the "rubbish pictures" of the Dadaists–included the materials of typography. The results that followed are observable today in a considerable body of printing, commercial photography, and advertising design, notably in some of the work of Lester Beall and the "montages" of Coutré Erman.

The force behind de Stijl and Constructivist art was that intangible "form-seeking" impulse which Sheldon Cheney, in *Expressionism in Art*, sees as the single unifying element in all the arts of the twentieth century. It is perfectly embodied in the deliberately abstract typographical compositions of Karel Teige, which we may take as representing in its purity the formal and abstract side of the New Typography. In the design and format of the *Bauhausbücher*, the "Futura" folder, the photographic poster by El Lissitzky [*USSR Russische Ausstellung*, 1929], and the other pieces shown this abstract form is given content without destroying the plastic-architectural quality. In direct line of descent from these are the selected examples of recent American work, culminating in the 1937 announcement folder of the Society of Typographic Arts, the cover of *Cue* magazine, and the current work of Moholy-Nagy for the New Bauhaus.

Attracted by the more diffused movement of Expressionism, which the work of Kandinsky had largely initiated, the two streams of influence –one from Holland and one from Russia and Hungary–would probably have been consolidated in Germany had the Bauhaus not been there. The Bauhaus was in the right place at the right time to catch them, fuse them, and transmute them into "utilitarian functionalism," which in printing and advertising design was to become known variously as "Elementary," "Constructivist," "The New," and, in the Danish edition of Jan Tschichold's latest book, "Functional" Typography.

5

The New Typography was a philosophy and not a style. It was largely the failure to understand this which produced around 1928 what the late Frederic Ehrlich called the "Dark Cloud Era" and retarded in America an international movement which may be said to have begun in 1925 with the publication, in *Typographische Mitteilungen*, of Jan Tschichold's "Elementaire Typographie." In the decade preceding this event typography had been lifted out of the tradition of printing and placed squarely in the dual "tradition" of abstract art and the New Architecture.

The basic element in its ideology is probably as old as man. It was a determining force in the mind of an American architect a half century ago. It was Louis Sullivan's dictum: "Form must follow function." It was the quite simple and altogether reasonable idea that there should be an organic relation between the inside and the outside of a building— between the materials out of which it was made, the purpose which it was to serve, and the outward visible form which it took. Though Sullivan himself prospered as an architect, America was not wholly hospitable to the idea. In Holland and Germany it found better soil in which to grow. It took root at the Bauhaus and was importantly illustrated in the Bauhaus building at Dessau, designed by Walter Gropius.

Just as architecture became a "machine for living" (or for doing business in or for learning things in), so typography became a machine for communication. In design for publicity the intention was to project a persuasive message into the reader's psyche with the highest immediacy of meaning and with the greatest possible psychological impact. The ammunition for this purpose often included asymmetrical relationships of masses, lines (conceived of as points or masses in motion), arrows,

bullets of color, oblique and vertical direction contrasts. The cue for using these devices and the ordering principle for handling them, apart from the intention to be architecturally simple and direct, was derived mainly from abstract painting. Jan Tschichold has developed the implied analogy:

> All abstract pictures, particularly the quite simple ones, show elements of painting or graphic art which are at once clearly defined in form and in plain relation to one another. From this to typography is no great step. The works of abstract painters are symbols of the subtle arrangement of simple yet strongly contrasting elements. Since the new typography sets itself no other task than the creation of just such arrangements, it is possible for many works of abstract painters and sculptors to act as inspirational models.

But there was more to the New Typography than merely organizing the visual material into an overall form that would be organically related to its content and purpose. For there were always alternatives, and neither architecture nor painting had much to say about the use of type faces. Beyond the functional requirements of a particular job there was a margin of creative freedom, within which the designer expressed his own peculiar sensibilities and sought, frequently if not always, to tie his work in with the *Zeitgeist*–the "form-seeking" impulse of the time.

It was in the effort to catch the "feel" of the machine age, and at the same time to create designs that would be economical of the mental and visual energies of the reader, that the New Typography developed an affinity for "constructed" type faces. The first preference was for a block letter similar to the "Venus-Grotesk" used in the Bauer booklet *Futura Schmuck* and in the folder announcing the *Bauhausbücher*. The first book on the New Typography was set in a light sans-serif midway between Venus and Futura. During the period 1925 to 1930 Herbert Bayer, Jan Tschichold, Karel Teige, and others experimented with reform alphabets, all working more or less on principles stated by Bayer:

> Geometric foundation of each letter, resulting in a synthetic construction out of a few basic elements. Avoidance of all suggestion of a hand-written character. Even thickness of all parts of the letter, and renumeration of all suggestions of up and down strokes. Simplification of form for the sake of legibility (the simpler the optical appearance the easier the comprehension).

The immediate outcome was Bayer's "Universal" type, after which the letters in the name "The New Bauhaus" were modeled by Moholy-Nagy. Close by in spirit was Paul Renner's first "Futura," more rigidly abstract than the version which reached America. Tschichold produced a design based on a phonetic alphabet, as radical, though in a different direction, as A. M. Cassandre's current "Peignot," which we may perhaps take as the final expression and modification of the geometric urge.

There was, however, never any absolute insistence on a type face whose design, like these, was based on the square-circle-line motif. "Bayer Type" is a case in point. Tschichold's *Typographische Gestaltung*, published in 1935, is set in Bodoni. On its title page a "bank" script is mixed with Georg Trump's "City," to which the author elsewhere accords the highest place among "Egyptian" faces. Not even the Cheltenham-like face used in the Danish edition, 1937, of the same book, though it forsakes the geometric ideal entirely, is inconsistent with the philosophy behind the New Typography. For it was recognized that type designs, as carriers of verbal meaning, could never depart too far from what people were used to reading however great might be the need for differentness or for falling in with the *Zeitgeist*. In the total design, using elements that had an immediate visual, rather than verbal, meaning, the typographer could make up for the lack of freedom which the necessity of using type imposed upon him.

If he chose a traditional type face, as he frequently did, it was because he thought he could do a better total job with it than without it. He still had no predetermined overall form into which he could pour his persuasive message, like water into a jug. Having traded tradition for a philosophy, his problem was one of analysis and experiment within the discipline of an ideology. His solution of the problem was not always clear. Looking at the final results from the outside, without his ideology, it was often impossible to rationalize many of the things which the analogy of typography to abstract painting and the New Architecture determined in his work. Surface characteristics were, therefore, widely imitated. In America the New Typography tended to become what it preeminently was not, a predetermined style. The New Painting and the New Architecture constituted a sharp break with the past. The gap between the "old" and the "new" was, as history goes, an enormous one. So also was the gap between the old typography and the new. Yet, in a sense, none of them was new. They were all in theory a return to a kind of original sanity–to a pristine unity of life.

6

The preliminary development of the New Typography at the Bauhaus was largely in the hands of three men–Walter Gropius, László Moholy-Nagy, and Herbert Bayer. They were the right men because they were prepared by training, inclination, and experience to view with an open mind the experimental typography then being done in Holland, Russia, Germany, Italy, Hungary, Czechoslovakia, France, and Switzerland.

Walter Gropius was first and last an architect. Though he did not himself venture into typography, he was, as director of the school, interested in it as one of many coordinated activities. Herbert Bayer, who had earlier been a student at the Bauhaus, was a self-taught painter with Surrealist tendencies before he joined the staff in 1925 to teach advertising design and typography. Moholy-Nagy had turned from the study of law to become a painter, photographer, typographer, and designer for the theatre and the film—in all of which fields he has made significant contributions. His pioneer work in developing the photogram, photomontage, and "negative" printing is only now beginning to take effect. Last year his "rhodoid" technique, illustrated in the jacket of the Gropius book [The New Architecture and The Bauhaus, n.d. 1936], was in evidence at the Art Directors Show in New York. His time at the Bauhaus was during the important formative period, 1923 to 1928, which produced, among other things, the Bauhausbücher, now to be continued in America under the same editorship.

It would not be quite true to say that this triumvirate created either the Bauhaus Tradition of the New Typography; but the work of Moholy-Nagy and Bayer was quickly noted throughout Central Europe. Among the first to feel its underlying sanity (though they may have rejected some of the surface characteristics) were Jan Tschichold and Karel Teige, to the latter of whom we owe the initial formulation of its ideology. Briefly it involved: (1) Freedom from tradition. (2) Geometric simplicity. (3) Contrast of typographical material. (4) The exclusion of any ornament that was not "functionally" necessary. (5) A preference for photography, machine composition, and combinations of the simpler primary colors. (6) A recognition and acceptance of the "machine age" and of the utilitarian purpose of typography.

Of this credo Jan Tschichold has from the outset been the chief protagonist, though little of his work has been translated from the original German. In the summer of 1936 Industrial Arts published a small portion in English of Typographische Gestaltung under the title "Abstract Painting and the New Typography." The following summer he discussed "Type Mixtures" in the new English quarterly Typography. His most recent writing

in English is included in Circle, an "International Survey of Constructive Art," published last year in England.

Though the Bauhaus closed its doors in 1933, its philosophy persisted through the work of individual men on the Continent, in England, and in America. In February of last year Walter Gropius was brought over to America to become a Professor of Architecture at Harvard University, from which point he now acts as adviser to the staff of the New Bauhaus. Josef Albers, who continued the work of Moholy-Nagy at Dessau following 1928, and Xanti Schawinsky have for some time been teaching at Black Mountain College in North Carolina.

The three men most influential in carrying on the Bauhaus tradition in typography have not been inactive. Bayer, as Director of the Berlin Dorland Studios, has wielded a continuous influence on the Continent. Tschichold continues to write from Switzerland. Moholy-Nagy now heads a New Bauhaus. Within the last two years all three of these men have exhibited their work at London galleries. All three of them have been featured recently in English periodicals. In the light of these facts one is tempted to agree with Paul Renner in thinking that "the wish is father to the thought" among those who still predict an end for the New Typography or who perhaps like to think of it complacently as decadent.

7

The New Bauhaus is the final result of efforts on the part of the Association of Arts and Industries, extending over a period of years, to create a school which would train young people to work realistically and significantly in that middle field between art and industry. This year only the basic training courses have been given. Next year the program will include typography and advertising design. Spiritually and philosophically the new school is carrying on from the point at which the old Bauhaus left off.

In Art and the Machine, which pays generous tribute to the pioneer work of the old Bauhaus, Sheldon and Martha Cheney venture the belief that "today, for the first time since the Middle Ages, we are at a new major beginning, with new dimensions, new proportions, new possibilities, new freedom . . . " If this be true it may not be too much to expect the new school to play in America a role comparable to the role played by its famous predecessor.

It may be that the New Bauhaus will find in America the right time, the right place, and the right men. Of the right men it already has one in L. Moholy-Nagy, whom Herbert Read believes to be one of the outstanding creative intelligences of our time. •

Article reprinted (without bibliography, illustrations, or captions) from PM: An Intimate Journal for Production Managers, Art Directors, and Their Associates, PM Publishing Co., New York, NY, Vol. IV, No. 7, June–July, 1938. Written by L. Sandusky, a faculty member of Commercial High School, New York. Original article layout by Lester Beall.

BIBLIOGRAPHY

Josef Albers

Albers, Josef. *Interaction of Color*. New Haven: Yale University Press, 1963.

Borchardt-Hume, Achim ed. *Albers and Moholy-Nagy: From the Bauhaus to the New World*. New Haven: Yale University Press, 2006.

Hermon, Nitzan. Interview by Steven Heller. January 13, 2015.

Tochilovsky, Alexander. "Albers in Command." Medium: Herb Lubalin Study Center. *VV6 Studio: Journal*, January 28, 2015. https://news .vvvvvv.co/albers-in-command -b3184edd7746#.

Weber, Nicholas Fox, and Martin Filler. *Josef and Anni Albers: Designs for Living*. London: Merrell, 2004.

Walter Allner

Heller, Steven. "Walter Allner, 97, Noted Art Director of Fortune Magazine, Is Dead." *New York Times*, July 24, 2006.

Lahr, John. "Computer Graphics at *Fortune*." *Print* 20, no. 6 (November–December 1966): 33–35.

Herbert Bayer

Bayer, Herbert, Walter Gropius, and Ise Gropius, eds. *Bauhaus, 1919–1928*. New York: Museum of Modern Art, 1938.

Chanzit, Gwen Finkel. *Herbert Bayer and Modernist Design in America*. Ann Arbor, MI: UMI Research Press, 1987.

———. *Herbert Bayer Collection and Archive at the Denver Art Museum*. Denver: Denver Art Museum, 1988.

Cohen, Arthur A. *Herbert Bayer: The Complete Work*. Cambridge, MA: MIT Press, 1984.

Müller-Brockmann, Josef. "The Bauhaus Tradition." *Print* 23, no. 1 (January–February 1969): 40–44.

Alexey Brodovitch

Grundberg, Andy. "1987 AIGA Medalist: Alexey Brodovitch." AIGA: The Professional Association for Design. www.aiga.org/medalist-alexeybrodovitch.

———. *Brodovitch*. Masters of American Design. New York: Harry N. Abrams, 1989.

Purcell, Kerry William. *Alexey Brodovitch*. London: Phaidon Press, 2002.

Will Burtin

Burtin, Will. "Integration: The New Discipline in Design." *Graphis* 5, no. 27 (1949): 230–37.

———. *Integration: The New Discipline in Design; An Exhibition of Design by Will Burtin from Nov. 9, 1948, to Jan. 14, 1949*. A-D Gallery, Composing Room, New York. [New York]: A-D Gallery, [1949]. Exhibition catalog.

———. "Burtin and Upjohn." *Print* 9, no. 5 (May–June 1955): 36.

———. "A Program in Print: Upjohn and Design." *Print* 9, no. 5 (May–June 1955): 37–60.

———. "From Where to Where?" In *Typography—U.S.A.: Forum, "What Is New in American Typography?"* April 18, 1959. 4–6. New York: [Type Directors Club], 1959.

Remington, R. Roger. *Will Burtin: The Display of Visual Knowledge*. Rochester, NY: RIT Cary Graphic Arts Press, 2009.

Remington, R. Roger, and Robert S. P. Fripp. *Design and Science: The Life and Work of Will Burtin*. London: Lund Humphries, 2007.

George Giusti

Drew, Ned, Brenda McManus, and Paul Sternberger. *George Giusti: The Idea Is the Heart of the Matter*. Rochester, NY: RIT Cary Graphic Arts Press, 2016.

Johnson, Fridolf. "George Giusti, Graphic Designer." *American Artist* 28, no. 10 (December 1964): 46–51.

Morse, Edward S. "The Man Who Signs His Work Giusti." *CA: The Magazine of the Communication Arts* 7, no. 4 (July–August 1965): 24–35.

Oeri, Georgine. "George Giusti, Graphic Artist." *Graphis* 5, no. 26 (1949): 148–53.

Remington, R. Roger. "Remembering George Giusti." *Graphis* 49, no. 285 (May–June 1993): 96–101.

Thomajan, P. K. "George Giusti." *Graphis* 11, no. 59 (May 1955): 266–71.

György Kepes

De Harak, Rudolph. "Gyorgy Kepes Revisits the Visual Landscape." In *Design Culture: An Anthology of Writing from the "AIGA Journal for Graphic Design."* Edited by Steven Heller and Marie Finamore. 139–151. New York: Allsworth Press, 2013.

Kepes, György. Interview by Rudolph de Harak. 1987.

———. Interview by Steven Heller. 1986.

———. *Language of Vision*. Chicago: Paul Theobald, 1944.

———. "The Task of Visual Advertising." Supplement, *PM: An Intimate Journal for Art Directors, Production Managers, and Their Associates* 6, no. 3 (February–March 1940): 08–16.

Kepes, György, et al. *Graphic Forms: The Arts as Related to the Book*. Cambridge, MA: Harvard University Press, 1949.

Kuh, Katherine. *Exhibition of the Advance Guard of Advertising Artists*. Chicago: Katherine Kuh Gallery, 1941. Exhibition catalog.

Leo Lionni

Heller, Steven. "1984 AIGA Medalist: Leo Lionni." AIGA: The Professional Association for Design, March 1, 1984. www.aiga.org/medalist-leolionni.

———. "Leo Lionni, 89, Dies, Versatile Creator of Children's Books." *New York Times*, October 17, 1999.

Lionni, Leo. *Between Worlds: The Autobiography of Leo Lionni*. New York: Alfred A. Knopf, 1997.

———. Interview by Steven Heller. March 11, 1985.

Herbert Matter

Eisenman, Alvin. Interview by Steven Heller. Spring 1983.

Heller, Steven, and David R. Brown. "1983 AIGA Medalist: Herbert Matter." AIGA: The Professional Association for Design, March 1, 1983. www.aiga.org/medalist -herbertmatter.

Purcell, Kerry William. "Herbert Matter: The Art of Photo-Graphics." *Baseline: International Typographics Magazine*, no. 49 (2006): 29–36.

Rand, Paul. Interview by Steven Heller. 1983.

The Visual Language of Herbert Matter. Directed by Reto Caduff. Zurich: PiXiU Films, 2011. DVD.

Erik Nitsche

Heller, Steven. "Erik Nitsche: The Reluctant Modernist." *Typotheque*, November 29, 2004. https://www.typotheque.com /articles/erik_nitsche_the_reluctant _modernist.

———. "Erik Nitsche, 90, Modernist Graphic Designer." *New York Times*, November 29, 1998.

Nitsche, Erik. Interview by Steven Heller. Spring 1994.

Niven, John, and Courtlandt Canby, eds. *Dynamic America: A History of General Dynamics Corporation and Its Predecessor Companies*. Fort Worth: General Dynamics; New York: Doubleday, 1960.

Thomajan, P. K. "Erik Nitsche Imagician." Special issue, *Design and Paper* (Marquardt & Company Fine Papers, New York), no. 34 (c. 1951).

M. Peter Piening

The Art Students League of New York. Prospectus and instructor biographies, 1946–47, 1948–49.

Piening, M. Peter. *Trademarks and Symbols*. Syracuse, NY: Syracuse University, 1964.

Schmeckebier, Laurence. *Introduction to Fourteen Prints*, by M. Peter Piening. Syracuse, NY: Syracuse University Press, 1965.

Schmeckebier, Laurence. "The Trademarks of M. Peter Piening." *American Artist* 29, no. 281 (January 1965): 52–57.

———. "The Trademarks of M. Peter Piening." *American Artist* 29, no. 281 (January 1965): 52–57.

Cipe Pineles

Ellis, Estelle, and Carol Burtin Fripp. *Cipe Pineles: Two Remembrances*. Rochester, NY: RIT Cary Graphic Arts Press, 2005.

Pineles, Cipe. Interview by Steven Heller. c. 1985.

Scotford, Martha. *Cipe Pineles: A Life of Design*. New York: W. W. Norton, 1999.

Ladislav Sutnar

Heller, Steven. "1995 AIGA Medalist: Ladislav Sutnar." AIGA: The Professional Association for Design, March 1, 1995. www.aiga.org/medalist-ladislavsutnar.

Schoener, Allon. *Ladislav Sutnar: Visual Design in Action*. Cincinnati: Contemporary Arts Center in association with Champion Papers, 1961. Exhibition catalog.

Sutnar, Ladislav. "The New Typography's Expanding Future." In *Typography—U.S.A.: Forum, "What Is New in American Typography?"* April 18, 1959. 32–35. New York: [Type Directors Club], 1959.

———. *Visual Design in Action: Principles, Purposes*. New York: Hastings House, 1961.

Fred Troller

"Geigy." *CA: The Magazine of the Communication Arts* 7, no. 3 (May–June 1965): 54–61.

Heller, Steven. "Fred Troller, 71, Champion of Bold Graphic Style." *New York Times*, October 24, 2002.

Janser, Andres, and Barbara Junod, eds. *Corporate Diversity: Swiss Graphic Design and Advertising by Geigy, 1940–1970*. Baden, Switzerland: Lars Müller, 2009.

Owens, Mark. "Soft Modernist: Discovering the Book Covers of Fred Troller." *Dot Dot Dot*, no. 6 (2002): 70–79.

George Tscherny

Heller, Steven. "1988 AIGA Medalist: George Tscherny." AIGA: The Professional Association for Design, March 1, 1988. www.aiga.org/medalist -georgetscherny.

Meggs, Philip B. "George Tscherny." *Graphis* 40, no. 230 (March–April 1984): 30–39.

Snyder, Jerome. "George Tscherny." *Graphis* 28, no. 161 (January 1973): 222–31.

Tscherny, George. Interview by Steven Heller. 1988.

Massimo Vignelli

Conradi, Jan. *Unimark International: The Design of Business and the Business of Design*. Baden, Switzerland: Lars Müller, 2009.

Heller, Steven, and Elinor Pettit. *Design Dialogues*. New York: Allsworth Press, 1998.

Vignelli, Massimo. Interview by Steven Heller. 1998.

———. *Vignelli: From A to Z*. Mulgrave, Australia: Images, 2007.

Dietmar R. Winkler

Winkler, Dietmar R. E-mail correspondence with Greg D'Onofrio. May–December 2016.

———. Personal notes: MIT Office of Publications, 1965 through 1970. 2015. PDF.

———, ed. *Posters: Jacqueline S. Casey; Thirty Years of Design at MIT.* Cambridge, MA: MIT Museum, 1992.

Rudi Wolff

Wolff, Rudi. "The Drug Market: A Graphic Design Challenge." *Industrial Design* 13, no. 3 (March 1966): 66–73.

———. E-mail correspondence with Greg D'Onofrio. September–October 2016.

———. Interview by Greg D'Onofrio and Patricia Belen. May 31, 2016.

———. "Psychotherapeutic Drugs and Their Graphics." *Graphis* 25, no. 142 (1969): 106–19.

Saul Bass

Bass, Jennifer, and Pat Kirkham. *Saul Bass: A Life in Film & Design.* London: Laurence King, 2011.

Bass, Saul. Interview by Steven Heller. c. 1989.

Friedman, Mildred S., et al. *Graphic Design in America: A Visual Language History.* Minneapolis: Walker Art Center, 1989.

Lillian Bassman

Aletti, Vince. "Junior Bazaar." *Aperture*, no. 182 (Spring 2006): 54–61.

Bouabana, Samira, and Angela Tillman Sperandio. *Hall of Femmes: Lillian Bassman.* Edited by Ika Johannesson and Hjärta Smärta. Stockholm: Oyster Press, 2010.

Himmel, Eric. "Bassman-Himmel." In *Lillian Bassman & Paul Himmel*, edited by Ingo Taubhorn and Brigitte Woischnik. Heidelberg, Germany: Kehrer Verlag, 2009.

Lester Beall

Belen, Patricia, and Greg D'Onofrio. "Lester Beall: A Significant American Corporate Identity Program." *Codex 3: The Journal of Letterforms,* Summer 2013, 52–69.

Remington, R. Roger. "The Creative Process of Lester Beall." *Step-by-Step Graphics,* July–August 1990, 120–129.

———. *Lester Beall: Space, Time & Content.* Rochester, NY: RIT Cary Graphic Arts Press, 2003.

———. *Lester Beall: Trailblazer of American Graphic Design.* New York: W. W. Norton, 1996.

Wills, Franz Hermann. "Lester Beall." *Graphis* 8, no. 40 (March 1952): 128–35.

Peter Bradford

Bradford, Peter. Chapters from unpublished memoir, portraits, and résumé. Sent to Steven Heller, May 18, 2016.

Robert Brownjohn

King, Emily. *Robert Brownjohn: Sex and Typography; 1925–1970, Life and Work.* Originated by Eliza Brownjohn. New York: Princeton Architectural Press, 2005.

"Robert Brownjohn." AIGA: The Professional Association for Design. www.aiga.org/medalist-robertbrownjohn.

Jacqueline S. Casey

Lupton, Ellen. *MIT/CASEY Exhibition.* New York: Herb Lubalin Study Center of Design and Typography, 1989. Exhibition catalog.

McQuiston, Liz. *Women in Design: A Contemporary View.* New York: Rizzoli, 1988.

Meggs, Philip B., and Alston W. Purvis. "The International Typographic Style in America." In *Meggs' History of Graphic Design.* 4th ed. 372–373. Hoboken, NJ: John Wiley & Sons, 2006.

Resnick, Elizabeth. "Woman at the Edge of Technology." *Eye: The International Review of Graphic Design* 17, no. 68 (Summer 2008): 26–28.

Winkler, Dietmar R. Personal notes: MIT Office of Publications, 1965 through 1970. 2015. PDF.

———, ed. *Posters: Jacqueline S. Casey; Thirty Years of Design at MIT.* Cambridge, MA: MIT Museum, 1992.

Chermayeff & Geismar

Chermayeff, Ivan. Interview by Steven Heller. 1987.

Heller, Steven. "Ivan Chermayeff and Tom Geismar: Partners, Chermayeff and Geismar." *Print* 61, no. 5 (September–October 2007): 32–34.

John and Mary Condon

Condon, Mary. E-mail correspondence with Greg D'Onofrio. June–October 2016.

———. Interview by Greg D'Onofrio and Patricia Belen. June 9, 2016.

Iachetta, Michael. "Subway Buffs Map Route to Riches." *Sunday New York Daily News,* November 1, 1964, section 2, 22.

Donald and Ann Crews

Crews, Donald. Interview by Greg D'Onofrio and Patricia Belen. June 24, 2016.

———. "Laura Ingalls Wilder Medal Acceptance Speech." Newbery-Caldecott-Wilder Awards Banquet, Association for Library Service to Children, San Francisco, June 28, 2015.

Richard Danne

Danne, Richard. *Dust Bowl to Gotham: Flashbacks of an Oklahoma Farm Boy Who Rose to the Top of New York's Design Profession.* Napa, CA: Richard Danne, 2011.

———. E-mail correspondence with Greg D'Onofrio. July–November 2016.

———. "The NASA Design Program." Published as "Space Odyssey" in *Dust Bowl to Gotham.* Reprinted in *Display.* Accessed January 17, 2017. www.thisisdisplay.org/features/the_nasa_design_program.

Louis Danziger

Danziger, Louis. Interview by Steven Heller. 1998.

Heller, Steven. "1998 AIGA Medalist: Louis Danziger." AIGA: The Professional Association for Design, 1999. www.aiga.org/medalist-louisdanziger.

Munari, Nicola-Matteo. "Louis Danziger." *Designculture,* September 23, 2013. www.designculture.it/interview/louis-danziger.html.

Rudolph de Harak

De Harak, Rudolph. Interview by Steven Heller. 1987 and 1992.

Heller, Steven. "1992 AIGA Medalist: Rudolph de Harak." AIGA: The Professional Association for Design, March 1, 1992. www.aiga.org/medalist-rudolphdeharak.

———. "Rudolph de Harak: A Playful Modernist." *Baseline: International Typographics Magazine,* no. 45 (2004): 25–32.

———. "Rudolph de Harak, 78, Artist and Environmental Designer." *New York Times,* April 30, 2002.

Louis Dorfsman

Dorfsman, Louis. Interview by Steven Heller. c. 2000.

Heller, Steven. "Lou Dorfsman, Design Chief at CBS, Dies at 90." *New York Times,* October 26, 2008.

Hess, Dick, and Marion Muller. *Dorfsman & CBS: A 40-Year Commitment to Excellence in Advertising and Design.* New York: American Showcase, 1987.

Smith, Virginia, ed. *Artograph 5: Lou Dorfsman.* New York: Baruch College, CUNY, 1985.

Ray Eames

Albrecht, Donald, et al. *The Work of Charles and Ray Eames: A Legacy of Invention.* New York: Harry N. Abrams in association with the Library of Congress and the Vitra Design Museum, 1997.

Neuhart, John, and Marilyn Neuhart, with Ray Eames. *Eames Design: The Work of the Office of Charles and Ray Eames.* New York: Harry N. Abrams, 1989.

Gene Federico

Federico, Gene. Interview by Steven Heller. 1987.

———. "Sight and Sound: Typography in Advertising." *Print* 40, no. 6 (November–December 1986): 56.

Heller, Steven. "Gene Federico, 81, Graphic Designer, Dies." *New York Times,* September 10, 1999.

———. "1987 AIGA Medalist: Gene Federico." AIGA: The Professional Association for Design, 1987. www.aiga.org/medalist-genefederico.

S. Neil Fujita

Fujita, S. Neil. *Aim for a Job in Graphic Design/Art.* New York: R. Rosen Press, 1968.

Heller, Steven. "Waxing Chromatic: An Interview with S. Neil Fujita." AIGA: The Professional Association for Design, September 18, 2007. www.aiga.org/waxing-chromatic-an-interview-with-s-neil-fujita.

"S. Neil Fujita." *CA: The Journal of Commercial Art* 4, no. 9/10 (September–October 1962): 62–69.

William Golden

Burtin, Will. "The Golden Touch—William Golden." *CA: The Journal of Commercial Art* 2, no. 6 (June 1960): 10–16.

Golden, Cipe Pineles, Kurt Weihs, and Robert Strunsky, eds. *The Visual Craft of William Golden.* New York: George Braziller, 1962.

Golden, William. "My Eye." *Print* 13, no. 3 (May–June 1959): 32–35.

Morton Goldsholl

Beste, Amy. "Designers in Film: Goldsholl Associates, the Avant-Garde, and Midcentury Advertising Films." In *Chicago Makes Modern,* edited by Mary Jane Jacob and Jacquelynn Baas. 59–75. Chicago: University of Chicago Press, 2012.

Even, Robert. *The Chicago Design History Project: Morton Goldsholl.* Northern Illinois University School of Art and Design. 1992. www.chicagodesignarchive.org/resources.php. Video.

———. *Morton Goldsholl: Moholy-Nagy and the New Bauhaus.* Northern Illinois University School of Art and Design. September 1992. https://www.chicagodesignarchive.org/documents/video_mortgoldsholl_bauhaus.php. Video.

Goldsholl, Morton, with Yoshi Sekiguchi. *Inside Design, A Review: 40 Years of Work.* Tokyo: Graphic-Sha Publishing Co., 1987.

Jacobson, Egbert, and Morton Goldsholl. *An Exhibition of the Work of Morton Goldsholl.* New York: A-D Gallery, 1950. Exhibition catalog.

Patterson, Rhodes. "Morton Goldsholl & Associates." *Communication Arts,* July–August 1963, 36–46.

Charles Goslin

"Charles Goslin: Graphic Design." *IDEA: International Graphic Art and Typography,* no. 124 (1974/75): 54–59.

Davis, Susan E. "A Burning Passion for Ideas." *Step-by-Step Graphics*, January–February 1997, 48–57.

Goslin, Charles. Interview by Paul Choi. StoryCorps audio recording, November 26, 2005. https://soundcloud.com/p-money-146641738/storycorps-interview-charles-goslin.

Hilten, Theodor. "Charles Goslin: Designs of a New York Free Lance Artist." *Gebrauchsgraphik*, no. 6 (1962): 14–19.

Santoro, Scott. "Scott W. Santoro on Charles Goslin." AIGA: The Professional Association for Design, May 27, 2004. www.aiga.org/scott-w-santoro-on-charles-goslin.

Snyder, Gertrude. "Charles Goslin." *Graphis* 39, no. 225 (May–June 1983): 84–89.

Irving Harper

Abercrombie, Stanley. *George Nelson: The Design of Modern Design*. Cambridge, MA: MIT Press, 2000.

Bravo, Amber. "Irving Harper: The Mediums Beyond the Message." Accessed January 20, 2017. www.hermanmiller.com/why/irving-harper-the-mediums-beyond-the-message.html.

Constantine, Mildred. "George Nelson & Associates." *Graphis* 9, no. 49 (September 1953): 370–76.

Lasky, Julie. "Irving Harper's World." In *Irving Harper: Works in Paper*, edited by Michael Maharam. 11–39. New York: Skira Rizzoli, 2013.

Makovsky, Paul. "Nelson & Company: Iconic Workplace, 1947–86." *Metropolis*, June 2009. www.metropolismag.com/June-2009/Nelson-amp-CompanyIconic-Workplace-1947-86.

Webb, Michael. *George Nelson: Compact Design Portfolio*, edited by Marisa Bartolucci and Raul Cabra. San Francisco: Chronicle, 2003.

E. McKnight Kauffer

Haworth-Booth, Mark. *E. McKnight Kauffer: A Designer and His Public*. London: V&A Publications, 2005.

Heller, Steven. "1991 AIGA Medalist: E. McKnight Kauffer." AIGA: The Professional Association for Design, 1991. www.aiga.org/medalist-emcknightkauffer.

Huxley, Aldous. Foreword to *Posters by E. McKnight Kauffer*. New York: Museum of Modern Art, 1937. Exhibition catalog.

Ray Komai

Blake, Peter. *No Place Like Utopia: Modern Architecture and the Company We Kept*. New York: W. W. Norton, 1993.

Bradford, Peter, and Tami Komai. E-mail correspondence with Greg D'Onofrio. June–November 2016.

Eidelberg, Martin P., ed. *Design 1935–1965: What Modern Was*. Montreal: Musée des Arts Décoratifs de Montréal in association with Harry N. Abrams, 1991.

Interiors (Interiors + Industrial Design) 107, no. 10 (May 1948): cover.

"Tokyo Library Certainly Isn't Dusty Mausoleum." *Panama City News-Herald*, February 27, 1974, 10.

Burton Kramer

Clarke, Ian. "Burton Kramer." *HeyThere*. www.heythere.ca/interview/burton-kramer.

Durrell, Greg, ed. *Burton Kramer Identities: A Half Century of Graphic Design, 1958–2008*. Lulu.com, 2011.

Janser, Andres, and Barbara Junod, eds. *Corporate Diversity: Swiss Graphic Design and Advertising by Geigy, 1940–1970*. Baden, Switzerland: Lars Müller, 2009.

Kramer, Burton. E-mail correspondence with Greg D'Onofrio. 2016.

Munari, Nicola-Matteo. "Charles Goslin." *Designculture*, October 19, 2014, and March 30, 2016. www.designculture.it/interview/burton-kramer.html.

Roy Kuhlman

Brower, Steven. "Roy Kuhlman." AIGA: The Professional Association for Design, December 11, 2014. eyeondesign.aiga.org/design-history-101-roy-kuhlman/.

Heller, Steven. "Roy Kuhlman Dies at 83; Designer for Grove Press." *New York Times*, February 5, 2007.

Rietschel, Barbara. *Roy Kuhlman and the Grove Press Covers, 1951–1971*. Albany, NY: Opalka Gallery, Sage Colleges, 2004. Exhibition catalog.

Matthew Leibowitz

Allner, W. H. "Matthew Leibowitz." *Graphis* 3, no. 17 (January 1947): 16–23.

Bresnick, Jan, and Lynn Leibowitz. E-mail correspondence with Greg D'Onofrio. September 2016.

Burns, Aaron, and Will Burtin. *Typography—U.S.A.: Forum, "What Is New in American Typography?"* April 18, 1959. 24. New York: [Type Directors Club], 1959.

Hölscher, Eberhard. "Matthew Leibowitz, New York." *Gebrauchsgraphik* 28, no. 5 (May 1957): 2–11.

Leibowitz, Matthew. "Dialogs on Graphic Design—V." *Industrial Design* 4, no. 1 (January 1957): 56–63.

Masaki Katsumi. "Selected Works of Matthew Leibowitz." *Graphic Design*, no. 7 (April 1962): 45–51.

Sachs, Sid. *Matthew Leibowitz: Philadelphia Modernist*. Philadelphia: University of the Arts, Philadelphia, 2007. Exhibition brochure.

Weill, Alain. E-mail correspondence with Greg D'Onofrio. September 2016.

George Lois

Heller, Steven. "Reputations: George Lois." *Eye: The International Review of Graphic Design* 8, no. 29 (Autumn 1998): 12–19.

———. "Revisiting the Work of One of the 20th Century's Best Ad Men." *Atlantic*, June 11, 2015. www.theatlantic.com/entertainment/archive/2015/06/70s-advertising-george-lois/395579.

Lois, George, with Bill Pitts. *George, Be Careful: A Greek Florist's Kid in the Roughhouse World of Advertising*. New York: Saturday Review Press, 1972.

Herb Lubalin

Heller, Steven. "Crimes against Typography." AIGA: The Professional Association for Design, August 4, 2004. www.aiga.org/crimes-against-typography.

Shaughnessy, Adrian. *Herb Lubalin: American Graphic Designer, 1918–81*. London: Unit Editions, 2012.

Snyder, Gertrude, and Alan Peckolick. *Herb Lubalin: Art Director, Graphic Designer and Typographer*. New York: American Showcase, 1985.

Alvin Lustig

Drew, Ned, and Paul Sternberger. *Purity of Aim: Book Jacket Designs of Alvin Lustig*. Rochester, NY: RIT Cary Graphic Arts Press, 2016.

Heller, Steven. "Born Modern." *Eye: The International Review of Graphic Design* 3, no. 10 (Autumn 1993): 26–37.

Heller, Steven, and Elaine Lustig Cohen. *Born Modern: The Life and Design of Alvin Lustig*. San Francisco: Chronicle, 2010.

Laughlin, James. "The Book Jackets of Alvin Lustig." *Print* 10, no. 5 (October–November 1956): 52.

Lustig, Alvin. *The Collected Writings of Alvin Lustig*. New Haven: Holland R. Melson Jr., 1958.

Elaine Lustig Cohen

Belen, Patricia, and Greg D'Onofrio. "Elaine Lustig Cohen: The Art of Modern Graphics." *Shelf Journal*, no. 2 (2012): 90–107.

Heller, Steven. "2011 AIGA Medalist: Elaine Lustig Cohen." AIGA: The Professional Association for Design, March 1, 2011. www.aiga.org/medalist-elainelustigcohen.

Lupton, Ellen. "Elaine Lustig Cohen: Modern Graphic Designer." *Eye: The International Review of Graphic Design* 5, no. 17 (Summer 1995): 8–9.

"The Lustigs: A Conversation with Elaine Lustig Cohen & Steven Heller." AIGA/NY on Vimeo, July 15, 2013. https://vimeo.com/69981714.

Sherin, Aaris. *Elaine Lustig Cohen: Modernism Reimagined*. Rochester, NY: RIT Cary Graphic Arts Press, 2014.

John Massey

Dougherty, Carissa Kowalski, ed. *John Massey: Vision*. Chicago: JMI Publications, 2014.

Even, Robert. *The Chicago Design History Project: John Massey*. Northern Illinois University School of Art and Design. 1991. https://www.chicagodesignarchive.org/resources.php. Video.

"John Massey." *CA: The Magazine of the Communication Arts 7*, no. 1 (January–February 1965): 18–29.

Massey, John. "New Direction for Designers?" *Print* 15, no. 6 (November–December 1961): 31–35.

Meggs, Philip B. "1994 AIGA Medalist: John Massey." AIGA: The Professional Association for Design, March 1, 1994. www.aiga.org/medalist-johnmassey.

Wallrapp, Yustin. "John Massey: Container Corporation of America." *Graphis* 24, no. 135 (1968): 8–19.

Tomoko Miho

Bouabana, Samira, et al. *Hall of Femmes: Tomoko Miho*. Stockholm: Oyster Press, 2013.

Vienne, Veronique. "1993 AIGA Medalist: Tomoko Miho." AIGA: The Professional Association for Design, March 1, 1993. www.aiga.org/medalist-tomokomiho.

Reid Miles

Adams, Wayne. Phone and e-mail correspondence with Greg D'Onofrio. August–December 2016.

Kinross, Robin. "Cool, Clear, Collected." *Eye: The International Review of Graphic Design* 1, no. 1 (Autumn 1990): 72–82.

Marsh, Graham, and Glyn Callingham. *Blue Note: Album Cover Art; The Ultimate Collection*. San Francisco: Chronicle, 2002.

———, eds. *Blue Note 2: The Album Cover Art*. San Francisco: Chronicle, 1997.

Watson, Gerald. "Jazz: Reid Miles; Courtesy of Wayne Adams." *New Ish: People, Places, Things*, November 3, 2010. https://gmoney77.wordpress.com/2010/11/03/jazz-reid-miles-courtesy-of-wayne-adams/.

Charles E. Murphy

"Charles E. Murphy." *Discogs*. Accessed January 21, 2017. https://www.discogs.com/artist/1374513-Charles-E-Murphy.

"Charles E. Murphy Obituary." *New York Times*, July 26–27, 2005.

Rolontz, Bob. "Sound Record Sales Boom after 3 Years of Stereo." *Billboard Music Week*, November 6, 1961, 15.

Tochilovsky, Alexander. "Albers in Command." Medium: Herb Lubalin Study Center. VV6 Studio: Journal, January 28, 2015. https://news.vvvvvv.co/albers-in-command-b3184edd7746#.

Georg Olden

Lasky, Julie. "2007 AIGA Medalist: Georg Olden." AIGA: The Professional Association for Design, March 1, 2007. www.aiga.org/medalist-georgolden.

———. "The Search for Georg Olden." *Print* 48, no. 2 (March–April 1994): 21.

Tony Palladino

Heller, Steven. "Tony Palladino, Designer of 'Psycho' Lettering, Dies at 84." *New York Times*, May 20, 2014.

Reynolds, Jamie. "The Concept of Tony Palladino's Universe." *Graphis*, no. 333 (May–June 2001): 116.

Paul Rand

Heller, Steven. *Paul Rand*. London: Phaidon, 1999.

———. "Paul Rand, 82, Creator of Sleek Graphic Designs, Dies." *New York Times*, November 28, 1996.

Rand, Paul. *Thoughts on Design*. New York: Wittenborn, 1947.

Alexander Ross

"Aaron Burns." Art Directors Club of New York, 1983. adcglobal.org/hall-of-fame/aaron-burns/.

Brown, Sylvia. "In Remembrance of Alexander Ross, 1914–1950." *AIGA Journal* 4, nos. 3–4 (c. 1952): insert.

Danziger, Louis. Phone and e-mail correspondence with Greg D'Onofrio. August–October 2016.

Thomajan, P. K., ed. "Presenting: Alexander Ross." *Friem's Four Pages* (A. I. Friedman, New York) May 1947.

"United States Government, Office of War Information, Bureau of Overseas Publications." In *23rd Annual of Advertising Art*. Edited by Art Directors Club of New York. 183–88. New York: Watson-Guptill Publications, 1944.

Arnold Saks

Caplan, Ralph. "Arnold Saks." *Graphis* 32, no. 185 (1977): 256–67.

Saks, Arnold. "Change–A Strength in Design." In *Speaking Out on Annual Reports: Commentaries by 50 Experts on the Organization and Creation of Annual Reports*. 84–85. New York: S. D. Scott, 1977.

———. *Folio 13: Graphics for Industry by Arnold Saks*. New York: Sanders, 1971.

———. Interview and e-mail correspondence with Greg D'Onofrio and Patricia Belen. July–October 2016.

———. Interviews by Greg D'Onofrio, Patricia Belen, and Paul Shaw. 2014–15.

"Special Feature: James Ward and Arnold Saks." *CA: The Journal of Commercial Art* 2, no. 1 (January 1960): 14–19.

Arnold Shaw

"Interiors' Cover Artists." *Interiors (Interiors + Industrial Design)* 108, no. 6 (January 1949): 10.

Moss, Tobias. "One Man's Fish Story." *CA: The Journal of Commercial Art* 1, no. 1 (August 1959): 60–62.

Shaw, Arnold. "Typography in Visual Communications." Notes on New York University course. 1959.

Shaw, Susan. E-mail correspondence with Greg D'Onofrio. August–December 2016.

Louis Silverstein

Heller, Steven. "Birth of a Style." *New York Times*, September 30, 1990.

———. "Louis Silverstein, Godfather of Modern Newspaper Design." *Print*, December 2, 2011. www.printmag.com/design-inspiration/louis-silverstein-godfather-of-modern-newspaper-design/.

Martin, Douglas. "Louis Silverstein, Who Gave a Bolder and Airier Look to the Times, Dies at 92." *New York Times*, December 1, 2011.

Silverstein, Louis. Interview by Steven Heller. 1987.

Barbara Stauffacher Solomon

Solomon, Barbara Stauffacher. E-mail correspondence with Greg D'Onofrio. September–October 2016.

———. *Why? Why Not? 80 Years of Art & Design in Pix & Prose, Juxtaposed*. San Francisco: Fun Fog Press, 2013.

Alex Steinweiss

Heller, Steven. "Alex Steinweiss, Originator of Artistic Album Covers, Dies at 94." *New York Times*, July 19, 2011.

———. "2004 AIGA Medalist: Alex Steinweiss." AIGA: The Professional Association for Design, 2004. www.aiga.org/medalist-alexsteinweiss.

Steinweiss, Alex. "An Artist's Odyssey." Unpublished manuscript, c. 1998.

———. Interview by Steven Heller. 1996.

Deborah Sussman

Heller, Steven. "She Made the World More Colorful." *Atlantic*, August 28, 2014. www.theatlantic.com/entertainment/archive/2014/08/how-deborah-sussman-made-the-world-more-colorful/379225/.

Prejza, Paul. E-mail correspondence with Greg D'Onofrio and Steven Heller. August 2016.

Bradbury Thompson

Heller, Steven. "Bradbury Thompson." *Baseline: International Typographics Magazine*, no. 11 (1989): 12–19.

———. "Westvaco Inspirations." In *Design Literacy: Understanding Graphic Design*, edited by Steven Heller. 201–3. New York: Allworth Press, 2004.

Purcell, Kerry William. "Westvaco: Inspiration for Printers." *Baseline: International Typographics Magazine*, no. 47 (2005): 05–12.

Thompson, Bradbury. *The Art of Graphic Design*. New Haven: Yale University Press, 1988.

———. Interview by Steven Heller. 1988.

Lance Wyman

Shaughnessy, Adrian. *Lance Wyman: The Monograph*. London: Unit Editions, 2015.

Selected Sources

Allen, James Sloan. *The Romance of Commerce and Culture: Capitalism, Modernism, and the Chicago-Aspen Crusade for Cultural Reform*. Chicago: University of Chicago Press, 1983.

Allner, Walter H. *Posters: Fifty Artists and Designers Analyze Their Approach, Their Methods, and Their Solutions to Poster Design and Poster Advertising*. New York: Reinhold, 1952.

Barr, Alfred H., Jr. *Cubism and Abstract Art: Painting, Sculpture, Constructions, Photography, Architecture, Industrial Art, Theatre, Films, Posters, Typography*. New York: Museum of Modern Art, 1936.

Black, Susan. *The First Fifty Years, 1926–1976*. Chicago: Container Corporation of America, 1976.

Blackwell, Lewis. *20th-Century Type*. New Haven: Yale University Press, 2004.

Clifford, John. *Graphic Icons: Visionaries Who Shaped Modern Graphic Design*. Berkeley, CA: Peachpit Press, 2014.

Cramsie, Patrick. *The Story of Graphic Design: From the Invention of Writing to the Birth of Digital Design*. New York: Harry N. Abrams, 2010.

Drew, Ned, and Paul Spencer Sternberger. *By Its Cover: Modern American Book Cover Design*. New York: Princeton Architectural Press, 2005.

Drucker, Johanna, and Emily McVarish. *Graphic Design History: A Critical Guide*. Upper Saddle River, NJ: Prentice Hall, 2008.

Eskilson, Stephen J. *Graphic Design: A New History*. New Haven: Yale University Press, 2007.

Fern, Alan Maxwell. *Word and Image: Posters from the Collection of the Museum of Modern Art*. Edited by Mildred Constantine. New York: Museum of Modern Art, 1968.

Friedman, Mildred S., et al. *Graphic Design in America: A Visual Language History*. Minneapolis: Walker Art Center, 1989.

Goldwater, Robert. *Modern Art in Your Life*. New York: Museum of Modern Art, 1953.

Gomez-Palacio, Bryony, and Armin Vit. *Graphic Design, Referenced: A Visual Guide to the Language, Applications, and History of Graphic Design*. Beverly, MA: Rockport, 2011.

Gottschall, Edward M. *Typographic Communications Today*. Cambridge, MA: MIT Press, 1989.

Hollis, Richard. *Graphic Design: A Concise History*. London: Thames and Hudson, 1994.

———. "The International Style and Italian Graphic Design." In *TDM 5: Grafica Italiana*, edited by Giorgio Camuffo, Mario Piazza, and Carlo Vinti. 34–41. Mantua, Italy: Corraini, 2012.

———. *Swiss Graphic Design: The Origins and Growth of an International Style, 1920–1965*. New Haven: Yale University Press, 2006.

Jacobson, Egbert, ed. *Seven Designers Look at Trademark Design*. Chicago: Paul Theobald, 1952.

Jubert, Roxane. *Typography and Graphic Design: From Antiquity to the Present*. Paris: Flammarion, 2006.

Moholy-Nagy, László. *Vision in Motion*. Chicago: Paul Theobald, 1947.

Remington, R. Roger, with Lisa Bodenstedt. *American Modernism: Graphic Design, 1920 to 1960*. New Haven: Yale University Press, 2003.

Remington, R. Roger, and Barbara J. Hodik. *Nine Pioneers in American Graphic Design*. Cambridge, MA: MIT Press, 1989.

Sanborn, Herbert J. *Modern Art Influences on Printing Design: An Exhibition Held in the Library of Congress, February 13–May 13, 1956*. Washington, DC: Washington Chapter of the American Institute of Graphic Arts, 1956.

Shaw, Paul. *Helvetica and the New York City Subway System: The True (Maybe) Story*. Cambridge, MA: MIT Press, 2011.

Trademarks/USA: A Retrospective Exhibition of American Trademarks from 1945 to 1963. Chicago: Society of Typographic Arts, 1968.

INDEX

Page numbers in *italics* refer to images.

IMAGE CREDITS

p. 2 Courtesy of Arnold Saks. p. 3 (right) Permission of The Xanti Schawinsky Estate. p. 9 Courtesy of Elaine Lustig Cohen. p. 10 Courtesy of Francis Nunoo-Quarcoo, permission of Carol de Harak. p. 12 Permission of Carol de Harak. p. 14 (top) Courtesy of the Graphic Design Collection at Fordham and Abby Goldstein. p. 20 George Giusti Collection, Cary Graphic Arts Collection, Rochester Institute of Technology. p. 22 Genevieve Naylor / Reznikoff Artistic Partnership. *001–007* © 2017 The Josef and Anni Albers Foundation / Artists Rights Society (ARS), New York. Photo: Tim Nighswander. p. 26 Reproduced from Walter Allner. *Posters: Fifty Artists and Designers Analyze Their Approach, Their Methods, and Their Solutions to Poster Design and Poster Advertising.* New York: Reinhold, 1952. p. 26, *008–019* Permission of Peter Allner. *014–019* Walter Allner Collection, Cary Graphic Arts Collection, Rochester Institute of Technology. p. 30 Courtesy of the Denver Art Museum, Herbert Bayer Collection and Archive. *020–031* © 2017 Artists Rights Society (ARS), New York / VG Bild-Kunst, Bonn. *020* Courtesy of the Herb Lubalin Study Center of Design and Typography at Cooper Union. *021* Courtesy of Tamar Cohen. *022* Courtesy of Swann Auction Galleries. *025–026, 030* Courtesy of Glenn Horowitz Bookseller. p. 36 George Karger / The LIFE Images Collection / Getty Images. *032–035, 040* Courtesy of the Herb Lubalin Study Center of Design and Typography at Cooper Union. p. 40 © Ezra Stoller/Esto. *041–055* Permission of Carol Burtin Fripp. *041, 044, 048, 053* Will Burtin Collection, Cary Graphic Arts Collection, Rochester Institute of Technology. *045* Courtesy of the Herb Lubalin Study Center of Design and Typography at Cooper Union. p. 46 Courtesy of the Collection of Robert Giusti. *057–069* George Giusti Collection, Cary Graphic Arts Collection, Rochester Institute of Technology, permission of Robert Giusti. p. 52 Courtesy of Juliet Kepes Stone. *070–080* Permission of Juliet Kepes Stone. p. 58 Reproduced from *Design and Printing for Commerce 1956*, New York: American Institute of Graphic Arts (AIGA), 1956. p. 58, *081–088* Permission of the Lionni family. *081–082* Courtesy of the Herb Lubalin Study Center of Design and Typography at Cooper Union. *083* Courtesy of Swann Auction Galleries. *084, 086–087* Leo Lionni Collection, Cary Graphic Arts Collection, Rochester Institute of Technology. p. 62, *089–100* Permission of Alex Matter. *090–091* Arts & Architecture © David Travers, used with permission. *094* Courtesy of Susan Shaw. *096* Courtesy of Swann Auction Galleries. p. 68, *101–110*

Permission of Renate Nitsche. *101, 106–108* Courtesy of Chisholm Gallery Vintage Posters. *105, 111* Courtesy of Glenn Horowitz Bookseller. *109* Courtesy of Swann Auction Galleries. *112, 115* Courtesy of Scott Lindberg. p. 74 Reproduced from M. Peter Piening, *Trademarks and Symbols,* Syracuse, NY: Syracuse University, 1964. *118* Courtesy of Art Students League of New York. *119* Courtesy of Sandi Vincent. p. 78, *128–135* Cipe Pineles Collection, Cary Graphic Arts Collection, Rochester Institute of Technology, permission of Carol Burtin Fripp. p. 82, *136–149* Copyrighted by Ladislav Sutnar, reprinted with the permission of the Ladislav Sutnar family. *137* Courtesy of ART . . . on paper. *138* Courtesy of Swann Auction Galleries. p. 85 Courtesy of Meret Troller Piderman. *150–161* Permission of Meret Troller Piderman. *150, 160–161* Courtesy of the Herb Lubalin Study Center of Design and Typography at Cooper Union. *151–153, 155–159* Fred Troller Collection, Cary Graphic Arts Collection, Rochester Institute of Technology. p. 94, *162, 176* Courtesy of George Tscherny. *163–175* Courtesy of George Tscherny Collection, Milton Glaser Design Study Center and Archives / Visual Arts Foundation, permission of George Tscherny. p. 100, *177–194* Permission of Beatriz Cifuentes and the Vignelli family. *177, 181–182* Courtesy of Beatriz Cifuentes and the Vignelli family. *180, 184, 186, 187* Courtesy of Massimo and Lella Vignelli papers, Vignelli Center for Design Studies, Rochester Institute of Technology, Rochester, NY. *183* Courtesy of Unimark International records, Vignelli Center for Design Studies, Rochester Institute of Technology, Rochester, NY. p. 106 Courtesy of Dietmar Winkler. *195–203* Architecture and Design Collection, MIT Museum, permission of Dietmar Winkler. p. 110, *204–218* Courtesy of Rudi Wolff. p. 116, *219–232* Estate of Saul Bass. *228 Arts & Architecture* © David Travers, used with permission. p. 122 © Estate of Paul Himmel. *233–238, 240–242* Courtesy of the Collection of Vince Aletti. p. 126, *254* Courtesy of Massimo and Sonia Cirulli Archive. *248–250* Lester Beall Collection, Cary Graphic Arts Collection, Rochester Institute of Technology. *255* Courtesy of Swann Auction Galleries and Art © Dumbarton Arts, LLC / Licensed by VAGA, New York, NY. p. 132, *259–268* Courtesy of Peter Bradford. p. 136, *271, 275–278* © Eliza and Rachel Brownjohn. *274, 279* Courtesy of Chermayeff & Geismar Collection, Milton Glaser Design Study Center and Archives / Visual Arts Foundation. p. 140 Reproduced from *Art Direction* magazine, 1966. *280, 282, 284, 285, 287* Architecture and Design Collection, MIT Museum. p. 144 Courtesy of Chermayeff & Geismar. *288–305* Courtesy of Chermayeff & Geismar Collection, Milton Glaser Design Study Center and Archives/Visual Arts Foundation. p. 150, *306–318* Courtesy

of Mary Condon. p. 154 Courtesy of Nina Crews. *319–330* Courtesy of Donald Crews. p. 158, *331–338, 340–341* Courtesy of Richard Danne. *339* Permission of Richard Danne. p. 162 Reproduced from *Graphic Designers in the USA/1*, Universe Books, New York, 1971. p. 162, *342–351* Permission of Louis Danziger. *342–348, 350–351* Louis Danziger Collection, Cary Graphic Arts Collection, Rochester Institute of Technology. p. 166, *357–358, 362, 364–366, 368–370* Courtesy of Francis Nunoo-Quarcoo. p. 166, *352–370* Permission of Carol de Harak. *352, 363* Rudolph de Harak Collection, Cary Graphic Arts Collection, Rochester Institute of Technology. *353–356, 360* Courtesy of the Herb Lubalin Study Center of Design and Typography at Cooper Union. p. 172, *372, 374–376, 378–379* Courtesy of the Herb Lubalin Study Center of Design and Typography at Cooper Union. p. 172, *371–379* Permission of Elissa Dorfsman. p. 176, *380–390* © Eames Office LLC, *Arts & Architecture* © David Travers, used with permission. *381, 383–390* Courtesy of Andrew Romano. p. 180, *391, 393–394, 396–397, 399–401* Courtesy of Gina and Lisa Federico. *391–401* Permission of Gina and Lisa Federico. p. 184, *410* Courtesy of Kenji Fujita. *402–411* Permission of Kenji Fujita. p. 188, *412–418* Permission of Carol Burtin Fripp. *417* Courtesy of the Herb Lubalin Study Center of Design and Typography at Cooper Union. p. 190, *419–427* Permission of Harry Goldsholl. *420* Courtesy Paul Carlos of Pure+Applied. p. 194, *428–445* Courtesy of Communications Design's Charles Goslin Collection, Pratt Institute, permission of the Estate of Charles L. Goslin. p. 200, *449, 451, 453–454, 457* Courtesy of Herman Miller, Inc. *446–457* Permission of Herman Miller, Inc. *457* (lower right) Courtesy Javier Garcia of Javier Garcia Design. p. 206, *458–468* © Simon Rendall. *458–460* Courtesy of Swann Auction Galleries. *466* Courtesy of Chisholm Gallery Vintage Posters. *461, 464, 465, 468* E. McKnight Kauffer Collection, Cary Graphic Arts Collection, Rochester Institute of Technology. p. 210, *475, 476, 479* Courtesy of Tami Komai. *469–479* Permission of Tami Komai. p. 214, *480–492* Permission of Burton Kramer. *480–485, 492* Burton Kramer Collection, Cary Graphic Arts Collection, Rochester Institute of Technology. p. 220, *493–513* Arden Kuhlman Riordan. p. 226 Courtesy of Lynn Leibowitz and Jan Bresnick. *514–528* Permission of Lynn Leibowitz and Jan Bresnick. *515, 517, 519, 524–527* Matthew Leibowitz Collection, Cary Graphic Arts Collection, Rochester Institute of Technology. *528* Reproduced from Walter Allner. *Posters: Fifty Artists and Designers Analyze Their Approach, Their Methods, and Their Solutions to Poster Design and Poster Advertising.* New York: Reinhold, 1952. p. 232, *529–539* Courtesy of George Lois. p. 236 Reproduced from *Print*

14, no. 4 (January–February 1958). p. 236, *541–542, 544, 547–549* Courtesy of the Herb Lubalin Study Center of Design and Typography at Cooper Union. *543, 545* Permission of the Herb Lubalin Study Center of Design and Typography at Cooper Union. p. 240, *550–568* Permission of Elaine Lustig Cohen. p. 246, *569–588* Permission of Elaine Lustig Cohen. p. 252, *589–591, 593, 594, 596–601* Courtesy of John Massey. *589–601* Permission of John Massey. p. 258, *602–608* Permission of the Tomoko Miho family. *602* Courtesy of Swann Auction Galleries. *605* Courtesy of Kent Kawakami. p. 262 Courtesy of Wayne Adams. *609–620* Permission of Wayne Adams, for the Estate of Reid Miles. p. 270 Courtesy of Terri Baker Weiss. *631* Permission of Terri Baker Weiss. p. 272, *632–642* Permission of Sabrina Palladino. *632, 633, 635, 637–639, 641, 642* Courtesy of Tony Palladino Collection, Milton Glaser Design Study Center and Archives/Visual Arts Foundation. p. 276, *643–655* Permission of Richard Klein on behalf of Marion Rand and as a Trustee of the Paul Rand Revocable Trust and the Marion Rand Revocable Trust successors in interest to the Estate of Paul Rand. p. 280 Reproduced from *AIGA Journal* 4, nos. 3–4 (c. 1952), American Institute of Graphic Arts (AIGA). *662, 665* Courtesy of the Herb Lubalin Study Center of Design and Typography at Cooper Union. p. 286, *670–687* Courtesy of Arnold Saks. *674* Courtesy of Matthias Gut. p. 292, *688–695* Courtesy of Susan Shaw. p. 296 Courtesy of Anne Silverstein. *696–706* Permission of Anne Silverstein. *696, 703, 705* Courtesy of the Herb Lubalin Study Center of Design and Typography at Cooper Union. p. 300, *707–721* Permission of Barbara Stauffbacher Solomon. p. 300 Courtesy of Hall of Femmes. *707–720* Courtesy of San Francisco Museum of Modern Art. Photograph: Don Ross. p. 304, *722–731* Permission of Leslie Steinweiss. *722, 724–726* Alex Steinweiss Collection, Cary Graphic Arts Collection, Rochester Institute of Technology. p. 308, *733, 734, 736, 737, 739, 740* Courtesy of Paul Prejza. *733–740* Permission of Paul Prejza. *735* Courtesy of Los Angeles County Museum of Art, Gift of Sussman/Prejza & Co., Photo © Museum Associates / LACMA. *738* Courtesy of Herman Miller, Inc. p. 312 Courtesy of the Estate of Bradbury Thompson. *741–751* Permission of the Estate of Bradbury Thompson. *742* Courtesy of the Herb Lubalin Study Center of Design and Typography at Cooper Union. *744–751* Courtesy of the Graphic Design Collection at Fordham and Abby Goldstein. p. 316, *752–765* Courtesy of Lance Wyman. p. 336 Permission of Architecture and Design Collection, MIT Museum.

ACKNOWLEDGMENTS

The Moderns began as an appreciation of designers known and unknown. We sought assistance and support from friends, scholars, and designers around the world. This book could not have happened without their encouragement and goodwill.

Most importantly, we are indebted to our publisher ABRAMS. We thank editor in chief Eric Himmel for his invaluable support and direction; design director John Gall for his continued enthusiasm; Richard Slovak for his thorough editing; Alicia Tan, our managing editor; and Darilyn Carnes, our design manager.

We are grateful to Patricia Belen of Kind Company for her significant contributions to the book and cover design.

An extra special note of thanks goes to those designers and their assistants who helped identify and locate work: Tom Geismar, Ivan Chermayeff and Marilee Scott, Elaine Lustig Cohen, Mary Condon, Donald Crews, Richard and Barbara Danne, John Massey, Louis Danziger, Burton Kramer, Arnold Saks and Anita Fiorillo, Dietmar R. Winkler and Megan Verdugo, Barbara Stauffacher Solomon, Peter Bradford, George and Luke Lois, George Tscherny, Rudi Wolff, and Lance Wyman.

During the research process, many family members and friends of families were consulted for information and materials. We are immensely grateful to the following: Peter Allner, Jennifer Bass, Eliza Brownjohn, Carol Burtin Fripp, Robert Fripp, Nina Crews, Carol de Harak, Elissa Dorfsman, Eames Demetrios, Gina and Lisa Federico, Kenji Fujita, Robert and Grace Giusti, Cathleen Falcione, Simon Rendall, Juliet Kepes Stone, Imre Kepes, Tami, Ken and Don Komai, Arden Riordan, Lynn Leibowitz, Jan Bresnick, Annie Lionni, Tamar Cohen, Alex Matter, Kent Kawakami, Wayne Adams, Harry Goldsholl, Terri Baker Weiss, Sabrina Palladino, Richard Klein, Marion Rand, Peter Reznikoff, Susan Shaw, Anne Silverstein, Leslie Steinweiss, Anne Ballard, Paul Prejza, Radoslav L. Sutnar, Elaine Sutnar, Mark and Dodge Thompson, Meret Troller Piderman, Renate Nitsche, and Beatriz Cifuentes.

A considerable amount of visual artifacts came from our own private collections, but archives, libraries, antiquarian sellers, and personal caches were also tapped. Thanks to Steven Galbraith, Amelia J. Hugill-Fontanel, and Kari Horowicz of the Rochester Institute of Technology Cary Graphic Arts Collection; Jennifer Whitlock of the Vignelli Center for Design Studies, Rochester Institute of Technology; Beth Kleber of the School of Visual Arts Archives; Milton Glaser Design Study Center and Archives; Alexander Tochilovsky and Laura Mircik-Sellers of the Herb Lubalin Study Center of Design and Typography

at Cooper Union; Amy Auscherman of Herman Miller, Inc.; Lauren Miller Walsh of Glenn Horowitz Bookseller; Rob Saunders and Tânia Raposo of Letterform Archive; Kathleen Creighton and Philip Graziano of Pratt Institute; Francis Nunoo-Quarcoo; Jeff Roth of the New York Times; Nicola Lucchi and Massimo Cirulli of the Massimo and Sonia Cirulli Archive: Alexandra Nelson and Ferry Foster of Swann Auction Galleries; Gail Chisholm and Alfra Martini of Chisholm Gallery Vintage Posters; Scott Lindberg of New Documents; David Hertsgaard of the Eames Office; Abby Goldstein of Fordham University; Philip Williams of the Philip Williams Poster Museum; Rebecca Race of the Josef and Anni Albers Foundation; Samira Bouabana of Hall of Femmes; John Dupuy of ART… on paper; Susan Reinhold and Robert Brown of the Reinhold-Brown Gallery; Staci Steinberger and Piper Severance of the Los Angeles County Museum of Art; Joseph Becker, David Rozelle, and Sriba Kwadjovie of the San Francisco Museum of Modern Art; David Travers of Arts & Architecture magazine; Stephanie Cassidy of the Art Students League of New York; Gary Van Zante and Ulrike Heine of the Architecture and Design Collection, MIT Museum; Marge Huang of the Philadelphia Museum of Art Library; Paul Carlos of Pure+Applied; Robin Benson; Javier Garcia of Javier Garcia Design; Matthias Gut; Andrew Romano; Vince Aletti; and Sandi Vincent.

Thank you to colleagues who fielded questions and provided time, assistance, support, feedback, and information—in no particular order: Stephen H. Van Dyk of Cooper Hewitt, Smithsonian Design Museum Library; David Lusenhop; Scott Santoro; Aaron Cohen of ProjectObject; Michael Skjei; Reto Caduff; David Stang of Ars Libri; Julian Montague; Elizabeth Resnick; Robert Wiesenberger; Steven Brower; Eric Breitoart; Andrew Alpern; Bill Bonnell; Armin Vit; Bryony Gomez-Palacio; Wayne Hunt; Perrin Drumm; Amy Chapman, and Heather Strelecki of the American Institute of Graphic Arts (AIGA), the professional association for design; Julie Lasky; Daniel Lewandowski; Paul Shaw; Jan Conradi; Doug Clouse; Pat Kirkham; Randall Ross; Susan Mayer; John Clifford; Nancy Watrous of the Chicago Film Archives; Susie Hoffmann of the Washburn University Alumni Association; Derrick Schultz; Gerald Watson; Louise Sandhaus; Alexandra Lange; Richard Poulin; Mártor Orosz; Alain Weill; Lisa Schoblasky of the Newberry Library; Erin Kinhart of the Archives of American Art at the Smithsonian Institution; Megan Keller of Special Collections and University Archives at the University of Illinois at Chicago; Renée B. Miller of the Denver Art Museum; Juliet Kinchin of the Museum of Modern Art; R. Roger Remington; Victor Margolin; Kerry William Purcell; and Adrian Shaughnessy of Unit Editions.

We have made every effort to contact the individuals and institutions that commissioned or were otherwise responsible for this work taking form. To all: You have our gratitude.

And finally, tips of the hat to friends and relations for being patiently and generously available whenever the need occurred: Louise Fili, Lita Talarico, Tom Bodkin, Seymour Chwast, and Mirko Ilić. And last but hardly least: I could not have done this book without my cohort Greg D'Onofrio. His energy, patience, enthusiasm, and expertise could fill a page of virtues. — SH

To my partner, Patricia: I'm grateful for your talents, judgment, and optimism. Thank you for your continual encouragement and love. — GD

To my coauthor, Steve: Thank you for taking me under your wing and providing the opportunity to collaborate. Your expertise and knowledge have always inspired me. Above all, thanks for your trust and friendship. — GD

MIT Alfred P. Sloan
School
of Management
20th
Anniversary
Convocation

October 26-28
1972

Self-mailer (shown flat, double-sided),
Alfred P. Sloan School of Management 20th
Anniversary Convocation, Oct. 26–28,
1972, Massachusetts Institute of Technology.
Designed as a self-mailer, when unfolded the
sum of the parts reveal the graphic arrows as
a total visual unit. Design: Ralph Coburn